SAP R/3
Implementation Guide

J. A. Hernandez

J. R. S. Elechiguerra

E. R. Bueno

S. A. Servera

McGraw-Hill

New York   San Francisco   Washington, D.C.
Auckland   Bogotá   Caracas   Lisbon   London
Madrid   Mexico City   Milan   Montreal   New Delhi
San Juan   Singapore   Sydney   Tokyo   Toronto

McGraw-Hill

A Division of The McGraw·Hill Companies

The sponsoring editor for this book was Simon Yates and the production supervisor
was Clare Stanley. It was set in Esprit by Patricia Wallenburg.

Printed and bound by Quebecor/Martinsburg.

 This book is printed on recycled, acid-free paper containing
a minimum of 50% recycled, de-inked fiber.

Dedication

My father Manuel and
my other father Charles David Bailey

Acknowledgments

I want to take this opportunity to offer my sincere thanks to the many people who helped and supported me through the sometimes painful process of making this book project a reality.

First, I want to thank my editor at McGraw-Hill, Simon Yates, for his patience, understanding, help, and support.

I want to thank all my friends at SAP Spain for providing me with insights and material: Rafael Cano, Javier Millares, José Manuel Nieto, Mario Daban, and Aurelio Rodríguez.

I want to thank my *knowledge network* colleagues: Jose Pablo de Pedro, general manager of RealTech Spain and Juan José Naranjo and Celia, from OkhtorLabs.

Many thanks again to E. R. Bueno and J. R. S. Elechiguerra from Compaq, and S. A. Servera and Marta Cantón from CSC/Ploenzke.

Thanks also to Jesus de Benito and his team of consultants from Soluciones y Proyectos (S & P), to my speedy friend and long time SAP consultant Johny Velilla.

A special acknowledgment goes to the people of the Hella project, because we all suffered and learned from a painful and finally successful experience: Rafael Sánchez, Juan Antonio Leon, and the Basis guys: Angel, Rosa, Carlos, Pilar, and also Carlos Calvo from Compaq.

Contributors

This book has been a real and very stressful challenge for me, dealing with most of the implementation issues addressed during SAP projects and after. I came from a technical background and have needed continuous help and contributions from many people and organizations; without whose assistance this book would not be as good as I have intended. This is the list:

❏ E. R. Bueno, a senior SAP consultant from Digital Equipment (now Compaq) who is one of the co-authors and contributed mostly to Chapter 3, the section about the Procedure Model. Several sections in Chapters 2, 4, 5, and 10 are also his.

❏ S. A. Servera, an experienced SAP functional consultant from CSC Ploenzke, was the author of most of Chapter 9, about R/3 application modules.

❏ J. R. S. Elechiguerra, a long-time manufacturing and SAP Basis consultant, contributed most of Chapter 5

❏ Marta Cantón, one of the best SAP Project System consultants in the world, from CSC/Ploenzke, contributed the description of the PS module in Chapter 9

❏ Rafael Barreda, a world expert in Change Management and director of the Change Leadership practice for Spain and Portugal at Deloitte Consulting. He contributed the state-of-the-art section on Change Management in Chapter 4.

❏ August Keller, long-time SAP consultant, founder, and manager of Offilog, an SAP partner, included an interesting section on the pull implementation approach on Chapter 2.

Autotester Inc., designers of world-class automated testing software, kindly contributed an extract from their excellent booklet "Best Practices in Automated Testing," included in Chapter 8.

CONTENTS

CHAPTER 2
SAP Projects and Implementation Issues   **45**

CHAPTER 3
Process and Methodology Issues   **77**

CHAPTER 4
People and Knowledge Issues in SAP Projects   133

CHAPTER 6
Technical Implementation   **243**

CHAPTER 7
Going Live, Continuous Change, and Productive Operation Issues

CHAPTER 8
Implementation Subprojects 329

CHAPTER 9
Overview of R/3 Applications 393

■■■ ■■■ ■■■ **CHAPTER 10**
Basis R/3: Architecture and System Management 445

Introduction

The Business World and the Standard Application Systems

The success of SAP is a fact. Read the figures about market share, revenue, and employee population accomplished by SAP in just a couple of years after the launch their flagship product, R/3, in 1992, which became the market leader and one of the most successful in the information technology industry. As much as Microsoft Windows has become the standard desktop operating system for an ever-increasing number of companies, SAP R/3 has become the "business operating system."

Issues and questions that arise when SAP R/3 is mentioned and discussed:

❑ Reinventing companies, reengineering business, redefining roles... rewriting software? Changing the rules: leading change, managing new practices, remodeling organizations... rechanging software.

❑ What to do with application software when you find out that there is a whole new way of conducting business with your suppliers, and it is more efficient and will save lots of money?

This book will not provide a new methodology for implementing SAP: there are already too many consulting companies in the market. Nor will it provide the right or best method to approach an SAP implementation project. However, our authors' experience and that of many SAP customers and projects in which we have been involved, has made us aware of the many topics and issues you will face during an implementation. That is what this book is about: providing knowledge of implementation issues, so they are taken into consideration and actions can be planned to deal with those issues.

We have tried not only to demonatrate our own experience, but learn from the experience of consultants, customers, and the general SAP community. The SAP user and consultant community has increased significantly during the last few years, and information and knowledge has grown exponentially. Though I tried to cover as many topics as possible, comments and suggestions are welcome at **implementation@k2p.com**.

Intended Audience

The language and approach to the issues described make reading this book appropriate for most people already familiar with R/3. The book is primarily intended for project managers, functional and technical consultants, IT managers, and project team members. It can be useful for those in the process of implementing SAP, but also for those in the planning stage.

For readers with little or no familiarity with R/3, the book includes three chapters, specifically Chapters 1, 9, and 10, which are introductory reference chapters for the world of SAP, the technical infrastructure, and the application modules.

Book Structure

This book is made up of ten chapters, which can be read independently:

Chapter 1, "Switching to Business Projects with SAP R/3," is a general introductory chapter on SAP and R/3, describing the features that made this *software* such a success and why it has become a "strategic solution." There is some history about the company and R/3 releases, as well information on the main strategic lines of SAP.

The aim of Chapter 2, "SAP Projects and Implementation Issues," is to depict the big picture of R/3 implementation projects, its problems, success factors issues, and tools. Drivers and risks for implementation are also analyzed and this chapter is the structural root for the rest of the book, since the issues are presented in an overview to later be explained in more detail in subsequent chapters.

Chapter 3, "Process and Methodology Issues," has two parts. The first deals with implementation issues: selecting and using a methodology, modeling business processes, performing a gap analysis, monitoring the project scope, customizing the system, auditing an implementation project. The second part of the chapter explains the solution sets SAP has designed as a methodological framework for R/3 implementations: the procedure model and AcceleratedSAP.

Chapter 4, deals with people and knowledge issues in implementation projects. Among those studied are Change Management, committing upper management, project management, and the project organization; communication strategy, training, dealing with consultants and customers, knowledge transfer, and documentation. Every project and project manager should consider the human resources problems and issues concerned with R/3 projects.

Chapter 5, "Development of SAP Projects," includes development of programs and reports, data migration, building interfaces, enhancing the R/3 system, applying patches, and personalizing the system. The second part of the chapter introduces the reader to the ABAP language and the main concepts and tools of the development environment.

Chapter 6 deals with technology and infrastructure issues in SAP projects, known as technical implementation. Among the issues explained are sizing and scalability, software installation and systems copy, choosing platforms, network infrastructure, backup and recovery strategy, printing strategy, contingency and high availability, batch strategy, systems landscape, and front-end distribution.

Chapter 7, "Going Live, Continuous Change and Productive Operation Issues," deals with the issues and problems that start with productive operation: activities to consider when going live, system management, performance, and tuning, support: troubleshooting and Help Desk strategy, upgrade projects, and implementation issues that must be dealt as continuous change issues.

Chapter 8, "Implementation Subprojects," covers implementation activities that fall between the technical and functional areas, and require a high degree of understanding and communication. They are often the hardest ones to implement. Among the topics explained are reporting strategy, testing, archiving, authorizations, security, and workflow.

Chapter 9 is a reference chapter containing a summary of the main features of the SAP application modules.

Chapter 10 is another reference chapter including a practical overview of the R/3 basis components, R/3 architecture, and System Management tools and common tasks.

CHAPTER 1

Switching to Business Projects with SAP R/3

If there is one word in the SAP world spoken and written more than SAP itself or R/3 that is *business*. It is at the center of the whole SAP strategy: software, services, functionality, evolution, mission, objectives, and so on. The marketing strategy for system components or elements includes Business Workflow, Business Framework, and Business Engineering. The B in ABAP programming language or in BAPI stands for *business*. And SAP has evolved the user interface into a *business client*. When Release 4.0 was introduced, SAP had evolved R/3 into a family of distributed *business* components.

Just as Microsoft became the de facto desktop operating system, SAP R/3 has become the *business operating system* of choice.

In the process of implementing the system and trying to grasp all the business benefits of R/3 applications, SAP projects cannot be handled as traditional IT projects, in which the computer literate interpret the needs of the users and design systems. Rather, in SAP implementation project users take control of configuring their business processes, leaving the IT departments for the support of the technical issues: basis system, middleware, and so on.

One well-known strength of R/3 is the solid integration of business processes that cross traditional departmental boundaries within companies.

These two features—a project led by users and horizontal approach—often need groundwork in reengineering (BPR) and lead companies to a continuous process of change; which will naturally engender resistance and difficulties. This is why implementing SAP must be seen and treated as a *business* project, led and sponsored by upper management, because its implementation can thereafter alter traditional company processes and organization.

In this book implementation is defined as a process ranging from making the decision to use SAP to the system's production start. It also covers all those issues that must be taken into consideration for productive operation and continuous change. These issues can have a significant impact on the usefulness and acceptance of the systems, and often do not appear on the radar of project managers.

This initial chapter is meant as an introductory guide to the R/3 world; it will be useful as a reference for understanding implementation issues.

Introduction to Business Applications

Although companies look for *business benefits* when implementing R/3, we will see in this and following chapters how SAP has made a major change in the way traditional IT projects are addressed and has changed how business projects are implemented.

In the world of business applications, there has been a strong movement towards *buy versus build* strategies, in part based on the idea that market trends and continuous business transformation can be realized faster and more easily in flexible standard applications than in custom-built ones.

The wave of *integrated systems* based on modular designs began during the '80s, though most of those systems were often highly *interfaced* applications and modules. The information generated by those systems was often restricted to the departments responsible for their respective business processes, resulting in lack of real integration.

The search for integration was not helped by the boom in networks, PCs, and relational databases at the beginning of the '90s, which often provoked the proliferation of user-with-PC-knowledge applications in every department of a company. The amount of data generated by hundreds of isolated or interfaced applications did not guarantee the right information for the decision-making process.

In traditional IT organizations, operational staff often discovered or required the development of new applications for their needs. This would be the start of a functional analysis or conceptual design that often took so long the initial requirements changed dramatically. Because change and transformation are not just an event, but the normal operative process in companies, business people eventually became aware that underlying technology for business applications must follow business directions and be able to react to those changes just as fast.

For this reason, business people should play the fundamental role in the implementation of IT systems to support the business process, as is the case of SAP R/3. While business people configure and design the SAP system, IT people are in charge of dealing with the technical aspects of SAP implementation, usually known as the *basis system*; this sometimes also includes dealing with development work in the ABAP language.

In the SAP world business management dictates the rules of business processes and IT systems. This process is achieved by assigning *super-users* to the project team.

Business super-users, also known as key users, are the people knowledgeable in business operational activities. They are the business people who specify business processes in SAP by configuring the systems to meet their requirements, or alternatively, use SAP's implicit business expertise to change the company's processes.

The market quickly recognized the value and significance of the R/3 application suite, but lengthy and costly implementation was a drawback. The usual reasons for long implementation times are the organization's resistance to changes and a lack of commitment by upper management. A section in the next chapter deals with typical implementation problems.

In any case, one of the main strategic goals of SAP for its R/3 applications has been to make the implementation easier, simpler and faster. As a result, the number of solution sets and implementation tools has been growing quickly since the introduction of release 3.0 in 1995, and ASAP in 1996.

SAP Success

One of the reasons for SAP's success is that because it is a standard package, it can be configured in multiple areas and adapted to the specific needs of a company. To support those needs, SAP includes a large number of business functions but leaves room for further functionality and enhancements adaptable to business practice changes. More and more, corporations are deciding to use standard software systems that are highly flexible and configurable and able to support most of the their business practices and information needs. This kind of package relegates the development of custom software to exceptional cases.

Along with the explosion of the Internet in the '90s and of Microsoft's Windows operating system, R/3 can be considered one of the hottest topics in the computing industry in the last years of the millennium, turning SAP AG into one of the most successful and important companies in the worldwide software market. R/3 has not been a revolutionary technology, but it has considerably shaken the consulting world.

As a business kernel, SAP R/3 is aimed at the majority of industries: manufacturing, distribution, chemical, automotive, health, utilities, oil and gas, telecommunications, and so on. SAP's customer list is huge and includes some of the largest and most important multinational companies.

All the factors that contributed to SAP R/3's immense success are a matter of analytical research, but SAP has become the leader in standard business applications; it is the business operating system of the future, just as Windows has become the desktop operating system of choice.

The coincidence of the announcement of the SAP R/3 client/server solution, the reengineering wave, and the downsizing approach as a cost-cutting method are all key factors for SAP success.

Other ingredients for SAP success have been:

❑ A well-oriented and swift strategy, in which the company dedicated a large amount of resources to research and development
❑ Partnership policies that account for the favorable reaction of hardware and consulting companies
❑ A position as software maker that leaves room for coordination with other business functions (especially implementation)
❑ A clear desire and effort to be present and innovative in every technological area, including Internet, data warehousing, business intelligence, cooperative tools (workflow), desktop application integration, business components, object orientation, etc.

The main hardware vendors as well as the largest international consulting companies, together with hundreds of smaller consulting firms, have committed to a strong partnership with SAP, knowing the benefits it can generate in hardware, software, and consulting services.

Additionally, SAP has developed a large number of technological partners including companies such as Microsoft, Informix, Oracle, Apple, Next, Adobe, iXos and Software AG.

Drivers for Implementing SAP

This section briefly summarizes the driving factors that influence the decision to start an SAP implementation project.

Each company implementing R/3 has different circumstances and different requirements and goals when making the decision to start this type of business project. A set of circumstances and requirements, the implicit change in the way of doing business, and a certain vision, constitute the drivers for starting an SAP implementation. Ultimately drivers are set goals which will engender measurable benefits to the organization.

There are several types of drivers:

❏ **Legal and technology drivers.** These include the effect of Year 2000, the euro currency, replacement of legacy applications and old systems, the search for real integration, and the support for standards.

❏ **Business drivers.** These include better cost control, a new way of doing business with partners and customers, optimization and automation of processes, and the search for survival and maximum efficiency.

❏ **Organization driver.** This is the search for productivity as a way to enable and support continuous changes in an organization and in business processes.

Finally, it is also interesting that some companies decide on an SAP implementation project without a real driver, or at least one which can be economically justified. These companies, acting as the early birds of technology fashions, usually fail to implement SAP. Companies without an urgent need or real driver can succeed only when the benefits of such a project are clear to the company, and supported by management.

Does SAP Have Competition?

SAP has a few competitors in the global ERP (Enterprise Resource Planning) application market. The most important competitors include Baan, PeopleSoft, Oracle Applications, JDEdwards, and QAD. All these standard application packages have also seen an impressive growth in terms of installations and revenues. SAP's popularity keeps increasing revenues, customers, employees, and benefits. Between 1994 and 1998, SAP revenue grew at a yearly average of 40%, positioning SAP as market leader after this short time span.

It must be observed that the monetary investment needed to implement a standard business software package requires a life cycle of at least 10 years; SAP heavily, continuously, and even frenetically invests in human resources and research to further increase its dominance.

Alternatives to SAP as the information system for business application are all those custom-built and designed programs generated by internal information technology people, or a combination of specialized packages with interfaces to local applications (a more common solution).

Since the emergence of SAP R/3, many SAP customers are progressively substituting a large number of individual applications and their interfaces with SAP. However, the total substitution by SAP of industry-specific software packages is not an easy objective to reach. These same industry-specific business processes are a clear target of SAP, for which it constituted the ICOEs (Industry Centers of Expertise). SAP is actively developing industrial solutions as a complement to R/3 core applications. These are known as *IS add-on packages* and are briefly described in a later section. By 1999 SAP industry solutions were present in 18 different industries.

SAP Consultants and Other Species

The qualification of an individual as an SAP consultant has been and still is synonymous with big money, as the following popular joke attests:

A tourist walks into a pet shop in Silicon Valley, and is browsing round the cages on display. While he's there, another customer walks in and says to the shopkeeper, "I'll have a C monkey, please." The shopkeeper nods, goes over to a cage at the side of the shop and takes out a monkey. He fits a collar and leash and hands it to the customer, saying "That'll be $5,000." The customer pays and walks out with his monkey.

Startled, the tourist goes over to the shopkeeper. "That was a very expensive monkey...most of them are only a few hundred dollars. Why did it cost so much?"

"Ah, that monkey can program in C, very fast, tight code, no bugs, well worth the money."

The tourist looks at the monkeys in that cage. "That one's even more expensive—$10,000! What does it do?"

"Oh, that one's a C++ monkey; it can manage object-oriented programming, Visual C++, even some Java, all the really useful stuff."

The tourist looks round for a little longer and sees a third monkey in a cage on its own. The price tag round its neck says $50,000. He gasps to the shopkeeper, "That one costs more than all the others put together! What on earth does it do?" "Well, I don't know if it does anything, but it says it's an SAP R/3 consultant."

In trying to reach universal and full SAP R/3 knowledge, we have often found newcomers to SAP asking for a way to "really know SAP" or how to become great SAP consultants. This question has been asked multiple times in a popular R/3 mailing list. This is the answer (copied from the reply in the mailing list):

> *As a Sr. SAP Consultant, you need to know the cross functionality within SAP, since SAP is an integrated software package and ERP. You can concentrate on SD, MM, and FI Modules. However, you need to get familiar with other modules such as PP and HR/Payroll since SAP has cross functionality with other modules. If you would like to be an application consultant, I would suggest that you study the Business Processes within SAP. You could look at the Business Navigator to start. Then, study the IMG (the customization with SAP). You should be able to customize for SD, MM, and FI modules. Then, study ABAP courses for programming because you need them for data conversion/interface (BDC), data dictionary, report writin, and dialog programming. If you're an EDI expert, take the IDOC/EDI and ALE courses. Also study Business Workflow for EDI transactions. Internet is also a good one to support SD and MM. If you would like to become a basis consultant, take the BASIS courses and be familiar with System Administration, Correction Transport System (Workbench Organizer), Security/Authorization, CCMS, and ORACLE/ INFORMIX/ SQL Server. Be familiar with the R/3 Instance parameter and all database, Windows NT, and UNIX kernel parameters. You should learn how to do performance analysis and tuning.*

There is no way we know of getting a grip on the SAP R/3 internals, because it means trying to cope with the coordination of close to 2000 people working on developing and improving a system that is constantly evolving new functionality, versions, and so on. It is enough to have a general knowledge of what SAP R/3 is, where its components are located, and its implementation issues, and then to specialize at most in a couple of the areas. Of course, consultants might change focus from time to time and become SD experts after learning MM, or specialize in CO or FI applications.

There are currently many different categories and jobs descriptions related to SAP implementation projects. Basically, consultants are known as either functional or technical. One might also find specialized SAP project managers, developers, strategic or management consultants, change management experts, trainers, and so on.

Functional consultants are those professionals with experience in various business areas, for instance, those with financial or logistics backgrounds, and with a knowledge of configuring SAP applications to meet customer needs in those areas.

On the other hand, technical consultants, also known as basis consultants, have the technical expertise and knowledge of the technical side of SAP to handle installation, operating system management, network design, database, sizing, monitoring, tuning, and so on.

ABAP programmers, although closer to the basis system, are positioned in the middle. Because they must do their job based on both functional or application needs, their work encompasses both programming and technical tasks.

The Role of Technology in Business Projects

The ability of integrated and standard applications in SAP R/3 to match and adapt to companies' business processes, and the flexibility to change those processes, has also introduced change in the leadership and management of projects. As the title of this chapter suggests, implementation projects have shifted toward business people and away from IT departments.

This does not mean that technology does not play a fundamental role in these business projects. Technical and technological advances have been mostly used for automating processes, using *time* as the main axis for enterprise efficiency. It is also a fact that technology can turn data into information, and information into *knowledge*, which is quickly becoming the most valuable asset any business can have.

Technology is one of the most critical enablers of business efficiency and profitability. Enterprises increasingly depend on technology for competitive advantages.

According to the Gartner Group "Applications, whether packaged or custom-developed, are influenced by technology and business requirements. When business and technology were both stable, functionality and costs were the prime considerations; however, stability no longer characterizes today's business and IT environments."

Projecting these theories into the R/3 world, technology is the area of opportunity that facilitates the availability of the business knowledge behind R/3 to companies and users, while maintaining focus on business-oriented projects.

In summary, technology makes enterprises able to adapt and change quickly to be competitive.

SAP AG: The Company

Four former IBM employees founded SAP AG in 1972. It is now a multinational company with a presence in over 50 countries, and headquarters in Walldorf, Germany. The company name, SAP, stands for Systems, Applications, and Products in Data Processing.

Since its foundation, SAP has made significant development and marketing efforts on standard application software. Before the R/3 boom, it was already in the market with its R/2 System for mainframe applications. After the introduction of SAP R/3 in 1992, SAP AG became the world's leading vendor of *standard* application software.

The maturity and solid experience of SAP in solving the information management problems of businesses around the globe is what has made the R/3 system the clear market leader in the development of standard applications.

The main reason for SAP's success is the fact that R/3 is a rock-solid standard application software package configurable in multiple business areas to meet the specific requirements of companies. In order to support those requirements, SAP includes a large number of business processes and functions; but it also leaves flexible room for introducing new processes or enhancements, and offers the needed flexibility for changing business processes as business itself changes.

With the clear tendency in the IT market towards the *buy* versus the *build* strategy, there is an ever-increasing number of companies opting for standard application packages that are configurable and flexible enough to support the majority of their core business processes and information needs. These packages use the development of custom-built software only for specific needs.

In 1997, SAP AG was the 4th largest independent software maker; between 1994 and 1998 there were annual increases of about 40% in revenue and profit, and employee growth of around 30% per year.

The number of SAP customers has constantly increased; there were more than 10,000 customers and about 20,000 R/3 installations in 1998, and more than 2 millions users of the R/3 system.

SAP AG values customer feedback highly and tries hard to meet customer requirements by constant enhancement of products and by offering valuable, state-of-the-art services, which combine to make a superbly integrated solution for enterprise applications.

SAP presence at the most important trade shows and the organization of many events attracting a growing number of attendees are a large part of SAP's marketing effort. SAP also participates in numerous user groups, organizing conferences and helping partners to market new products and solutions complementary to the SAP environment.

SAP has its own events, including SAP Universe, SAP InfoDays, SAP TechED, and the biggest, SAPPHIRE, which are organized on a European, American, and Asia-Pacific basis, as well as in specific countries. SAPPHIREs gather large numbers of top executives, engineers, consultants, partners, and others to take part in workshops, presentations, exhibits, and conferences; here major releases and announcements are made.

SAP also offers an extensive range of training courses and consulting services for customers and partners.

SAP has two main products on the business software market: mainframe system R/2 and client/server R/3. Both are targeted to business application solutions and feature a high level of complexity, business and organizational experience, strength, and integration. SAP software systems can be used on different hardware platforms, offering customers flexibility, openness, and independence from computer technologies. The SAP AG base software market is concentrated around the R/3 product, although it will continue to enhance and support the R/2 system up to the year 2004.

Both R/2 and R/3 aim to provide a core framework and solution to companies' business applications, incorporating an internal complexity, solid experience, and knowledge of companies' organization and best business practices. The adequacy of these application suites is based on integration as well as in the proven benefits derived from the installed base.

SAP products can be installed using multiple hardware platforms and with different database management systems, and offer customers the flexibility, openness, and independence of the different hardware and software vendors' technology.

The functionality of R/3 and R/2 software is based on the concept of *business process*, a complete functional change within a specific business practice, whatever software module has to handle or manage that process. This concept means that the chain of business processes can be managed by different application modules. This feature is sometimes referred to by SAP as the *internal data highway*.

An example of this definition is the fact that, whether the process is a sales order, a purchase order, an expense claim or the paycheck, all the processes will probably finally be connected with financial modules, updating the general ledger or cost center accounting.

With the release of R/3 3.0 at the end of 1995, SAP included more than 800 predefined business processes from which customers can freely select, to use them in their own way to manage companies and conduct business. With the release of 4.0 and 4.5 in 1997 and 1998, the number of processes now exceeds 1000, and in every new major release, more processes and features are incorporated as standard in the system.

SAP knows quite well how companies frequently change both organization and processes, and gives the system enough flexibility to customize those changes in a rapid manner.

SAP's competition argues that changing the system is not easy, and that there is no such flexibility. While one might agree that

changes could be easier, it is also true that since R/3 is a system intimately connected to the business, the flexibility to customize the system is second to the flexibility to effect process changes in companies. One full section in chapter 5 deals with the issue of change
management.

Strategy and Releases

SAP invests about 20 % of its annual sales revenue in research and
development to remain at the cutting edge of technological innova-
tion. With about 25 % of employees working in the research area,
SAP wants to ensure a constant dialog with customers and users,
exchanging with them experiences and ideas to enhance systems and
service offerings. This information exchange is vital so that SAP can
maintain a long-term relationship with its customers and attract new
ones into the R/3 sphere.

International applicability is an important part of the strategy to
meet today's complex and global business. For SAP it means not only
having software in different languages, but also covering different
aspects for each country: currency, taxes, legal practices concerning
human resources, import/export regulations, etc. Users in a multinational company in different countries can work simultaneously in the
same system with their own language, currency, and taxes.

An additional aspect of the software integration capability is *real
time*. In fact, the R in R/3 originally meant real time. When new
input is made into the system, the logical application links concur-
rently update related modules, so that business can react immediately to that information and those changes. This type of updating
reduces the overhead of manual processing and communication and
enables companies to react quickly in the nonstop and complex business world. This makes SAP software systems a valuable tool for
executive planning and decision making.

SAP R/3 technology is the logical evolution of the SAP R/2 system and is the product that really fueled the expansion of SAP after
its introduction in 1992, when SAP established itself as the leader in
standard applications in the industry. R/3 has become the system of
choice for those companies anchored in character-cell legacy applica-

tions wishing to downsize their centralized mainframe-class computer system to new and cheaper client/server technology.

The implicit complexity of the R/3 systems is explained by SAP's dictum that the business world is complex; a standard system must include a large number of functions. SAP included not only business functionality, but also efficient implementation tools, a comprehensive development environment, and a full-featured set of tools for efficient monitoring and management of the system.

SAP Release 3.0

3.0 was a major release for SAP, providing the application with many technical improvements and new features, as well as with the introduction of an easier implementation path. With the release of R/3 3.0, SAP concentrated its strategic efforts and directions on the following points:

❑ Application Link Enabled (ALE) technology. With this interface technology and different business scenarios to link different SAP systems and external application systems, SAP overcomes the problem of having a unique centralized database server, and allows big companies to distribute their business processes without loosing integration.

❑ Interaction and integration with standard PC applications, mainly with the Microsoft Office suite. Although in previous releases there were options to connect R/3 with PC applications, with version 3.0 SAP included standard links to interact with MS-Excel, MS-Word, MS-Access, and others, using OLE technology.

❑ Enhanced Graphical User Interface (SAPGUI) with many new options, buttons, captions and images. There is also a set of utilities for interacting with SAP such as SAP Automation, RFC interfaces, and so on, included in standard Desktop SDK.

❑ Technological enhancements in the architecture of the system, like new memory management features, easier installation and upgrade procedures, user exits, online download of patches, and so on.

❑ New APIs and standard calls for software developers, further
opens the system and broadens the spectrum of functionality,
with add-ons like archiving, EDI, forms management, external
workflow, plant data collection devices, mail fax solutions, etc.

❑ First steps to a more business object-oriented system with an
enhanced SAP Business Workflow and the introduction of business objects.

❑ The introduction of the Business Framework Architecture with
the goal of making it faster and easier for customers to introduce
new functionality into the system, as well as to making the system even more flexible and open.

Internet Release: SAP R/3 3.1

By year-end 1996, SAP announced the availability of release 3.1.
This version was known as the Internet release, since the main new
features and capabilities made it possible to expand the capacity of
the R/3 systems using the Internet, while preserving the functionality and support of the core R/3 applications. Users are able to make
transactions directly into the system from Internet browsers. R3.1
allows for efficient communication in the business world between
companies, customers, and providers.

SAP R/3 Release 3.1 was the first to broaden the typical three-tier
client/server architecture to a multitier architecture by introducing a
new layer, known as Internet layer, located between the presentation
and application layers.

Figure 1.1 shows a schema of these new levels. With this
approach SAP claims potential access to the system of thousands of
"users" or "business partners."

To support this new architecture, SAP introduced several modifications to the application level, based on the *thin client* concept,
reducing data transfer between presentation and application levels.
This is a vital concept considering the limited bandwidth often
found on Internet connections.

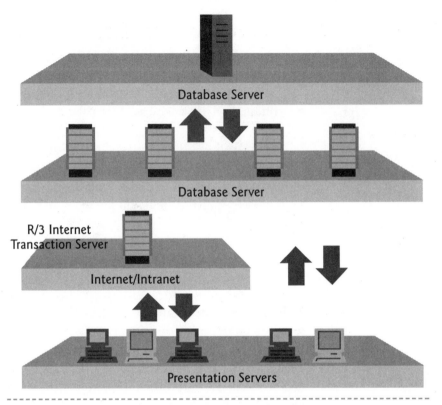

FIGURE 1.1   *Multilevel architecture with Internet layer after Release 3.1*

R/3 Release 3.1 offers the same functionality as R3.0 but enables business processes to use both intranet and Internet. Some of its features are:

❑ Java enabling, with the possibility of avoiding the code for the presentation server in clients and facilitating presentation software distribution.

❑ Support for new presentation platforms such as Network Computers (NCs) and NetPCs.

❑ Introduction of BAPIs (Business Application Program Interface), which can be used as a communication mechanism between R/3 and external applications using the Internet. BAPIs are object-oriented definitions of business entities. The concept behind BAPI is key to the overall SAP R/3 Internet and electronic commerce strategy, as BAPI is the object-oriented interface to integrate external applications. Based on business objects, such as company, vendor, employee, material, and so on, a BAPI defines the methods which can be used to interact and communicate with those objects. Release 3.1 included more than 100 predefined BAPIs ready to integrate R/3 with third-party solutions and applications.

❑ Internet Application components (IACs), new components of R/3 application servers which allow the use of software modules to support business transactions through an Internet layer. Initially SAP provided a small number of IACs (around 40) including components for Human Resources applications.

❑ Web Browser, an Internet browser including Java-enabled components, becomes a new user interface (a new presentation). Most typical browsers such as Netscape Navigator and Microsoft Internet Explorer are fully supported.

❑ Web server, the typical Internet server with which R/3 applications facilitate communication between the Internet or intranet world and SAP business processes.

❑ Internet Transaction Server (ITS), located at the Internet level in the architecture, connects the Web server with SAP Internet Application Components.

❑ SAP Automation, the programming interface which allows Internet components and other applications to interact with R/3.

Besides total support for Internet layer within business engineering tools, release 3.1 incorporated new process configuration based on models. This feature allows for a quicker and more dynamic configuration of business processes and includes several "industry" models, which can be used directly by customers, thus reducing the time needed for configuring and customizing the system.

SAP and Electronic Commerce

One of the biggest and most important challenges that the Internet unleashed was the opportunity to broaden the information system availability of companies beyond their internal frontiers to allow 24-hour access by their customers, consumers, or general business partners.

With the introduction of the R/3 solutions for supporting business processes through the Internet, companies can increase their business by providing a new communication channel for other companies and customers.

Standard with release 3.1 of SAP R/3 was the possibility of using three different types of Internet and intranet scenarios for supporting electronic commerce:

- Intranet corporate applications
- Intercompany applications, extending the possibilities of the supply management chain
- Applications from consumers to companies, enabling ultimate customers to use a simple Internet browser to communicate and trigger transactions with an R/3 system

Toward Componentization: R/3 Release 4.0

With the introduction of Release 4.0 and in the context of the Business Framework, SAP's strategy for enterprise computing was to develop R/3 into a family of integrated components that can be upgraded independently.

A study by the Gartner Group was the basis for SAP's close monitoring of the survival of enterprise software vendors. Four trends were indicated:

- Componentization in products and sales force. This move is clearly reflected in the emergence of R/3 release 4.0.
- Addition of consulting content. SAP quietly introduced this concept so as not to provoke their legion of consulting partners. According to SAP figures, 1997 and 1998 have seen a substantial growth in people services and consulting
- Industry-specific components or templates. This is no new strategic direction for SAP, although for years there was more marketing than actual products. With Release 4.0, industries like retailing and the public sector can find additional, specific business processes (although telecom companies have been waiting since 1995 for their piece of the cake).

❑ Focus on fast implementation: methodologies and solutions. ASAP and TeamSAP are excellent examples of SAP's reaction to criticism of long implementation times and over-budget projects.

Beyond the logical evolution in technological aspects and the growth of functionality in release 4.0, two features should particularly be highlighted: componentization and inclusion of industry solutions. We should also add the increased accent on the use of solution sets for rapid implementation, such as AcceleratedSAP or ASAP.

Componentization is a practical consequence enabled by the Business Framework architecture. When SAP introduced release 4.0 it was obvious that R/3 had evolved into a family of distributed business components.

Among the new components and functional add-ons to the kernel R/3 application modules are:

❑ Introduction of new distributed scenarios using ALE and integration using BAPIs.
❑ Enhancements for the management of global supply change (from the provider of the provider to the customer of the customer). This is done with the launch of the SCOPE (Supply Chain Optimization Planning and Execution) and APO (SAP Advanced Planner and Optimizer) initiatives.
❑ Introduction of new specific functionality for particular industry solutions, starting with retailing and the public sector.
❑ New Business Framework architecture components. With these new components customers can add enhancement to the system independently of other R/3 functionality. For instance there are many new Internet scenarios which can be used for business processes.
❑ Business components including PDM (Product Data Management), ATP Server (Available-to-Promise), the Business Information Warehouse, and a system of catalogue and purchase requisitions using the Internet.

It was SAP's goal to include substantial improvement for implementing R/3 more quickly, making it an easy to use and easy to upgrade business solution. With the new R/3 Business Engineer components, the system includes an advanced mechanism for model-based configuration (business blueprints) and for continuous change management.

Technologically, the programming language ABAP/4 has evolved towards a completely object-oriented language based on ABAP Objects. These new objects allow interoperability with other types of external and standard object architectures.

There are also enhancements in security and data integrity by means of authentication and electronic signature techniques.

The extension of the SAP Business Workflow was accomplished with the addition of new wizards for rapid workflow scenario configuration and deployment as well as the ability to launch workflows from the Internet using forms with HTML formats.

Full-flavored Business Framework: R/3 Release 4.5

Release 4.5 was announced in 1998; with it SAP continues the process of introducing new functional components for logistics, financial management and human resources modules, many of which are based on a new open standard provided by the Business Framework architecture.

Strategically, Release 4.5 is SAP's strongest bet to introduce and enhance industry solutions. This version is specifically valuable for automotive, distribution, and consumer products.

Among new and enhanced technological features of this release are extensions for centralized systems management; new GUI components for integration with PC applications, including new ActiveX controls; more BAPIs; enhanced, easier use and configuration of the Business Workflow; enhanced features for object-oriented ABAP; and the ability to access archived documents from the Internet using an enhanced Web ArchiveLink interface.

There are also major changes in programs and utilities used for systems installations as well as for upgrading.

By using the architecture provided by the Business Framework, release 4.5 introduces new possibilities for extending the system using third-party solutions, via BAPIs, in many R/3 areas: enhanced system administration and control with CCMS, human resources management, enhanced global supply chain, report generation, and more.

EnjoySAP: R/3 Release 4.6

The EnjoySAP initiative was announced by SAP at SAPPHIRE'98 in Madrid. It is targeted to receive as much feedback as possible on R/3 *usability*, with a view to enhancing the system from an end-user point of view. The resulting customer and user feedback, and new strategic and marketing campaigns such as the New Dimension Solutions and the Next Generation, have established the cornerstone for Release 4.6, known as EnjoySAP Release.

Previous R/3 releases included many new components, functionalities, add-ons, industry solutions, and technological improvements, but few revolutionary user features. EnjoySAP Release has dramatically changed the user interface, going beyond designing appealing and colorful features to fundamentally distinguishing between different types of users and delivering a role-based user interface. One of the features included in EnjoySAP most demanded by users is the ability to tailor the interface by adding icons for most-used functions to the application toolbar.

Figure 1.2 shows an example of a screen from the EnjoySAP Release for the Implementation Guide.

Products Complementary to R/3

It has always been a good strategy for SAP to maintain and increase its leadership in business applications with R/3 by integrated third-party software that adds value to SAP solutions.

For several years now, SAP has run a certification program for interfacing SAP applications and third parties. The purpose of the program is to guarantee that solutions and products developed for SAP applications are really proven and can really help mutual customers. All third-party products and programs must be certified by SAP using this program; hundreds of third-party solutions have been certified in the areas of Plant Data Collection interfaces, CAD systems, Geographical Information systems, LIMS (Laboratory Information Management Systems), archiving, system management and so on.

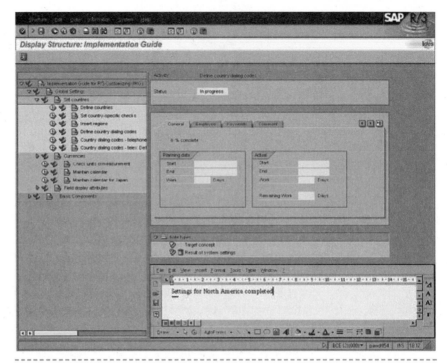

FIGURE 1.2   *Implementation guide with enjoySAP release   Copyright © SAP AG*

More information about the certification program or available complementary products can be found at **http://www.sap.com/products/compsoft/index.htm**.

WEB

Rapid Implementation Solution Set: ASAP

AcceleratedSAP (ASAP) is a solution for making rapid and efficient SAP implementations. It was introduced in the United States in 1996 and soon became available worldwide. ASAP is based on coordinating all necessary SAP implementation elements to guarantee quick deployment and success.

ASAP is also known as the *Process* component of TeamSAP, and can be seen as a methodology, although it goes beyond just methodology. ASAP is made up of three main elements:

❑ The *ASAP Roadmap* is a project plan with five phases, from project preparation to production start and support.

❑ ASAP tools, also known as Accelerators are included on the ASAP CD-ROM and are based on the R/3 Business Engineer. There are also Question & Answer database models for a semiautomatic configuration of the system, tools for the management and control of the project, documentation, white papers, and more.

❑ SAP Services, which provide help with related areas from training to remote consulting.

Chapter 3 is devoted to the SAP Solution Sets, including ASAP, and provides details about each of the project phases and the main uses of the tools.

WEB

More information on ASAP can be found at **http://www.sap.com/products/ imple/index.htm**. There is also very useful information and tools on the Simplification group Web site. This is a group in charge of developing tools and documentation which can help simplify and accelerate R/3 implementations. Visit **http://207.105.30.51/simpweb/ toolarea/frames21.htm**.

Partnership Strategy

SAP standard software and services are strongly supported by a partnership policy and a close relationship with an extensive group of companies to help mutual customers, as well as to cope with a strong demand for implementing and supporting R/3 systems. It is also through technological and customer partnerships that SAP designs and develops additional industry solutions (IS), new complementary products and tools, training, and reengineering consulting programs, outsourcing guidelines and so on.

SAP has established several types of partnerships:

❑ **Hardware partners.** These include all large computer hardware companies whose equipment is certified to run SAP R/3. They work closely with SAP and have competence centers to help mutual customers in tasks such as sizing, installation, maintenance, technical consulting, availability strategy, and tuning.

❑ **Consulting partners.** All the largest worldwide consulting firms and hundreds of the integration system divisions in multinational companies have some type of alliance with SAP, providing a great deal of expertise in R/3 technology, industry solutions, and strategic and business process reengineering consulting. This strength is aimed at SAP implementation projects. Because of the size and international presence of many of these companies, they are known as *global logo partners*. At a national and regional level, there are smaller service and consulting companies specializing in SAP projects, in customizing some of the modules and in specific industry areas. These companies are known as *logo partners*.

❑ **Technology partners.** These are mainly software companies who make databases, network software, operating systems, and R/3 complementary products that add value or functionality to the core R/3 system.

❑ **Development partners.** These companies and organizations help with SAP's constant development and enhancement of the R/3 product suite, including new releases and industry solutions add-ons.

❑ **Value-added resellers.** These service companies specialize in providing implementation support for SAP projects in small and medium-sized companies.

As the last significant step in the SAP partner policy and strategy, and to increase efficiency when implementing R/3, SAP introduced the TeamSAP concept in 1997 as a symbol to distinguish the best SAP and partner resources. TeamSAP includes persons, processes, and products.

SAP R/3: Software and Beyond

SAP R/3 is not only software: R/3 is a strategic solution. This slogan becomes true for companies deciding to implement R/3 as their core business application. It is also true that for the enormous and growing number of consultants around the R/3 world, SAP has become almost a religion.

SAP differs from other types of applications in many respects, the most fundamental of which is that SAP has modified the way companies do "software" projects, and has made a significant shift toward moving the responsibility of process design to process owners and not to IT departments.

Information Technology groups are now responsible for supporting the technical base or technological system infrastructure, not in process design or development, as was common in older information systems. In traditional IT projects, the information systems departments was in charge of fulfilling user needs based in functional specifications written using business terms which often were not correctly understood by technicians. This situation often led to communication problems and naming convention misunderstandings; these are avoided by implementing systems such as R/3.

In order to fulfill complex information needs as well as accomplish business management automation, the R/3 application suite includes the following features:

❑ Multi-tier client/server architecture
❑ Middleware basis for supporting open systems technology
❑ Business Framework Architecture, open to total integration with other components and applications, including the Internet world; this is achieved by the use of standard BAPIs
❑ Homogeneous user interface among applications
❑ Comprehensive development environment
❑ Total application integration
❑ Solution sets for configuring the system
❑ Wide range of services including hotline support, training, consulting, and quality checks
❑ Complete support for solving all the problems which arise because of Y2K and the new European currency, the euro

Figure 1.3 shows different levels or components of R/3 from the point of view of the functions for which they are designed. Globally, the SAP R/3 system is represented by everything included inside the ellipse.

The lower level is composed of the computer operating system, the database management system (normally included in the R/3 kit), and the network. Above this is the middleware layer, which interfaces with the lower layer and integrates the R/3 applications above it. This intermediate layer is often known as the R/3 kernel or Basis system, and includes components such as the ABAP development workbench, the system administration utilities, the background system, the authorization system, and many of the cross application modules.

NOTE

For technical consultants and basis people, the R/3 kernel is the collection of runtime programs (non-ABAP) located at the operating system level and *not* in the database, as are the R/3 application programs (ABAPs).

ABAP/4 is a fourth-generation programming language used to develop all R/3 application modules. When releases 4.0 and 4.5 were introduced, and SAP strategy focused on object orientation, it was decided to rename the programming language to ABAP.

The role ABAP and the development environment of SAP implementation is dealt with in Chapter 4.

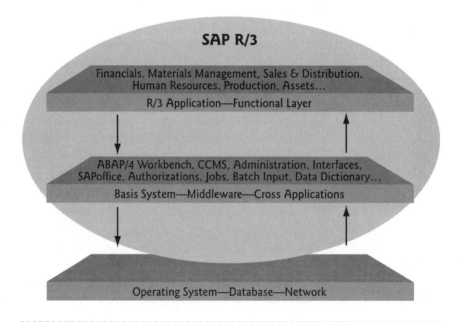

FIGURE 1.3   *Layers and components of the R/3 system*

Normally, *middleware* is the computing term used for those software components that facilitate the development of client/server applications which can be used on different vendor platforms. The R/3 basis system is the R/3 middleware.

The upper or *functional layer* is where the many functional applications are located: general ledger (FI module), cost accounting (CO module), human resources (HR module), logistics applications such as sales and distribution (SD module), materials management (MM module), production planning (PP module), and so on. Chapter 9 includes an overview of the SAP functional modules.

The integration of all these functional applications is based both on the R/3 reference model, which describes the business processes and their inter-relationships, as well as in the technology provided by the Basis system.

SAP also defines the client/server concept from a business point of view as a technology concept which leverages computing power in order to integrate key business processes with software, generating a close relationship between different business areas such as finance, logistics, and human resources.

Figure 1.4 shows the most typical way in which SAP represents the R/3 system from an integrated and logical point of view. The R/3 kernel as ABAP/4 client/server is located in the center of the diamond, providing the infrastructure and integration for the R/3 applications.

For communicating with the operating system and the relational database management system, the R/3 kernel uses standard application programming interfaces (APIs) and standard communication protocols. As stated previously, the kernel layer is located under the application logic level and system data, and works exactly the same no matter what the applications are. This type of architecture allows for quickly changing the system configuration, as well as installing new systems (for example, new application servers) without altering or interrupting any of the existing applications.

The next sections describe in more detail each of the main features of the R/3 system. More information about the systems architecture can be found in Chapter 10 and an overview of the functional modules is included in Chapter 9.

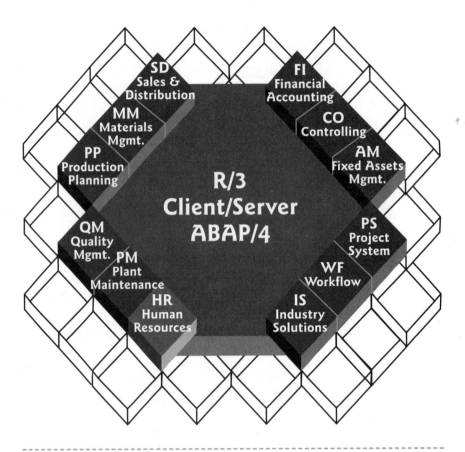

FIGURE 1.4   *R/3 integration model representation by SAP   Copyright © SAP AG*

Client/Server Technology

In general, *client/server* is a class of computing technology that allows for distributing the load of applications among several cooperating programs. This type of technology makes possible separation of user tasks from application logic and from data management. Client/server must be understood as a software concept, which includes a set of "service providers" and "service requesters." In client/server computing, the individual software components act either as "service providers," "service requesters," or both at the same time. The software service communicates among them using predefined standard interfaces.

The main advantages of the client/server architecture are:

❑ **Flexible configurations.** With standard communication interfaces there are multiple choices for planning and distributing a
client/server installation: from a centralized configuration to a
highly distributed system, even with an additional, huge Internet
layer between the presentation and application servers. Refer to
Figure 1.5.

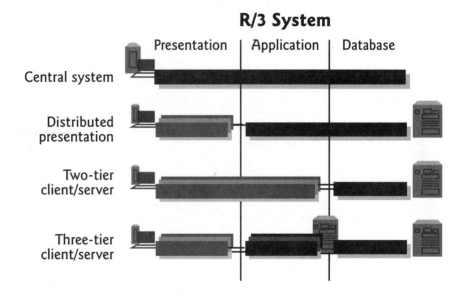

FIGURE 1.5 *R/3 client/server configurations   Copyright © SAP AG*

❑ **Workload distribution.** Becuase the application servers work
simultaneously and in parallel and communicate with the database server, both users and services can be distributed and shared
according to task types and applications used. It is also possible to
use application servers dedicated to specific business areas.

❑ **High scalability.** By deploying client/server systems architecture, both the capacity and hardware power can be progressively
adjusted according to the evolution of performance needs or the
growth of the company, as when the number of end-users
increases. This is a very useful feature that can easily be applied
to add new application servers when there is a significant
increase in the number of application users, when new modules
are configured, when there is a database growth, and so on. The

scalability of this type of architecture allows companies to protect their software and hardware investments.

One of the most-deployed configurations of SAP R/3 is the three-level client/server architecture (see Figure 1.5), which distinguishes three types of servers according to function: presentation, application and database. As stated previously, client/server is mainly a software concept, and an application server will run those software components that make up the service providers for the presentation servers, acting as a server; but it also includes all the needed components for requesting the services offered by the database, and therefore is also a *client*.

With the three-tier architecture, every group is configured to support the requests of its own functions. The central server contains the database (the database management system), and is generally known as the *database server*. The *application servers* contain the system process logic (it is simpler to consider this the *programs*), and include services such as printing, dialog servers to answer interactive requests by users, services for processing background jobs, and so on. Finally all tasks related to user interface and the presentation of information are handled by the *presentation servers*, usually PCs or workstation, which facilitate access to the system.

Communication between these three levels or types of servers is through use of standard communication services or protocols, such as TCP/IP.

Open and Standard Systems

Another of the important features and a key success factor for SAP R/3 is the strategy for making solutions technologically *open*. This means basically that the applications could work on top of multiple operating systems, multiple database management systems, and communication protocols. Also, the ABAP source code is completely reusable and transportable among heterogeneous systems.

This type of technology allows SAP customers a certain degree of independence from hardware and database providers.

What makes the systems open is the use of standard formats for data interchange, and the use of standard communication interfaces among systems and among programs. In the generic concept of open systems, SAP includes the following values:

❏ **At the system level.** Support for multiple hardware platforms and operating systems, such as most UNIX flavors, Windows NT, AS/400, S/390, and so on. Support for a large number of graphical user interfaces (GUIs), such as for all Windows flavors (Windows 3.11, Windows 95, Windows 98, Windows NT), Macintosh, OS/2, Motif, Internet browsers, and so on. In 1999 SAP announced support for the Linux operating system.

An updated list of the supported and certified systems by SAP can be provided by any local SAP subsidiary.

WEB

This information can also be found on the Internet link from the Information Center for Technology Infrastructure: **http://www.sap.com/products/techno/index.htm** selecting **Platforms** and then **Hardware**.

❏ **At the database level.** R/3 supports most popular relational database management systems such as Oracle, Microsoft SQL-Server, Informix, Adabas D, and the several variants of IBM DB2. It is possible to access the data managed by R/3 using standard SAP programs or other SQL tools and applications such as ODBC, remote SQL tools, and so on. SAP incorporates the use of standard SQL, known as Open-SQL, as the database data manipulation language (DML), which allows both users and programmers to store, display, or extract data from and to the database management systems.

NOTE

Not all database are supported in all different platforms. The previous list included platforms supported as of the beginning of 1999. For more information contact SAP directly, or call the hardware or database provider.

❏ **At the application level.** The R/3 system is open to possible enhancements and add-ons for specific business requirements. Both the ABAP Repository and the Reference model allow business users to better understand the relationship between the R/3 applications. The programming interface allows external systems and other R/3 systems to communicate, share information, and execute function modules using standard RFCs or (Remote Function Calls), RPCs (Remote Procedure Calls), or by using BAPIs. SAP includes the RFC development kit, known as RFC SDK, which is an standard interface for customers and software vendors (ISVs) that allows them to develop individual complementary products or tools as enhancements to core SAP applications. It can support direct communication with the R/3 function modules.

WEB

In the URL **http://www.sap.com/bfw/index.htm** (Business Framework Main information center) and then **Open BAPI Network**, SAP provides a repository of BAPIs with all the information needed for use.

❑ **At the PC tool level.** By using Microsoft OLE (Object Linking and Embedding) technology, R/3 also makes it possible for PC application users to access SAP data from many different OLE client programs. With the introduction of R/3 release 4.0 and especially with 4.5, SAP leveraged the concept of integration with PC programs, mainly with the technology provided by ActiveX and JavaBeans.

❑ **At the communication protocol level.** SAP can use standard communication protocols such as TCP/IP, SNA-LU6.2, CPI-C, and OSF/DCE/DME both for program-to-program communication and for network data transfer.

❑ **At the external communication level:**
  ❑ R/3 includes supports for EDI (Electronic Data Interchange) for automating the interchange and transfer of data (invoices, orders, and so on) between R/3 and other information systems used by company business partners.
  ❑ It incorporates MAPI (Messaging Application Program Interface) technology, with support for standard protocols such as X.400 and SMTP. Using these standards R/3 users can communicate with other messaging systems, including Internet mail.
  ❑ From release 3.1 and with BAPI technology, SAP has actively supported electronic commerce through the Internet, enabling

business transactions between R/3 systems and Internet users.

❑ With ALE (Application Link Enabling) technology, SAP also permits communication between distributed applications, for instance, between different R/3 systems, between R/2 and R/3 systems, and also between R/3 and external systems.

❑ Finally, using development environments based on programming languages such as C, C++, Visual Basic, Visual Studio, Java, Delphi, etc. developers can easily integrate external applications with the R/3 systems, interchanging information at the business object level.

User Interface

The R/3 user interface (GUI) was designed for simplicity and easy use for any employee in a company. The typical and most common SAP graphical user interface is known as SAPGUI, and acts as the client for the application servers. It is available for many different desktop operating systems, such as all Microsoft Windows flavors, Macintosh, Motif, and OS/2, and others. All have an identical look, despite their underlying operating system.

SAPGUI includes all the features available in modern, Windows-oriented graphical user interfaces such as buttons, icons, menu bars, tool bars, active descriptions, hypertext, right mouse-button options, and so on. Basic functionality and the design of the graphical interface is homogeneous and common to all R/3 applications, which makes training much easier for all types of end-users.

Depending on the functions and R/3 applications to be implemented in a company, the screens can be very simple or might contain many fields and graphical elements.

SAP customers also have the opportunity of designing and configuring their own screens and creating new ones using the help and utilities offered by the ABAP development environment.

It is also important that the communication protocol between the user interface (client or presentation server) and the application server has been greatly minimized/optimized, so that there is good response time over both LANs and WANs, and even when using phone lines and modems.

In R/3 release 4.x the new GUI was designed to be able to show several types of information at the same time. It is also possible to transfer the presentation components on demand from R/3 to the workstations because of enhancements in the architecture introduced using ActiveX under Windows, or JavaBeans.

As introduced previously, one of the biggest changes/improvements in EnjoySAP Release is the user interface strategy.

More information on SAPGUI strategy and the implementation issue of personalizing the system can be found in Chapter 5.

Integration of Business Applications

The data from the different SAP functional applications are shared and integrated to create what is often known as an *internal information highway*. This integration can be seen as implicit applications workflow.

One of the main benefits of the set of R/3 applications is the capacity for making a perfect integration between different business processes in companies. It is that integration between applications which ensures that all business and management information is available to all areas of a company.

A concomitant feature that makes application integration stand out is the capacity for working in *real time*. This means that information is constantly updated, so when a manager requests a report on the current balance, the system provides instant information about the status of the financial statements, avoiding the difficulty of running end-of-period reports and programs from a traditional legacy system, which must search for and incorporate needed data from other applications.

From the point of view of business processes, the integration of the R/3 application modules is represented using the tools available within the *R/3 Business Engineer*. At the level of data models, this integration can be accessed using the functions included in the *Data Modeler*.

Development Environment: ABAP Workbench

The ABAP development environment includes all tools needed for the design and development of programs, screens, menus, function modules, and more. It also includes the utilities for program debugging, performance and runtime analysis, and testing.

ABAP/4 was SAP's own fourth-generation programming language. From release 4.0 it was known simply as ABAP; it is exactly the same language with several technical improvements, mainly in the field of adding features to make it an object-oriented language.

The name comes from "Advanced Business Application Programming Language" and signifies the programming language used by SAP for the development of all standard business applications included in the R/3 suite.

Around the ABAP programming language, SAP designed a complete development environment, like a CASE environment, known as *ABAP Development Workbench*. This is totally integrated with the R/3 system and is available to customers to enable them to develop specific solutions to their requirements, or to use for improving or enhancing the standard applications.

At the center of the ABAP development environment are two core components: the ABAP Data Dictionary and the ABAP Business Object Repository, typically known as BOR.

The *Data Dictionary* contains all system *metadata*, that is, the descriptions of the data structures which are used in the programs. The dictionary is the metadata repository, and thus includes tables definitions, values permitted for fields, views, data elements, and so on; most importantly it defines table relationships. An in-depth knowledge of navigation and use of the Data Dictionary is very important not only for database administrators and developers, but also for customizing consultants.

The *Business Object Repository* contains all the development objects from the ABAP Workbench: programs, dictionary data, *dynpros* (screens with dynamic programs), documentation, and more. The repository is an essential component for controlling and testing developments.

From release 3.0 on, the development environment also included the *Workbench Organizer*, an additional component to the transport system. The Workbench Organizer and the Customizing Organizer are in charge of controlling the development and transition of development objects and customized settings, in order to transport them to other systems.

Features of the Workbench Organizer include version management, program modification control, coordination of team development, object locking and unlocking, among others.

Transport systems are in charge of the physical transport between systems of the development and customizing settings. For instance, SAP application patches and upgrades are really massive object transports between SAP's own systems and customer systems. This is a vital tool with which developers, customizers, and system administrators must be familiar.

Since release 3.1H of SAP R/3 and with general availability since release 4.0, there has been a new transport system known as TMS (Transport Management System), which introduced the concept of transport domains and groups. It allows for the graphical definition of systems in transport groups and the import of change requests from within the system, avoiding access to the operating system.

TIP

For those using release 3.1H, where there is no direct menu for TMS, this system can be accessed by typing transaction code STMS in the command field.

Chapter 5 deals with implementation issues related to development, and includes an overview of the transport system.

Configuration and Implementation Tools

The configuration process, known in SAP as *customizing*, is the cornerstone of SAP R/3 implementation project activities, and is basic to the *realization* phase of an implementation project.

In the software kit, a SAP customer gets the core R/3 functional modules, which include a large number of predefined business processes based on best business practices.

When the organizational aspects of a project are defined and the business processes of a company have been analyzed, the next step in the implementation project is to *customize* the system in order to match standard business processes to the needs of the company. This is the method for implementing and enhancing the R/3 system, as well as for upgrading SAP releases.

Some of the customizing activities are as easy as introducing the country or countries where the company operates. As simple as it sounds, this will make an automatic impact on the currencies that can be used, applicable taxes, legal requirements, and so on. Other customizing activities are much more complex, oriented to specific business areas or even industries, and can be much more difficult to define; these will require not only customization techniques, but also a broad knowledge of specific business activities.

Customizing the system used to be one of the longest phases in SAP implementation projects, but this was often for reasons unrelated to the actual process of customizing, and had more to do with the availability of key process users, the decisionmaking process, and politics. This area of activity should normally be done by expert users with the help of knowledgeable consultants.

Often, before or during the selection of SAP as the strategic and core business solution, companies start a project for reengineering their business processes. R/3 customizing will later try to reflect the result of that reengineering effort, with remodeled business processes, their functions, and new organization.

With every new release, and within the environment provided by the R/3 Business Engineer, SAP includes new tools and utilities to help both customers and consultants in the customizing process. As part of its strategy, there is constant incorporation of new industry "blueprints" which can quickly be used to adapt specific R/3 functions and processes to the corresponding best business practices.

Some of the tools and documentation provided by SAP are:

❑ The **Procedure Model**, a hierarchical project structure designed to help customers in their implementation projects. Introduced in release 3.0, it can be considered the first integrated solution set that SAP included within the R/3 system. The Procedure Model has been integrated into the R/3 system, but is quickly becoming less used than ASAP methodology.

❑ The **IMG (Implementation Guide)**, an interactive model for helping users and consultants to customize the system by entering the needed entries for matching required parameters and definitions with specific needs for conducting the business. The IMG can automatically manage and create all organizational activities and can start the implementation project. It works like an electronic manual for consultants, and includes hypertext links to documentation for the customizing process, as well as direct links to execute the needed transactions for making the customization entries.

❑ The **Transport System**, an important component of systems configuration, is used to monitor, manage, and transfer the configuration and settings from the development or integration environment to the production systems.

❑ Tools for managing and upgrading of systems releases.

Some customization like defining the printing infrastructure, copying clients, configuring the transport system, and so on, is the responsibility of system administrators and basis system consultants.

R/3 Business Engineer

SAP provides the R/3 Reference Model to help depict and describe business processes, the possibilities offered by the R/3 software, and the relationship between different processes and application modules. This model is vital to R/3 projects, since it allows customers and consultants to select which processes, alternatives, workarounds and system components will be necessary to meet an organization's requirements and technological infrastructure needs. The R/3 Business Engineer is a graphical tool used to document business processes included within R/3, providing a clear vision of their integration.

Together with the customizing tools, the R/3 Reference Model is one of the essential components for implementing SAP. Figure 1.6 shows the relationship and role of the Reference Model as the intermediate layer between R/3 business practices and processes and the specific needs of companies.

The Reference Model can also be used for other SAP project tasks, including end-user training, project scope analysis, integration tests, systems reengineering, and gap analysis.

When there is no SAP R/3 system installed at the customer site, the Reference Model is available as an independent PC tool, such as the ARIS toolset, LiveModel for SAP R/3, Visio or Micrografx Enterprise Charter. All these tools can be used to analyze and model the business processes of companies and can be helpful in simulation, prototyping, training, and documentation.

Since release 3.0, the Reference Model has been integrated into the R/3 system. It is better known as *Business Navigator*.

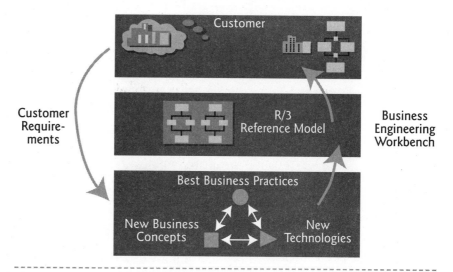

FIGURE 1.6 *R/3 Reference Model and Business Processes*   *Copyright © SAP AG*

SAP Services

SAP has put in place a comprehensive set of quality services to help customers in the process of implementing and supporting the R/3 system. These services include product information, training, installation, upgrades, consulting, etc. SAP has based its services mainly on remote connections with customers through international networks.

Services are considered some of the additional components within the ASAP methodology, and SAP continues to introduce new and enhanced SAP R/3 Service Packages to complement the full implementation process.

Administrators, support personnel, and consultants should be particularly familiar with SAP's *Online Service System* (OSS), which is the primary source for service and support.

SAP offers a certification process in the technical, functional, and developing areas of the system , and an extensive number of training courses worldwide.

Generically, SAP provides the following types of services:

❑ **Consulting Services.** This type of individualized consulting service can be given onsite or via a remote connection to SAP. With remote consulting, customers can receive immediate and updated technical support and have answers to their questions. SAP also gives weekend support when upgrades or installations must be done outside regular working hours. Customers open the connection so SAP consultants can directly access customer systems and evaluate problems online. Once the consulting session is finished the customer closes the connection.

❑ **Maintenance Services.** This is the basic and most common type of support for customers in the preproduction and production phases of an R/3 implementation. This service deals with answering questions and giving help to solve errors or problems with the system. For maintenance, SAP has set up a HelpDesk or Hotline, which monitors calls and resolves them or directs them to the appropriate SAP expert. A First Level Customer Service team is in charge of resolving problems, prioritizing calls, and, if needed, referring the matter to other experts. Customers can obtain this service via phone, fax, and the OSS 24 hours a day, 7 days a week. As an example, if you have a severe problem at 5:00 AM, log it in OSS, and give it a "Very High" priority (it means "my system does not work"). You might expect a fast call back from Japan, Philadelphia, Walldorf, or other international location.

❑ **Information Services.** The various information sources for receiving detailed information about the R/3 system are marketing brochures, system documentation, training information, an events calendar, etc. As the main information service SAP introduced SAPnet (**http://sapnet.sap-ag.de**) for customers and partners. It can be accessed though the Internet. SAPnet has become a key site not only for information, but also for requesting notes, services, and so on.

❑ **Preventive Services.** The most important is EarlyWatch™ Service to ensure successful and efficient installation of the R/3 sys-

tem in all phases. This service makes regular (monthly, bimonth-
ly, or other requested period) performance checks and analyzes
the system to identify potential problems and help system managers and SAP administrators tune the system to its full potential.
Soon after an EarlyWatch session, SAP sends the customer a
report with the results of the analysis, and recommendations for
avoiding potential problems, like a database becoming full, short-
age of system parameters, buffer tuning, etc. Recently SAP introduced the EarlyWatch Alert service, meant to automatically send
to SAP, via the remote connection, the main parameters of productive installations.

SAP provides additional services like Development Request Service,
to submit enhancement requests, and First Customer Shipment
(FCS), which gives selected customers the opportunity to test new
R/3 version functionality before the product is officially released.

Since 1997 SAP has been introducing new Service Packages
including services such as OS/DB migration (for changing the operating system or database), remote upgrades, remote archiving, Going
Life Health Check, and so on.

More information about current SAP service offerings can be found at
http://www.sap.com/services.

WEB

The Online Service System: An Introduction to the OSS

The Online Service System (OSS) is the main door for customers to
SAP services. It is itself a special customized R/3 system that customers with remote connection to SAP support servers can use free.
(It is included in the maintenance fee). The main goal of the OSS is
to provide a two-way communication channel so customers can try
to solve problems before logging a call to SAP, or requesting service.

This is a brief list of what is available at the OSS system:

❑ Problem and information database (Hint notes), so that a user
can try to find the solution to a problem, before calling SAP or

sending a problem report. Reading OSS notes is a good way not only to solve problems but also to learn about the many complexities of R/3.

❑ The latest SAP news, patches, and service announcements in the HotNews section.

❑ Up-to-date release, installation, and upgrade information. These latest notes are mandatory in any installation of upgrades to R/3.

❑ Online help. Users can register problems or questions online, and be treated the same way (and sometimes better) and with the same priority as if this were done by telephone.

❑ Look-up database for training offerings and course descriptions.

❑ Since release 3.0, access to the SSCR system (SAP Software Change Registration), used for registering both developer and system objects before making any modification to the system.

❑ Online registration for customer systems or knowledge products.

❑ Customized OSS user administration.

❑ Training calendars, locations, and availability.

❑ License keys.

OSS is the star service system provided by SAP, and the most widely used by SAP customers and partners, especially consultants and administrators. The OSS interface is intuitive and very easy to use and learn.

SAP provides an initial OSS user ID and password for a customer administrator; you can obtain additional OSS accounts by entering the request in the OSS system.

EarlyWatch: The Preventive Maintenance Service

EarlyWatch is SAP's offering for preventive services, providing online diagnosis and analysis. This service connects SAP experts into the customer system to get all information needed for preparing a report that is later sent to the customer.

Soon after or even before production starts, SAP recommends a first session to verify the quality of the installation.

The first thing visible in the EarlyWatch report is a summary diagnosis with a "traffic light" that indicates the level of severity of system problems.

Administrators always like to see a green light, which means that most parameters are well tuned and the system is running fine. The yellow light indicates that some problems have been detected, and a red light indicates that there are critical problems to be solved as soon as possible.

EarlyWatch checks on potential problems in the SAP R/3 application, as well as in the database and operating system. It provides information on tablespace capacity, SAP system log error messages, buffer tuning, database parameters, and more.

R/3 systems have hundreds of parameters, and many of them directly affect other values. The EarlyWatch team analyzes the evolution of the system, and if they detect bottlenecks or an increase in processing time, they usually recommend new values for the profile parameters.

CHAPTER 2

SAP Projects and Implementation Issues

The usual meaning of *implement* is to fulfill or accomplish something, whereas a *project* is usually defined as a *problem scheduled for solution*.

In SAP implementation projects, the problem is usually the implementation itself. SAP implementation does not begin and end with simply installing SAP R/3 on your system. Implementation issues expand beyond the implementation project to encompass both pre-implementation planning and post-implementation upgrades. The reasons are threefold: First, because change is a continuous process in most businesses, SAP implementation is often an ongoing process to incorporate change into existing systems.

Second, SAP implementation requires the development of both support and systems management strategies for optimum results. And third, because not many companies implement SAP via a "Big Bang" strategy, but rather follow a phased implementation plan, some application modules start production before others. Upgrading releases, connecting additional business components, and adding features to the SAP system also expand the process of implementation. In a large, complex project of this nature, you will find numerous problems, tasks, and activities that were not initially anticipated. These, too, become part of the ongoing implementation process.

To be successful in SAP implementation, you must have a clear framework or roadmap that shows what the end result will be—before you begin. This book is not intended to depict or design new implementation methodologies. We are concerned instead with addressing those issues that are needed to accomplish a successful SAP implementation. Choosing a methodology, although extremely important, is just one issue that must be addressed.

Every project has a goal of reaching its expected results. In computing projects, these results are usually defined by a requirements analysis. In a business project, these results are often defined by the results of previous attempts at business-process reengineering. Any implementation that attempts to incorporate the results of this reengineering process must be supported by upper management because it will affect the entire organization and will require critical decisions to be made.

SAP R/3 projects might cover every area of the company and all the critical information for the business. Taking into consideration global approaches, it is obvious that a SAP R/3 implementation is not a trivial collection of activities, but rather a complex and critical collection of projects which can directly influence financial results: the cost of R/3 implementation extends from project initiation to the going-live phase to succeeding product operation and maintenance phases, and can be quite high.

Scope of Implementation Issues

As we noted in the previous chapter, implementing SAP R/3 is far from just running the setup for a software program and starting to enter data. Implementing SAP is a business project, a strategic solution for companies.

Implementation issues spread beyond implementation projects: a SAP implementation project with an explicit goal and objective might end, but normally the business project does not, mainly because of the process of continuous change. Projects might be similar but are basically different by nature, as are implementation paths.

Whatever path, methodology, or scope is chosen, *implementing SAP* means embracing a business project and envisioning the future.

When companies decide to confront the challenge of implementing SAP, one of the first hurdles recognizing where to start. This is due in part to the lack of SAP knowledge or experience; most companies contact and contract with external consultants who sometimes have more experience in SAP methodologies.

NOTE   A methodology is a practice or discipline which is formal and structured; it typically includes phases/paths, activities/tasks, inputs/outputs, and should have been proven efficient when appropriately used by project managers.

The most methodologies developed by multiple SAP partners are good, but whichever methodology is chosen, most important to project success is that the project manager and consultants working in a methodological framework are experienced and capable.

In this book only SAP methodologies—a part of solution sets—are discussed, in order to help readers understand the methodological framework of SAP implementation.

In the introductory chapter we noted how SAP competition criticizes the cost and difficulty of implementation, how long it takes for successful implementation and how many consulting services are needed. These criticisms should be considered in perspective.

The SAP response to these criticisms has been to ease the path to implementation, mainly with the ASAP solution set and the Team-SAP initiative for providing quality services.

Another critical factor of implementation, from a business point of view, is the expected return on the investment (ROI). The ROI must be measurable and as swift as possible. This factor will be a challenge for the project team and supporting management, and will actually be the most significant factor by which to measure the degree of success of the implementation.

Frequently the costs of aSAP R/3 implementation project of the nature of SAP R/3 are increased by the difficulties of defining a realistic and achievable project plan. Factors influencing planning have to do with heterogeneous project team members and project methodologies.

According to the extent of an SAP R/3 implementation, the project might affect one, two, three, or all application modules, or might be a release upgrade. There are natural differences in company sizes where implementation is taking place. There are also differences in geographical location, and social and cultural organization.

One process of business engineering or reengineering might lead to choice of the full standard SAP functionality, while other projects might need to modify parts of the standard software.

Introduction to SAP Implementation Projects

This section covers general notes about R/3 projects, and will contain an overview of the process of implementing SAP. These topics are covered in more detail later in the book.

A project can be considered as a set or group of activities to be done or developed, within a time frame, with a schedule, with the purpose of reaching an objective or result previously established. Besides specific and measurable objectives, the goal of the project is to succeed, so that the company implementing R/3 is satisfied with the results. To reach that goal the set of activities must be accomplished according to defined project plans, within the set time frame and budget, or with a justifiable and acceptable deviation.

The success of a project is ultimately measured by the degree of satisfaction of the end-users.

The project is done by a group of individuals, properly organized, so that each member of the team knows the precise content and goal of her/his work, the schedule and planned time for activities, and the global objective and mission of the project.

No two projects are equal. Even when an attempt is made to replicate an implementation already done in a division of a big company, for it becomes necessary to make various adjustments.

From a SAP R/3 methodological point of view, the implementation of these types of integrated business systems, both functional and technical, is described within the "Procedure Model," which is provided and included within the software. To a great degree, AcceleratedSAP is equivalent to the Procedure Model.

SAP R/3 includes a large number of tools and much documentation to ease the implementation of the system. (The details and thousands of pages of documentation are often necessary, but at the same time are overwhelming.) The implementation tools and manuals are online and directly accessible from the system, mostly from the menu options **Tools → Business Engineering**.

Many satisfied SAP customers recommend that companies interested in SAP invest part of their time and money in getting a correct R/3 perspective before they start implementation. This can save money and hassles later.

At the same time, an implementation project does not have much chance of succeeding when upper management is not strong enough, does not have a clear vision, or hesitates about the business processes which must be changed. If management does not commit to change, it cannot make quick decisions, and the project will find itself in a deadlock or labyrinth.

Companies should also estimate the need to undertake a reengineering process before starting an implementation project. Customizing and reengineering at the same time often creates delays in the implementation process.

Identifying Implementation Needs

Different companies have many different needs and will face different implementation issues when approaching business projects like implementing R/3.

An implementation project is heavily influenced by generic factors such as the number of potential users, the size of the company, the time, the budget, and the expected return on investment. For some companies data conversion and migration from a legacy system can be a big issue. For many companies, leading the cultural change will be of core importance, while for other companies, such as small, new, or recent enterprises—the issue might not be crucial. Finally, some companies will decide to replace most of their business legacy applications with SAP, while others will just replace some of them and live with different types of periodic interfaces.

These different needs engender other implementation issues. For instance, for monitoring the SAP systems some companies might decide to get third-party tools to integrate the monitoring of R/3 with other types of systems, while for others CCMS is enough. In any case filling needs will require identifying cost-effective solutions company-wide.

Identifying needs leads to many different configuration scenarios. One example is when R/3 is selected for implementing a single application module to solve a specific business problem, usually from an independent business area. Companies might find this a suitable solution, maybe the starting point of a bigger project. But in doing so, the real value of SAP—the integration of processes—is partially lost.

Implementation Risks

If there is some work to be done to identify implementation requirements and define the project scope, there should be corresponding effort to identify implementation risks. This is usually a process of risk assessment that can be conducted as part of change management. Before getting to that point, some risks can be identified by lessons learned in many previous customer installations, mainly by analyzing typical problems in the implementation, and by considering critical success factors. If some of the points for success cannot be met, this is a clear risk; they must be removed or their impact eliminated.

Generically, there are three types of risks in any implementation:

❑ Risks related with human factors, like availability of skills and resources, impact of cultural change, or commitment of the company leader
❑ Risks that have to do with the technical infrastructure and resources needed for the project
❑ Methodology risks, related to the proper way of doing implementation projects, process modeling, project management, and so on.

A secure knowledge of implementation issues can be the best way to address risks. Providing that knowledge is one of the main goals of this book.

SAP Implementation Solution Sets

SAP provides many tools and complementary applications to help in the implementation process, covering every aspect involved in such an enterprise. There are two main solution sets, the Procedure Model and AcceleratedSAP. There are called solution sets because they include more than a simple methodology for implementation; they try to provide a global solution for the project. Differences may not be clear, and may be confusing if they are influenced by marketing messages. Detailed information about both solution sets is contained in the next chapter; what follows is an introduction.

Procedure Model is a key implementation tool in a SAP project. The Procedure Model defines, from a generic point of view, all the activities needed for SAP implementation. It has a mission to provide a detailed project plan, with all the phases, steps and activities not only for customizing but for all other SAP implementation issues. The model is accessed from within the system by selecting menu options **Tools → Business Engineering → Customizing → Basic functions → R/3 Procedure model**.

The Procedure Model includes active links to the documentation, to R/3 transactions, notes, customizing, and so on and allows for project management monitoring and analysis. Figure 2.1 shows the main diagram of the procedure model in a hierarchical form.

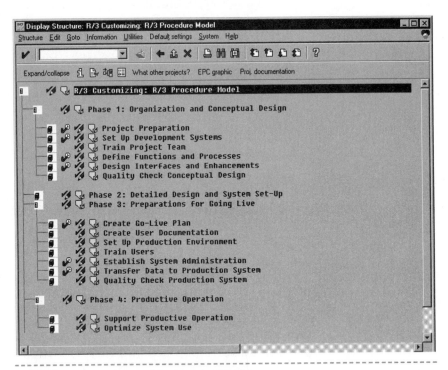

FIGURE 2.1   *Overview of the Procedure Model*

Additionally and fully integrated with the R/3 Procedure Model, for a general approach to implementation issues, SAP provides the following help:

❑ **Customizing Manual.** Customizing is the process of adapting the SAP R/3 software to business needs. This manual provides a detailed guide to customizing activities, including references and links to other manuals and system tools. Functions needed for adapting the system are under menu option **Tools ➜ Business Engineering ➜ Customizing**.

❑ **The IMG or Implementation Guide** includes a step-by-step guide to customizing, with direct links to all necessary transactions to adapt the selected R/3 modules or applications. Using the IMG, it is possible to train end-users (especially key users) in customization techniques and options so they can configure the system themselves according to their business and organizational needs.

The IMG includes utilities to manage the "customizing projects." Using these project management utilities, consultants decide which part of the system is to be customized. They generate projects for which the system automatically produces a hierarchical list of the necessary customizing steps for the selected application modules. IMG is accessed from the customizing main menu. Select the necessary functions or utilities under the Implementation Projects menu.

Figure 2.2 includes an example of the Implementation Guide, within an IMG project.

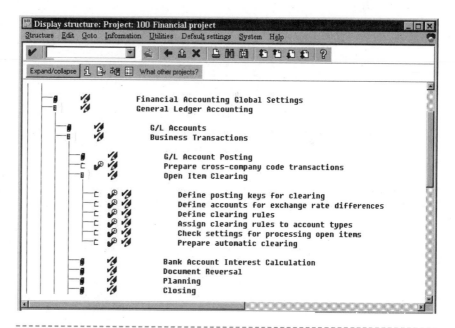

FIGURE 2.2   *Example of IMG*

The IMG is the tool used for configuration, and includes about 10,000 configuration objects in the latest versions. There is no need to customize settings except those resulting from business process modeling or reengineering. Subsets of the IMG are set up using IMG projects that can be generated by selecting and including applications or components that are part of the project. The tool will automatically choose any previously required customizing object even if it was not selected.

❑ **The R/3 Reference Model** is the data model describing the business processes and business components included in the standard SAP R/3 system, as well as the relationship between different functions and application modules. The Reference Model is accessed using the functions of the Business Navigator.

The AcceleratedSAP solution set is very similar to the Procedure Model, and also makes use of the available tools for customizing and implementing the system. They are generically known as *Business Engineer*. ASAP is further explained in the next chapter.

Implementation Issues: The Big Picture

Out of my own and customer experiences, and from Internet forums and mailing lists, I have compiled a list of implementation issues. In this book we will consider this list of implementation issues, why they are important, how can they influence the success of implementation projects, and how to deal with these issues.

The immutable issues of any implementation are cost, time and expected benefits. Beyond this many implementation issues are related to more than one business area, for instance, technical and functional problems (i.e. archiving), people and knowledge (i.e. helpdesk strategy), and so on. The implementation issues covered here address as many variants as possible, to cover as many unique situations as possible. Most implementation issues can be grouped as follows:

❑ **Processes and Methodology Issues.** These are the implementation problems related to the "how to." Among these issues are questions about the methodology and solution sets available for implementing, how to customize, and so on. The issues included within this category are:
   ❑ Selecting and using a methodology

❑ Modeling business processes
❑ Performing a gap analysis
❑ Monitoring the project scope
❑ Customizing the system.

Chapter 3 deals with these implementation issues, explaining in detail the Procedure Model and the ASAP Solution Sets, the two main methodologies for solutions to these topics.

❑ **People-related Issues.** These are issues related mainly to project organization and change management and include:
   ❑ Project organization
   ❑ Commitment of upper management
   ❑ Project management
   ❑ Dealing with consultants
   ❑ Dealing with key users
   ❑ Change management.

These topics are extensively explained in Chapter 4, which also includes the following category.

❑ **Knowledge-based Issues.** These have to do with problems caused by wrong communication policies, training, transfer of knowledge or lack of documentation, which can clearly affect other implementation tasks such as end-user training or helpdesk strategy. They include:
   ❑ Communication
   ❑ Training
   ❑ Project documentation
   ❑ End-user documentation
   ❑ Procedures
   ❑ Knowledge transfer.

❑ **Technology and Infrastructure Issues.** In every implementation project there must be a solid technical base for supporting the installation. The fact that SAP is a business project does not mean that technology issues must be underestimated; a poor infrastructure and technical consulting can lead to implementation chaos. Gartner says that an enterprise application is a business project with an IT component. The following list outlines the main infrastructure issues in SAP implementations:

❑ Systems landscape
❑ Sizing and scalability
❑ Choosing platforms
❑ Network infrastructure
❑ Software installation and systems copy
❑ Front-end distribution
❑ High availability
❑ Backup and recovery strategy
❑ Printing strategy
❑ Batch strategy.

This technical category includes such issues as System Administration, Performance and Tuning, and System Troubleshooting; these topics are dealt with in Chapter 7 because they have a bigger impact during the completion phase of the project.

❑ **Development-related Issues.** These are issues related to change or enhancement of the system, as well as to activities that require development knowledge; they include:

❑ Programs and reports development
❑ Data migration issues
❑ Building interfaces
❑ Enhancing the system
❑ Applying patches
❑ Personalizing the system.

These topics are explained in Chapter 5.

❑ **Going-Live and Support Issues.** An implementation project might be considered to end when end-users start productive work on SAP systems. However issues which must be taken into consideration after going live, and which must be addressed and planned for ahead of time include:

❑ Going live
❑ System management
❑ Performance and tuning
❑ Supporting SAP: troubleshooting

❑ Supporting SAP: helpdesk strategy
❑ Upgrade projects
❑ Continuous change.

Chapter 7 is devoted to explaining the implications of these issues.

Finally I have distinguished an additional group of implementation issues which do not belong to a particular group but rather relate to all of them:

❑ **Subprojects or Cross-application Issues.** These include those problems that must be resolved by both technical and functional teams; these often include many organizational problems. The main issues identified under this category include:
❑ Reporting
❑ Archiving
❑ Authorizations and profiles
❑ Testing
❑ Security.

Upgrade projects also fall into this category but this issue is covered in Chapter 7 on post-implementation issues.

The following chapters deal with all these implementation issues, focusing on importance, repercussions and how to deal with them, with emphasis on available documentation, tools, and best-known strategies.

Tools, Utilities, and Applications for Helping Implementation Projects

Since the last section included an overall picture of the main implementation issues, here I have tried to compile and briefly describe the SAP helpers available for the implementation. These include system components, utilities, tools, applications, documentation, and even architectures. Besides the SAP tools, there is an ever-growing number of complementary products and solutions covering many implementation issues as well as daily operations.

For instance there are third-party tools and applications which can be used for:

- **Testing and scripting.** Automated testing can be used in the testing phases of the project to potentially save money.
- **Business process modeling.** Tools like ARIS toolset, Micrografx Enterprise Charter, Intellicorp LiveModel, or Visio can be used when documenting and designing the business processes, whether a BPR is underway or not, and can be used later to customize the R/3 system. They can also be used for prototyping, end-user training, and so on.
- **Barcoding.** Special tools connect barcode printing devices with the system.
- **Form design.** Design tools either as substitute for or complement to the SAP standard SAPscript, can be used to design and realize printed forms, such as invoices, payrolls, or warehouse labels.
- **Systems monitoring.** These tools complement SAP Administration functions and the Computer Center Management System (CCMS) and often work as part of a company's global administration and monitoring strategy.
- **Backup solutions.** These are designed for demanding backup and restore installations, such as those with very large databases, or with little or no time for stopping the system.
- **EDI subsystems.** These tools communicate some of the SAP logistics processes to companies' business partners, customers, or providers.
- **FAX integration.** Fax links can be used as direct output of process, for requests for quotes, invoices, etc.
- **Output management.** These tools handle large print volumes.
- **Archiving.** Archieving tools can be used either for removing obsolete data from the database or as a means to store scanned documents in an optical archive system.
- **Tools for integrating CAD, GIS, LIMS, PDC.**

A complete list of complementary products can be found on the following URL: **http://www.sap.com/products/compsoft/index.htm**.

WEB

Within and around R/3 there is a huge list of tools, applications, helpers, and technology enablers, which can be used directly or indirectly to address many project and implementation issues. Some of them are:

❑ **ABAP Workbench.** This is the SAP complete development environment, where new programs can be designed and others enhanced or modified. The Workbench integrated components include the ABAP Data Dictionary, Testing Workbench, ABAP Editor, Debugging Facilities, Workbench Organizer and more. See Chapter 5.

❑ **ALE (Application Link Enable)** technology is part of the Business Framework Architecture, and can be used to solve the problem of distributed installations with a semantic business process integration, as for example, a central headquarters and local subsidiaries.

❑ **APO (Advance Planner and Optimizer)** is an independent and fully integrated SAP component, part of the SCOPE (Supply Chain Optimization Planning and Execution) initiative. APO includes advanced features in complex environments for demand forecasting, a comprehensive planning engine for the full supply chain, and process optimization.

❑ **ArchiveLink**, the R/3 standard interface definition for connecting external archive servers for optical document archiving or application data archiving.

❑ **ASAP Accelerators**, an ever-growing collection of tools, documentation, programs, and templates used as helpers in many of the tasks and activities of ASAP-based implementation.

❑ **Authorization system/Profile Generator**, has been available since release 3.0F for easing the process of designing profiles and authorization for users.

❑ **BAPIs (Business Application Program Interfaces)**, the standard interfaces (methods) of SAP business objects; one of the main pieces of the Business Framework Architecture.

❑ **Business Framework**, the SAP open architecture for integrating independent components of R/3 with other SAP and non-SAP software products and technologies. These products can have their own life-cycle and release independence. Business Framework is based on standard interface technology provided by BAPIs and business objects.

❑ **Business Information Warehouse**, SAP's data warehouse solution, a component of Business Framework and fully integrated with R/3; it can be used for consolidating data from R/3 and external systems.

❑ **Business Navigator**, the collection of tools used for displaying and working with the R/3 Reference Model. It can be used for the process analysis phases of implementation and can be accessed from within R/3. There is also a Web version.

❑ **SAP Business Workflow.** SAP's solution for workflow management. A Workflow Management system is designed to automate the procedures within business processes, managing and controlling the sequence of work activities involved, communicating to the related job positions, and triggering the corresponding events and subsequent steps and activities to complete the process.

❑ **CATS (Cross Application Time Sheet)**, SAP's solution for recording the time sheets of employees; it is used in several R/3 applications such as PS, PM, PP, HR, Travel Expenses, and so on.

❑ **CCMS (Computer Center Management System)**, R/3 application for systems management, monitoring, and control.

❑ **GuiXT**, a third-party SAP-supplied tool that allows easy personalization of SAPGUI screens without programming.

❑ **Hot Packages/Legal Change Packages**, a collection of changes and corrections to R/3 application programs. Hot Packages do not include Human Resources-related corrections, which are contained in the Legal Change Packages.

❑ **IACs (Internet Application Components)**, used for linking HTML forms with R/3 application business scenarios.

❑ **IMG (Implementation Guide)**, the SAP step-by-step guide to activities related to customizing settings, and directly connected to both the Procedure Model and ASAP.

❑ **Implementation Assistant**, the main tool of the ASAP solution set, used independently of the R/3 system, although it includes certain functions for performing several implementation tasks directly over the R/3 systems.

❑ **Installation tools**, such as R3SETUP and R3INST, for the process of easing and automating the installation of R/3 systems.

❑ **Interface Adviser**, a collection of documents to help customers design and maintain their permanent interfaces with non-SAP systems.

❑ **ITS (Internet Transaction Server)** middleware for connecting Internet and Intranet applications with R/3.

❑ **Knowledge Warehouse (InfoDB)**, an independent SAP component, part of the advanced training solution in the Knowledge Management initiative. It is based on a repository of training courses and documentation, with many possibilities for editing, authoring, searching, etc.

❑ **LSM Workbench (Legacy System Migration)**, available directly in R/3 since release 4.0 and helpful for Data Migration-related activities

❑ **Made Easy guides**, by the Simplification Group, are excellent manuals providing step-by-step procedures for learning and performing the most common operations in the R/3 system. Available guides include: Authorizations Made Easy, Administration Made Easy, Data Transfer Made Easy, Printing Made Easy, and Reporting Made Easy.

❑ **Modification Assistant**, a tool within the R/3 system that can be used for managing enhancements and modifications in development work.

❑ **OSS (Online Service System)**, the main service offering of SAP; it includes a problems database, hotline support, online correction system, training availability, service connections, and more. Chapter 1 gave an overview of the OSS.

❑ **Pre-configured clients (PCC)**, by the Simplification group (**http://www.saplabs.com/simple**), are a set of transports with customizing settings, and a guidebook that gives customers a direct start for implementation projects where the system is already customized for most standard application business processes. PCCs are only available for U.S. and Canada.

❑ **Procedure Model**, SAP's first solution set for implementing R/3, is included in the system. Chapter 3 describes the Procedure Model in more detail.

❑ **Profile Generator**, the R/3 tool that can be used for implementing the authorization concept to enable system security, user access, and privileges for accessing systems transactions.

- ❏ **Project IMG**, a subset of the Implementation Guide, contains activities defined for a particular part of the R/3 application.
- ❏ **Quick Sizer**, an Internet-based tool that helps customers and prospects to size the hardware platform according to customer requirements in terms of number of users per module, or by workload transaction profile.
- ❏ **R/3 Business Engineer**, a collection of tools (R/3 Business Navigator, R/3 Reference Model), included within the R/3 system.
- ❏ **RRR: R/3 Ready to Run**, a preconfigured, preinstalled hardware, software, and network system for running R/3 out of the box. This solution is intended for small- to medium-sized companies, and is offered by many SAP hardware partners.
- ❏ **RFC (Remote Function Call)**, a standard communication protocol and interface for carrying out remote calls between programs or applications of different systems (SAP and non-SAP). Functions supporting RFC can be remotely called by other programs.
- ❏ **SAPDBA**, the SAP database administration tool that includes all the functions for managing ORACLE and INFORMIX databases.
- ❏ **SAPnet**, a central repository of SAP information for customers and partners available on the Internet (**http://sapnet.sap-ag.de**); it includes not only documents, but also access to many of the functions and services available in the OSS.
- ❏ **SAPconnect**, another communication interface, that behaves like a middleware layer, to link R/3 with other systems or applications, for example with mail systems, fax, Internet, and so on.
- ❏ **TeamSAP**, SAP and partners' initiative for supporting mutual customers in total lifecycle implementation and operation of the R/3 systems. It is made up of the Triple P: People, Products, and Processes.
- ❏ **TMS (Transport Management System)**, the tool used for copying and moving objects and customizing settings between systems; it is also the R/3 standard way of organizing development work.
- ❏ **Test workbench and Computer Aided Test Tool (CATT)**, a collection of tools that permit recording and performing testing procedures, included in the R/3 system.
- ❏ **Upgrade tools**, R3up and others, used to help prepare and carry out release upgrade projects.

These are just some of the many available utilities that can be used for streamlining the process of implementing SAP systems.

Problems and Success Factors in SAP Implementation Projects

One of the most common reasons for problems in SAP implementations is that customers often do not understand the nature of this type of project until several months after the project has started. By then, lots of problems are in the waiting queue.

SAP R/3 is not meant as a quick software solution for solving basic business problems, such as the lack of information. Many of the problems with implementation have to do with the mistaken or incomplete concept of what it means to implement SAP. Companies often think that when they decide for R/3 they are just buying software, without understanding that the road ahead can lead to immense benefits, but must be correctly followed so that companies don't get lost in the way.

An R/3 implementation project can be seen as a process consisting of an initial reengineering effort, followed by a configuration process and user training, with the support of a technical and infrastructure layer, and under the umbrella of an accompanying management change project.

Stories about the problems choosing consultants are common, but many SAP customers find that expert consultants were very expert.

The issue of "choose your consultants well" can be also phrased (sometimes) as "choose your customers well." Whatever the situation, to work successfully in implementation projects customers and consultants must be fair to one another, and above all, make an integrated team, where everybody looks at exactly the same goals and objectives to make the project successful.

The business side of SAP implementation projects must also be considered. Just as the title of the first chapter stated, with SAP there is fundamental switch from IT to business projects. It was very common in traditional software packages and custom-built legacy systems for project teams to be based mainly on technical specialists and not real business users. In SAP implementation, the number of technical personnel used to be much lower than for business users and business consultants. Beware of forgetting to provide enough technical support: IT does not define or design business processes, but there must be a stable infrastructure environment and technical support for consultants.

The Cost of an Implementation Project

Project or implementation costs exert considerable influence on the decision to get an integrated application suite.

Costs will be difficult to plan, especially indirect costs difficult to budget. The list below should give an idea of various cost elements in SAP implementation projects:

❑ **Software package license costs** include R/3 licenses plus operating system, base software, and database.
❑ **Hardware and infrastructure costs** include servers, storage, backup devices, PCs, printers, faxes, network hubs, and so on.
❑ **Consulting** costs include business process modeling, customizing, knowledge transfer, change management, and even project management. Other consulting services will be required for technical tasks such as installation, upgrade, systems management, infrastructure setup and testing, and so on.
❑ **Training costs and the corresponding logistics** include documentation preparation, facilities, and so on.
❑ **Complementary products** costs like automated testing software, data migration, online interfaces, reporting tools, archiving solutions, and so on, must be factored.
❑ **Development costs** are accrued when new programs or reports are needed, or an existing process must be adapted or enhanced.
❑ **Time spent by end-users**, outside their normal work and productive operations add costs to implementation.
❑ **Time spent by managers** learning the new system costs money.
❑ **Maintenance costs** for hardware, software and support must be considered.
❑ **Miscellaneous costs** include facilities, logistics, material, travel, mail, and others.

Also plan for the cost of the resources needed to support the system (Helpdesk) and the continuous management of change (i.e. new or additional projects, training, and others).

Costs will be a function of the balance needed between the quality of the project and the time needed to achieve it. However as the risks of the project are assessed, and problems ahead are identified, the three factors—costs, quality, and time—can be significantly improved.

What *Sappers* Say About the Problems They Had

This section contains a large collection of problems related by people working on SAP projects, both customers and consultants. If you are in the process of implementing SAP, don't despair. Implementation circumstances can be quite different, and thousands of SAP customers have succeeded in their efforts, with more or less pain. Consider the list as a "lessons learned" summary. Problems can be avoided if they can be anticipated and actions can be planned.

Below is the list of reasons for implementation problems and project difficulties. Many are closely related to one another:

❑ **Wrong understanding of SAP Implementation:** A mindset that the project is an IT project, like the installation of a new software system, instead of a business project with an IT component. A project of this nature and magnitude needs to be user-led as opposed to being systems-led.
❑ **Vision:** Lack of a clear vision resulting in a badly designed future goal coupled with ever-changing scope.
❑ **Tendency to over-customizing:** Users want the system to look and act just like the old system.
❑ **Lack of focus** on core functionality instead of uncritical enhancements.
❑ Problems with management and organization:
  ❑ Lack of management support. Without support and buy-in, working in a project of this nature—change of culture—is high-risk.
  ❑ Upper management commitment to the project is not clear
  ❑ Management does not communicate effectively

- ❏ Lack of senior management support
- ❏ Senior management not visible
- ❏ Project decisions not supported
- ❏ Lack of leadership
- ❏ Lack of direction and common objectives
- ❏ Lack of a commitment to change and re-engineering
- ❏ Management does not get user involvement
- ❏ Unclear role of the end-user community
- ❏ Management does not know how to retain project members
- ❏ Problems with project management
- ❏ Problems with scarce resources:
  - ❏ Not enough consultants (functional and technical)
  - ❏ Key users not available for the committed time
  - ❏ Lack of hardware resources
  - ❏ Insufficient budget
  - ❏ Inadequate hardware
  - ❏ Problems with the network
  - ❏ People not available
  - ❏ Lack of skills for required tasks
  - ❏ Training not available (budgeting)
- ❏ Problems with consultants:
  - ❏ Over-reliance on consultants
  - ❏ Lack of knowledge transfer to employees
  - ❏ Lack of trust in own people instead of consultants
  - ❏ Inexperienced consultants
  - ❏ Lack of teamwork
  - ❏ Differences in objectives
- ❏ Wrong project management:
  - ❏ Unrealistic planning, usually too aggressive
  - ❏ No clear mission, goals, and measures; project team doesn't know where they are in the project path, what the next step is and whether or not they met expectations
  - ❏ Undefined scope
  - ❏ Scope creep: different projects and different budgets
  - ❏ Wrong personality for project management
  - ❏ Project manager lacks communication skills
  - ❏ No leadership
  - ❏ Inability to motivate project members

- ❑ Inability to control project scope
- ❑ Lack of project management skills
- ❑ Lack of communications
- ❑ Lack of oversight (of what people are doing)
- ❑ No process of issue resolution
- ❑ Unrealistic implementation schedules
- ❑ Lack of a change management process
- ❑ Roles and responsibilities not clearly defined, or not defined at all; this makes it hard to find people in charge of particular activities or those who must take a decision
- ❑ No or insufficient communication:
  - ❑ Problem communicating within project team
  - ❑ Restriction on communication flow
  - ❑ Users not informed
  - ❑ Upper management not informed
  - ❑ Decisions not communicated to all interested parties
  - ❑ No communication procedures
- ❑ Lack of technical skills:
  - ❑ Not enough technical people to do the job
  - ❑ Difficult to find and retain technical people
  - ❑ Keeping technical staff motivated
  - ❑ Non-technical people driving technical decisions
  - ❑ Changing SAP supplied source code
- ❑ Problems with people in general:
  - ❑ No change management program
  - ❑ Lack of recognition
  - ❑ Incorrect reward system
  - ❑ Employees leaving for better job before finishing project
  - ❑ Inappropriate skill sets
  - ❑ Negative and unenthusiastic people
  - ❑ People retention and project continuity problems
  - ❑ No incentives for supporting project
  - ❑ No planning for premature departures of project members
  - ❑ Very stressful environment
  - ❑ Burnout
- ❑ Technical problems:
  - ❑ Problems with data conversion and migration
  - ❑ Incorrect sizing

- ❑ Bad performance
- ❑ No system management
- ❑ Equipment not on time or inadequate
- ❑ Dependent projects not delivering on time
- ❑ Too much development work
- ❑ Lack of proper controls and procedures in the Transport System
- ❑ Problems of not dealing with change management:
  - ❑ Internal and political problems
  - ❑ Insufficient sponsorship to make the change happen
  - ❑ High resistance to the project
  - ❑ Lack of proactive organizational change strategy
  - ❑ Lack of communication of the changes
  - ❑ Users not prepared/not trained for change

The next section includes what sappers say to avoid these problems.

What *Sappers* Say About the Success Factors

The previous list includes key indicators to watch for, to avoid undermining the path to success, so that actions can be planned and corrections to those problems provided. Not all of the problems can be easily addressed. For instance, in the case of external consultants, dealing with the "inside politics of a customer" is very risky business, and can only be addressed within a global change management program.

These are some of the issues *sappers* (I am included in this group) think will streamline the implementation process:

- ❑ Commitment of upper management:
  - ❑ Efficient and active sponsorship of the project
  - ❑ Corporate-wide buy-in of the project
  - ❑ An efficient decision process
  - ❑ The role of Project Manager is key to the project: select carefully and then empower
- ❑ Ownership and organization of the project:
  - ❑ The project team must understand the methodology, standards, and procedures of the whole process
  - ❑ Have realistic and measurable objectives
  - ❑ Design and document roles and responsibilities
  - ❑ Provide an issue and problem resolution procedure

- ❑ Establish an approval process for the most important implementation steps
- ❑ Establish an organization to support the project
- ❑ Empower team members to make decisions
- ❑ Create a pleasant working environment
- ❑ Compensate hard work
- ❑ Efficient communications:
  - ❑ This includes personal communication by project and organization leaders
  - ❑ Awareness of the project and SAP in the organization
  - ❑ Communicate clearly and with trust
  - ❑ No hidden messages
- ❑ Maximum teamwork and proactive collaboration:
  - ❑ Clear and common objectives of all team members despite their company affiliation
  - ❑ Involve legacy system people to make the new system also theirs
  - ❑ Involve user community
  - ❑ Give users, developers, and the technical team an environment (playground) where they can test and learn the system
- ❑ Manage the change:
  - ❑ Assess the implementation risks
  - ❑ Provide as much training as possible to team members
  - ❑ Address early the issue of end-user training
  - ❑ Manage the knowledge
  - ❑ Give incentives for knowledge transfer
  - ❑ Include an HR person in the project team
- ❑ Provide technical support:
  - ❑ Adequately size a proper hardware configuration (sappers insist on this point: double size, triple size, and so on)
  - ❑ Have an appropriate master load
  - ❑ Do not underestimate data migration
  - ❑ Install and test all technical components as soon as possible
  - ❑ Configure the System Landscape and Transport System as soon as customizing and development start
- ❑ Test:
  - ❑ Involve end-users in testing from the beginning
  - ❑ Offer cross application testing

❑ Test technical infrastructure (printers, fax, EDI, network, servers)
❑ Test for peak workloads (stress)
❑ Test backup/recovery procedure
❑ Test data migrations, loads, and interfaces
❑ Test a disaster recovery

❑ Manage the knowledge and document:
    ❑ Document problems and resolutions
    ❑ Document best practices
    ❑ Document decisions

❑ Treat consultants with respect
❑ Treat customers with respect
❑ Involve end-users and operational people while defining the scope and business requirements.
❑ Consider business engineering
❑ Select consultants carefully
❑ Avoid changing SAP standard code
❑ Avoid overcustomizing the system just to please end-users
❑ After implementation:
    ❑ Establish a support organization for handling future projects or changes
    ❑ Plan for the management of continuous change
    ❑ Plan for upgrade projects
    ❑ Plan for additional training needs.
❑ Have fun

This list of advice comes from many sources, but the question is: how to address key issues. What to do to be in line with other people's recommendations?

The answer to those question is *knowledge*: useful information that can be applied in particular circumstances.

These are the questions addressed by the following sections and chapters on this book.

ASAP Conditions for Effective Implementation

According to the ASAP solution set, there are four main requirements for succeeding in performing an efficient SAP implementation. These are:

❑ The full commitment of the whole company toward the success of the project, including the need for a fast decision-making process
❑ A clearly defined and stable project scope
❑ The realization of only a referenced-based reengineering
❑ Completely basing the implementation on SAP standards.

There are many advantages to staying within the limits of the SAP standard functionality, and these will increase as more functionality is added to the system. However, it is also true that when studying certain business processes, customers will miss certain functionality needed for their operations.

Implementation Strategies

There are many ways of approaching SAP implementation; these are closely related to expected objectives. They are dependent on customer requirements, current IT systems and infrastructure, and business organization such as divisions affected, number of users, geographical locations. These factors will influence what the implementation strategy will be, and will heavily influence the project plan.

There are three generic implementation strategies:

❑ **Phased Implementation.** This strategy means that some R/3 business processes or applications are being implemented while legacy systems are still in use, either permanently or temporarily. It may happen that a company starts with R/3 financial applications like the general ledger and accounts payable, then adds cost center accounting, and later the purchasing application from Materials Management is implemented, then Sales and Distribution and so on. This type of strategy has the advantage of taking less cultural and technical risk with the changes. On the other hand, interfaces with legacy systems must be developed and maintained, and the benefit of integration inherent in the R/3 system is only partly achieved. In any case, this is the strategy selected by most SAP customers.

❑ **Big Bang Implementation.** With this type of project, a multiple of R/3 modules are implemented at once in an organization or business unit. This type of approach can involve more risk since much effort is involved, both technically—training end-users—and in support and the management of the change. The benefit is that companies get the advantage of business process integration and fewer interfaces are required.

❑ **Roll-out Implementation.** This is a mix and match of the two previous strategies. In this approach, some modules are implemented in some parts of the company, for example in a business unit or geographical location, and later "roll out" to other divisions, geographical locations, or subsidiaries. The advantage is that lessons learned in the first implementations will help to ease the process of starting to operate the system in other parts of the company.

The Pull Approach to SAP Implementation

Below we describe the strategy for SAP Implementation of Agust Keller, a long time SAP consultant, and founder of his own consulting and reputed company, Offilog, that has been a national logo partner of SAP for several years. He calls this strategy the Pull Approach, and although not revolutionary, he has proven this to be very efficient in his many successful implementations.

Pull strategy means that a company implements the system itself with the necessary help of experts, whereas a *Push strategy* means that an external consultant implements the system in the name of top management and explains it to the end-users at the end of the project.

Usually, the process leading to the decision to implement SAP in a company is a complex project guided by a large consulting company. The arguments which lead to the acquisition of the system are on two levels: first, an organizational level documented by "process-reengineering" studies is designed to convince top management of the necessity to invest in an ERP; and second, a technical level to select a concrete system.

Nowadays, in most cases, SAP is chosen, not only because it fits the requirements better than other systems, but perhaps also because it is "fashionable" and "state of the art". The consulting companies in the sector then sell the idea of the "turnkey project" to achieve the goals described in the first step, with a price and implementation time guarantee. The customer, who has no experience in SAP projects, is tempted to buy this service basically to avoid risks. Nobody wants to risk his job for a failed data processing project, and the situation is classic: little to gain and much to lose for everybody in the company in times when changes are afoot. When changes are announced, everybody knows that there must be a return on the usually large investment related to the project.

The organizational concept describes a scenario where costs or lead times are reduced and other well-known advantages must be achieved in order to justify the investment. The payback period is a critical factor behind these decisions. This leads to "big-bang" approaches with huge project teams that are difficult to manage; their ultimate and decisive success keys are top management support and implementation time. The more "unconditional" the top manager, the longer the possible implementation time for the project. And when the project finally comes to an end, nobody wants to know anything more about SAP for a long time. The worse the experience, the longer this time will be. That is basically the push approach.

The pull approach to implementing SAP in a company is based on the following two simple facts which are not usually considered:

1. SAP is *recognized* as the basis for business applications for at least the next 10 years.
2. The *company* that acquires the system is *responsible* for the project.

The first important point is that SAP is recognized at top-management level as a strategic decision about data processing. The extent of the organization involved, the applications installed, and the time scale are all discriminators. The initial SAP project is seen as part of a process that will last for at least the next 10 years. Even in the case of a big-bang for the whole company there will be release changes, new modules, changes within the structure of the company, and other reasons for new SAP projects. The first project is almost provisional, a basis for the next projects, and something alive. That is one of the two basic reasons to realize the first SAP project as soon as possible once the decision has been taken to go ahead. The other main reason is motivation. The sooner you get results in a productive system, the more content, and sometimes even happy, users and management will be. The question is not primarily a problem of cost and resources in this approach. It is not a disaster if the project lasts a month longer than foreseen. If you see it as a first step on a long road, it is more important to learn as much as possible as soon as possible. Effective learning is done in a productive system by trial and error, not on courses and in test environments.

The easiest way to get it done as soon as possible is to make no substantial changes in the first project, either in the organization or in the software. In case of conflicts, exclude the subject from the first project if you can, or make some additional provisional development. That way it is less expensive, as a first step, and convinces the user to wait for a second step.

The conclusion from this first fact: do not mix a reengineering or other organizational project with your first SAP experience. *Do the reorganization once you have SAP installed.*

The reasons for this are:

1. In the first project the consultant does not yet know the company at the level he will know it after having installed the system; he may make assumptions that do not reflect the real situation of the company.
2. The company has no idea about the possibilities offered by a system like R3 and will sometimes require functions to be implemented in a way that will be useless once the system is known.
3. The parallel reengineering project delays and complicates the initial step.
4. Later changes resulting from an organizational project are not only possible to implement, they will happen anyhow.
5. One of the strongest points of SAP Software is the ability to adapt a working system to new requirements.
6. Any delay in the first ROI period will be more than compensated, even without taking into account the other advantages of the pull strategy.

The second crucial point is that the customer does not buy the responsibility for the project's success. He assumes it. This is a point that practically defines the approach. It is crucial for several reasons:

1. It is much less expensive, and therefore there is much less pressure on the initial project because the investments to justify it are much lower.
2. The customer controls the project day by day and not via monthly meetings prepared to show him the results he expects to see as long as possible. There are fewer surprises.
3. The consultant does not drive a project from outside, which costs much more than from inside the company, he is responsible for his specific knowledge.

It is less expensive because the price for a closed project has to be higher because the consultant takes the risk for failures and, usually knowing little about the customer, has to protect himself. A factor of two or more in an turnkey offer is not unusual, not only because the environment is unknown, but mainly because everybody knows that the cost to implement a system against the resistance of low-level (and sometimes even not too low-level) users is high. There is a reason for consultants to offer this kind of approach: it serves to sell a team where juniors are learning the system; they can then be sold in another project as experts and so pay back the investment. The other point to remember: obviously it is less expensive because the project is simpler without the reorganization.

There are fewer surprises for the customer because one of his people leads the project day by day, and is responsible for project success. It is possible that someone from outside supports him, but the crucial point is that he is responsible for the success or failure of the project. This requires a team leader within the company who has the confidence of top management. Experience indicates that the higher the last hierarchical level involved in a decisive way in the project, the more difficult the implementation. A worst-case scenario: Top Manager buys an SAP system from a service company responsible for implementing the push scenario. Best-case scenario: the IT-department is also convinced and has the confidence of end-users that it can change the actual system as usually happened in the past. The easiest way to convince the IT department is to offer the possibility of being SAP experts in a reasonable time! Even if it is obvious that a SAP Project is something for end-users, the easiest way to implement it is via the IT department (instead of against them), if they have user confidence.

Why does the IT department of a company not install the system without outside help? Because it is inefficient. SAP is a complex system and specific know-how is needed to install it. Education and training are vital. The most practical way to learn about the system is to watch it working in productive systems. Also useful are specific or general courses during the project with a partner who not only customizes the system, but also shows you how to do it. This makes it possible to be more independent and ask for specific support when you need it. It requires a partner who knows the system and is willing to give that knowledge to his customers.

Key Success Factors for a Pull Strategy

Factors or requirements to be met for a successful implementation based on a pull strategy include:

1. **Top-management support to launch the project and in critical moments.**
   It is impossible to implement a SAP system without this.
2. **An easy concept for the first project.**
   This point is not so obvious. It helps to get fast success. SAP tends to become a large system. It is easy to make huge concepts with the system, and consultants tend to feel more important the larger the books they write. Apply a step-by-step method not only within projects, but also for the projects themselves. Be confident that the important things are not realized at once, SAP will last for years and one learns on the way.
3. **The customer can manage the project himself.**
   It is clear that you need somebody inside your company who is able and willing to manage the project with the help of an outside expert. This is a question of responsibility. In this approach it is the customer who assumes the risk of project failure.
4. **A partner who knows the system, ready to share his knowledge.**
   The project will not work with a partner who wants to train his own people on the project without the customer's getting to know it.

CHAPTER 3

Process and Methodology Issues

This chapter presents issues that are concerned with the full implementation process. Methodology issues deal with selecting and following a framework or roadmap for the project. Process issues have to do with analysis, definition, and realization of actual processes that will be implemented.

Dealing with these issues is the highest priority of an implementation project, and only when these issues are solved is there a solid base or framework for the successful completion.

As we discussed in Chapter 2, this book does not deal with implementation issues in a sequential manner, as a methodology usually does, but rather in categories. Issues are intimately related to project organization and preparation, are categorized as *people* issues, and dealt with in the next chapter.

However methodology issues should be considered key for starting and carrying out the project, and for finishing it in a successful and timely manner; they are also vital in planning for support and continuous change.

For dealing with these issues SAP provides two similar *methodologies* that I prefer to call *solution sets*, because they act as a framework for helping not only with a phased project plan and set of activities, but also for dealing with issues which go beyond the structured plan. These solution sets are the *Procedure Model* and *AcceleratedSAP*, commonly known as *ASAP*. Later in this chapter the differences between them are presented and explained.

This chapter begins by explaining the issues introduced in the previous chapter, and then there are several sections introducing the SAP Procedure Model and ASAP.

The implementation issues covered in this chapter are:

❑ Modeling Business Processes
❑ Performing a Gap Analysis
❑ Monitoring the Project Scope
❑ Customizing the System
❑ Checking the Quality of an Implementation Project.

Selecting and Using a Methodology

There are many reasons to use a methodology in an implementation project. These are even stronger when the project's weight is more on the business side than on the technology side, as is the case with SAP R/3.

When the activities to be performed by a project team in pursuit of the planned objective are accomplished without any methodology, the most probable result is chaos, or in the best case, a slip in the execution schedules which will affect costs and customer satisfaction. Without method it is almost impossible to guarantee that final project results will meet the agreed-on requirements established at the start of project. Because so much information is handled by an SAP project, and the number of team members is usually large, the need for a method is still more obvious.

There are many methodologies, and several of them are equally good, if objectives and goals are reached with the same or similar level of quality and satisfaction.

What follows is an example, whose project objective is to release a successful new musical as yet unwritten. The work plan and required resources can be quite different. For instance, an opera to be performed in a church may run into space difficulties: how to position the orchestra, the choir, and the singers will be a problem in a confined space and the success of the project may not be assured. A project is therefore developed with a large number of tools and resources (orchestra, instruments, singers, mechanics, producers, dresses, etc.) to perform a concert in the church. If the music is written for a quartet to be performed on the field of an outdoor stadium, it probably will not have the problem of the physical space, though there might be problems of reaching the expected audience with good-quality sound.

R/3 can be implemented for the quartet version or for the full opera; what will be different will be the project scope, the tools, and resources. The methodology to be deployed in each case will be also different. To help the implementation process, SAP provides a set of functions and tools.

The first methodological framework introduced is the SAP Procedure Model. The Procedure Model is one of the best methods for the SAP implementation projects because it evaluates the environment where it is to be integrated. Procedure Model functions and linked activities have been developed by SAP, as with R/3 core applications, and SAP should know all the particulars, the scope, and even hidden limitations.

The second, popular method, especially for quick implementations requiring less engineering effort, is provided by the AcceleratedSAP (ASAP) solution set. ASAP is positioned as the *Process* component within the TeamSAP initiative. ASAP is a software application including an *Implementation Assistant*, a *Question & Answer Database*, and templates, tools, documentation, and utilities (*accelerators*) for helping in the planning and realization of a full implementation project. ASAP is closely linked with the R/3 Business Engineer and with the IMG.

Other methodologies that can be used are those offered by consulting companies that target business projects and ERP packages; these should include those that deal with aspects such as change management or the technological side of the project.

The chart below summarizes why selecting a methodology is important for an SAP implementation project.

Why deal with this issue	Other issues affected	Solutions
❏ To provide a project framework for planning, designing, realizing, and supporting	❏ Project organization ❏ Control of scope	❏ ASAP (AcceleratedSAP)
❏ To avoid chaotic project realization	❏ All technical, process, and people issues	❏ Procedure Model ❏ Methodologies targeting business projects
❏ To provide credibility	❏ Time and costs	
❏ To organize the project team		

Modeling Business Processes

Implementing R/3 basically means to setup and configure the standard SAP R/3 software to resolve and supply the information needs of a business.

Although there may be many tasks and conditions before the final implementation goal is reached, one of the factors which heavily influences R/3 projects is the extent to which the standard software, without further modifications, resembles the actual requirements of company. From the opposite point of view, the problem can be presented as the extent to which a company can accommodate or modify itself into an open and integrated information system like SAP R/3.

Modeling Business Processes automatically brings to mind the intimidating word BPR (Business Process Reengineering). Michael Hammer introduced reengineering in 1990, and the key concept was a *radical* change in business processes, meaning that companies had to revise from the beginning the design of their processes. In 1997, Hammer's book *Beyond Reengineering* stated that instead of *radical*, "the key word in the definition of reengineering was *process*: a complete end-to-end set of activities that together create value for a customer."

SAP has said that R/3 includes a large number of business processes based on industries' best practices. The implementation issue of modeling business processes means that companies must decide which of those processes are appropriate for operating their business.

It is a debatable whether SAP is or is not designed for automating processes and making incremental improvements in companies, or whether the engineering or reengineering of processes is a must. We would suggest a mix and match, allowing SAP to help automate less efficient but valid processes and reengineer those that are not valid or operative any more.

In any case a company must clearly define the targeted processes, which usually involves the rethinking and redefinition of all or most of its business processes.

This issue is the typical analysis phase of traditional IT projects, with the difference being that the *modeling of processes* must precede customizing work, instead of the design and programming phases of traditional projects coming before customizing.

SAP R/3 is not initially designed as a software system made of components which can be individually deployed, but rather it tries to show business processes and companies as a whole, from above, where there are no boundaries between divisions or departments. As we noted in Chapter 1, this means integration; this is not only one of its main features, but is the main benefit of R/3.

The modeling of the business processes will have repercussions for many other implementation issues. It is the base for later customizing, which is the main task of translating business models or blueprints into a customized setting to make the system behave as expected by the company.

For instance, a switch in the way business processes are perceived will probably affect the way jobs are performed; *change management* will be required to avoid resistance to change and to deal with the human factors involved.

The difference between the SAP standard processes and functionality, and the customer's expectations for business processes is usually known as gaps. There is an implementation issue known as *Gap Analysis* that provides a way to identify and close those gaps. This issue should be included in the modeling of business processes. In fact, the same tools can be used to address both issues. Here the issues are described separately because Gap Analysis starts with an as-is situation, which might not be the case for newly created companies. Gap Analysis can be considered a subset of the overall Process Model design.

Other issues affected by business process modeling are:

❑ **Controlling the implementation scope**, which can hardly be delimited without a clear vision of the company structure and business processes targeted.
❑ **Project organization**, which is also heavily dependent on business processes, because it will involve key users, expert consultant, and the sponsorship of managers.

Other implementation issues that can benefit from business process models are testing, training, and project documentation.

Having a proper definition or map of the business process not only adds value and consistency to the project but also can save time and effort in implementation. This fact is sometimes hard to realize in the initial phases, and often SAP customers are very reluctant to do this work.

In order to deal with these implementation issues, SAP and other complementary software partners have developed useful tools and applications. But tools are just helpers and will not solve this issue by themselves. It requires cooperation within the organization and the help of experienced consultants.

To deal with implementation issues SAP provides the *R/3 Business Engineer* configuration tools, introduced in Chapter 1. The Business Engineer includes the R/3 Reference Model, a graphical representation of the business processes included in R/3. The Business Navigator is used for navigating the Reference Model and directly accessing the transactions and data models of R/3.

The ASAP Solution Set is largely based on the R/3 Business Engineer, and includes both the Reference Model and interactive configurations using the Question and Answer database.

Figure 3.1 shows an example of the Reference Model as seen from within R/3. Figure 3.2 shows an example of the Q&A database from ASAP.

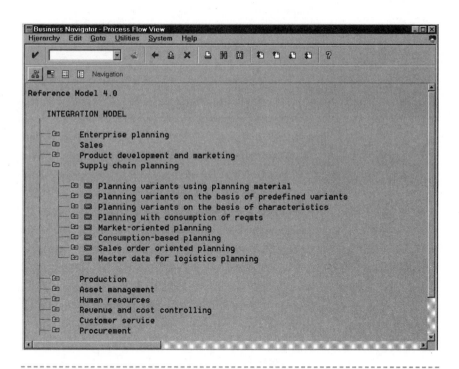

FIGURE 3.1   *R/3 Reference Model*

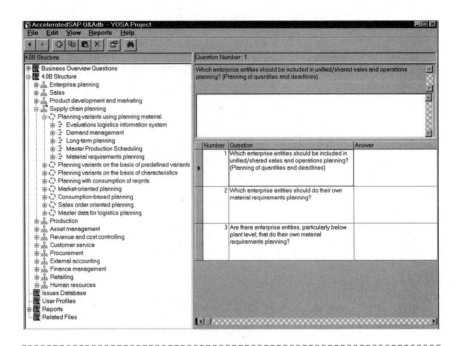

FIGURE 3.2   *ASAP Questions & Answer database*

Among the tools for modeling business processes are the ARIS toolset, VISIO, LiveModel, and Enterprise Charter. These are based on the R/3 Reference Model and permit many modeling functions, including a live link with a real R/3 system for rapid and iterative prototyping of business processes, simulation, testing, automatic generation of documentation, and so on.

WEB

More information about these tools can be found at **http://www.sap.com/ products/compsoft/certify/modeling.htm**.

Whichever methodology or tool is used for modeling processes, it is important to define a procedure for standardized process modeling which is easy to follow and understand for all team members. For that purpose the R/3 Reference Model and other modeling tools usually use EPC (Event Process Chain) diagrams for representing business processes by describing the process flow. Figure 3.3 shows an example of an EPC for the process "Processing receipt of application."

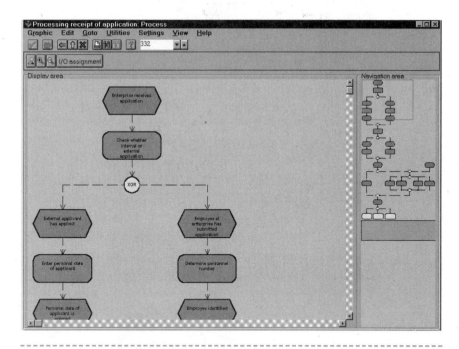

FIGURE 3.3   *EPC for vendor document parking*

Figure 3.4 below includes the basic objects for representing EPCs.
Objects used in EPCs are:

❑ **Events**, for describing a business process that can trigger one or
more functions, or that can be the result of a function.
❑ **Functions**, the smallest units of functionality; these describe a
operating activity or business task.
❑ **Process paths**, logical connections to other business processes
❑ **Linking operators.** Three linking operators are used:
   ❑ AND (∧): when events are linked by AND operators, all of
   them must have occurred so that the successor function can be
   carried out.
   ❑ OR (∨): for events connected by OR operators, it is necessary
   that at least one of them occurs so the following function will
   be performed.
   ❑ XOR or Exclusive OR (XOR): when events are connected by
   the exclusive OR operator, then only one of them must occur
   for the successor function to be triggered.

❏ **Control flows**, which are the broken arrow lines that connect one object above to another below, except in the case of logical operators that can enter or leave objects from the side.

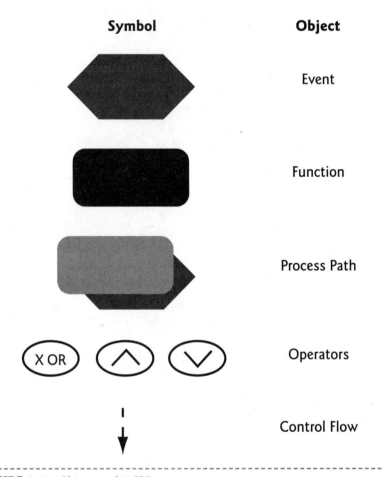

Symbol	**Object**
	Event
	Function
	Process Path
	Operators
	Control Flow

FIGURE 3.4   *Objects used in EPCs*

There are other graphic elements in process modeling, for business organization and scenarios, and data flows. More information can be found at the R/3 online help within the manual for "R/3 Process Model."

The chart below summarizes the issue of modeling business processes.

Why deal with this issue	Other issues affected	Solutions
❏ Effectively design the way business operates	❏ Customizing	❏ SAP Business Engineer
	❏ Gap Analysis	
❏ To define the blueprint needed for later customizing and realization	❏ Control of Scope	❏ Third-party modeling tools
	❏ Change Management	
	❏ Project Organization and Project Plan	❏ ASAP Accelerators
	❏ Time and Costs	❏ Experienced consultants
	❏ Others: Training, Testing, Documentation	❏ Management commitment
		❏ Key-user involvement

Performing a Gap Analysis

The *Gap Analysis* can be defined as a comparison of what is required—what has been defined as needed—by the business, and what is included within the standard R/3 system. Gaps are those functions or business processes not part of the standard R/3 applications.

The work of gap analysis consists of identifying and dealing with the missing functionality in SAP that is considered *important* for the implementation. The adjective *important* is quite ambiguous and when possible, should be replaced by *critical* or of *highest priority*. Gap analysis can become a burning issue to be addressed, since it might create political, organizational, and even legal problems.

The most typical approach for gap analysis is to define the "AS-IS" and the "TO-BE" situations. "AS-IS" analysis consists of identifying and describing current functions, business processes, and organizational structure. Once the current business and organizational status is depicted, then it is necessary to identify best business practices in the areas thought to need change or improvements, in order to give form to future and better business processes and organizational structure. This analysis of the future shape of processes and business organization is known as the "TO-BE" analysis.

The mapping between the "TO-BE" of the company and the standard R/3 business processes is needed to identify the gaps in needed functionality.

Although there will probably be some required functions missing, and those gaps must be addressed, it can also happen that during gap analysis standard R/3 processes will fit the requrement, rather than a custom-designed one. In these cases, gaps are automatically eliminated.

When approaching an SAP implementation using the ASAP methodology, the Questions and Answer database will be the tool to use to find out customer requirements using the Customer Input Templates, and to generate important documents such as Business Blueprints, that are used to verify that customer requirements have been properly understood.

Starting Point: Analyzing "AS-IS"

The analysis of current business status, processes, and organization is normally done on three levels:

❑ **Analysis of functional requirements.** The functional view of the business corresponds to traditional business organizations based on functional areas or divisions, such as accounting, controlling, sales, purchasing, and so on. Functions are identified and are evaluated to select those that are considered critical.

❑ **Analysis of business processes.** Business processes are analyzed at a cross-functional level, as with purchase requisition, order fulfillment, or materials requirements planning. The result of the analysis will be a list of the most critical business processes, which will be refined later to exclude processes which do not add value to a company's business objectives. This is the activity that will be most closely related to the overall R/3 implementation strategy, project plan, and project scope.

❑ **Analysis of the organizational structure.** It is also important to analyze current organizational structure to provide a view of the company at the organizational level: business areas, divisions, departments, management levels, responsibilities, and so on.

The results of the analysis provide the project team with a general perspective and understanding of company business and structure. They should also provide a picture of current applications and data flow.

The Vision: Analyzing the "TO-BE"

The "TO-BE" analysis is the vision of how the business will operate in the future. When envisioning or designing business processes and organization, the analysis should take into consideration the company's business objectives This is the best time to consider SAP R/3 applications and business processes as the model for the best business practices that companies can adopt as required. The R/3 Reference Model and modeling software including those business processes can be used as base tools for depicting the "TO-BE."

The R/3 Reference Model includes more than 1,000 business processes based on best practices, both for generic industries and for vertical industries. A simple way to avoid gaps is to consider the proposed R/3 processes as those to be adopted.

Gaps are found when the proposed R/3 process differs from the one required by a company. In these cases it is essential that only those gaps considered critical be addressed, otherwise the level of additional development or enhancements might become the greatest implementation effort; this could affect project time and costs.

The "TO-BE" analysis must consider the same levels as the "AS-IS," so a comparison can be made by mapping current status with future needs:

- **Functional requirements**, to find functional gaps
- **Business processes**, to depict future business operations
- **Organizational structure**, to define the required organization for supporting the new model.

Filling the Gaps

Filling functional and business process gaps leads to BPR (business process reengineering).

As we noted, a detailed analysis of the R/3 processes for the "TO-BE" processes must be carried out to find all possible matches. To do this, the help of experienced consultants with knowledge of R/3 can be key, if not critical. An outside view is often valuable and can help companies learn about other possibilities for business operations.

When gaps are discovered there are several ways to address them:

❑ Enhance the system by deploying user exits
❑ Leaving less-than-critical gaps for a subsequent refining project; often what seem gaps at the beginning of the projects, disappear in the integration of business processes
❑ Use third-party complementary solutions or interfaces
❑ Use workarounds
❑ Modify standard SAP; or copy it first and then modify (not recommended but possible)
❑ Last but not least, and most recommended, rethinking the business process with the possibility of making a major change in business operations or organization, so that a different business process is selected. This seems radical, but an objective and measurable analysis should help to identify possible benefits. If no improvements are found through the analysis, another solution should be used.

The chart on the next page summarizes some of the topics in gap analysis during SAP implementation. The main addition to process modeling is that gaps may have a big impact on development and enhancements to standard R/3 systems.

Monitoring the Project Scope

The project scope is the definition of the final outcome of the project: which functions and business processes will be implemented in the new system and which will not, which activities will be included in the project plan and which will not. The task of monitoring project scope will be hard, mainly because of the difficulty of clearly defining scope before the actual implementation project starts. A very specific definition of project scope can be completed just before the realization phase, when process modeling and gap analysis have been conducted.

Why deal with this issue	Other issues affected	Solutions
❏ To analyze functions and processes not covered by standard applications	❏ Customizing	❏ SAP Business Engineer
	❏ Process Modeling	
	❏ Control of Scope	❏ Third-party modeling tools
❏ To be better able to plan project realization	❏ Change Management	❏ ASAP Accelerators
❏ To have a better view of and design for how business will operate	❏ Project Organization & Project Plan	
	❏ Development and Enhancements	❏ Experienced consultants
❏ To prepare a plan for enhancements, workarounds, or other solutions for filling gap	❏ Interfaces	❏ Management commitment
	❏ Time and Costs	❏ Key-user involvement
	❏ Others: Training, Testing, Documentation	❏ Third-party complementary products

For instance, when using ASAP as the implementation solution, it is not until Business Blueprint documents and the Business Process Master List are ready that the detailed scope of the project is actually defined.

Changes are common and scope modifications can start conflicts, mainly when dealing with consulting partners. Internal difficulties also result because the budget horizon is not precisely known.

What many companies do to overcome the initial problem of determining the project scope is to perform the detailed analysis of processes and gaps as an independent project, often *before* the full project plan is made. They may do a full plan but condition termination dates, detailed planning, and budget on analysis of the business processes.

There are subsequent problems as well, because even in the case of a detailed analysis of the "TO-BE" of the business, unplanned-for issues will crop up during the realization phase and even when getting ready to going live. These may include additional enhancements or developments, additional reporting or printing requirements, fine tuning of business processes, or even a different system landscape.

The project manager and project sponsors must play an active role in managing problems arising from sudden changes in scope. Monitoring the project scope is closely related to the processes of managing issues and problems during implementation. The plan for managing issues is normally established during the initial project phase, within the definition of standards and procedures.

Scope control is only one of the important issues to be addressed. Resolving issues means review by project team members, documentation, exposing possible solutions. If none are found or none are considered satisfactory, the issue must be brought to the project manager, steering committee, or project sponsors.

Within the Question and Answer database, ASAP includes an issue database, where issues are identified and classified and people are assigned responsibility. Documentation can be attached to issues to help in the resolution process.

In order to avoid excessive changes in project scope, the following points and suggestions have demonstrated effective results:

❑ Prioritize changes, according to the impact they might have
❑ A change in scope must be aligned with the project and business objectives; if it is not, it should be reconsidered
❑ Leave a detailed definition of project scope until the gap analysis has been carried out or the business process master list is ready
❑ Negotiate any changes in project scope fairly with all interested parties
❑ Communicate efficiently to all affected team members or partners.

Why deal with this issue	Other issues affected	Solutions
❑ To avoid legal problems with customers/ consultant companies	❑ Project Management	❑ ASAP (AcceleratedSAP)
	❑ Customizing	
	❑ Gap Analysis	❑ Procedure Model
❑ To provide a stable project framework	❑ Testing	❑ Methodologies targeting business projects
❑ To be able formally to finish a project and start production operation	❑ Training	
	❑ Time and Costs	❑ ASAP Q&A database and Issue Resolution process
❑ To resolve project issues quickly		

Customizing

Customizing *is not* a method or a collection of tools for helping to modify the standard R/3 functions. *It is* a way or method of working in the R/3 environment to help to implement and improve the R/3 functionality. Customizing provides the tools for configuring the system and the project documentation for implementation projects. It also furnishes needed tools for managing and evaluating the implementation using the Customizing Project, while making recommendations for the configuration of the system.

Customizing provides help and tools for migrating the system configuration from development systems to productive systems, and also for the release of upgrade projects.

Actual customizing activities are derived from previous process modeling and gap analysis, using the R/3 Reference Model. Both the Procedure Model and ASAP include the structure of R/3 implementation projects, and are also used for defining and navigating customizing activities. The main tool for customizing is the Implementation Guide (IMG), which is used to carry out the actual configuration of R/3 applications.

The IMG

IMG is the main tool for the customizing work, providing a guide for consultants and users of customizing transactions. Figure 3.5 shows an example of the IMG.

The IMG has a hierarchical tree structure, divided according to business applications. Within the different applications, configuration activities appear in the correct sequence, so each entry in a customizing transaction is set up by previous customizing steps. Each IMG activity has four icons, which have links to:

❑ Accessing the customizing transaction

❏ Accessing the SAP documentation

❏ Accessing status and project management

❏ Accessing notes for project documentation.

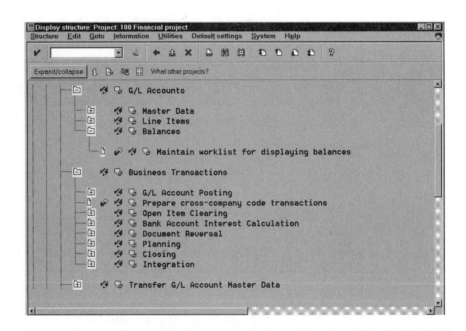

FIGURE 3.5   *The Implementation Guide*

The scope of customizing can be defined by choosing the applications and components to be configured. In order to do that, SAP offers several options or IMGs:

❏ The **SAP Reference IMG** contains all the settings for all business applications.
❏ The **Enterprise IMG** is a subset of the full Reference IMG, in which customers choose the application components and coun-

tries to be configured during implementation. This, and generating the Enterprise IMG, should happen at the beginning of customizing.

❏ Later, R/3 allows for filtering or dividing the Enterprise IMG into various **IMG projects** that can be used, for example, to assign different projects to different teams, each in charge of an application component.

❏ Projects can be further filtered into **Project Views** where the R/3 system automatically selects different types of activities: *only mandatory*, *only critical*, *optional*, or *all*. Users can define additional views by a manual selection of activities.

The project features of the IMG make it possible to reduce the scope of the settings needed for customizing by organizing those tasks by projects or views that are subsets of a larger Enterprise IMG. This is a subset of the SAP Reference IMG, which is the superstructure that includes the full R/3 configuration.

Checking the Quality of an Implementation Project

In the context of an implementation issue, *auditing* the project is the process of checking the quality of what is being implemented and how it affects the cost of ownership. The terms of reference are the initial implementation process, operation, and support, and the management of continuous change, such as additional projects or system reconfigurations. An audit of an implementation project can also be held just before going live, or even when the system is in productive operation.

Both the Procedure Model and ASAP include a quality check as the last work package of every phase, so that a review and validation is held before proceeding to the next phase. It is common that this type of activity is not carefully considered, so that a very light check is performed, or often one is not done at all.

For checking the quality of every project phase and every deliverable, a recommended solution is to create an auditing team, led by an external Quality Auditor and an Internal Auditor.

Areas to be audited for quality should include:

- ❑ Methodology chosen and how it is being used
- ❑ Risk factors
- ❑ Documentation
- ❑ Functional areas
- ❑ Cross-application areas
- ❑ Technical areas.

An implementation audit or quality assurance process is useful for:

- ❑ Early identification of problems and risks
- ❑ Ensuring a successful implementation project
- ❑ Preventing large budget increases by controlling project scope
- ❑ Gaining confidence in new business applications
- ❑ Determining that change management, effective communication, and knowledge transfer are taking place
- ❑ Increasing the probabilities of reaching project objectives, and therefore the expected benefits.

The ASAP solution set includes several elements to help guarantee a certain level of quality:

- ❑ The use of a methodology that includes quality assurance reviews for every major phase
- ❑ The support of qualified consultants for the full R/3 implementation and life cycle
- ❑ The role of project manager as a quality leader reviewing decisions, documentation, results, and deliverables. The project manager should be in charge of monitoring the success factors in implementation and should take a positive attitude toward problems.

SAP offers several auditing tools and services in the full implementation cycle, including ASAP Concept Check, GoingLive Check, or EarlyWatch.

In many ways the content of this book addresses most of the areas that must be checked for quality. As a way to ensuring quality and success, knowledge of implementation issues and success factors is extremely important, so that plans can be made and actions can be taken to avoid problems.

This section does not have a summary because quality affects, and its affected, by all implementation issues and circumstances. It is an overall process during the length of the implementation.

Implementation Solution Sets

We now introduce in more detail the two implementation solutions offered by SAP summarized earlier.

The Procedure Model was introduced in 1995 and was a giant step toward facilitating and providing a framework for the implementation process. It was included in release 3.0 of R/3.

ASAP was introduced in the United States in 1996 as a solution for quick implementations, but has evolved into a full-flavored solution.

There are obvious differences between the two methodologies, and confusion has been fostered by SAP marketing, which provided quick and sometimes misleading messages to the market, as a reaction to competitor criticism. Table 3.1 shows some of the differences between the two solutions.

TABLE 3.1   *The Procedure Model and ASAP*

Procedure Model	ASAP
German model	American model
Integrated in R/3	Independent tool
General view at a high level	More detailed view of activities and tasks
Four phases	Five phases
Includes Project Management	External Project Management
Online Help and Hypertext	Accelerators: documents, templates, tools, presentations, models, databases
R/3 Reference Model	R/3 Business Engineer (includes Reference Model)
Implementation Solution	Complete Implementation Solution
Considers Reengineering/BPR	Little Reengineering

continued on next page

Procedure Model	ASAP
Long project?	Quick projects? (6 months / 9 months)
—	Question & Answer Database
Will be supplanted by ASAP?	Will supplant the Procedure Model?

Let us move on to consideration of general and common R/3 concepts well known to the SAP community. These must be understood in order to further comprehend the issues surrounding an SAP implementation.

Client Concept

A client is defined as a legally, financially, and organizationally independent unit within the R/3 System, for example, a company group, a business unit, or a corporation. At the technical level a client is like a subset of the physical database, because it is part of the primary key of most of SAP tables.

The R/3 System includes tools for creating, copying, transferring, resetting, deleting, and comparing clients. When the loads of individual clients differ, the buffer manager of the application service is able to respond and allocate resources appropriately. The *client* is the first field when logging on to the system.

This information structure allows, for instance, for more than one implementation by individual and independent companies, and for division by modules. There is also information which is client independent; it will be common to all defined clients of the same SAP system.

All the ABAP programs, transactions, and data structures defined in the dictionary (tables, views, data elements, etc.) are client independent so that R/3 functionality is available throughout the system, to all clients.

All application data, master data, documents, and most customizing settings are client dependent, and therefore can only exist within the client where they were defined, or to which they were *transported*.

SAP systems are commonly delivered after installation with three standard clients: 000, 001, and 066 for the EarlyWatch and maintenance functions.

Client 000 is a client with a complete information structure. It contains entries for all tables of the organization structure (an example or model one). SAP does not recommend making any customization work in this special client, except when indicated otherwise in OSS notes or official SAP documentation. This client is automatically updated and modified on each release upgrade. The following objects can be affected by an upgrade:

❑ Table contents and structures
❑ Programs
❑ Screens
❑ Forms
❑ Online help
❑ The SAP Reference IMG.

This client always has the most current status. Information contained in client 000 is defined for a German model company with the code 0001 and according to legal German specifications; for instance, taxes are calculated on a German model.

Client 000 contains a simple organizational structure of a test company, with parameters for all applications, standard settings, configurations for the control of standard transactions, and examples to be used in many different profiles of business applications. For these reasons, 000 is a special client for the R/3 system since it contains the client-independent settings.

Client 001 is identical to 000, but customization work can take place to adapt and configure the standard system to the specific implementation project.

Client 001 is a copy of the 000 client, including the test company. If this client is configured or customized, its settings are client dependent. It does not behave like 000. It is reserved for the activities of preparing a system for the production environment. SAP customers usually use this client as a source of copies for other new clients.

Country-specific Standard Settings

Predefined values and settings for clients 000 and 001 are determined by the legal requirements and the business practices in a specific country. The SAP Standard Delivery System initially provides the German requirements. When there is the need for other settings, those specific country settings must be generated.

This is one of the first customizing activities. When the customizing transaction is executed, the initial parameters established for German settings are automatically replaced by those corresponding to the country selected.

Transport System

Customizing work and ABAP development, including new dictionary object definitions, forms, programs, and so on, are initially performed in the development environment, within one or more clients. The Transport System is the SAP solution for moving or copying all the required information from the development environment to any other system, either quality assurance or production. Using the Transport System, it is possible to copy the elements of one SAP environment to another. This includes copying client-dependent objects between clients of the same SAP system as well as between different ones; client-independent objects can be copied between different SIDs (within the same SID it does not make sense since client independence is available to every client).

A transport system must be previously defined or configured using transaction SE06 and the new Transport Management System (STMS) after release 3.1H. Transport strategy should be defined as part of development strategy and the system landscape architecture.

Client Copy

Among useful tools for the technical aspects of SAP implementation projects is the set of transactions in charge of copying, exporting, importing, and deleting clients. A client copy can be made within the same SID (local copy) or between different SIDs (remote copy, or client export/import). In any case technical and functional requirements must be considered.

The following requirements should be adhered to when performing client copies:

❑ Source and target system must be on the same R/3 functional release
❑ Target client must be empty
❑ Target system must have enough database space for receiving copy.

The Procedure Model

The Procedure Model is more than just the methodology for the implementation of the SAP standard business software. It is also a step-by-step guide through each project phase, providing the needed software tools for efficient development of the project using the proposed methodology. From the point of view of the method, the Procedure Model offers an implementation model by phases, with three levels of detail:

❑ On the first level are the *project phases*
❑ The second level includes the *work packages*
❑ The third level is made up of *project activities*.

At the first level, the Procedure Model has four phases:

❑ Phase 1: Organization and conceptual design
❑ Phase 2: Detailed design and system setup
❑ Phase 3: Preparations for going live
❑ Phase 4: Productive operation.

All project activities are hierarchically structured within each phase. Every phase includes several *work packages*, and every work package is made up of a group of activities with a predefined execution sequence.

The *method* describes the objectives and scope of each phase, as well as the generic structure and specific functionality of every work package and the relationship among them (work package information flow) within the same phase.

For every activity described in a phase and its corresponding work package, the Procedure Model provides recommendations for execution, additional information, and practical examples.

Each of the phases includes a set of tools and utilities oriented to the activities to be performed in that phase, with the objective of easing development within the context of the implementation project.

As described in the R/3 Procedure Model manual, the utilities are conceptually grouped in two classes:

❏ **Customizing R/3.** Among the customizing elements that could be used during the project life, are:
   ❏ Customizing projects
   ❏ The SAP Reference IMG
   ❏ The Enterprise IMG
   ❏ Project IMGs
   ❏ The standard delivery system
   ❏ The client copier
   ❏ The transport system
   ❏ The countries program and
   ❏ SAPoffice for project documentation.
❏ **R/3 Reference Model.** This has the following elements:
   ❏ The Component view, which includes
      – The business application component hierarchy
      – The process selection matrix
      – Processes and functions for input/output assignments of business objects/entities and system organization units
      – The system organization diagram
      – Information flows
   ❏ The Process Flow view, which includes
      – The communication diagram
      – Scenarios
      – Processes for input/output assignments of business objects/entities and system organization units.

The Procedure Model also includes project management activities as well as specific work packages for system maintenance and release upgrade.

Work Packages

A work package usually corresponds to a Procedure Model transaction. As stated in previous sections, the SAP Procedure Model includes a hierarchically structured activity plan which establishes the order for performing tasks and the relationship of activities for system customizing.

Since work packages are used as structural elements for globally planning and managing the implementation project, its advisable to know how they are organized.

- ❑ **Work package description:** summary of the tasks to be performed and support tools
- ❑ **Requirements or triggers:** prerequisites to fulfill in order to start working with the work package
- ❑ **Needed information:** documents, models, manuals, and guides which can be used with the work package
- ❑ **Work package contents**: a detailed description of the activities within the work package
- ❑ **Deliverables:** the work package output information, and
- ❑ **Results**.

At the same time, work packages are made up of several activities or working steps. The Procedure Model includes Project Documentation tools for documenting the implementation project. This documentation is included within SAPOffice as Shared Documents, where project documents are inserted. By default it includes nine folders as shown in Figure 3.6: system problems/errors, open general questions, project standards documentation, meeting reports, status reports, interface descriptions, external documents, enhancement descriptions, and other documents. Project team members can create additional folders as needed.

Every folder can include as many documents as required. Documents might be of many types and natures, such as Microsoft Office files (Word, Excel, Powerpoint, Project, etc.), text files, distribution lists, business objects, or even programs or transactions.

It is important that before starting work with the Procedure Model and the implementation project, we have correctly configured the system.

There are two ways to access the Procedure Model: either graphically or as a list structure. The menu path is **Tools → Business Engineering → Customizing → Basic Functions → R/3 Procedure Model**. Users must then choose either **Display Graphic** or

Display Structure. Figure 3.7 shows the Procedure Model displayed as a structure.

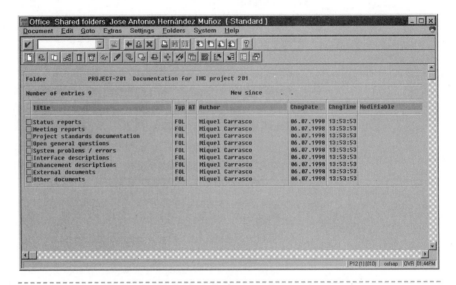

FIGURE 3.6 *SAPoffice shared folders for documenting implementation*

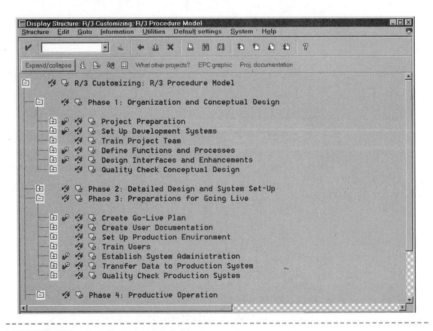

FIGURE 3.7 *R/3 Procedure Model*

Work packages are made up of several elements. The graphic representation of the Procedure Model shown in Figure 3.8 is an example of these elements, which are also available in the list structure representation.

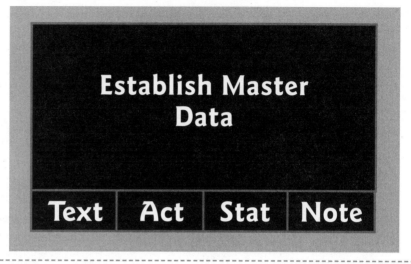

FIGURE 3.8   *Graphic representation of Procedure Model Work package*

A work package always has:

❑ **Documentation.** Clicking on **text** reveals the work package description and SAP recommendations for carrying it out.

❑ **Activities.** Clicking on **Act (Activities)** shows the customizing tasks associated with the work package. This is the link between the Procedure Model and the IMG.

❑ **Status Information.** Clicking on **Stat (Status)** shows the work package status maintenance screen for entering project management information such as degree of advancement, project status, resource assignments, or dates. This information can later be used for project analysis.

❑ **Project Documentation.** Clicking on **Note** reveals a dialog box for choosing note types for documenting work package activities. Several types of notes are defined when generating the Enterprise IMG. R/3 provides the chance to document using either SAP-script or Microsoft Word.

If we choose to view the procedure mode in list-structure mode instead of graphical, the system includes exactly the same functions but uses other symbols, as can be seen in Figure 3.7.

In addition to those work package elements, the system also includes EPC graphics for representing the overall work package process and relationships with other work packages. This can be accessed by clicking on the **EPC graphic** button located on the Application toolbar.

Project Management with the Procedure Model

The Procedure Model acts also as the project management tool provided by SAP within the R/3 system to guide users through the implementation activities. These activities can range from full R/3 implementation in a company, to configuring a new module in an already productive operation, or for release and upgrade projects.

The problems related to the issue of managing SAP implementation projects are described in more detail in the next chapter. This section introduces the available project management functions within the Procedure Model.

The Procedure Model is a four-phases plan; two generic work packages apply to Project Management and System Maintenance and Release Update.

The degree of integration of the procedure model with the other tools and utilities used in implementation projects should be highlighted. Its versatility of use in different projects is important. Integration with customizing allows for starting customizing activities from the Procedure Model, granting the right sequence of configuration steps.

In order to manage the project efficiently with Procedure Model functions, it is essential to have a certain discipline, and use the Status function within each of the work packages and activities. Using Status functions on items of the second detail level (immediately under the phases) can help carry out the initial planning of the project. Later, a detailed planning of dependent activities is performed; it can be adjusted with corrective measures as the project advances.

The system includes utilities to pass Status information from a work package to dependent activities and from activities to the relevant work package. It is possible to select what information will be transferred—for example Plan Dates, Status, Resource, or Selection Field—or we can aggregate Plan Dates, Actual Dates, Plan Work, Current Work, or Remaining Work.

Another possibility is to use external tools such as Microsoft Project to plan a project. Microsoft Project can upload to the Procedure Model or, you can feed data into the Procedure Model and download to MS Project.

The main functionality of Project Management within the Procedure Model is with the *Project Analysis* functions. Figure 3.9 shows a window with the different pushbuttons corresponding to available project analysis options.

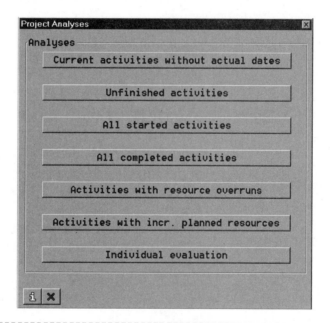

FIGURE 3.9   *Project Analysis in the Procedure Model*

From data entered in each work package activity, project managers can use these functions to evaluate status of tasks and activities, resources, dates, and so on. This information provides current snapshots of project problems or bottlenecks to allow project managers to take corrective action or focus on problems found.

The next section introduces each of the Procedure Model work packages.

Phase 1: Organization and Conceptual Design

This phase has two objectives: the organization of the project and the elaboration of the conceptual design of the solution that will be implemented. At the end of the phase this design should be correctly documented and must be approved by the project management team; all needed resources must be organized. Once the team is dedicated to a project, the first activities should focus on getting organized for the whole project. Once the organization is defined, the team will be in charge of starting the rest of the work packages within the first phase.

The conceptual design should include how company business processes are supported by the new system of information (R/3 in this case), those that could be supported in the near future, how they are going to be handled, and everything related to the best solution for the company.

The six work packages included within this first phase are:

Project Preparation

Before starting an R/3 implementation project, certain requirements must be verified. There are five important questions to be addressed: a definition of the objectives for implementing R/3, what parts of the system are being implemented, how the system will be implemented, what the planning will be, and who will be responsible.

This work package is closely related to Business Modeling and Gap Analysis, so use of the R/3 Reference Model is recommended. To modify or extend BM & GA, the project team can use a modeling and documentation tool such as ARIS, Visio, LiveModel, or Micrografx EnterpriseCharter.

Activities within the Project Ppreparation work package include:

❑ Initializing the project: checking the status of previous analysis, choosing the team, and initial planning for training. The first decisions or the reasons for project are communicated to the organization.
❑ Defining company objectives for using R/3.
❑ Defining the "AS IS" situation.
❑ Making project team members familiar with R/3 functions and processes.

❑ Identifying and defining the business processes to help specify the scope of implementation.

❑ Carrying out a gap analysis: functional requirements versus R/3 application component functionality.

❑ Establishing the organizational model. The objective here is to detect possible organizational changes related to the organization defined during the "AS IS" situation.

❑ Defining the objectives and level of standardization.

❑ Establishing implementation strategy.

❑ Defining the hardware architecture.

❑ Defining project structure, to establish the organization of the project team, roles, and responsibilities.

❑ Defining project procedures and standards.

❑ Defining the system landscape.

❑ Creating a preliminary project plan. Using the R/3 Procedure Model, a preliminary project plan can be created and an initial estimation made of time and resources required for the realization of every work package. During this activity all the resources needed for the implementation project must be determined and the initial project plan established. Budget and expense planning must be set out, based on the established plan and resources. Training courses and the calendar must be designed. All this must happen while trying to be as realistic and cautious as possible when estimating.

❑ Approving the report for project preparation.

❑ Creating the project charter.

❑ Kicking off the implementation project.

Set Up Development Systems

The objective of this work package is to install and configure the development systems, based on the infrastructure previously defined using the standard models provided by SAP in clients 000 and 001. The event that triggers the activities of this work package is the approval of the previous Project Preparation work package.

This system can be used for initial training, testing, and prototyping after a new client has been created and copied.

In this phase the following activities should be carried out:

❑ Defining the required clients for the development systems.

❑ Creating a user profile for project staff, and developing required users with their corresponding authorization profiles.

❑ Defining the system as designed in the previous phase, that is, with the settings for the clients, the definition of the Correction and Transport System, and so on.

❑ Guaranteeing the correct functioning of the technological environment, such as the network, communications with other systems, and access to shared resources or printers.

❑ Establishing communications with SAP for getting provided services such as the SAPnet/OSS, Earlywatch, or remote consulting.

❑ Generating the "country version" for customizing the first client from a copy of one of the standard SAP clients.

❑ Creating the Implementation Guide for the company model, known as Enterprise IMG, which comprises the full project. The base for generating the Enterprise IMG is the selection of the processes during the execution of the previous work package. Generating the Enterprise IMG also provides a SAPoffice folder structure for associated documentation and a set of filters for working with Business Navigator.

❑ Defining Customization Projects and the Project IMG. Project management is in charge of modeling the project structure according to the most appropriate model of implementation for customizing projects. It is possible to define filters for working with the R/3 Reference Model within Business Navigator. If necessary, a project can be further divided into smaller parts, generating partial views of customization projects.

Training of the Project Team

The objective of the Training Project Team work package is to guarantee both quality and efficiency when implementing R/3. The plan must include R/3 training for every member of the project team according to their current profiles, experience, previous training, or project role. These training sessions will foster a common language among project team members and set a common standard for the solution being analyzed.

Training is basic for the design and testing of project prototypes. With prototypes or blueprints, the selected business processes can be simulated so that end-users can see and feel how R/3 handles daily operations and information needs.

Define Functions and Processes

The result of this work package will be a verified/checked conceptual design approved for the implementation of SAP R/3 in the company. This work package carries out detailed analysis and definition of functions and business processes affected by implementation. The R/3 Reference Model and Business Modeling tools can be used. Activities within this work package include:

❑ Performing a detailed specification of company business processes versus those provided by SAP. R/3 applications should be seen as a model; the company's requirements should be matched against those business processes included in the model. The R/3 model is represented in the Reference Model.

❑ Defining responsibility for processes and functions, to identify organizations and project team members responsible for different processes.

❑ Checking Input/Output data objects, so that significant information objects are correctly assigned to functions and processes.

❑ Establishing reporting requirements.

❑ Defining requirements for interfaces and enhancements.

❑ Defining the enterprise structure.

❑ Creating a prototype for selected functions and processes, so they can be configured and demonstrated in R/3.

❑ Creating the technical design.

❑ Agreeing on process and technical details.

Define Interfaces and Enhancements

An organization usually has several related business applications that exchange data or are highly dependent. When a company decides on a business solution like R/3, it is common that the R/3 applications replace one, several, or all existing business applications. However, it is common that during a certain period, several applications coexist and need to communicate with each other to exchange information.

Interfaces in R/3 are programs that must usually run in both environments for transferring and sharing data and information that needs to be integrated. The need for interfacing within a SAP implementation necessitates considering those external systems, the data that must be shared, and the functionality to do this. The main activities within this work package include:

❑ Detailed definition of the interfaces: describing the systems to be interfaced with R/3 and the type of data to be exchanged.
❑ Detailed definition of enhancements for evaluating the cost and complexity of modifications, add-ons, or enhancements required in the R/3 system.
❑ Overview of data to be transferred. This activity consists of identifying the applications to be replaced by R/3, and what data must be transferred to R/3.

Quality Control of Conceptual Design

For the last work packages of any phase it is convenient and necessary to perform a quality check or audit of the work performed during that phase. The objective is to ensure the quality of results so that implementation can proceed smoothly to the next phase.

Typical activities of the quality work package are:

❑ Verifying the plan for the project infrastructure. Every member of the organization and project team must know her/his role, and should be aware of the common objective for the project.
❑ Verifying that all team members know and agree with the standards and procedures established.
❑ Validating the systems environment. Needed hardware is available, user accounts are created, the environment is stable and work can be performed.
❑ Validating the conceptual design. The application end-user of every affected division or department has reviewed the main processes on the prototype and agrees with the design.
❑ Validating the definition of interfaces and enhancements.
❑ Validating the project plan.
❑ Creating a verification report.

❑ Getting agreement from steering committee to proceed to the next phase.

Phase 2: Detailed Analysis and System Setup

In this phase detailed conceptual analysis is carried out, by:

❑ Configuring the system according to the requirements of the customizing client.
❑ Testing the business processes in this configuration.
❑ Integrating external applications with R/3.
❑ Presenting the system, configured and documented, for approval.

The result of the detailed analysis and systems setup phase and the approval will be an R/3 system verified by the customer and prepared for going live.

This phase includes ten work packages:

Establish Global Settings

Among global parameters to set are the country or countries, currencies, units of measurement, calendars, and so on. A requirement for performing this work package is that the conceptual design be finished and approved by the steering committee.

It is important to highlight the fact that the global settings provided by SAP comply with international ISO standards organization, so usually there is no need to change them.

Establish Company Structure

In this work package, a company structure model is created using the "system organization units" previously defined in the project. Each of the R/3 applications uses one or more system organization units to portray functions and processes. Relationships among the organization units can be hierarchical or networked. A system organization unit can be the company codes, the controlling areas (in the case of finances), and so on. As a result of this work package there will be a system configuration for a specified company structure.

Establish Master Data

R/3 business processes depend on the quality of the master data. These data are normally provided by the legacy applications to be replaced with R/3. It is necessary to describe the data structure of those legacy applications, to establish and define the methods for loading the data in R/3, and to guarantee that these data, once loaded into the system, are valid and complete.

Establish Functions and Processes

Each of the R/3 application components includes functions to be used in business processes. System settings are used for adapting functions to company requirements. The functions and processes configured in this work package will be performed according to the requirements established during the initial project phase. This and the previous activity are closely linked and are performed together.

Create Interfaces and Enhancements

The interfaces and enhancements defined in the previous phase are now created, as are the programs needed for data transfer. For the realization of this work package, it is vital to have information such as the programming requirements for data transfer, descriptions of interfaces and system enhancements, and programming standards, as well as the project IMG. The work package includes activities to verify programs, interfaces, and enhancements.

Establish Reporting

Companies implementing SAP as their business strategic solution might previously have had a reporting system more or less integrated with legacy applications. When end-users are asked about their reporting needs or enhancements to their existing reports, this is the moment when many new reports are requested. Although it is not always possible or convenient to fulfill all user requests, this is a good time to improve the existing reporting system, by better addressing the application end-users' reporting requirements. Among the main activities of this work package are:

- ❑ Identifying what information is required and who needs it.
- ❑ Finding out what parts of the required information are available in the R/3 system.
- ❑ Designing reports and forms.
- ❑ If required, updating the R/3 spool and printing system, for instance, by adapting or adding new devices, formats, print controls, device types, printer drivers, or character sets.
- ❑ Defining the system reporting organization for an effective distribution of information. What reports must be available for what users, how those reports will be accessible, for how long, and so on.

Establish Archiving Management

The objective of this work package is to describe a solution for data archiving to address the critical situations that can be generated over time, due to growth in data volume and the online availability of data. Archiving Management also addresses the issue of types of access to archive data, analysis, and management. The database cannot grow indefinitely, since it might become unmanageable. The legal, fiscal, and business requirements that define the need for a specified range of data online and immediately accessible help to fix the limits for database growth. However it becomes necessary to establish methods for moving information whose business process is complete to alternative "near-line" systems that permit managing the information moved, although without the same access speed or management possible when the data are online. Data that will never or rarely be used should be moved to historical data archive files. The archiving solution allows a limited growth of database volume; this will improve the performance of processes that do not need to scan unnecessary data. Database growth also has an important effect on common operations and system management activities, such as backup and restore, database reorganizations, and so on.

The main activities within this work package are:

- ❑ **Design Archiving Management.** It is important to establish what documents can be archived and in which circumstances. There is also a need to select hardware and software solutions compliant with ArchiveLink specifications. This activity defines whether the archiving solution could also be used for optical archiving of original documents linked to R/3 business documents.

❑ **Configure Archiving Management.** A view of project IMG is generated for this activity, and the IMG activities are carried out. The system is documented according to project documentation standards.

❑ **Test Archiving Management.**

Establish Authorization Management

R/3 modules or business applications provide many options for controlling access to functions and transactions by using the authorization concept and profiles. A more detailed description of the security and authorization concept in SAP projects is found in Chapter 8.

Activities of this work package are aimed at defining and implementing the authorization system. They also define authorizations needed for executing functions, and to whom they are assigned. Authorization and profiles are created, and their correct assignment according to the established organization model is verified, as is the fact that they work as intended.

Perform Final Test

The goal of this work package is to perform a global test of all previous activities. This means not only partial tests of each activity done while carrying out tasks, but tests of all components and designs. This is normally known as the integration test.

Quality Check Application System

The objective of this work package is to review the results of this project phase. If results are satisfactory, a project report is sent to the steering committee for approval, so that the project can proceed to next phase.

Phase 3: Preparations for Going Live

The objective of this phase is to have a productive systems environment ready for the process of going live and for productive operation. The following work packages are included in this phase:

Create the "Going Live" Plan

Activities within this work package are:

- ❑ Finishing configuration of productive systems. Based on sizing and performance tests done in previous phases, a hardware architecture is defined, including elements such as:
  - ❑ Application and database servers
  - ❑ Printing requirements
  - ❑ Network infrastructure (LAN, WAN, Ethernet, FDDI, Token Ring, and so on), and network software and protocols (TCP/IP, Novell, Windows NT, and so on)
  - ❑ Desktop computers and equipment
  - ❑ Disk volume and storage requirements
  - ❑ Backup and restore strategy
  - ❑ High availability requirements: switchover or cluster systems, critical element redundancy to avoid single points of failure, disaster recovery, and so on
  - ❑ Remote connection requirements: ISDN, X25, Frame Relay, Internet, and so on.

  At this point initial configuration and hardware requirements are to be verified, and if needed, modified or completed. It is critical that early size estimates approach the requirements for the final systems landscape, otherwise the plan for going live may suffer delay in the time needed for delivery of new equipment, hardware, or software.
- ❑ Procuring the hardware and software required for going live
- ❑ Setting up master data for application users; at this point user master records must be created and authorization profiles assigned
- ❑ Creating a plan for data transfer to the productive system. A detailed, step-by-step plan for the data transfer must reflect data volume, complexity, and consistency. It is also vital to describe the sequence of data transfer since some master data can require a previous load. Once the plan is completed, the project team can proceed to actual load or transfer, as well as to verify consistency, and perform any required configuration action after the data are loaded. This will be done in a later work package.

Create User Documentation

At this point project teams must generate the documentation that application end-users need for their work. It must be clear and easy to understand, and should be sorted by functions or business processes, as well as by user job tasks. Documentation must enable a quick and easy search. This user documentation will form the basis for the end-user training. Some of the main activities of this work package are:

❑ Defining structure, content, and presentation format. The objective of this activity is to establish how to structure the information to be included in user documentation, such as by application areas, task profiles, and so on. This activity is used for defining the content and scope of the documentation, as well as the design and format, and how will it be shared and distributed.

❑ Preparing creation of user documentation. This activity sets the responsibility for creating each identified structure, as well as the plan for elaborating each part of the documentation.

❑ Creating the change concept. Since any documentation may be frequently updated and enhanced, the procedure for making required corrections to user documentation must be established.

❑ Creating user documentation. This is when user documentation, is created: help files, HTML, Word files, or others. If required, the users' working environment must also be set up, so that there is easy access to documentation, for instance by setting up initialization files or shortcuts to online documentation.

Set Up Production Environment

Activities within this work package include:

❑ Installing and configuring the network
❑ Installing and configuring any additional hardware and software for going live, such as the presentation interface (SAPGUI) or any additional components
❑ Installing and configuring the R/3 productive system.

As a result of this work package, the production system should be ready.

Train End-Users

The objective of this work package is to train users in the R/3 business applications that they will be using, to avoid problems related to knowledge or skills needed for job duties. This training should be provided on conceptual and operative bases: users must know how to perform their tasks, but also how to understand the processes. Activities within the work package are:

❑ Creating training plan
❑ Preparing training
❑ Delivering training.

Extensive information on the training issue can be found in Chapter 4.

Establish Systems Management

All activities related to administration of systems are developed in parallel to the use of the application. The objective of activities within this work package is to guarantee a stable system environment and application performance, availability, and security. Among the activities are:

❑ Defining the organization for systems management. According to the size, complexity, and requirements of the implementation, the following profiles should be among those considered when defining systems management:
  ❑ Operating system administration
  ❑ Administration of the network
  ❑ Administration of R/3
  ❑ R/3 operations
  ❑ Database administration
  ❑ Archiving administration
  ❑ R/3 monitoring and tuning
❑ Training the system administration and operation team.

Transfer Data to the Productive System

This is one of the last steps before actually going live and starting productive operation. Activities in this work package include the final preparations of the productive environment such as the transport of authorizations, profiles, users, printers, and so on, as well as new developments (repository objects) and customizing settings. These are common activities performed using the Transport System to transport change requests generated in the development environment to the selected client in the productive system. Finally, data transfer starts, using available automatic methods such as Batch Input, Direct Input, or Client Copy, or by manually entering data. An alternative way of setting up the productive system and loading data can be by making a complete client copy, or a complete systems copy, and then performing a set of complementary configuration activities. More information on this topic can be found in Chapter 7.

A final activity in this work package is performing a test of the configured productive system before going live, so that all required preparations are verified and the integrity of loaded data is ensured.

Quality Check Production System

This is the final work package of the preparation phase. The objective is to have a report on the validity of the phase for approval, so that the environment is ready for productive work. Some of the activities within this work package are:

❑ Verifying end-user documentation
❑ Validating the productive environment
❑ Verifying successful end-user training
❑ Validating the systems management organization
❑ Validating data transfer
❑ Validating the project plan
❑ Creating a validation report
❑ Agreeing to proceed to next phase by presenting the report to the steering committee for approval.

Phase 4: Productive Operation

Phase 4 of the Procedure includes five main functions or work packages for productive operation:

- ❑ Support users at start of live operation
- ❑ Establish and organize help desk
- ❑ Monitor and improve system use
- ❑ Update and change user documentation and system settings
- ❑ Formally close the project.

When going live, it is critical to guarantee exhaustive support to end-users starting to use and operate the R/3 applications. There will be many doubts, errors, problems, or mistakes, which must be quickly answered or solved. This is a temporary phase within the overall project, but is demanding on resources and time-critical. After this temporary phase, once users are familiar with the new application and working environment, there will be a more stable situation in which most incidents are already known and classified. For this process it is vital to organize a Help Desk for dealing with user questions and problems and for solving them or referring them to more specialized support personnel or external sources. Support issues including the Help Desk are described and explained in Chapter 7.

A server's configuration and parameters are usually not perfectly tuned during the first weeks of productive operation, since it is difficult to estimate or test the actual workload profiles. For this reason, it is convenient to monitor the workload, statistics and resource consumption, so that the greatest problems or performance bottlenecks can quickly be detected and corresponding tuning or configuration actions can take place.

To analyze the systems performance and do some tuning, SAP has several services such as EarlyWatch, described in the previous chapter. EarlyWatch provides a detailed report of system status and gives recommendations for improving performance and solving detected problems.

At this time, requests for changes to system settings or documentation are common. A certain type of user may need to perform a specific transaction and cannot for lack of proper authorization, or because the authorization did not include all possibilities within the transaction. Often, when user menus are developed, these must be adjusted to better address requirements.

Finally, there is a formal closing of the project. The question of a real ending to an SAP implementation project can be a point of intense debate. Chapter 7 includes an overview of this issue.

For the formal closing of the project, the Procedure Model includes the following activities:

❑ Creating a report of project closing
❑ Project review with the steering committee
❑ Publishing the success of project implementation
❑ Informing SAP of the success of the implementation.

Final project reports should include general details such as project name, authors, application modules implemented, project charter, and so on. This would encompass the project and business objectives, results, costs, implementation problems and issues, solutions, and lessons learned. This report is basic for reviewing the project, so that the steering committee can make a final evaluation. Once the report is accepted, the project manager's responsibility is finished.

Introduction to ASAP

AcceleratedSAP (ASAP) is SAP's implementation solution to R/3 projects. ASAP goes beyond just methodology by providing a large number of tools and utilities to simplify the implementation process. It is backed by extensive SAP and SAP partner implementation services, such as training, support, consulting, and so on.

One of the main goals of ASAP is to guarantee the ROI, a term SAP coined to merge Return on Investment and Return on Information. The faster a business gets an ROI, the better. The path proposed by SAP to reach the goal is based on the idea of facilitating a quick implementation of SAP R/3 and guaranteeing quality. To achieve both a fast and quality implementation, ASAP is based on the following issues:

❑ Clearly defining the mission and scope of the project; a clearly defined project scope is key to adjusting time planning and to making project cost plans approach real costs.
❑ Increasing the feasibility of realizing a detailed plan at the beginning of the project
❑ Standardizing and establishing a single project or implementation methodology, as defined by ASAP itself

❑ Creating a homogeneous project environment.

To realize these objectives, ASAP provides the project team with a methodology, tools, training, and services, as well as a process-oriented project plan, known as the ASAP Roadmap.

Some of the tools provided by ASAP are:

❑ Implementation Assistant
❑ Question & Answer Database
❑ Business Engineer
❑ SAP project team training
❑ SAP support and services
❑ Knowledge Corner

The ASAP solution set is delivered in a CD-ROM that is installed independently of R/3, although there is a connection between some of the tools and the IMG. ASAP is release dependent and is constantly updated. SAP provides periodic updates on SAPnet.

SAP has also launched the TeamSAP initiative for providing coaching and training to partners, as well as a certification program so that customers can be confident about the quality of consultants who help them. TeamSAP is normally positioned as a three-component solution, or as a coordinated network of:

❑ Processes, represented by the ASAP solution set
❑ People, including prepared and certified consultants
❑ Products, represented by the R/3 Business Framework architecture.

TeamSAP is SAP's commitment to its customers' implementation success and encompasses full application life-cycle support with ongoing changes. In this line, SAP plays an important role in coaching and auditing the quality of projects.

This chapter has dealt only with the process component of the TeamSAP, although it has referred to the role of TeamSAP consultants.

Figure 3.10 below shows the initial screen of Release 4.0B of ASAP.

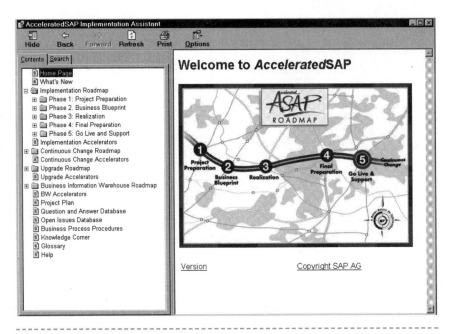

FIGURE 3.10   *ASAP Implementation Assistant and Roadmap*

In line with SAP strategy, the ASAP method of implementation is positioned according to the following objectives:

❏ ASAP is the first SAP R/3 implementation solution directly developed and supported by SAP where the contribution from the TeamSAP consultants is critical.

❏ ASAP offers a preliminary planning of the resource needs—time, costs, people—based on initial customer information and requirements

❏ ASAP provides an optimal environment for SAP R/3 upgrade projects, since it is aimed at and specially suited to implementation projects where the number of changes to standard SAP is reduced to a minimum. As Figure 3.10 shows, there is also an ASAP upgrade project roadmap.

The following sections introduce some of the main features of ASAP. The remainder of this book will explain some of the tools, documents, and ASAP approaches in greater detail for specific implementation issues.

The *ASAP Roadmap* is the project plan of the methodology. It is a well-defined and clear process-oriented project plan, providing a step-by-step guide during the life of the implementation project.

The Roadmap is made up of four major phases, each one describing the work packages, activities and tasks needed to achieve the expected results. Together with activities, and tasks, ASAP provides all the process description, tools, training, services, and documentation that will be usefd to carry out these activities.

The next sections briefly introduce the Roadmap phases.

Phase 1: Project Preparation

In this first phase, the project mission and scope are defined. Key issues of this phase are:

❑ Defining clear project objectives
❑ Reaching total agreement among involved parties on project issues
❑ Establishing an efficient process for making decisions and resolving conflicts
❑ Preparing the company for accepting cultural and process changes.

In this phase ASAP provides tools such as the Project Estimator, which helps and guides the project team using predefined questionnaires aimed at company upper management. Using the results of those questions, a TeamSAP consultant can evaluate answers and provide a high-level evaluation of the project scope, as well as an initial estimation of required resources and planning. This is the project starting point.

The outcome of the phase includes two documents essential to the implementation: the project charter and detailed project plan. The management team or steering committee is responsible for evaluating this plan and approving it, if no objections are found. This will trigger the start of next phase.

ASAP pays particular attention to ensuring quality in the whole project process and in decisions taken throughout the execution of this phase, since any error or wrong decisions can negatively affect the subsequent flow of the project and might produce delays leading to a longer time frame and higher costs.

Phase 2: Business Blueprint

In the second phase of the Roadmap, the project team undertakes a complete and comprehensive analysis of requirements and business process, while documenting and defining R/3 implementation in the company. To achieve these results ASAP provides a group of predefined questionnaires, group sessions, individual interviews, and so on.

Information gathered is critical and extremely useful for the TeamSAP consultants, who can analyze and help to document business processes and future business requirements for the company. SAP Business Engineer includes the tools used for this phase, mainly the R/3 Reference Model and Question and Answer database, that will be used for generating Business Blueprint documents and the Business Process Master List. ASAP includes a "business application repository" with tools that allow users to interact with and test the business process of the SAP R/3 application.

This phase of the project provides a specific methodology for analyzing business processes from an R/3 perspective and facilitates process documentation. The result is a complete blueprint of the business. Initially ASAP was not designed to be applied to projects requiring much reengineering.

Within an overall implementation project, this is probably the most challenging phase. In a typical nine-month implementation project, this phase could last five or six weeks.

This phase combines the analysis and documentation of business processes with first-level training of project teams in the different functionality of SAP R/3 modules. Within this phase there is also a work package for developing the system environment; this includes the design of the system landscape, the technical infrastructure, and the start of defining and testing system administration procedures. At this point, development and test clients are set up, and the IMG is initialized for the starting customizing activities.

Finally, an extremely important addition to this major phase is the inclusion of the Change Management program, in charge of dealing with all human and organizational factors that influence the implementation project. An extensive section on this issue can be found in Chapter 4.

Phase 3: Realization

With the Business Blueprint documentation generated as result of the previous phase, the project team should be in good shape to start the realization phase that includes a collection of work packages where actual implementation of business processes takes place.

Figure 3.11 shows the work packages included in release 4.0B of ASAP.

```
⊟ 📂 Phase 3: Realization
    ⊞ 📁 Project Management Realization Phase
    ⊞ 📁 Sustaining Change Management Processes
    ⊞ 📁 Project Team Training Realization Phase
    ⊞ 📁 Baseline Configuration and Confirmation
    ⊞ 📁 System Management
    ⊞ 📁 Final Configuration and Confirmation
    ⊞ 📁 Develop Conversion Programs
    ⊞ 📁 Develop Application Interface Programs
    ⊞ 📁 Develop Enhancements
    ⊞ 📁 Create Reports
    ⊞ 📁 Create Forms
    ⊞ 📁 Establish Authorization Concept
    ⊞ 📁 Establish Archiving Management
    ⊞ 📁 Final Integration Test
    ⊞ 📁 End User Documentation and Training Material
    ⊞ 📁 Quality Check Realization Phase
```

FIGURE 3.11   *ASAP Realization phase*

From the Business Blueprint documentation generated as deliverable from the previous phase, consultants and project team members have enough information to make a valid proposal covering most business processes (usually about 80%), reports, and daily business transactions, trying to match those of the SAP standard. The remaining processes (around 20%) which do not seem to cover the company's business process report, or transaction requirements, will be a matter for fine tuning.

The most important work package activities within Realization include:

- ❑ Reviewing project management activities such as planning, reviews, schedule, and scope
- ❑ Providing advance training to the project team
- ❑ Establishing the system management strategy and configuring the technical infrastructure and system landscape
- ❑ Sustaining the change management program
- ❑ Configuring and testing an initial prototype (baseline) for major functions and processes
- ❑ Developing conversion, interface, and data transfer programs
- ❑ Developing enhancements for scenarios not fully covered by standard R/3 applications
- ❑ Configuring and verifying the final R/3 system; this can be based on a iterative approach to the prototypes
- ❑ Creating forms and reports
- ❑ Establishing the authorization concept and strategy
- ❑ Planning and designing archiving strategy
- ❑ Performing a final integration test
- ❑ Preparing end-user documentation and training material.

As in every major phase, the last step is a quality assurance realization process, where every element of the project phase is checked and verified.

This phase will be the longest in terms of time, effort, and resources needed.

Phase 4: Final Preparation

This phase, where all implementation elements and configurations are tested to finish the preparation for going live, requires a close collaboration between the full project team and the end-users. The main objectives of this phase can be summarized as follows:

❏ **Strict implementation verification.** The team and the users should test that all requirements defined in previous phases are met, and that the behavior of the implemented business processes is correct. This phase is the appropriate time for doing stress tests, which are important not only for verifying sizing, but also for optimizing the system's performance. It is also convenient to undertake simulations of real operation as the most important point of integration tests. In this phase it might be convenient to request SAP help through available services such as a GoingLive Check, which analyzes configuration and makes recommendations which can be evaluated and implemented.

❏ **End-user acceptance.** This is the main requirement for any project that is going to be deployed by a number of end-users. Without wide final user acceptance, the project success is far from guaranteed.

❏ **End-user training.** This is another key factor since end-users must receive the appropriate training, according to their job profiles and the applications they need to use. Training helps users to become familiar as soon as possible with the new environment; this can provide optimal user operation in less time.

❏ **Initial Data Loads and Cutover.** At the moment that application and systems are ready for going live, all necessary data still resident in legacy or other systems must be transferred to R/3. All those load and interface programs should be prepared, tested, evaluated, and optimized, as should the quality of data to be transferred, and the time it takes to load.

❏ **Help Desk Strategy.** From the first moment of productive operation, every system user should know where and how to call to resolve doubts or handle problems. A support group, usually known as the Help Desk, should be created to answer end-user questions and solve or refer both technical and application problems. Problems and doubts which might arise can be classified according to their nature, for instance:
  ❏ SAP R/3 application modules
  ❏ Interfaces with external applications
  ❏ Technology infrastructure
  ❏ Communications
  ❏ Hardware

❑ Printing.

Refer to Chapter 7 for more information on Help Desk strategies and support issues.

Phase 5: Go Live and Support

In this phase the productive operation starts. The initial period after going live is also the best evaluation period for everything done and designed in previous project phases. In most cases, a progressive productive start is recommended so that there is time to react to typical problems like:

❑ Not enough physical resources such as network printers
❑ Problems when printing reports, spool saturation, repetitive sending of the same output by the same users, etc.
❑ Wrongly configured PC or SAPGUI, wrong server, deleted files, help files not reached, etc.
❑ Reports and transactions not completely meeting user needs
❑ Bugs in the standard R/3 system requiring patches or repairs
❑ Database or runtime problems when running reports or transactions with real data
❑ Adding new users to the system
❑ Lack of end-user training
❑ Help Desk strategy is not well defined or not defined at all
❑ Many others.

The degree of success or failure (unfavorable user reaction) in this initial period of productive operation will be a factor of the completeness and accuracy of work done in the previous phases and of how possible problems were addressed.

In this phase a good procedure for communicating with SAP or partners to request their services may be important, for example, to realize EarlyWatch—preventive maintenance—services. This is also the phase for testing the quality of operation and system administration procedures.

Soon the most frequent types of problems will already be classified and can be quickly solved.

From the technical and administrative point of view, after the initial adaptation to the productive operation, there is time for managing different activities of a productive R/3 system such as:

❑ Managing transports and change requests
❑ Applying Hot Packages (collections of corrected programs and transactions)
❑ Installing SAP R/3 Kernel Patches
❑ Planning EarlyWatch sessions
❑ Making changes and configurations as recommended by EarlyWatch reports
❑ Watching systems performance and tuning the most critical reports and transactions
❑ Others.

Chapter 7 devoted to the issues related to going live and productive support.

CHAPTER 4

People and Knowledge Issues in SAP Projects

If you carefully reviews the critical success factors and the reasons for failure presented in Chapter 2, it is clear that most problems have to do with people. It is therefore obvious that people issues are extremely important factors in SAP implementations. This is also probably one of the most difficult issues to address since behavior and reactions are often unpredictable and conditioned by personal and organizational circumstances.

The main issue of this chapter is *management of change*.

From an organizational business standpoint, people can be severely affected by major changes in the company. It is vital to deal with the cultural impact of the changes before, during, and after the implementation, in order to reduce the risks inherent to the project by reducing resistance and increasing credibility.

From a SAP project viewpoint, people need to train and be trained, people make decisions to manage the project and the systems, develop reports, and so on. In the integrated world of SAP applications, these factors will invariably affect human relationships, and there will be a need to establish standards and procedures.

This chapter explores the most significant people related issues in implementation projects, starting with higher positions in the hierarchy of the decision-making process.

The Commitment of Upper Management

The commitment of upper managers to the implementation project is of vital importance to make it not only successful but also cost effective. This second reason is probably better understood and supported. This commitment is more a critical success factor than an implementation issue, but its significance to the project is so important that clarification is a must.

Even when project managers are hierarchically dependent on company management they must constantly look for the active support of decision makers. Upper management must clearly understand the nature of SAP projects. It is a mistake to consider SAP as "just another systems project." A SAP implementation project, as introduced in Chapter 1, is more a business or strategic project for companies.

According to proposed methodologies like ASAP, managers may have several roles in global project organization. They are not only project sponsors, but also involved in the steering committee. These functions require that management provide support and credibility to the project, participate in the communications strategy, take decisions, lead the changes, and also act as a force to be periodically consulted to erase doubts.

The lack of commitment of company leaders will have a tremendous influence during implementation, especially with project organization and the overall change management process and methodology. Upper management will probably more clearly understand that without their active support, the time and cost of the project can and will increase dramatically.

Among possible ways to actively involve upper management are:

❑ The project manager, with the support for project sponsors, must have the ability to forge a close relationship and communication channel with company management at the top level.
❑ If applicable, the SAP counterpart to the project manager must have the same efficient and close communication.
❑ The use of organization, change management, or strategic consultants with knowledge of reengineering and ERP implementation can be very helpful for fostering an active attitude in managers.
❑ There must be a clear definition of approved roles and responsibilities during implementation.
❑ Top leaders should be involved in short and effective meetings about project progress, status, and open items.

These points form a set of actions led by the project manager which need to be integrated into an efficient communications and knowledge strategy sharing during the implementation project.

Table 4.1 summarizes the issue of upper management commitment during SAP implementation projects.

TABLE 4.1 *The Issue of Upper Management Commitment*

Why deal with this issue	Other issues affected	Approach and Solutions
❏ Because decisions have to be made to solve issues	❏ Methodology	❏ Information with effective communications
❏ To assign budget and resources	❏ Project Organization	❏ Project management involvement
❏ To provide credibility	❏ Customizing	❏ Strategic consultants
❏ To diminish the implementation risks	❏ Change Management	❏ Definition of roles and responsibilities
❏ To succeed in the project in a timely manner	❏ Communication	❏ Other
	❏ Time and Costs	
	❏ Others	

There is the additional question of when to deal with this issue. The obvious, although not simple, answer is: always. The project manager, and project sponsors must closely watch the involvement of top company leaders.

The Issue of the Project Organization

In any project and, of course, in the case of SAP implementations, the need for people to realize the project is obvious. Because there will often be a mixture of different types of people, and even different types of cultures, the project team can be made up of consultants from different companies: there might be SAP consultants, as well as hardware experts, IT personnel from the end-customer, end-users, maybe BPR experts, strategic consultants, and so on.

The scope of the implementation, in terms of business areas, users affected, and the project budget, will be important factors for configuring the right team to achieve the goal of a successful implementation.

The main questions arising from the process of defining and selecting the project team are:

❏ What are/will be the project tasks and activities?
❏ What skills or competencies are needed for performing those tasks?
❏ How many resources are necessary for the planned time for completion?
❏ What are the roles and responsibilities?

The following paragraph comes from an excellent paper by the Gartner Group (*Next-Generation Enterprise Applications*, 1997).

> *Even the best processes and tools will not lead to successful projects without clearly defined roles and responsibilities. For each project phase and each deliverable produced, the role of end users (e.g., core end users, occasional end users, and end users indirectly affected by the project), the various areas within the IS organization (e.g. operations, the help desk, or security), and anyone else who is critical to or significantly affected by the project, must be understood clearly (preferably up front).*

In a later paragraph from the same Gartner paper talking about the problems and challenges of implementing enterprise applications there is this group of clarifying ideas about the importance of keeping the "right people" in projects:

> *Earlier, clearly defining roles and responsibilities was listed as being key to a successful application-acquisition process. In addition, efforts to ensure continued involvement of the right people throughout the project are needed to ensure that defined responsibilities are fulfilled. If a key project team member is unable to spend the amount of time needed to keep the project on schedule or is pulled off the project, one or more of the following actions must be taken to keep the project on track:*

❑ *Replace the person*
❑ *Distribute the person's workload to other project team members*
❑ *Reduce the scope of the project*
❑ *Extend the timeline.*

This implementation issue is closely related to Project Management, though its essential importance lies in the fact that it has a direct impact on the full project—on all organizational and technical areas—of the implementation and ongoing production.

There is no single solution, since there are different degrees of project complexity and implementation scope. Therefore communication and clear description of objectives and scope, as defined in a project charter and translated into a project plan, become a must.

The next sections describe approaches to project organization on SAP implementation projects.

ASAP Approach to Project Organization

Phase 1 of ASAP includes the work package "Determine Project Organization," just after the project charter has been defined and the implementation strategy decided.

This ASAP activity has five steps:

1. Refine organization and roles
2. Assign people to roles
3. Assign people to core change roles
4. Conduct project team transition meeting
5. Create the extended change team.

Notice how steps 3 and 5 include activities dealing with the change management issue. This will be extensively described later in this chapter.

The number of roles and types of activities to be performed on SAP projects is extremely large, ranging from Project Manager to Power User, from Layout Developer to Help Desk Provider. They are all described in the ASAP paper on Organization and Roles, which defines not only functions but also the time commitment expected, depending on the project's complexity.

ASAP also includes a Team Organization Chart Template. Figure 4.1 shows this template at the first level of the organization.

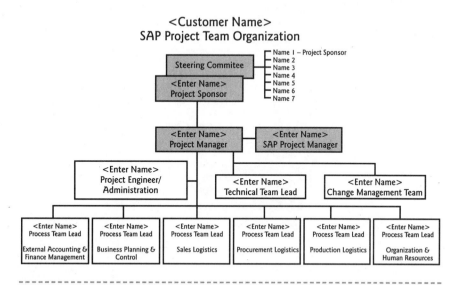

FIGURE 4.1   *SAP Project Team Organization Template   Copyright © SAP AG*

An Approach to Roles and Responsibilities

Next, Figure 4.2 shows a simplified example of a possible organization for the group of people playing a role not only in the implementation phase, but also in the use and the support of the SAP R/3 system.

Theoretically, this approach should not differ much from the IT organization set in place for supporting other types of demanding and critical business information systems. There are, however, factors which make the technical aspects of R/3 different from other business applications.

The number of people and the actual management organization to which they belong will depend on the size and budget of the company, and the size, scope, and complexity assigned to SAP R/3 as a strategic business application.

Depending on the complexity and size of the project, some of the roles could further be divided into more detailed ones, although typically several roles are assumed by one person or organization. In small installations, several of the generic roles presented below can fall to a single person; other sites will require several people to cover them.

Many companies decide to have their Help Desk, or even the whole IT department, outsourced to external and competent organizations.

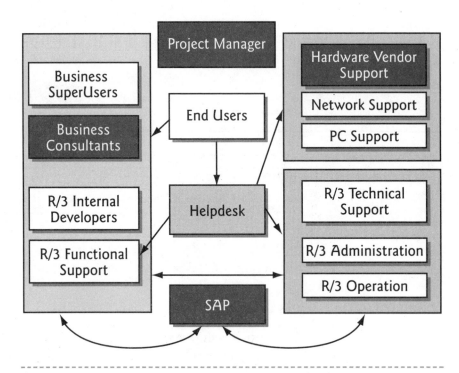

FIGURE 4.2   *An Approach to Project Use and Support Organization*

Figure 4.2 shows some of the roles commonly seen in SAP R/3 projects.

It would also be possible for part of the existing IT department in a company, with some additional R/3 training, to combine some of the tasks with new ones. For instance, there is no need for a network administrator just for SAP. Network managers need only add additional systems to monitor and watch for a correct network layout and configuration.

The most important entities that every person or role in the organization must consider are the *business* and the *mission*. SAP R/3 might be implemented because corporate management made a strategic decision to support a new business model, maybe as the result of a reengineering process to support changing business needs to compete in a global market. What is obvious is that no company invests in a new system like this without expecting to get some benefit from it.

Looking at the arrows that connect different roles in the figure, consider that one of the most important aspects for successful productive operation and organization among all the entities is a fast and efficient communication path among them. The left side of the figure represents functional roles, while the right represents technical ones. Dark boxes with white letters indicate entities normally "external" to the company. In the center and above all, there is the central figure of the Project Manager (or Project Managers).

The following is an overview of the roles pictured above:

End-users. Users of business applications do the work of feeding the system with information and obtaining results to help in the decision process. End-users usually have a partial but important vision of the business, and are sometimes those who know the specific details of business processes. For this reason, end-users also feed information to business super-users in the implementation phase.

This will probably be the largest group in terms of people, and is the main requester of training, functional, and technical support. In a good organization, end-users should not directly call the application experts. They should depend on a form of Help Desk, which can be a first-line support that redirects the call to the appropriate person or organization.

Business super-users (known frequently as *key users*). This group of expert users has a comprehensive knowledge of the business. It is usually the *driver* of the whole SAP R/3 project and should be formed of people who can make fast decisions. Normally they belong to the *steering committee* for the project and assign a project manager or project leader for each of the business areas on which the implementation is based. For example, there will be one leader for the FI Treasury module, another one for Materials Management, Sales, etc. It is also important to get the involvement of key users in the change management process.

In medium-sized to large companies, many times a business requests an impartial view of the business, or help in implementation techniques, know-how on R/3 application software, or the ability for knowledge transfer. Because of the business-oriented nature of such projects, it is quite common to find *external business consultants* in most SAP projects. These consultants, might also have the responsibility for project management or project management assistance. As Chapter 1 stated, SAP has a large number of consulting partners, including the biggest consulting firms, plus hundreds of smaller local consulting companies.

Some of the participants in the group of business super-users make up the next group in the picture, the *SAP functional support*. The function of this group is to help in customizing the system as well as in solving those users' problems which directly relate to business processes and applications. It is also this group's function to effect corrections, enhancements, or new developments in the system according to user requests. Usually these people are in charge of training end-users in their specific modules, as well as receiving support calls that might relate more to functional system aspects rather than to technical problems. Examples of their support activities might be when a user gets an error when posting a financial document, a user needs a higher customized report of the inventory. R/3 functional support might rely on an internal or external development team, as well as on the overall support of the technical group.

The *development team* will only be necessary in case new developments are needed to fill identified and critical gaps. When only the development of simple reports is required, the technical support group could assume some of the simple development functions. However in pre-production stages of the R/3 implementation, some help might be needed for tasks such as massive data load from legacy applications, development of batch input programs, business customized menus, screens, etc. Developers need close contact with the functional group, since this group is supposed to know the business and user requirements. At the same time, developers will often need the help of the technical group for things such as system requirements, database resources, transport requests, etc.

The *SAP technical support* group is in charge of all the technical aspects of R/3 installations. They give continuous support to the development and functional teams, participating actively in the technical parts of R/3 projects. They are usually the second-level line for solving users' technical problems. This group can be subdivided into R/3 technical specialists, R/3 system administrator, and operation personnel. In small R/3 installations a single person can assume all functions if the procedures to maintain the system are well documented and mostly automated.

The technical group must have a wide range of skills, including client-server computing, operating systems, database and R/3 expertise, as well as a good knowledge of PC technology and networking. These technologies can be totally or partially supported by existing technical groups (as shown on the upper right side box in the figure) like the network support or PC support groups; there can also be maintenance contracts with and support from the corresponding hardware vendors. Some of the functions of this group could be handed over to existing IT resources; for example, operating system managers, could assume the management of new servers once the architecture of R/3 is introduced to them.

A summary of functions normally assumed by the R/3 technical and administration group includes:

❑ Administration of the operating system, database, and sometimes even the network. This includes such things as doing all typical functions of DBAs, such as reorganizing the database, monitoring storage, backups, etc.
❑ Administration and monitoring of R/3, including management of background jobs, users, the authorization system, printing system, interfaces, correction and transport system, remote communications, profile and instance maintenance, tuning, etc.
❑ Defining and implementing the system backup and recovery strategy
❑ Solving and reporting technical problems as they are logged in the system
❑ Support for new modules going into production by allowing sufficient space, checking technical settings of tables, doing previous exports/imports, etc.

❑ Support for all kinds of maintenance upgrades
❑ Support for and implementation of new technical or cross-functional projects in the R/3 environment, such as the implementation of the Workflow, EDI server, Archive Link, Internet, fax and mail integration, and so on.
❑ Implementing EarlyWatch suggested recommendations and corrections into the system
❑ Always observing the highest system availability.

The *R/3 Operation* staff can be responsible for checking system-critical log files, such as backup logs, the system log, etc. and reporting observed problems. They can also be responsible for system and database backups as well as doing daily backups of archived redo log files. Even when this process is automated without manual intervention, someone has to check the log and change the tapes. They can also periodically check some of the system monitors, and the state of spool and background systems.

In any case, the administration and operation group should design a comprehensive guide, such as an administration and operation manual, which can easily be followed by anyone who could eventually substitute in or help this group.

The *Help Desk* is the central support location in charge of receiving user calls and doing first-line support. This group must be actively in touch with the rest of the support groups, so if for any reason network lines are not available, the SAP system has been shut down for maintenance reasons, etc. they know the situation and quickly react to and answer user queries. This group might normally use one of the many available Help Desk software applications that include features such as automatic call transfer, keeping problem logs, record incidences, etc.

As to the role of *SAP* itself in the big picture, the need for is SAP services throughout the installation and implementation of the R/3 systems is understood. SAP's extensive range of services, specially OSS and EarlyWatch, should be of active help in overall support, both functional and technical. SAP's role might include the following activities (and perhaps others):

❑ Providing on-site and remote consulting (both functional and technical)

❏ Being the main source for project team training
❏ Helping in stress testing definitions
❏ Collaborating in a quality check before going productive.

Finally there is the central figure of the *Project Manager*, with overall responsibility for the success of the implementation project, support after going live, and continuous change management. Project management itself constitutes a vital implementation issue that it is dealt with in another section of this chapter.

A Simple Knowledge-based Approach to Project Organization

Figure 4.3 shows an alternative, simple approach to organizing people involved in a SAP implementation project.

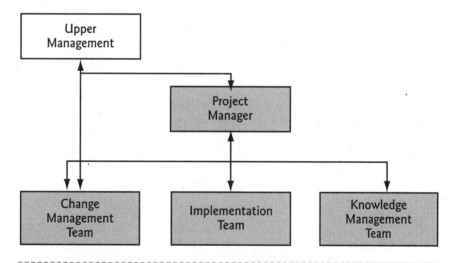

FIGURE 4.3   *A knowledge-based approach to SAP Project Organization*

It is based on three not necessarily hierarchical levels:

❏ On the top level are the top leaders and sponsors for implementation; their function is described in the section on the commitment of upper management
❏ The project manager plays a central and fundamental role, since her/his function will be coordinating of the team members in dif-

ferent groups and enabling knowledge sharing across teams. The project management issue is described in a subsequent section of this chapter.

❑ On the third level are three teams that cooperate closely and even share members:

  ❑ The Change Management team, in charge of the Change Process, is described in a subsequent section of this chapter.

  ❑ The Implementation team is in charge of the technical activities of projects, such as customizing, development, and technical infrastructure. Members of this team also have responsibility for training and support.

  ❑ The Knowledge Management team can be composed of experts from the other two groups; its main task will be to gather the best practices from the implementation, and use them for active communication to all levels, end-user training, issue resolution, procedure definition, documentation preparation, support, and knowledge sharing. This team may be compared to a customer competence center, though the key is a tight integration with other project team members.

Project Organization Summary

The organization of the project and the definition of roles and responsibilities are primary and essential tasks of the project prepa-

Why deal with this issue	Other issues affected	Approach and Solutions
❑ To create the project team	❑ All	❑ ASAP Accelerators
❑ To avoid organizational gaps		❑ Experienced and competent project managers
❑ To assign tasks to responsible people		❑ Clear objectives and scope
❑ To keep the right people involved		❑ Clear project plan

ration phase. Caution must be exercised, since the organization may change as new responsibility gaps are discovered.

Project Management

Effective Project Management is the central role of any implementation project and without doubt, the toughest work in an SAP implementation. Two complementary people often play this role: a customer project manager, and an external project manager or person experienced in implementing SAP or other ERP projects.

The following paragraph from the Gartner Group paper *Next Generation Enterprise Applications* includes an excellent description of project management:

> Project management *is a subset of process management and is both a discipline and a technology. As a discipline, it involves the functions of planning, estimating, organizing, launching, monitoring, managing, and delivering a project. As a technology, project management tools help the project manager develop the schedule; however, that is only a small part of the benefit. Good project management tools also help track the project, adjust the schedule, and report project status. Active management of projects after planning is critical. For example, the rocket ship to the moon allegedly was off course 95% of the time, but it still reached its target because of frequent in-flight corrections and adjustments. Successful business and IT projects must be managed in a similar fashion, because developing the perfect project plan is virtually impossible. Project planning and management are key skills for successful IS organizations.*

The project sponsors, and sometimes the top company leaders, are usually in charge of selecting the Customer Project Manager. Among the responsibilities of the project manager will be to provide leadership, not only to the project team, but also to upper management.

A word of caution in the project management selection process. This manager plays a fundamental role, and therefore, the selection criteria must include technical *and* personal skills; when internal politics rather than candidate skills influence the decision, project management might be biased in taking decisions and solving issues.

Top leaders usually require project managers to fulfill project goals as cheaply and fast as possible. However, as James P. Lewis points out in his book *Project Planning, Scheduling & Control*, if you pick two constant requirements, the third must be allowed to vary. In other words "Cost is a function of Performance, Time and Scope."

A project manager is not the greatest expert in PC scheduling software. A project manager is responsible for the planning, execution, and control of the full project—and that includes the supervision of deliverables and daily activities. This will cover solving issues related to budget and resources, as well as assigning priorities.

Among additional responsibilities of the typical project manager on SAP projects are:

❑ Providing a methodology framework
❑ Anticipating implementation issues
❑ Demonstrating leadership in solving problems
❑ Communicating objectives, milestones, status, deviations, changes, and so on, not only to sponsors, but to all project team members
❑ Negotiating constantly.

In order to accomplish those functions, SAP project managers require knowledge, experience, and a set of skills that are often difficult to find in the SAP customer companies.

Among the skills and knowledge required are:

❑ Negotiation skills at all levels: management, consultants, end-users, IT, hardware and software vendors, etc.
❑ Power to make decisions
❑ Ability to communicate
❑ People leadership
❑ Knowledge of company business processes
❑ Experience in consulting projects
❑ Technology know-how
❑ Knowledge of SAP implementation solution sets.

The issues of project management and selection of a project manager have a direct impact on many other identified SAP implementation issues and indirectly affect all of them.

Project management directly influences the commitment of upper management, the definition of roles and responsibilities for the project, the project plan, the communications strategy, and all people-related issues (the change management process). It also controls the scope of the project.

It has an indirect responsibility for the rest of the implementation issues, since project managers are in charge of identifying and anticipating those issues, planning and scheduling their resolution, and assigning resources.

The list below provides advice for dealing with the issue of project management on implementation projects:

❑ Carefully select Project Managers, avoiding internal politics; search for personal skills as well as ability to perform

❑ Obtaining support from experienced or external project manager or implementation consultant can be very helpful, especially in identifying and anticipating issues specific to SAP projects.

❑ Use project management tools, not only planning and scheduling software, but also tools provided by SAP solution sets, such as ASAP or the Procedure Model.

❑ Finally, training R/3 project managers should receive includes R/3 basics, implementation training, ASAP, Going Live training and even some overview of core functional modules. This training can be supplemented by sharing experiences with other PMs who have already undergone R/3 projects, or are in the process of doing so. There are many lessons to be learned from the experiences of others and it is one of the aims of this book to reflect some of those lessons.

The next chart summarizes the issue of project management on SAP implementations.

Why deal with this issue	Other issues affected	Solutions
❑ Drive the project and provide leadership	❑ Upper management commitment	❑ Careful selection of PM
❑ Ongoing maintenance of project plan	❑ Project organization	❑ Support from experienced external SAP PM
❑ Anticipate and solve implementation issues	❑ Communications	
	❑ Control of scope	❑ Project Management tools
❑ Manage budget and resources	❑ Change management	
	❑ Consultants and key users	❑ Training on SAP implementation
	❑ Time and costs	❑ Visits to other SAP projects
	❑ And…indirectly, all the rest	❑ ASAP knowledge

Dealing with Change Management

Business and technology are in a state of continuous change. A famous line from a company CEO says that "change is the only variable that remains constant."

Change is an implicit, continuous process, a result of the need to survive or improve so that business can react and respond better, in a more efficient and competitive way, to customers, to shareholders, and to employees. There are market trends, financial figures, new products, new technology, new competitors, new needs, and so on. It is undeniable that change is important for business growth.

Change is often translated into the need to implement new systems and new technology aimed at fulfilling company objectives. Currently, the need for change and improvement influences the budget for projects where standard application packages such as SAP are implemented.

Even if SAP projects must be handled and managed as business and strategic projects, a solid technological background has been the real enabler of this type of package. The importance of technology for driving change must be acknowledged.

Ability to Change as a Key SAP Feature

SAP technology has enabled a milestone in business applications, the possibility for a (sometimes not so) quick reaction to constant changes in the organization, structure, or objectives of companies. This feature might seem secondary, but has made R/3 the leading standard-application system, especially when management has understood the inherent link between business processes and supporting information systems. This link was virtually impossible in previous legacy systems, and huge programming departments were more occupied solving yesterday's problems that providing for tomorrow's needs.

Another reason for SAP's success is due to the fact that a standard application package can be configured in multiple business areas, adapting to a company's specific needs. In order to support those needs, R/3 integrates a large number of built-in business processes and functions; at the same time it is open to improvements and supports continuous change in business practices.

More and more, in late '90s companies have decided on the "buy" strategy and use standard, flexible and customizable application packages to support the majority of their business processes and information needs. This type of package leaves custom software development to very specific cases.

SAP is quite aware that companies are in a process of constant change in organization and processes, and every release has increased system flexibility for supporting those changes in a swift and cost-efficient manner.

With release 4.0, 4.5, and EnjoySAP (4.6) and the tendency toward componentization, there have been important improvements to enable R/3 implementation in less time, with a growing focus on positioning R/3 as a solution easy to customize and use, and quick to change and upgrade. With the new components of R/3 Business Engineer, the system includes an advanced mechanism for model-based (business blueprints) configuration and continuous change management.

Top Leaders in Project Success

Many factors such as cost, time for implementation, return on investment, and so on, influence the decision to implement SAP.

However, more important than the decision to implement is the capacity of companies to achieve the goals of the project.

Project success is a matter not only of methodology or technical/functional work, but also of diminishing the risk of future changes; there is a critical need to get upper management to understand the basic nature of SAP.

Upper management must understand the nature, scope, repercussions, and changes implied in implementing a package such as SAP. This does not mean that upper management must know how to configure the system, but at least they must be aware that a change in a business process is not programmed but customized, and that a change in the way people work must be managed and led.

With SAP, companies are buying not only software, but something broader—the flexibility and ability to adapt to new business processes, to change existing ones, and to always seek best business practices, efficiency and business benefits.

Only with the basic knowledge of the nature of implementing this type of packages can a project team get the necessary support from top management; decisions can then be made in a quick and efficient way, without compromising project success. Only with this knowledge will it be possible to manage the change deriving from these types of systems and to overcome natural resistance to such change.

Change Management as an Implementation Issue

As a generic process *change* might have many objects or elements in companies, but managing the change refers only to the most critical focus point: people.

Fear of change is intrinsic to human nature; it is actually fear of the unknown. People change for two main reasons: when we find ourselves in a confined situation, or when there is a model we want to follow. In the second case, the *unknown* transforms into the *known*. People behave in a mimetic way, and the second reason we mentioned is comparable to the process of learning: explicit knowledge becomes tacit. There has been a transfer of useful information. The learning process is the key to effectively managing changes.

When there is a significant or radical change in business processes, this change will be not just a patch to satisfy everyone. Changes cannot exist in a poorly defined gray area.

As we have stated, people issues are extremely important agents in SAP implementation projects. From an organizational business point of view, people will/can be severely affected by major changes in the company. These issues are the object of the strategies and processes of change management.

From an SAP project point of view, it is people who need to train and be trained, people who make decisions and manage the project and the systems, who develop reports, and so on. In the integrated world of SAP applications, these factors will invariably affect human relationships, and there will be a need to establish standards and procedures.

Under a process of change management, people fear the unknown in their positions, their jobs, their careers. The mushroom clouds of departmental power tend to disappear at the same time that vertical information flows turn into a company-wide information flow.

Independently of the fact that a business implementation project like SAP takes place, companies know they have to change, either because of requests coming from inside or because of the dictates of balance sheets. Companies that need to change the most are usually those presenting more resistance to change. Companies more willing to adopt changes quickly are those better prepared to ensure success in their SAP implementation projects.

There is much fear and pain associated with a change process and some companies lack the strength, or the ability, to undertake that process. Changes are unavoidable in an SAP implementation and success can only be guaranteed when companies are able to overcome the problems and risks associated with change.

Often in an effort to soften the changes, companies fall into the *over-customizing* problem, customizing the SAP system in a way that looks like the old style of doing business, even changing standard codes and screen. Although this practice can satisfy certain user needs, in the long run it is another hurdle to a successful implementation and might involve more cost and time.

Change management is an implementation issue that must address human factors, search for ways to involve employees in the change process, and deal with the cultural impact of change.

A Word about Change Leadership

A Change Management initiative within an SAP implementation might involve a large number of people, including consultants, executives, site-level managers, key users, and so on. This will be a systematic and constant effort throughout the project, and to sustain the expected benefits, it would be a mistake simply to react to changes instead of to lead in creating them; this is the only way the problems and risks of an implementation can be assessed and planned for before they actually become project hurdles.

Change leadership has been acknowledged as an important area of business by many of the large, respected consulting companies, some of which have a well-defined solution map.

Leading change involves new management principles, as Douglas K. Smith suggests in *Taking Charge of Change*: "To change others, change yourself."

ASAP Approach to Change Management

Since release 3.0 (late 1995) SAP has been incorporating more and more tools and methodologies for the process of implementing R/3. The first solution set was the Procedure Model, which is included within the software. In 1996, the AcceleratedSAP (ASAP) program was introduced, first in the United States and later on a worldwide basis, as a solution set for quick and efficient implementation.

ASAP can be considered a methodology framework that includes an implementation roadmap for the different project phases: Project Preparation, Business Blueprint, Realization, Final Preparation, Go-Live, and Support. It also includes tools, documents, white papers, a question-and-answer database to enable quick configuration of processes, and so on.

ASAP Release 4.0 (1998) and later ASAP upgrades included a comprehensive Change Management methodology in the form of a work package within the Business Blueprint phase, specifically targeted to SAP implementation projects. Figure 4.4 shows this work package. This section presents a summary of methodology. The full methodology can be found on the ASAP software included in every R/3 kit since release 4.0B. The methodology is complemented by many white papers, guidelines, interview templates, and other useful information.

```
☐ 📂 Implementation Roadmap
   ⊞ 📁 Phase 1: Project Preparation
   ☐ 📂 Phase 2. Business Blueprint
      ⊞ 📁 Project Management Business Blueprint Phase
      ☐ 📂 Change Management
           📄 Create a Business Impact Map
         ⊞ 📁 Complete the Baseline Leadership Risk Assessment
         ⊞ 📁 Develop Sponsorship Strategy
         ⊞ 📁 Complete the Baseline Project Team Risk Assessment
         ⊞ 📁 Complete the Baseline Organizational Risk Assessment
         ⊞ 📁 Establish Change Communications Framework
         ⊞ 📁 Establish Management Structure for Skills Development Process
         ⊞ 📁 Establish Management Structure for Knowledge Transfer Process
      ⊞ 📁 Project Team Training Business Blueprint Phase
      ⊞ 📁 Develop System Environment
      ⊞ 📁 Business Organization Structure
      ⊞ 📁 Business Process Definition
      ⊞ 📁 Quality Check Business Blueprint Phase
   ⊞ 📁 Phase 3: Realization
   ⊞ 📁 Phase 4: Final Preparation
   ⊞ 📁 Phase 5: Go Live and Support
```

FIGURE 4.4   *Change Management Work Package within ASAP*
Copyright © SAP AG

According to ASAP, R/3 change management must address three strategic issues for a successful implementation. It must:

❑ Minimize the implementation risks
❑ Accelerate the R/3 implementation process
❑ Align SAP with the organization to ensure the return on information that SAP delivers.

From the perspective of the project team and organization, there is a change team responsible for the change management process.

The change management procedure is based on 8 steps.

Step 1. Create a Business Impact Map

This map will become the starting point for change management. The purpose of this step is to define the impacts of R/3 implementation in the organization. In order to create this map, managers of departments must rank their perceptions on the influence of R/3 implementation on the different divisions of the company.

Step 2. Complete the Leadership Risk Assessment

In this step, the change team will try to find factors in leaders of the organization which can influence implementation: resistance or acceptance will undermine it or accelerate it. ASAP proposes a *Risk Assessment Tool* that can be used to measure the project implementation risks at each point of the R/3 implementation. The objective of the assessment is to anticipate risks and prepare the change program. The result of the assessment is used as a critical element in the change program. It is also very important for this and other types of assessments to translate the results into efficient communications.

Step 3. Develop Sponsorship Strategy

The strategy for getting sponsorship at the top level, and from there to site manager levels, is aimed to sustain the *credibility* of the project by means of effective communication of the key benefits of an R/3 implementation. It must also be able to address those issues which can have a negative impact on the project. The ASAP change methodology considers the engagement of local site managers extremely important, because of their closer relationship with people affected by changes. A real commitment and corresponding supporting actions are needed, sustained by communicating project status and updates.

Step 4. Complete the Baseline Project Team Risk Assessment

This task also involves identification and qualification of implementation risks, although this time it targets the project team. This becomes a critical issue in the change process, since the project team is responsible for most project realization and support. This step is undertaken using a risk assessment tool provided by ASAP, which will need to be efficiently administered. One or several workshops will be conducted during this step. As a result of the risk assessment an action plan defines clear roles and responsibilities, as well as measurable results.

Step 5. Complete the Baseline Organizational Risk Assessment

In this final step of risk assessment the target is the full organization, including its divisions. Tasks, tools, and activities used for this assessment are similar to those used in previous steps. The differential factor here is the number of people involved, and the number of workshops, meetings, and interviews needed. This will largely depend on the size of the company.

An important part of this step is that employees tell their views and concerns about the implementation and the changes. This will separate useful information for targeting issues and risks through the communication program.

The results of this step will include the identification of key risks for the implementation in the organization, as well as an action plan to target those risks.

Step 6. Establish the Change Communications Framework

Paradoxically, rumors usually are a far more efficient communication than "official" channels. The difference is the accuracy of transmitted information. It is critical to prepare for constant communication throughout an SAP implementation project, and possibly even before the project starts. The communication framework will be the background controlling strategy against the implementation risks assessed in previous steps.

ASAP includes some rules for the success of the communication efforts, and defines six stages for a cumulative process of communication. In stage one, the organization has no knowledge of the ASAP project, and in every following stage, organization members become aware. They begin to understand the project basics, later the strategic view, then the project impact on the business, and finally the impact on their own personal jobs.

There are also guidelines to measure the effectiveness of a communication strategy.

Step 7. Establish Management Structure for the Skills Development Process

The purpose of this step is to implement a training strategy covering the main aspects of the skills needed in a change management program. ASAP establishes three areas of skills development: concept training, process-level training, and impact training. This training should be conducted simultaneously with the end-user training on

SAP applications. This step involves several activities. Besides logistics and training resources, one important point to consider is the selection of an external training delivery partner.

Step 8. Establish Management Structure for the Knowledge Transfer Process

The last step in the change management program for ASAP implementation deals with the definition of a knowledge-transfer team in charge of developing knowledge-transfer processes. This step will result in the creation of a central source of information and knowledge, available to all people involved in the implementation and to the rest of the organization.

In this set of tasks ASAP introduces many opportunities for learning, both from internal and external sources. Most important, a knowledge-transfer process ensures that valuable experience resulting from implementation is kept within the organization and not just within individual people's heads. A *knowledge-management* practice is useful not only as a step in the change management program but also in the SAP implementation as a whole, in every phase and every task of the project. It can become an essential strategy for a rapid implementation.

Conclusions to be Drawn from the ASAP Change Methodology

The Change Management work package included in the ASAP methodology is the logical response to a common need in SAP implementation projects. It is a group of tasks which demand a great deal of involvement and work, and it is not easy. Communicating and dealing with people is not easy.

ASAP provides a framework; customers and implementation partners must choose how to satisfy their needs from this framework and commit to it.

One of the key lessons is that Change Management is about leading the change rather than reacting to it. Companies should seriously consider getting outside and expert help for this critical and difficult task.

An Approach to Change Leadership: Realities in SAP R/3 Implementation Projects

The following sections on Change Management and Change Leadership are the direct and expert contribution on the subject by Mr. Rafael Barreda Martínez, Deloitte Consulting Director of Change Leadership for Spain and Portugal, and author of other books on the subject.

How Change Affects Organizations and Persons

Companies currently need large transformations. They have to redesign their processes to make them more efficient and competitive, to get closer to their customers and end-users, and to assume a stronger commitment to quality and to their own employees.

Changing business processes, work habits, information systems, or communications is not enough to reach those ambitious objectives, nor is having the right management or organization charts. There is need for a true cultural revolution within each entity, a change in the people, in their way of thinking, and in their way of acting.

One of the most important transformations companies can make is the implementation of integrated business software packages, such as SAP R/3. However there are not many companies that can find a correct focus and anticipate the changes caused by these implementations. In many cases, the consequences can cause constant delays and a continuos process of conflicts and inefficiencies over a long time period.

Many managers who were successful during the implementation of SAP R/3 had a vision of the impact that such a project would have in the organization as a whole. When software like R/3 is chosen, benefits can be tremendous. The organization can gain the ability to make rapid business decision; but at the same time people need to gain new abilities to be able to take advantage of those benefits. Sometimes this exchange of information throughout the organization necessitates to adapting the business processes to the new flow of information. This can be the origin for reorganization in departments, local subsidiaries, or divisions.

Often the risks that these change originate are completely ignored. On other occasions these risks are minimized and are almost always underestimated when assigning budgets. Why do we care about the plane and not the pilot? Are not human failures the main causes for plane accidents? In the case of business changes there is a similar process. There is a great investment in changing the technology, much less in changing the business processes, and almost nothing in the change for people. But people are the ones that must initiate the new changes, manage new technology, accept the changes in their work habits, and sometimes in the practice of their whole work life.

It should not be forgotten that all people have two cerebral hemispheres that direct different aspects of life. We use our logic and reasoning to accept new, sometimes indispensable challenges; but our feelings sometimes play a decisive part in our behavior.

However, most of people's actions are evaluated in terms of our logical capacity. We speak of the necessity and the imperative for the change; it can be the only road to survival, the challenge of our careers—and so many other ideas that don't convince our sentimental side. Our moving, affective capacity is not taken into consideration. How many times is solidarity with colleagues rejected? How can we anticipate the reality of a new scenario that is still only sensed, since we have no reliable data on it?

Those who plan changes in the organizations must take into account people's reluctance to change. Change Management offers training activities, sometimes quick and unplanned, to users, interest groups, and on occasion to the organization. But it always communicates in a single direction, without considering the communication needs of the recipient. We really need to know the feelings of people affected by the change. We should never forget that people are the ones who will start or will slow down or undermine the benefits of the change.

All this may seem obvious, since hundreds of published articles speak of the critical mission to adapt to the necessities of people and company culture as a key part of the success of the project of organizational transformation. However, most of the CIOs who are responsible for leading the implementation of software packages that affect different functions or processes agree that the most relevant problems they must solve—that in some case put at risk the success of the project—are those related to Change Management.

In a survey carried out by the Deloitte and Touche Consulting Group in 1995, which polled CIOs of important companies, among the ten most important barriers to success in implementation, four had to do with change. The "resistance to the change" was selected as the main obstacle by 82%; second place was occupied by "inadequate sponsorship and support" (72%). The fifth barrier was that "the change was not considered compelling or necessary" (46%) and last, almost half the answers (43%) attributed the lack of success to not having a "program for managing the change." Figure 4.5 shows the result of the Deloitte & Touche survey.

FIGURE 4.5   Deloitte & Touche survey of CIOs opinions of business transformation: barriers to Success.   Copyright © Deloitte & Touche

These opinions are derived from real experiences; if we are sure that the main barriers to the success in implementation are related to the management of change, the general tendency to consider this a secondary activity seems unreasonable. How can something considered "the peak" of the project, be an activity in which project costs can be saved?

At a minimum, managers find resistance to the changes, active or passive, produce considerable delays whose cost was not initially estimated. Managers also worry about the repercussions that change will have on the morale and motivation of the employees.

When managers ask for opinions from experienced colleagues these topics are much more common than technological problems.

This lack of focus in the planning and execution of programs of change mainly occurs because of erroneous ideas and misunderstandings about change. A manager might consider valid statements such as the following: "we don't need to spend effort on this, time will take care of everything," "during the change, those persons who seem to agree with it really do," "the change can be carried out quickly and effortlessly," "most of the employees want to contribute and adopt innovative ideas," "the behavior of the upper managers of the company is invisible to the rest of the organization," "the change is always adjusted according to a plan," "our personnel are accustomed to the changes and will adapt effortlessly," "having clear ideas and exercising solid leadership is enough for successful change," "the pressure and stress will be understood as something reasonable that it is an integral part of this type of project," "people will behave in a logical way and won't have emotional reactions to the changes."

We have all heard statements like these more than once. They suggest risks to the project. One of the major risks is the deterioration of communications between the project team and the company. Employees, the manager, and the project team members start acquiring degrees of uncertainty that undermine the strategic objectives of the project. Battles for power and internal wars between areas begin to appear, causing difficulties for teamwork. They provoke, at a minimum, loss of competitiveness. The initial impulse of the project declines, the integration of all the people is not accomplished, and as a consequence the employees are demoralized and some of the "talents" of the organization react by inhibiting change.

Most of these errors crop up due to the lack of sensitivity of management. Other administration or business areas would not suffer from this lack.

One of the most important problems is that managers are unable to transmit their confidence in the project to their collaborators, and on occasion, to their own management team. This does not foster enthusiasm in people, and it becomes impossible to generate substantial positive changes. Most of such changes demand great personal effort, achievable only when people understand the situation and commit to it. This understanding and commitment can only be achieved through knowledge of the necessity of the proposed change.

The logical consequences of the beliefs discussed are that many managers carry out activities that impede success in the project of implementing SAP R/3. Undesirable management behavior might include:

❑ Proclamation of unconditional support at the beginning of the project, but lack of presence in the practice

❑ Not distinguishing risky situations that require special planning

❑ Considering that the change is just another event and trying to look for and implement a technical solution; feeling uncomfortable with ambiguity and, therefore avoiding any of it

❑ Allowing change to vanish in a black hole

❑ Evading the ongoing change initiatives and allowing those initiatives to get lost or diluted in ineffective programs

❑ Using a superficial and inconsistent control, frequently not in the topics that affect change the most

❑ Underestimating the role and importance of implementing a communication plan in the company; some consider that "using the company newsletter will be enough"

❑ Considering people's restlessness as a defect; instead of acting to prevent or to cure it, restlessness is excluded or punished, an attitude that makes people hide their feelings and leads to lack of collaboration as expected

❑ Underrating or avoiding assessment of the level of commitment in managers, interested groups, team members, and employees in the project—if commitment exits at all

❑ Implementing changes without considering if they are necessary, the interdependencies that exist, or the work loads of employees, team, and managers. Without assigning priorities, there is little strategic planning, and increased risk, uncertainty, and stress

❑ Failing to understand the importance of the company culture and consequently, only providing superficial attention to change programs, without understanding that these should be quickly integrated into the company culture

❑ Giving agents of change and project team members an ultimatum and beginning to impose changes without keeping in mind:
  ❑ The resistance to change among end-users and even managers
  ❑ The good ideas contributed during the project by affected personnel
  ❑ That it is necessary to insist on and achieve the participation of all personnel.

Managerial Transformation and Change

All the activities and behavior discussed are detrimental to transformation, and of course, to the success of any implementation of more-or-less-complex integrated software packages.

Remember that, in the reality, any initiative for managerial transformation argues a significant and fundamental change in the organization, change that must at least make people ask themselves the following questions:

How will people affected carry out their work with the changes that will be introduced?

Although everyone is conscious that the implementation of a package like SAP R/3 will affect people's daily work, planning for the work environment, from technological and sociological points of view, is sometimes neglected. Little consideration is given to relationships with colleagues, the physical location of new work positions, equipment, and so on.

How will change affect work positions, qualitatively and quantitatively?

Work positions will change, in some cases in a substantial way, and publicizing the changes required in the new environment should not be left until the end of the project.

What will the new reporting system be? Is the current structure valid?

Often flowcharts will be different, because operational changes introduced with the software make obsolete hierarchical relationships and existing functional reports. This should be foreseen, and there must be a plan for the new situation.

What will the work tools be, and how will employees relate to them?

Generally, people will have a work position computerized with a workstation PC, or perhaps a portable PC, with connection to the net; the work style maybe different from the previous one. This change will be greater as the difference between the current and the proposed situations increases. It is not uncommon to find positions with little or nothing computerized, with individual spreadsheets on the users own PCs, with gathering of data and information in local offices prior to its transmission for consolidation at central head-quarters, and so on.

What new abilities, knowledge, and behavior will be required in the new situation?

New job profiles will provide hints about new competencies that will be needed. Those people who are indispensable must correctly perform their new jobs.

What people will be appropriate for the new work?

Once the required competencies are known, it is necessary to discover which people will be suitable to carry out the new work positions.

What is the current situation of employees in connection with the required new abilities, knowledge, and behavior?

Know in-depth the current situation of employees who hold the positions that will be modified because of the installation of the package or because of processes that change. This is required from the rational point of view and also from the emotional perspective.

What training plans will be needed?

The situation of the current employees will indicate what training, coaching, and development plans should be undertaken before, during, and after the implementation. Training strategy should be planned at the beginning of the project. Often members of the project team will need to be absent from the project in order to acquire knowledge in some specific area; user training strategy is also often improvised (when the project has been going on for months). Decide if project team members will be trainers; maybe advanced users or mixed groups can be. Other questions include: will there be any on-line help? What about functional help desks?

Are we willing to invest in this area?

This may seem an obvious question, and the answer should be affirmative; but in our professional experience we have met with companies that will try to save in this budget area. Perhaps they are not aware of it, but in reality they do it, and then question the success of the project implementation. Many times planned training is a pure formality; on other occasions training is help just before or after the right moment; occasionally the user has help when he needs it. There is a tendency to save in this effort: we must remember that training takes time (a learning pill has not yet been invented), but the company has to continue working. A training plan has to be perfectly coordinated with the necessities of operation and, of course, with the project. Training plans cannot be either anticipated too much or delayed; training much ahead of going live would be a loss of time, because it would be necessary to repeat it later. After going live it would be catastrophic, as much for the lack of user motivation as for the hyperactivity required for trainers and applications experts. This latter burns them out, making the first weeks and even months, true chaos, with consequent inefficiency.

Will we have to train inside or outside of working hours?

A continuation of the above is the question of whether workers will be trained inside or outside working hours. The most efficient way is inside because it is part of work! Training is not a secondary activity; if it were, its success would be compromised. It will sometimes be necessary to train management outside working hours.

Will this new training, coaching, or necessary development be compensated in some way?

There will be different circumstances, but always study this situation in a generous way. Do not forget that employees are facing changes and uncertainties in their work positions, and do not need situations for additional controversy. Although pecuniary compensation is not necessary, look at other options to find an appropriate, negotiated alternative for each situation.

How and when will the adaptation of people to the new resulting job positions take place?

It is absolutely necessary to have a Transition Plan for ensuring correct transition during this more-or-less turbulent period. This plan will serve as a guide to conquering the restlessness and latent anxiety in the organization, the employees, and management, whether or not they are affected by the new situations.

Will we need new competencies? Do we have them? Will we need to recruit outside people with the new competencies? Do they exist? Can they be easily found or be recruited in the job market? How long does it take to select them?

The new profiles, training, and personnel development for those currently in the organization have been discussed. In some cases, it will also be necessary to incorporate external competencies, because either the organization doesn't have them or because they are not available at the required moment. This will provoke the need to carry out external searches that must be scheduled and planned for, because some of those competencies might be in demand on the job market. People who have these skills are not easy to incorporate, much less in a short time. A quality selection process needs time until the selected person is on board. Even more time is required to fill positions that are in high demand. Each individual hired will need a reasonable period of time to be incorporated into the company.

In summary, an organization must know as soon as possible if it will have to carry out external recruiting and must immediately communicate this fact to human resources.

Will getting these new competencies increase salary mass significantly?

More than increasing salary mass, new job descriptions can lead to a modification of compensation policies, since many needed competencies are usually overvalued in the market, and the urgency of the recruiting forces companies to modify salary ranges. This can produce misalignments in compensation policies.

How will the information be distributed? How will it be obtained? Who will provide it? With whom will it be shared? If a there is a cultural change in this process, will we need a new system of values anda cultural model?

The change that takes place in the handling of information in SAP R/3 implementations is much underestimated. Some companies change, almost without transition, from excessive hierarchical and bureaucratic controls, with several levels of management, to a much more agile system, with information shared by many users. Employees need to adapt to this change, especially the intermediate management; it has often been considered an important part of their job to coordinate, transmit, and filter the information that passes through their hands.

Do we need a new alignment of the systems and processes of Human Resources?

It is not usually necessary to change the Human Resources systems, but it might be convenient to adapt them to some of the new situations. For example, if we want to establish more teamwork it would be advisable to change job performance assessments and to incorporate group objectives with individual objectives.

How will the changes be communicated to upper management, middle management, employees, union representatives, customers and suppliers, shareholders, interest groups, and so on?

A critical factor for success in all projects of this type is to have a communication strategy for the whole duration of the project. Elaborate communication plans can be adapted to each phase. Sometimes these report on project status, or they can combat rumors, or they simply requesting feedback, to interest and involve future users and interest groups. A newsletter or colorful magazine is not enough; there should be two-way communication and use of personal contacts during the project.

Will there be resistance to changes? How and when will we know it? How will we act? Are there any preventive or contingency plans?

Most changes will not be equally accepted by all. While some people quickly adapt to change, and some are even its most fervent defenders, at least half the affected population are expectant, doubtful, waiting "to see what happens." It is not effective to have half the employees expectant, when there is a good opportunity to involve them as "champions of the coming change." In some cases, a very influential and noisy minority is opposed to any modification or change, often through ignorance or lack of previous involvement.

The risks in this area should be assessed to discover potential problems and formulate preventive plans for avoiding the problems or minimizing their consequences.

What to Do Before this Change?

Any transformation a company undertakes in its processes, technology, systems, infrastructure and, of course, its employees, is an important change.

This process of change should not be approached like a juxtaposition of activities more or less related to each other. It should be addressed as a global program, perfectly coordinated with the Transition Project that iso the main imperative of change.

Why a Global Program? Could we not just include modifications here and there? To answer this with an example, we would say that a sick person cannot only be treated for fever, which is a result and a symptom, but never a cause; it is necessary to discover the true cause of the fever and to diagnose the root of the problem, keeping in mind the secondary effects of any medicines.

For the same reason, we cannot address just one aspect of a company without keeping in mind that it is a complex, dynamic system, in which processes, structures, technology and people have to be aligned with strategies to complete the company mission and vision.

When involved in a process of change management, a company must be accounted as an entity. A prescription drug can alleviate fever but can also damage other organs of the sick person. Experts in processes of change are needed to act in "all the systems." To ignore the group and to act locally will in most cases can cause serious problems or, at best, undesirable delays in starting the project.

The change should be undertaken with appropriate methodology and techniques, and with tools suited to the final objective. Keep in mind that planning the roadmap and the change process is key to its success or failure. It is vital to plan these processes while keeping in mind the end of the program, not only the first phases.

Many poorly planned SAP R/3 implementation projects have been called "Pandora's boxes." Once they are opened, it is impossible to manage their content.

Of What Change Are We Speaking?

So far, we have considered a change that makes it possible for people and groups in an organization to commit to a new situation and to develop the potential they possess. The processes and the technology by themselves can do nothing; the participation of the employee is required. Usually most employees formally accept the changes, although there is always some resistance. In general, changes are tacitly admitted. When there is no commitment to change, the human potential used does not go beyond 20 or 30%. It is well known that people working just "to management's order," are not really aligned with the final objective; they work without hope and usually do not excel, especially in those functions whose modifications are not well understood by the employees doing the job.

People usually understand change in a conceptual way; they even rationally accept change, but we would be misled if we thought this meant total acceptance. Besides this logical and rational component, there are also feelings; people are emotional, and there is not always a match between what we think and what we feel. There can be deeply buried rejection producing behaviors that do not appear in a simple and spontaneous way. The process of change must take this into consideration, since resistance is emotional in many cases; visceral and irrational rejections must be treated as such.

Why Are Change Programs Useful?

A change program is useful because it has rules for behavior that repeat in many entities; people usually respond to changes in a predictable way. The only secret is to approach the Change Program from a systemic perspective that keeps in mind the four levels that are intertwined in any project of this type. These four levels are the leaders of the organization, the project team, the employees, and the infrastructure.

With the organization's leaders it is necessary to develop continuous and long-lasting support for change during the length of the project, so that after the project goes live they are able to sustain and strengthen the change.

The project team is less well taken care of. It contains a mix of consultants, on occasion coming from different companies; technicians who support the new teams, the most permanent members in the project and; especially, the end-users. Continuous and effective communication is needed, so that each of the questions from the interest groups affected by the changes can be addressed early.

The employees of the company are a key element in the project's success. The various different abilities, knowledge, and practices required for success must be identified so that these new abilities can be acquired within the time allotted. These new abilities are not acquired overnight. Time and planning are a must. The human resources department should be involved in the project from the beginning to ensure that the company has the necessary competencies for the new work environment before going live.

Another element often forgotten in these projects is the existing infrastructure. Carry out an evaluation in the first stages of the project to understand the changes needed in the organizational environment as well as in the affected systems. It is sometimes necessary to realign the existing system of human resources to adapt them to new profiles, job descriptions, evaluations, salary modifications, employees' mobility, performance assessments, recruitment systems, and selection. Each case will be different. The culmination will be implementation of the changes, with initiatives that will continue after the project goes live.

Vision and Direction

In the words of John P. Kotter, any leader should have and must transmit a vision as well as pointing out a direction. This is essential in a project of strategic span, not only for the company leaders, but also for all company management, who should follow these rules:

- ❑ Manifest solid and constant support during all phases of the project
- ❑ Make rational estimates when a specific plan is required
- ❑ Understand the process of change and, consequently, tolerate and manage ambiguity
- ❑ Develop levels of sponsorship in cascade throughout the company, aligning and harmonizing performance
- ❑ Commit, remain involved and guarantee a continuous effort
- ❑ Understand the critical role played by a global communication plan and apply it conscientiously
- ❑ Understand and respect honest and sincere opinions
- ❑ Make and support difficult decisions
- ❑ Evaluate the level of commitment required by interest groups and plan accordingly
- ❑ Develop effective control and feedback mechanisms
- ❑ Plan the estimated changes as imperatives, postponing those of lesser weight
- ❑ Detect the deficiencies in the culture of the company and then plan the values that sustain the company culture, changing them as required
- ❑ Develop the abilities of project team members and other agents of change, and give them status, information, and appropriate encouragement
- ❑ Establish methods and a climate for interest group involvement in order to reduce restlessness and effect the best implementation
- ❑ Adequately relocate project team members when the project concludes.

The attitudes and performances of companies in which SAP R/3 has been implemented with success reinforce the message that effective leadership, together with good planning and appropriate management of change support continuous employee performance during and, more important, after implementation.

Planning and Management of Change

No change is carried out easily. To effect the strategies that drive companies toward their vision depends on the specific necessities of each project, the attainment of milestones, on things that must be done well, on intermediate objectives that should be reached along the road, and on the critical factors for the success. Some of these are:

❑ **Creating an imperative for change.** This is necessary for much of the company staff. Everybody who has lived in some situation of change can corroborate that most people expect to see "how things go," that some are opposed to change, sometimes viscerally, and that others quickly "get in." The efforts must address getting and increasing this favorable and motivated minority, making converts from the doubtful ones. Sometimes it is only necessary that people understand the necessity for change.

❑ **Creating a vision and a strategy.** What direction can be followed without a strategy? Why begin changing without analyzing what the final products will be? What about the side effects of change and their consequences? Both the vision and the main strategies should be clear and simple to understand for all components of the organization. We don't want an international prize in marketing. We want collaborators to understand the vision, assume it, make it theirs, and work together to achieve it!

❑ **Creating and developing a group of leaders.** Many "bosses and traditional managers" start changes, but only the good leaders finish them with success. This makes it essential to create a group of leaders who commit to the project, execute the strategies, and work toward the proposed vision.

❑ **Getting the changes consolidated in the culture of the company.** This is one of the main tasks of the sponsor and the group of leaders: permanently communicating the vision, successes, and so on. It is essential to involve middle management.

❑ **Changes that are born with military discipline, with rigid rules and procedures, and promulgated from above, are difficult to undertake.** It is much more convenient to *allow and stimulate particular initiatives* that enrich the project and make the vision "belong." Everyone who contributes something to a project feels like a co-owner.

❑ **Generating continuous feedback.** Celebrate early successes, without exaggerating, when they are evident and attributable to the ongoing project.

When changes affect and conflict with traditional company systems, those traditional systems must either be adapted or changed to the new culture. A sensation of incoherence must be avoided. It can destroy any belief in the change.

Change Management Summary

The following table summarizes the Change Management issue in SAP implementation.

Why deal with this issue	Other issues affected	Solutions
❑ To sustain support throughout the implementation	❑ Project organization	❑ ASAP Change methodology
❑ To overcome resistance and minimize implementation risks	❑ Communications strategy	❑ ASAP Risk Assessment tools
❑ To align the organization with changes imposed by SAP software	❑ Training	❑ Knowledge Management program
❑ Because it is a CSF	❑ Time and costs	❑ Strategic consultants
❑ Others		❑ ASAP Change methodology
		❑ ASAP Risk Assessment tool

Dealing with Consultants and Key Users

People problems in implementation projects were discussed above. We must now briefly describe the problems arising from the relationship between consultants and the customer's key users. These concern *integration* and *teamwork*. Consultants are needed because companies usually lack the required product knowledge and SAP project experience to effect implementation on their own. Key users are needed to help during the implementation. They usually are the people who later become application administrators and supporters.

Whatever marketing message gets out, it is difficult to find a consulting company which excels at every aspect of an implementation; if it does, what are the probabilities of getting all the experts at the same time for "your project?"

Choosing the right consultants is difficult, or at least costly and time consuming. The search is mainly directed to discrete facts such as implementation time and costs. Selection becomes mainly a budget decision, without much evaluation of individual skills, previous experience, affinity for teamwork and knowledge transfer.

On the other hand, there is not much work involved in choosing the right customers, and of course, none in choosing key users. In this case it is usually a business decision, hard to back away from.

The potential problems, some of which are on the list of typical implementation problems in Chapter 2, are:

❑ Customer users think there is too much confidence in consultants rather than in their own people
❑ Companies become consultaholic
❑ Key users do not have enough time for the project and are reluctant to give information to consultants
❑ Consultants do not know how to transfer their knowledge
❑ Information is not shared among groups
❑ Disputes and disagreements occur among consultants and key users about customizing specific business processes
❑ Priorities are not the same
❑ Consultants seem to be acting as key-user bosses
❑ Key users seem to be acting as consultant managers.

Does this list seem familiar? When there is a stressful atmosphere, the list can grow even longer. These are big reasons that increase risks in the implementation as a whole and to specific parts of it, as listed on the following summary chart.

The project manager will be responsible for dealing with this problem. Project Management skill in motivating teamwork and culture integration can alleviate part of the problem. It is most important to set clear and common objectives: everybody works for the same goal of successfully implementing the new system (as described in a project charter), and gets benefits from it. Managerial attitudes should be avoided, and companionship through knowledge sharing should be encouraged.

Some companies use some type of compensation for teamwork and knowledge sharing: monetary, milestone bonuses, release time parties, etc.

The chart below summarizes points in the issue of dealing with consultants and end-users.

Why deal with this issue	Other issues affected	Solutions
❑ Avoid implementation risks	❑ Project realization	❑ Compensate integration and teamwork
❑ Increase project efficiency	❑ Project management	
❑ Avoid people burnout	❑ Control of scope	❑ Set common objectives
	❑ Knowledge transfer	
	❑ Training	❑ Project management
	❑ Time and costs	❑ Knowledge sharing

Knowledge Management Issues in SAP Implementation Projects

Coming from scientific areas related to semiotics and philosophy, Knowledge Management is one of the latest buzzwords in the management world. Because the talents of most of today's workforce are based on knowledge, this has been recognized as one of a company's biggest assets. The business goal for knowledge management is to transform individual knowledge into corporate knowledge.

The theoretical value of consultants on SAP projects is in their knowledge. Knowledge is generally considered to be the technical ability to perform and accumulated experience. Often the capacity of consultants to share their knowledge is not sufficiently valued in the selection process.

Sharing, as a process of communicating, teaching, and learning, is considered a key ability on any project. In SAP implementations of complex and strategic business projects, sharing is increasingly important. The main reasons for this are:

❏ To avoid ambiguity
❏ To deploy best business practices in any tasks or activities
❏ To avoid reinventing the wheel
❏ To obtain overall company involvement
❏ To gain credibility
❏ To communicate effectively.

Sharing knowledge must always enable bidirectional communication, so that attitudes are not considered impositions. Projects must always welcome constructive suggestions.

Most issues in implementation can be considered knowledge-based, and as such can be managed. In the following sections we discuss these knowledge issues:

❏ The Communications Strategy
❏ End-User and Project Team Training
❏ Project Standards, Procedures, and Documentation
❏ Knowledge Transfer

The Communications Strategy Issue

A well-defined and efficient communication strategy can make a huge difference in projects of a business nature, such as SAP. Lack of communication is considered one of the most typical implementation problems. It is typified by such remarks as: I didn't know. When was that decision made? Who said that? When are we starting? What do we have to do? How does this work? What is the project goal? I have not been notified; I am not responsible for that, ask somewhere else; anyway, who are you?

Remove all these sentences and questions from a project and see if it makes a difference. That's what a communication strategy is about.

In the context of implementation, there are additional reasons for dealing with communications. The most important are:

❑ It is key to managing change.
❑ It provides credibility to the project.
❑ It is another way to assure teamwork and get user involvement.
❑ It is another way of providing training.

Communication strategy is closely linked to other implementation issues, as listed on the summary chart. Project management and the change team must rapidly address this issue. The ASAP method includes a communication strategy to be used from the first phase of the implementation.

There are many ways and an ever-growing number of interesting initiatives to accomplish communications strategies and knowledge sharing, especially since the boom of collaborative software and intranets. As fancy and efficient as new technology might seem, personal contact and meetings should not be forgotten, since it is direct relationships that generate more trust.

The next section summarizes the ASAP approach to project communications.

ASAP Approach to Effective Project Communications

The ASAP approach to communications is intended to support the Change Management process, and positions the communication strategy as an activity to carry out even before the actual project starts.

According to ASAP, this issue includes all forms of communications that project leaders (project management, sponsors, change team, etc.) direct toward forwarding the goals of the organization. The goal is to send "key messages" to an intended audience, mainly employees. The objective is to gain employee support.

To do this, ASAP introduces a "communication team," that will be in charge of ensuring confidence, credibility, positive attitude, preparation for change, and that the benefits from implementation are known at all levels.

The approach is based on a push/pull marketing strategy. The *push* strategy is a top-down approach where an internal marketing campaign is conducted to create awareness and provide credibility. The *pull* method is a bottom-up strategy, where there is interactive communication with employees, to engage them as part of the project success.

ASAP defines communications as a cumulative process consisting of six different stages, indicating different levels of comprehension. For instance, in stage one the organization has no knowledge of the project, but in stage six the organization population understands the strategic objectives of the project and is confident about the message that the new system will provide "more gain than pain."

Every stage is identified not only by awareness status but also by communication focus. Stage one is the starting point; the focus is on delivering and emphasizing the basic and key message. Every new stage tries to communicate additional benefits, first overall, then in organizational areas and finally individual benefits, up to a level (stage six) where communication objectives have been achieved.

Finally, the ASAP approach includes mechanisms for measuring the effectiveness of the communications strategy by conducting different types of surveys. Results from surveys can be used to strengthen weak points in communications.

The ASAP approach to communication, although effective, is basically intended to gain support for the change initiative. This is important, but seeing the project as whole, with communications channels and strategies in place, could be used for other implementation issues, such as training, knowledge sharing, or documentation. Also, except for the pull approach and the surveys, ASAP is quite restrictive about making the strategy a one-way process from management to employees.

Employees' (end-users') suggestions can be useful in many implementation activities. If they are not accepted, the reasons should be understood. Truth generates trust.

The following chart summarizes the issue of communications in SAP implementation projects.

Why deal with this issue	Other issues affected	Solutions
❑ To provide credibility to the project	❑ Change management	❑ ASAP Approach
	❑ Documentation	❑ Collaboration software
❑ To assure teamwork	❑ Project management	
❑ As a key to manage change	❑ Project organization	❑ Communications Office
	❑ Training	
❑ To get user involvement		❑ Personal communications
		❑ Project newsletter

Training in SAP Projects

Training is a simultaneous process of teaching and learning, a *knowledge-sharing* process. It is a common error to consider training as discrete or one-time events rather than as an ongoing process. It is also a mistake to think that training is based on fixed content. Training is a serious implementation issue in every SAP project, and as such, requires not only an effort and a budget (training is very expensive), but a whole strategy. The training issue must be considered in the initial stages of SAP implementation projects.

A training strategy must start with a training plan, define goals, the target population, the content, the logistics, and the tools.

The *training plan* can be designed as a step program that should include:

1. Overall understanding
2. Project team training
3. End-user training
4. Advanced and follow-up training.

The following is a list of some of the *objectives of a training program*:

❑ To prepare the organization for the changes of the new system
❑ To prepare team members for project realization
❑ To be ready for support and administration

❑ To prepare end-users for the why, the what, and the how-to
❑ To communicate sources of help, support, and documentation.

Finally and most important, training is a way for users to produce the expected output from the new system and thus achieve business goals.

The *target population* for training in SAP implementation is all project team members and all identified end-users. Upper management should get at least some brief training sessions on SAP basics. The plan must also include how to provide training for new users. At this level, it is important to identify requirements by user type; for instance, while operational users need to understand processes and actions, the project team must be trained in how to customize applications, and the technical staff on how to manage the base system.

Training content is a function of the role of project team members. There should be training, in the form of efficient communication, on project standards and procedures for project team members. There must be general awareness about change initiatives. In addition, the content for the project team is based on getting knowledge of functionality and acquiring skills for customizing.

There should also be focus on horizontal business perspectives, showing the integration of functions and processes, for instance, when there are business processes that run across different application modules. Courses that combine the content and material of several modules are needed. Some standard courses do cover the overlapping areas of applications.

The development team should be familiar with ABAP Workbench and programming language, and maybe with other helpful SAP tools such as SAPscript, CATT, and others.

Training for the base team should focus on the technical areas of administering and supporting R/3 systems, including operating system knowledge, the database, and R/3 specifics. The technical staff must acquire skills for proactive systems management and monitoring, as well as for troubleshooting.

Finally, there is the end-user training, which should cover an overview of the system, expected business goals, and specifics on business processes and functions. This is a process of teaching concepts, how the system works and how to navigate through menus and screens, with live demonstrations of real scenarios and hands-on experience.

A word of caution about the computing skills of end-users: there are cases where end-users have not used computers before, in which case there is need for additional basic training.

It is not a good idea to leave the *logistics* of training to the last moment. It is common to find implementation projects with no appropriate system for end-user training. Logistics include the planning and procurement of external and internal training courses and material, training rooms, flowcharts, computers, training documentation, training tools, and, of course, teachers.

Some companies have a dedicated R/3 server for training. It is also common to use the integration system and provide training on a specially configured client, with some data loaded for doing labs.

Sometimes it is difficult to schedule SAP's standard courses: first because of availability, and second because of the time needed. SAP Education Services must be viewed as a helpful aid for those courses in line with organizational needs and training plans. There will be many times, however, that in-house training needs to be developed, mainly in the area of end-user training.

Because of time constraints, it is difficult to shorten the length of courses without compromising quality and the expected acquired knowledge and skills.

A common approach to end-user training, especially where there is a large end-user population, is to start with training the trainer (normally key users and local managers responsible for business areas). These key users can later train the end-users in their area of management.

Finally, in the area of training tools and services, SAP has in place a large Education Service with a global Knowledge Management initiative, which includes a comprehensive training program, as well as several advanced applications and tools. The two most important are the IDES system and the Information Database, now called SAP Information Warehouse. These products go beyond the training issue to address others such as knowledge sharing and documentation. The following sections contain an overview on these products.

Training Strategy within ASAP Roadmap

The ASAP Implementation Roadmap sharply focuses on training by including training tasks and activities from the first phases of the project.

In the Initial Project Planning of Project Preparation (Phase 1), ASAP includes the "Create Project Team Training Plan" activity, with the objective of creating a plan for the initial training of the project team doing the R/3 implementation. Also in Phase 1, between the activities of defining implementation standards and procedures, ASAP includes the "Overview of End User Documentation and Training," aimed at making project management aware of the training strategy to be developed and performed during and after implementation.

In Phase 2, the Business Blueprint phase, there are two main training activities: "Conduct Project Team Training" and "Draft End User Training and Documentation Plan," to start the actual learning process.

In the Realization phase, there is additional project team training with a focus on technical and functional knowledge, as well as on the change process and implementation risks. This implementation phase also includes all the activities related to the preparation of end-user documentation and training material.

End-user training is one of the main work packages of the Final Preparation phase, where actual training is conducted.

On the Continuous Change Roadmap, ASAP also includes "Follow-up Training" including: "Advanced Training" (new features, optimization and support, etc.), as well as the strategy for training new employees.

SAP Knowledge Management Initiative

Although SAP had worked on knowledge-based tools, especially in the area of training and support, it was not until 1999 that SAP launched the first Knowledge Management (KM) initiative, including a three-level solution map: Knowledge Development, Knowledge Transfer, and SAP Content. Each of these levels includes its own processes.

Figure 4.6 shows the 1999 Edition of the SAP Knowledge Management Solution Map.

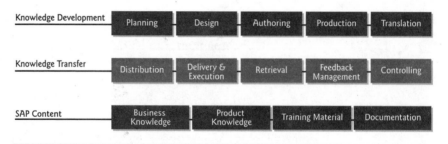

FIGURE 4.6   *SAP Knowledge Management Solution Map (1999).*
Copyright © SAP AG

The goal of the SAP KM program is to provide a permanent learning solution so business can have a long-lasting training program that capitalizes on knowledge.

More information on SAP Knowledge Management can be found at **http://www.sap.com/km**.

WEB

Knowledge Transfer as an Implementation Issue

The transfer of knowledge between the people who know and the people who need to know requires a considerable effort in any implementation. Knowledge transfer is a core process of Knowledge Management.

This process is important for saving time in any implementation project, since it can help avoid "reinventing the wheel." It is also the way to help organizations benefit from the experience and knowledge obtained from previous implementations.

Knowledge transfer is another method, maybe the most efficient, for providing training. Efficient transfer of knowledge can save a tremendous amount of time and money by decreasing the need for support. Handling a knowledge transfer process consists of identifying potential knowledge sources, both inside and outside the organization, so that this knowledge can later be distributed.

Knowledge sources can be found using different methods, before, during, and after implementation: by queries, searching, benchmarking, visits, and so on. The goal is to gain as much experience and useful information as possible, to collect lessons learned, working models and procedures, tips, FAQs, and so on.

A word of caution about information overflow. Only useful information can be considered as knowledge. For this reason, the collection of knowledge needs to be evaluated, filtered, structured, and indexed. Otherwise, the delivery process is in danger of failing.

The distribution of knowledge is handled using a delivery process, which must take into consideration the target population and methods for storing, sharing, and retrieving information.

Intranet applications and collaborative software are the most frequently used tools for information sharing. SAP provides several applications to help with the global process of knowledge management. The next sections describe IDES and InfoDB, now known as SAP Knowledge Warehouse.

International Demo and Education System (IDES)

IDES is one of SAP's solutions for quicker access to R/3 training, and it is available in several languages. IDES is a standard R/3 system that also includes customizing and master and transaction data, based on a model fictitious company. R/3 standard training courses are based on the IDES system, which also includes process-oriented online help with step-by-step instructions on how to carry out processes.

The IDES system is an integral part of the SAP Knowledge Management solution. Its goal is for users with little R/3 knowledge and experience to run and/or simulate actual business processes.

IDES includes standard scenarios with actual data that can be used for running core application R/3 standard business processes; it is also prepared for Internet transactions, ALE, and Workflow. There is even a IDES Notebook with a complete R/3 system preinstalled; details can be found on SAP Web pages or SAPnet.

InfoDB: SAP Knowledge Warehouse

Release 4 of SAP Information Database (InfoDB) has been renamed SAP Knowledge Warehouse. It is a special system based on SAP's open architecture and designed to contain a repository of information for storing content and distributing information. It can be used for providing online and on-demand training material. It also includes the tools needed for creating, distributing, and managing content.

The SAP Knowledge Warehouse is the central masterpiece of the SAP KM initiative for providing business and individuals with continuous learning solutions and knowledge transfer. This system is usually delivered with standard SAP content including documentation, training courses, and materials, including instructor guides. It also includes many role-based education courses for end-user training, focused on specific job tasks. There are many advantages to using this type of system: not only there is a cost reduction because of the reuse of content based on best practices, but there is also a great savings on documentation and end-user support.

Summary of the Training Strategy Issue

The following table summarizes the main points of the importance of training on SAP implementation projects. Consider training a continuous process, starting at the beginning of the implementation project and never ending. For going live, it is critical that end-users be completely trained and knowledgeable in using the system.

Why deal with this issue	Other issues affected	Solutions
❏ To prepare team members for project realization	❏ Customizing	❏ Knowledge Management tools
❏ To prepare the organization for changes in the new system	❏ Project Realization	❏ SAP Education products and services
	❏ Systems Landscape	
	❏ Change Management	
❏ To be ready for support and administration	❏ Documentation	❏ Training systems, IDES, Knowledge Warehouse
	❏ Communications	
❏ To prepare end-users for the why, the what, and the how-to	❏ Support/Help Desk	❏ SAP and external training partners
	❏ Time and Costs	
		❏ In-house training development

Documentation, Standards, and Procedures

Any type of project, whatever its nature, needs to be documented. Documentation of SAP implementation projects is critical, and this issue must be taken into consideration from the earliest stages of the project. Documentation is important because project team members need to have a reference on project status, decisions, process descriptions, and project standards and procedures. Documentation becomes essential for communications strategy, for solving issues; it is therefore a tool to be used in the change management process. Documentation is also essential for helping the project team during implementation, and for helping end-users get answers to their questions.

The implementation project needs to include all the activities related to documentation that a company might need during and after the project. The documentation issue relates to deciding what is needed in a particular SAP project.

SAP includes much documentation on standard software kits, mostly compiled in Online Documentation. These help files (in HTML format on the latest releases) include not only a reference manual on all modules and system components but also several practical tutorials. The objective of the online documentation is to cover reference and training needs, mainly for the project team, and then for end-users.

The documentation needed in each particular project may differ widely from that supplied by SAP. The ASAP solution map, however, includes virtually hundreds of document templates ready for use.

Types of Documentation

One of the goals of companies implementing SAP is attaining a competitive advantage over competitors by using the best information system that supports their business processes. The type of documentation must also be aligned with the goal of best supporting company business processes, both during the implementation phase and after. The following general types of documentation will be needed:

❑ **Project Documentation**, for description, management, and control during implementation.

❑ **Support Documentation**, for system management needed in the ongoing operation and support phases of the project.

❑ **Procedures Documentation**, to provide a reference framework on how the R/3 implementation project is carried out, how it is later supported and how continuous change will be managed.

❑ **End-User Documentation**, to provide knowledge on concepts and skills in how to navigate the system and perform their processes.

All four types are closely related; for instance, there are procedures documents that are also project and support documents. Project documentation is essential at the beginning of the project and during realization phases, but its relevance is minimized when a project finishes. Often though, the end of the project is valuable as a starting point for future projects, in particular for service and consulting firms where the best practices on projects can become a valuable knowledge asset.

Project documentation includes all documents on planning, assignment of resources, meeting minutes, communications, and those issues presented to the steering committee for discussion and approval. This category also includes customizing notes and documents, business process modeling, gap analysis, and so on.

Support documentation for the new information system can be divided into two groups:

❑ **Technical documentation** is useful primarily in aspects directly related to the application, the technical infrastructure of the system, and its maintenance: system architecture and topology, new enhancements and developments, description of interfaces with other systems, software used, hardware, and other tools used.

❑ **Operation documentation** are technical procedures documents. Their main utility lies in a description of operation and system management procedures, the description of procedures for supported operation functions and processes, and the assignment of roles and responsibilities. For example, for the backup and recovery process, the documentation must include what is to be done, when, with what procedure, and by which people.

The Problem of Defining Standards and Procedures

We could say that any project with more than one person involved, and even with only one, needs to have a framework for carrying out tasks and activities. In the case of SAP implementation projects, standards and procedures are essential for aligning team member roles and responsibilities.

For instance, during the implementation phase it is important to have a standard for creating status reports, as well as for documenting customizing settings and other required procedures and standards such as:

❑ Development guidelines
❑ Enhancement requests
❑ Authorization standards
❑ Problem escalation and issue resolution procedures
❑ System problems.

After going live, during the support and continuous change phase, it is important to have an Operations Manual with procedures on how to maintain and manage the system and solve problems. The guidelines of this manual are introduced in a following section.

It is also crucial to establish procedures for solving end-users' problems. This issue is closely related with the Help Desk strategy described in Chapter 8.

Documentation Aids

The amount of work involved in documentation can be huge, and usually more time is used for documenting that for actually realizing the project. The project needs to include facilitating tools for easing and speeding up this process while maintaining required quality.

All documentation is carried out with certain support; it is normally written or recorded on paper, computer files, audiotapes, etc. Do not forget that a great deal of required documentation, especially for project realization and reference and for end-user training, is contained within SAP Online Help, accessible directly from the R/3 system.

SAP R/3 provides tools to ease the process of documenting. There are hyperlink buttons for including notes while customizing, and shared folders within SAPoffice for including generated documentation. These folders can include most types of PC applications files, such as Microsoft Word, PowerPoint, etc. There is however a trend toward using external collaboration tools such as Lotus Notes, Microsoft Outlook, and so on, with the support of an intranet and intranet-based applications.

A superb aid for documentation is provided using ASAP templates. These are included in many of the work packages and activities and act as accelerators for implementation. Other aids are found in third-party tools, like those of business process modeling, that usually have some type of automatic documentation generation.

As we noted earlier, the SAP Knowledge Warehouse can be used not only for storing information, but also for creating and managing documents.

Introduction to the R/3 Operation Guide

The goal of the R/3 Operation Guide or Operating Procedures, is to define "the rules of the game" for working and operating the SAP system. Its target is the technical support group that manages and operates the R/3 systems landscape. It should include clear norms for answering questions such as what, when, why, and by whom.

This manual should identify roles and responsibilities in the implementation and operation of systems. It should not be confused with an "administration and operation manual" which goes into more specific detail about system architecture operation and administration, providing clear "how-to" steps for daily operation.

The rules in the procedures guide might range from a clear definition of the R/3 implementation goal to who is allowed to enter the computer room (data processing center).

The following list provides an approach to the contents of a procedures guide:

❑ Introduction to the procedures guide:
    ❑ Goal of the implementation and operation of the system
    ❑ Project scope

- ❑ Team roles and organization
- ❑ Systems and application architecture description
  - System landscape definition
  - Business applications definition
- ❑ User management procedures:
  - ❑ User master administration
  - ❑ Naming conventions
  - ❑ Authorization and profile security measures
  - ❑ Management of users leaving the company
- ❑ Functional implementation procedures:
  - ❑ Enhancement and change requests management
  - ❑ Developing methodology
  - ❑ Guide for implementing new modules
  - ❑ Functional test procedures
- ❑ Technical implementation procedures:
  - ❑ System administration and operation rules
  - ❑ Backup and recovery strategy
  - ❑ Front-end installation and distribution strategy
  - ❑ Batch management
  - ❑ Printing strategy
  - ❑ Networking procedures
  - ❑ Systems failover procedures
  - ❑ Daily operation tasks
  - ❑ Rules for implementation of new technical projects
  - ❑ Load balancing
  - ❑ Technical test procedures
- ❑ Cross-functional application procedures:
  - ❑ Workbench and transport system rules
  - ❑ Use of SAPoffice and Business Workflow
- ❑ Migration strategy:
  - ❑ Hardware upgrade procedures
  - ❑ Software upgrade procedures
  - ❑ SAP R/3 application upgrade
- ❑ User support management and organization:
  - ❑ Support guidelines
  - ❑ Help Desk organization
  - ❑ Keeping a record of problems and incidences
  - ❑ Escalation of problems

- ❑ Personnel issues:
  - ❑ Training procedures
  - ❑ People backup and holiday permissions
- ❑ Contingency procedures:
  - ❑ System crash procedures
  - ❑ Emergency situation guidelines
  - ❑ Disaster recovery procedures
- ❑ Security issues:
  - ❑ Passwords
  - ❑ Super-users
  - ❑ Remote connection procedures
  - ❑ Access to OSS
  - ❑ Access to the computer room
- ❑ Procedure for changing and updating this guide

This is an example of an index of subjects which a procedures guide can include. Extend or compress its contents as the scope of your installation requires. Add guidelines included in the SAP procedure model or in the Operations Manual template included in ASAP if you need them. Preparing this document should be the collective work of the project team with the consent and approval of company managers.

The Administration and Operation Manual

The goal of this manual is to provide technical support personnel easily and quickly with systems information and step-by-step instructions on how to perform the most common administration and operation tasks. This guide can help the system function properly, and can also be useful for a backup person in case someone from the technical team must be absent for any reason.

This manual must comply with the rules and procedures established in the procedures guide. It will include two types of information: detailed descriptions of the systems and step-by-step instructions. You can decide to put them all together or enter an instruction code within the descriptions, leaving the instructions ordered by code at the end of the manual.

If you intend to describe *all* the administration and operation tasks it can become a very large manual; an effort must be made to include only those descriptions and instructions most important for the system. Others can be referred to either in another manual or official documentation. Diagrams and pictures can be useful for this type of guide.

Just as in the procedures guide, the following is an approach to the possible contents of this manual:

❑ Systems information:
   ❑ Hardware and software inventory
   ❑ Physical layout of disks and file system configuration for every system
   ❑ Support hotline numbers
   ❑ Hardware maintenance
   ❑ Software maintenance
   ❑ Instructions for computer and operating system startup and shutdown
   ❑ Instructions for handling disks: adding, removing, etc.
❑ Error situations:
   ❑ Logging and escalating problems
   ❑ Instructions for notifying users with system messages
❑ SAP R/3 startup and shutdown:
   ❑ Normal procedures
   ❑ Error situations
❑ Backup procedures:
   ❑ Tape management: labeling, schedules, types
   ❑ Starting backups
   ❑ Checking backups
   ❑ Recovery procedures
   ❑ Archiving backup procedures
   ❑ Backup error conditions
   ❑ Backup problem and incidence log
❑ System Monitoring:
   ❑ Alerts definition
   ❑ Systems
   ❑ Network
   ❑ Processes
   ❑ System logs
   ❑ Backups

- ❑ Batch input
- ❑ System performance quality (buffers, workload, etc.)
- ❑ Storage and free space
- ❑ SAP R/3 general maintenance and administration tasks:
  - ❑ Cleaning procedures
  - ❑ Background processing management
  - ❑ Handling priority jobs
  - ❑ Changing a system parameter: profile maintenance
  - ❑ Printers and spool management
  - ❑ Archiving management
  - ❑ Definition of operation modes
  - ❑ Authorization management
  - ❑ General accounting control
- ❑ SAP R/3 database maintenance:
  - ❑ Checking database state
  - ❑ Adding space to database
  - ❑ Reorganization procedures
  - ❑ Export/import instructions
- ❑ Administration of the transport system:
  - ❑ Performing imports
  - ❑ Checking imports
- ❑ SAPGUI and SAPlogon:
  - ❑ Installation instructions
  - ❑ Upgrade and software distribution policies
- ❑ User management:
  - ❑ Users at operating system level
  - ❑ User master records: add, change, delete
  - ❑ Changing passwords
  - ❑ Locking user access to the system
  - ❑ Unlocking users
- ❑ Security management:
  - ❑ Security at presentation: virus protection and access restrictions
  - ❑ Security at the server level
  - ❑ User password control
- ❑ Accessing OSS:
  - ❑ SAProuter configurations
  - ❑ Registering new users

❑ Enabling remote access to the systems
❑ Guide change management
❑ Guide availability
❑ Quality controls

Summary of the Documentation, Standards, and Procedures Issue

The following chart summarizes the issue of documentation before, during, and after an SAP Implementation project.

Why deal with this issue	Other issues affected	Solutions
❑ To have written reference for the overall project description, status, activities, decisions	❑ Project Management	❑ Online Help
	❑ Project Organization	❑ Knowledge Warehouse
	❑ Training	
❑ To describe the framework for implementation and teamwork	❑ Change Management	❑ Intranet and collaboration software
	❑ Communications strategy	
❑ To get answers	❑ Help Desk strategy	❑ ASAP Accelerators: documentation templates
❑ To help in learning processes and to distribute knowledge		
❑ To communicate		❑ Process Modeling and documentation tools
❑ To help operate and support the systems		

CHAPTER 5

Development-related Issues in SAP Projects

Development and development-related activities in SAP projects may be of great help for the overall project, but may cause many problems, with bad effects on the overall project.

Everyone approaching SAP R/3 projects must clearly understand the business nature of this type of project, as it was explained in Chapter 1. R/3 is a system that is mainly customized, and not developed, as traditional systems used to be. The main question addressed by this chapter is the circumstances under which development is necessary.

The most dangerous part of development-related activities is *over-customizing*; the natural tendency of the project team to build a new system that behaves and looks just like the old system. The only advantage to this approach is that users accept the system more readily. On the other hand, it will certainly cause problems in project scope, in support, in performance and, of course, in time and costs.

There are development issues related to change or enhancement of the system, and these might have an impact on or may be influenced by gap analysis, user acceptance, migration, project organization, and activities requiring development knowledge.

Within an SAP project, development can be considered a "middleware" activity, an interface between functional and technical activities.

This chapter is divided into two parts. The first introduces the implementation issues related to or involving development work or development tools. The second is a reference section introducing readers to ABAP Workbench tools, the Business Framework, and some of the main features of ABAP language.

Now we introduce readers to the following implementation issues related to development:

❑ Program and Report Development
❑ Data Migration and Data Load
❑ Building Interfaces
❑ Enhancing the System
❑ Applying Patches
❑ Personalizing the System

Program and Report Development

Before we discuss this topic, readers should clearly understand a basic concept in SAP development environment, the difference between a program and a report, terms which are often used interchangeably.

A *report* is an ABAP program that outputs a listing, obtained from a search and a selection from database data. The search and selection might have user interaction or it might be included within the report logic. In the SAP environment, these listings can be static or interactive, allowing users to modify the search selection criteria.

The report is held in system memory and displayed on the screen. End-users or developers can decide whether the report should be printed using the SAP spool system.

A report is not restricted to making the database read operations. It can also perform database updates.

A *program*, on the other hand, can be compared to an interactive transaction, in which the user interacts with a module pool (ABAP program) that contains the transaction logic using screens or dynpros, menu options, function keys, icons, pushbuttons, and other controls that can be defined for that transaction.

This user interaction includes the possibility of modifying the flow of the transaction logic, and can make the decision of whether or not to activate the database updates.

In summary, a *report* is a type of ABAP program with the goal of "selecting from the database" to obtain an output listing that is independent from user interaction; a *program* (or transaction) is an ABAP program that processes database information and reacts to user interaction (transactions) or to specifically developed logic (batch input).

Report development is mainly targeted toward reporting needs, while program development is targeted at adding, modifying, or enhancing business transactions.

Before identifying times when there is the need for performing development activity, we must emphasize how R/3 *customizing* covers most of the objectives of business process implementation; in classic systems development most of the implementation is covered in custom development of programs, report screens, or transactions.

Table 5.1 shows the different approaches or tools for development arranged by their level within SAP R/3.

TABLE 5.1   *Development Approaches*

Development level	Development approach/tool
The customer business process is included within the SAP reference model	Perform customizing to adapt the behavior of standard transactions to the customer business process
A specific customer business process is partially included in standard SAP, and differences can be covered by using "user exits" for the remaining components (transactions, screens, menus....)	Use the enhancement tools (user exits)
Differences are not covered, and user exits do not exist, but the business process is included in SAP	Use ABAP Workbench tools for adding or modifying standard programs
The business process (or part of it) is not included as standard SAP	Perform the development of new programs, data dictionary elements, reports, screens, and other needed objects

Customized Reporting Using ABAP

As a consequence of the great versatility supported by R/3 in the reference model, tasks that have the most impact during the realization phase of implementation are customizing activities and the creation or adaptation of reports. SAP offers several reporting tools from the development environment and also ad hoc reporting options such as ABAP Query, Report Painter, Report Writer, SAP EIS, and the many standard reports included within the R/3 Information System.

Within the ABAP Workbench and closely linked to the reporting environment, R/3 offers the possibility of using and/or creating *logical databases*, ABAP programs with the mission of obtaining database data in a predefined structure and sequence to speed up searches and to foster quick generation of reports and interactive reports. The advantage of using the logical database is that the generation of reports is independent of an efficient access logic in the database.

To summarize, an important aspect in the success of implementation, concerning and affecting system performance, is to find the required logical database for the project's reporting needs. Logical databases can also be developed, but this can be quite costly. A good analysis in the initial phases of the project and the use of an efficient logical database can provide following benefits:

❑ Less time is needed for developing reports
❑ Report runtime is minimized
❑ Performance problems during production phases are minimized.

The reporting issue is covered in more detail in Chapter 8.

The Issue of Enhancing the System

Despite the widespread functionality of R/3 applications, their flexibility and possibilities for adapting SAP business processes to customer requirements, there is hardly any SAP customer project that does not at some time contemplate performing some type of enhancement to adapt SAP processes to business operations.

The process of including enhancements must be managed within the implementation and development project, with the actual standards and procedures defined for the development methodology. The inclusion of unnecessary or noncritical enhancements should be avoided, except in cases where enhancements come from official standard SAP channels.

There are several possible ways to modify, improve, enhance, or include new components in R/3 systems:

1. **New local programs, transactions, or components.** These are customer programs, components, or other Repository objects, completely new and developed using the ABAP Workbench tools, or by using BAPIs and the Business Framework architecture. These types of enhancement usually do not present problems when there are SAP official functional release upgrades, except for the possible connection or interface with current R/3 applica-

tions. In these cases naming conventions must be strictly followed.

2. **Modifications to SAP standard programs, data dictionary objects, and transactions.** These are known in Workbench Organizer as system repairs. This type of change is completely inadvisabe for SAP, except for advanced corrections, described in OSS notes, which are usually either for solving existing bugs or for increasing the functionality of later releases.

3. **Improvements and enhancements to standard SAP without modifications.** This method is provided by SAP through user exits or customer exits. By using standard user exits it is possible to enhance the system in an orderly and structured way so that no problems between standard SAP developments and customer ones arise, especially when there is a release upgrade or standard patches (Hot Packages or Legal Change Packages) are applied.

Introduction to User Exits

User exits are standard links on the system which customers can use to place enhancements without altering the SAP standard. As part of enhancement functionality, the R/3 system provides a central function for managing these changes which can be accessed from the main menu by selecting **Tools → ABAP Workbench → Utilities → Enhancement → Project Management**, or typing the transaction code **/NCMOD** in the command field.

These links can be compared to hooks in the standard programs, with the guarantee that you can hang up your material. Even if the standard programs change, the same hooks and also your material will remain.

SAP enhancement functionality distinguishes several types of user exits. These are:

❑ **Function Exits.** These can be used to add enhancements to existing functions and for linking new functions or programs, while following the syntax and options allowed by the particular available enhancement.

❑ **Menu Exits.** These can be used to insert new menu options into standard menu bars.

❑ **Field Exits.** These are a special type of user exit; they facilitate performing different types of functions associated to the data element allied to the fields, for example some type of additional field verification or authorization.

Another type of enhancement to the standard system is to add new fields to existing standard SAP tables, without modifying the tables' original structure. This can be done by using append structures. Functions for handling *append structures* are located within the ABAP Data Dictionary.

With release 4.x, SAP included the Modification Assistant, used to control and manage all the changes made to the ABAP development environment and thus minimize the time needed for adjusting changes and version management.

A Word of Caution about Nonstandard Enhancements

Often modifications to standard programs are done by first copying the original SAP program (called a Z program) and then changing it, while also changing the transaction and flow logic. What happens when a release upgrade must be performed? If the original program was enhanced, either the Z program must also be modified, or customers must do without the modifications. Whatever the case, this can be costly because modifications to programs and functionality must be assessed.

Another way, usually even less useful, is directly to repair original SAP objects and programs. The risk here comes from standard patches and upgrades. This method is not recommended by SAP.

What To Do When Changes are Needed

To avoid possible problems caused by developments, the tendency to overcustomizing just to please end-users should be avoided. Changes should be approached either through change management, or by studying the possibilities of using standard customizing.

Sometimes missing functions may be present in the next R/3 release. An evaluation of whether to wait for the new upgrade is also a good idea. The use of different user exits is recommended.

Whatever method is used, the tools within the ABAP Workbench and the transport tools must be used efficiently. This makes it easier to address performance problems, tests, or successive modifications

If needed changes apply to reporting requirements, there are many options. These are explained in Chapter 8.

Summary of Program Development

The following chart summarizes the issue of program development in SAP implementation projects.

Why deal with this issue	Other issues affected	Solutions
❑ To develop unavailable custom reports	❑ Reporting	❑ Ensure the function is not covered by customizing
❑ To extend SAP functionality	❑ Customizing	
	❑ Gap analysis	
❑ To solve programming problems and bugs	❑ Performance	❑ Avoid over-customizing
	❑ Systems Landscape	
	❑ System Management	❑ User exits
	❑ Transport Management	❑ ABAP Workbench tools
	❑ Testing	❑ Ad hoc reporting tools
	❑ Upgrade	
		❑ Third-party add-ons
		❑ Change Management
		❑ Upgrade

Data Migration and Data Load

Data migration is the process of extracting data from old systems and loading it into the R/3 system. This is often known as *data load*, although data migration is actually part of the overall data load.

The migration or initial data load from legacy systems to R/3 is probably one of the biggest problems to be faced. It requires the greatest effort and has the highest cost in many SAP implementation projects.

It is a complicated process mainly for the following reasons:

- ❏ The knowledge gap and difficult communication between the SAP project team and those responsible for the maintenance and management of legacy systems applications
- ❏ Problems with quality of data from the legacy applications
- ❏ Large volumes of information
- ❏ The process of testing and simulating data migration is often underestimated and not sufficiently planned for
- ❏ Synchronizing the data load, the customizing settings, and the planned enhancements is difficult
- ❏ Difficulties in using tools designed for easing the migration process
- ❏ Organizational and business process problems related to the cutover.

Cutover is the set of activities that must be performed just before going live so that the production system is prepared with the required customizing of business processes and data.

Before deciding how to approach the cutover process, consider the additional factor of complexity if the implementation project team has planned a period when both the new systems and the legacy applications must operate in parallel. The best approach is, if possible, not to include parallel operation of two systems. Two parallel systems implicitly create problems and can also affect change management.

The cutover process can include the following set of activities:

- ❏ Enhancement and customizing settings performed on the development environment and tested on the Quality Assurance system must be transported to the SAP productive systems using SAP standard transport tools
- ❏ Make an initial massive data load of master data
- ❏ Perform massive data load of transactional data of pending or open items

❑ If convenient, perform data load of usable historical data

❑ Make automatic and/or manual data entry into the R/3 of nonexistent data in the legacy system, not only for application data, but also for user master data, printers, and so on.

Performing a massive data load requires:

❑ Establishing the team, which must be composed of those knowledgeable in the basis technology, developers, and the functional team of the corresponding R/3 application

❑ Establishing the R/3 business objects to identify mandatory fields and those which are needed for the business processes

❑ Establishing the method for data transfer:
  ❑ Standard SAP data transfer programs (standard batch input, standard direct input program, Data Transfer Workbench)
  ❑ Custom-developed Batch Inputs
  ❑ Third-party data migration and data transfer tools

❑ Studying in detail the meaning and use of the input from the legacy systems

❑ Carrying out (assigning and defining conversion rules) the mapping between the legacy systems and R/3

❑ Establishing the correct order and synchronization for the data load

❑ Performing data conversion from the legacy system to a sequential file

❑ Carrying out the data transfer from the sequential file to the SAP system.

It is important to remember that data transfer must always be performed using tools that guarantee the system's integrity and consistency. For this reason using direct transfer to native database tables is not recommended.

Data Transfer Methods: Batch Input and Direct Input

Batch input is one of the standard methods for carrying out data transfer to the SAP system and consists of exactly emulating the steps and input a user would do to enter that data manually and interactively. The data is stored in batch input sessions for later processing (classical batch input). Corresponding transactions are executed and system integrity is maintained. The processing of batch input sessions can be performed either online or in the background using the transaction SM35.

In a second type of classical batch input, the session is not created, but the processing is done online by directly calling the corresponding transaction using the ABAP statement CALL TRANSACTION USING... .

Any of the methods above ensures the integrity of the electronic data load. SAP includes a group of tools to ease the process of creating batch input programs, such as by using the recording of an interactive transaction to create batch input sessions, or by using the Data Transfer Workbench to speed up checking and verification before the actual data load. Programs thus generated require only small modifications according to the sequential file generated by the data transfer program.

Figure 5.1 shows the batch input method.

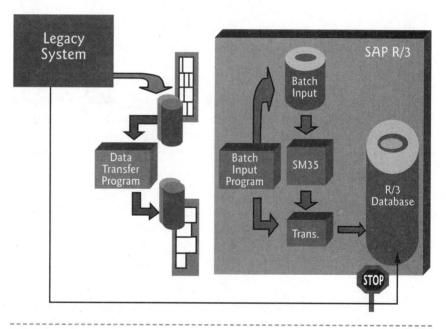

FIGURE 5.1   *Batch input method for data transfer*

Direct input is a variant of the batch input process. The difference is that no sessions are created and processed. Instead data are directly loaded into the relevant tables, using special function modules that guarantee all necessary verifications. R/3 includes many standard direct input programs, and also several tools for managing them and data load error processing (transaction BMVO). This method is advisable for initial data load when the following conditions are met:

❑ There are programs and function modules that can verify the consistency of the data load. Usually, every R/3 application includes some standard program for this purpose; it can be found in the relevant module documentation.
❑ There is a large data volume to load, and running standard batch input could be lengthy and costly.

LSM (Legacy System Migration) Workbench

The LSM Workbench is a tool currently not integrated into the R/3 system. It has been developed on the basis of the SAP R/2 to R/3 migration tools. It can be downloaded free from SAPnet. The main features of LSM Workbench are:

❑ It allows for defining external legacy data in the R/3 system
❑ It can migrate *data objects* instead of single tables
❑ It can be used for defining flexible conversion rules
❑ It is able to generate conversion programs from defined conversion rules and automate the whole process
❑ It goes with more than 20 steps
❑ It supports batch input and direct input methods
❑ It lets you check the data for migration against the customer R/3 customizing

Figure 5.2 shows an overview of how the LSM works.

Summary of the Data Transfer Issue

Any form of data transfer in an SAP project is a costly business. The recommendation is to plan ahead and test carefully, especially the quality of the source data.

Besides SAP tools there are many other third-party tools available for data extraction and migration. The table on the next page shows the summary of this issue.

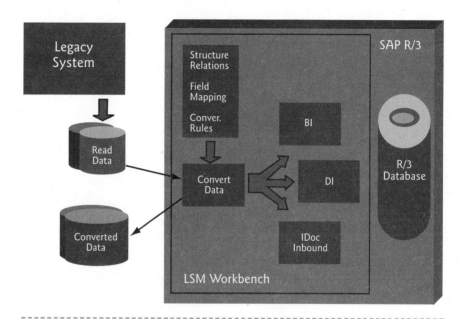

FIGURE 5.2   *SAP Legacy system migration workbench*

Building Interfaces

Although the SAP R/3 application suite offers a comprehensive solution for managing business applications, there are many occasions when R/3 must coexist for a while with other systems. This means that SAP implementation must address the issue of creating a group of interface programs to establish communication with other systems for exchanging data. This communication is often bidirectional.

Depending on the level of integration demanded by the system, including R/3, these interfaces can be designed to be used in an asynchronous way by exchanging files (file access). They might instead require a synchronous level of integration (task-to-task integration).

Why deal with this issue	Other issues affected	Solutions
❏ To be able to continue with critical business information and operations	❏ Project Go Live	❏ Batch Input/Direct Input
	❏ Customizing	
	❏ Interfaces	
	❏ Development	❏ LSM Workbench
❏ To clean up and adjust data structures in the new system	❏ System Management	❏ Data Transfer Workbench
	❏ Cutover	
❏ To transfer data from the previous system to the new SAP system		❏ Data extraction, mapping and migration tools
		❏ Third-party tools
		❏ Document: Data Transfer Made Easy

From the point of view of the implementation plan, the design and development of interfaces must address the following issues:

❏ Interfaces must be tested before productive operation. This is not always easy since the external connecting systems are often productive systems and sometimes have other operating interfaces. This issue is even more difficult in the case of online interfaces.
❏ Performance problems must be anticipated and the data volume that can be generated by the interface activity must be evaluated.
❏ Appropriate skills must be available to match interfaces requirements.
❏ Interface testing and execution must be planned for periods of time with less user-interactive processing.
❏ The responsibilities for managing and validating the results of the interface execution should be clearly defined.
❏ Interface process execution scheduling must be perfectly synchronized.
❏ A procedure must be established for restarting interfaces in case of problems (broken communication lines, systems down, and so on). This includes taking into consideration aspects of data security and integrity, like avoiding entering or processing data twice.

❑ When possible, standard and certified interface programs must be used.

SAP Online Interface Techniques

Of the data transfer methods mentioned previously (file access and task-to-task) only the last one is appropriate for doing online interfacing.

R/3 online integration can be carried out on three different levels of the architecture:

❑ Application server
❑ Front-end
❑ Database.

The last (database) level is only possible if using tools provided by the database vendor (embedded SQL, ODBC, and so on.). It is not recommended since it might cause integrity problems with R/3 applications.

Table 5.2 includes the list of SAP-supported techniques, although not all of them are appropriate for every situation, and may not be available for all platforms and all R/3 releases.

TABLE 5.2   *SAP Interface Techniques*

Online Interface Techniques	Description
Remote Function Call (RFC)	❑ Based on the CPI-C technique
	❑ Can be used at the presentation or application server level
	❑ Similar to the UNIX RPC
	❑ There are libraries for ABAP, C/C++, Visual Basic, and others
	❑ SAP includes an RFC template generator using standard R/3 function modules

continued on next page

Online Interface Techniques	Description
Common Programming Interface for Communication (CPI-C)	❑ Tool for basic programming of online applications ❑ Works at the application server level ❑ Libraries exist for ABAP and some operating system platforms
OLE/ActiveX Components Technology	❑ OLE/ActiveX clients can make calls to SAP function modules which are enabled for calling with ActiveX Controls ❑ ABAP includes OLE instructions ❑ Only for dialog work process ❑ Works at the desktop level
GUILIB/GUI Component	❑ Tools that can be used for developing applications that behave like the SAPGUI interface ❑ Supports C and Visual Basic ❑ Works at the application level
IDOC interface for EDI	❑ Message interchange with external business applications using standard protocols (EDIFACT, X.21, etc.) ❑ Uses the SAP IDOC message structure ❑ Not every module supports IDOC ❑ Works at the application level
IDOC interface for Application Link Enabling (ALE)	❑ Business Framework component, allows integration between applications (either SAP or external) at the business process level ❑ Can use IDOCs, RFC, files, and CPI-C ❑ Works at the application level

continued on next page

Online Interface Techniques	Description
SAP Business Workflow	❑ Can be used for further integration of processes between different R/3 applications within the SAP system
	❑ Can be integrated with external applications using ALE
	❑ There is a Workflow API (WAPI)
	❑ Can be used for integrating external forms using ActiveX components and the SAPforms tool with the SAP Business Workflow
	❑ Works at the application and desktop levels
Business Application Programming Interface (BAPI)	❑ Standard SAP Interface for accessing data and business objects
	❑ There are libraries for BAPI C++ and BAPI ActiveX Control
	❑ Can also be accessed using RFC (not recommended)
	❑ SAP commitment of long-term and stable technique to guarantee future compatibility
	❑ Works at the server and desktop levels
Internet Access Components	❑ Complete solution for connecting SAP with the Internet using Internet browsers
	❑ Access using ITS (Internet Transaction Server)
	❑ IAC (Internet Application Components) are objects developed in ABAP but with dynpros that can interchange data in real time with HTML pages from the ITS
	❑ Works at the server and front-end level

continued on next page

Online Interface Techniques	Description
Additional SAP application interfaces	❑ There is an extensive set of specific interfaces, by module, business activity, or cross-application component, like:
	❑ SAP Archivelink (optical and data archiving)
	❑ CAD interface for CAD systems
	❑ PDC-interface (for data collection devices)
	❑ QM-IDI (Quality Control and Management systems)
	❑ MM-MOB (Mobile data capture terminals)
	❑ PP-PCS (Devices for plant control)
	❑ POI (Specialized systems for scheduling and production planning)
	❑ RWIN (financial interface for carrying out postings in SAP from external applications)
	❑ These interfaces use basic techniques and protocols such as RFC, EDI, or CPIC

The following chart summarizes the issue of dealing with interfaces during SAP implementation projects.

Why deal with this issue	Other issues affected	Solutions
❑ Coexistence with legacy systems	❑ Development	❑ Interface Advisor
❑ Data integration with other applications	❑ System Management	❑ Third-party data mapping and application connection tools
	❑ Data Transfer	
	❑ Performance and Tuning	

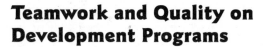

Teamwork and Quality on Development Programs

Checking the quality of custom development programs and transactions is something many SAP customers strive for, but very few achieve. The quality of development is closely related to the software quality theory, but discussing that would require a full book.

This section focuses on SAP implementation projects and the management of development-related continuous change. Checking development is meant to ensure:

❑ Error-free program execution
❑ The best performance
❑ Data integrity and locking
❑ Development maintenance and reusability
❑ Development project coordination.

The first three points will require effort and resources for comprehensive testing, the fourth point is related to developing procedures and methodology, and the fifth is geared to the coordination of the development team and teamwork.

Getting error-free programs means avoiding not just syntax errors (the program just doesn't run), but also logic errors. The program and transactions must achieve the desired application goals. There are several tools within the ABAP Workbench for addressing this issue, of which the most useful is the Debugger.

Getting the best performance out of programs (tuning) might be the most arduous task, mainly because it is quite difficult to simulate real conditions for program execution: data volume, sharing resources with other processes (online users, batches, etc.), performance bottlenecks, and so on. The best approach to this issue is to try to simulate conditions by testing, or using testing automation tools. There are also several tools within the ABAP Workbench and the CCMS that can be used for this purpose, among them Runtime Analysis, SQL Trace, CATT, and Workload Analysis.

The issue of data integrity and avoiding locking problems is concerned with the fact that sometimes wrongly designed programs provoke undesired locking (normally on tables or table rows); or they do not plan for a required locking mechanism. Locking at the row or table level is almost guaranteed because of the uniqueness of the primary indexes of database mechanisms; the same holds true in the ABAP program's lock objects and associated ENQUEUE/DEQUEUE statements. However, there can be situations where massive updating causes conflicts with other programs or transactions. Therefore addressing quality of programs will require drafting a testing plan where locking conditions can be simulated.

The question of maintenance and reusability of development is closely related to the methodology and conventions used for development projects, as well to the cost of maintenance and support. An important side effect is the impact that local development might have on upgrade projects. Reusability is typically closely linked to the modular design of programs and is one of the main features of object-oriented programming. A valid approach to this issue is to establish standards and procedures for development, including the best documentation possible, and to start taking advantage of features of object-oriented ABAP. R/3 also includes a Style Guide within Online documentation that can be used as the basis for software design, mainly in the area of user interfaces.

The issue of testing in SAP projects is discussed in Chapter 8. Upgrading is introduced in Chapter 7. The coordination of development projects across SAP systems is the leitmotif of the Correction and Transport System.

Modifications to existing programs and development of new programs are not carried out on the production system, but on the development system.

According to the size and complexity of the SAP project and the user community, there is a system landscape than can be composed of following roles:

❑ Development system
❑ Quality Assurance system
❑ Production system
❑ Training system
❑ Test system.

These system roles need not be performed on different physical systems, but if they are, they must to be clearly defined in the Transport

Management System. The issue of System Landscape is explained in Chapter 6. What follows is a brief introduction to the Workbench components related to the issue of the Transport System and its main concepts.

Teamwork: The Workbench and Customizing Organizer

The Workbench Organizer is the tool within the ABAP development workbench that is used for performing the important functions of managing and coordinating development in a group of SAP systems. Among these functions are administration and control of new development requests, modifications and corrections to Repository objects, the configuration of development classes, version management, and documentation.

In a distributed SAP systems environment, the Workbench Organizer uses the Transport System for orderly copying and moving, of development or customizing objects among different SAP systems, usually between the systems used for development and testing, and the productive system. Figure 5.3 shows a simple diagram of the Transport System used for inserting, deleting, substituting, and protecting the development objects of the target R/3 system. The transport system also takes care of logging the results of transports and indicates reasons for errors.

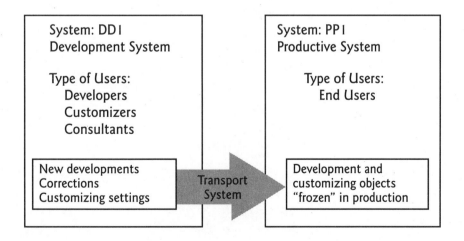

FIGURE 5.3   *Simple diagram of Transport System*

Transport to the target systems is carried out at the operating system level using the transport control program, *tp*. With the introduction of the TMS (Transport Management System) on release 3.1H, imports can also be made from within SAP using RFC mechanisms, without having to resort to the operating system terminals.

Complementary to the Workbench Organizer is the Customizing Organizer, which is used for managing *change requests* generated while configuring or customizing the R/3 applications.

The Workbench and Customizing Organizers and the Transport System include a comprehensive information system that can be used to find information about tasks, change requests, objects, repairs, transports, and so on.

Transport System Concepts

As we have noted, R/3 includes several tools for orderly control and management of the development and transport of customizing and development objects between systems in a consistent way. These tools are:

❑ **Change and Transport System (CTO).** This is composed of the transactions SE01 (Transport Organizer), SE09 (Workbench Organizer), and SE10 (Customizing Organizer), used to register modifications done on Customizing and Repository objects.

❑ **Transport Management System (TMS).** TMS manages and controls the transport of development objects (Repository and Dictionary) and customizing settings between systems belonging to an SAP systems group, using predefined transport routes. This transport process consists of exporting objects from the source R/3 system and importing them to the R/3 target system; this is achieved by the programs R3trans and tp at the operating system level or via RFC.

The functionality of these tools is based on the following concepts:

❑ **Development Class.** This is the concept used to group all related development objects with the same integration system (development system) and consolidation system (quality assurance system).

❑ **Original Object.** Every Development Object has an attribute indicating its system owner. When a Development Object is located in the same system where it was originally created (usually the integration system), then the object is original to that system. This is an extremely important concept because of the effects that modifications can cause. When an original object is modified in a system different from its original one (for example, R/3 standard objects), then this modification is known as a *repair*.

❑ **Transport Layer.** This is a central concept for the Transport Management system and is used for grouping all the development objects within the same development system that will always use the same transport routes. Transport layers are assigned to all the objects that come from specified development system.

❑ **Transport Routes.** Transport Routes are used to define the different routes that exist between two systems within the same system group. There are two types of transport routes:

  ❑ *Consolidation routes* link a source system such as the integration (development) system, with a target system, such as the consolidation (quality assurance) system. Every consolidation route is assigned to a transport layer.

  ❑ *Delivery routes* are used to link a source system such as consolidation (quality assurance systems), with a target system such as the recipient (productive) systems. The delivery routes are not assigned to a transport layer, but every object using a consolidation route (transport layer) arrives at a consolidation system that is also the source of a delivery route and is automatically sent, using the delivery route, to the specified target system.

With release 4.x, any system from the group can be the source of a delivery route, which makes it possible to establish complex transport routes among a group of R/3 systems.

If there is no consolidation route assigned to a transport layer or the transport layer does not exist for the system where objects are modified or repaired, then this modification is considered local and cannot be transported to other systems.

All these concepts we have just explored emphasize the importance of having a well-defined transport and development strategy between a system's groups, their roles, transport layers, and routes. It should be used to manage and automate the process of distributing the development or customizing of objects between the systems belonging to a group. This is crucial when people plan an upgrade project in a systems group, since those phases where modifications must be adjusted must be done in several systems; those adjustments then must be transported among the various systems to be upgraded.

Summary of Teamwork and Quality

The following chart summarizes the issues of managing the quality of development projects and how to handle teamwork using the Transport System and related ABAP tools.

Why deal with this issue	Other issues affected	Solutions
❑ To verify expected results in development areas	❑ Performance	❑ ABAP Work-bench tools: debugger, trace, runtime analysis
❑ To optimize systems performance and make better use of available resources	❑ Testing	
	❑ Support	
	❑ Gap Analysis	❑ CCMS Workload statistics
❑ To avoid locking problems	❑ Reports/Program Development	
❑ To saving costs for development	❑ Upgrade	❑ Workbench, Customizing Organizer, and TMS
	❑ Costs	
❑ To automatically distribute developments		
		❑ OSS
❑ To prepare for upgrade projects		❑ Training

Getting Rid of Bugs: The Issue of Applying Patches

To support systems like R/3, with a high degree of integration at the data and functional level, and taking into consideration the fast pace of the technology market, SAP has established an efficient and swift way to address the issue of correcting bugs and problems in the many programs included within R/3. SAP offers two different ways of correcting errors according to the size of the problem or whether there is a preventive or reactive action for resolution.

When there is a specific problem in a reactive situation, SAP offers the Online Service System (OSS), SAPnet, and the support servers (sapservX).

When there is a need to update the system in a preventive way to avoid problems or correct program errors, in order to have the system at the required correction level, there is the Online Correction System (OCS), which can also be accessed from the OSS or SAPnet. Alternatively these corrections are periodically sent to customers in CD-ROMs.

According to the level within the SAP architecture that a customer needs to maintain, there are different mechanisms for correcting errors and problems. Table 5.3 shows these different methods and tools.

TABLE 5.3 *Correction Methods*

Level	Release Identification	Correction Mechanism	Source	Method/ Tool
SAP Application (ABAP Repository Objects)	Maintenance Level or R/3 Release Version	❑ Hot Package ❑ LCP ❑ CRT ❑ Full Patch ❑ FCS Final Delta Patch (FFDP)	❑ OSS/OCS ❑ SAPnet ❑ Package Collection	SPAM
Kernel SAP (executable programs binaries, closely linked to OS and DBMS)	R/3 Kernel version	R/3 kernel patch level	ftp sapservx	Substitution

continued on next page

Level	Release Identification	Correction Mechanism	Source	Method/ Tool
SAP Tool: SAPDBA, RFC API, SAPgui, SAProuter, etc.	Tool version	New version	ftp sapservX	Substitution
DBMS	Release version	Patch	ftp sapservX	Native tool
O.S.	Release version	Patch	ftp sapservX	Native tool

The following are definitions of the main tools and concepts used for solving problems by applying patches and other types of corrections:

❑ **Hot Package (HP).** Hot Packages are a collection of corrections for serious errors with a broad range of applications to ABAP Repository objects. Normally, errors that appear in the OSS notes as either "Hot News" or "Corrections with high priority" are solved by applying the appropriate Hot Packages.

❑ **Hot Package Collection.** The Hot Package Collection is one or more CDs containing all the available Hot Packages for a specific date. The collection is periodically and automatically sent to SAP customers, often with new SAP correction releases.

❑ **Legal Change Patch HR (LCP).** LCPs include, in addition to all the corrections contained in the Hot Packages, the modifications and adjustments required by several areas of Human Resource Applications, which are affected by the impact that different countries' laws have on the HR application settings and programs.

❑ **SAP Patch Management (SPAM).** SPAM is the R/3 tool used for managing and controlling the transport and import of Hot Packages and Legal Change Packages in an orderly and secure form.

❑ **Online Correction System (OCS).** The OCS includes several tools that, in conjunction with SPAM, are used for acquiring SAP patches that can be automatically downloaded and applied. OCS manages the following types of patches:
    ❑ Hot Package

- ❑ Conflict Resolution Transport (CRT)
- ❑ Full Patch
- ❑ SPAM update
- ❑ Legal Change Patch HR (LCP)
- ❑ FCS Final Delta Patch (FFDP)
- ❑ **Online Service System (OSS).** As introduced in the first chapter, the OSS is the system SAP offers to customers and partners to access an information and knowledge database for solving problems. The OCS is also part of the OSS. The OSS is a major SAP service that offers support for solving customer problems, with 24-hour, worldwide support.

Independently of the implications of quick solutions to R/3 problems for daily systems operations, these important points regarding the issue of applying patches must be noted:

- ❑ HPs or LCPs should not be applied when the system is being used by end-users.
- ❑ It is necessary to analyze the relationship between objects that have been modified by customers (repairs) and objects included in the HP or LCP before they are applied to the productive system. OSS notes and the SPAM tool should be used.
- ❑ When possible, it is desirable to have the same patch level (HP or LCP) in a group of systems. Usually, patches are applied in development and quality assurance systems to test their effects.
- ❑ HPs and LCPs are not perfect either and may produce consequences such as the loss of R/3 table entries. It is important to read the related OSS notes before applying patches, so that procedures for saving and restoring certain tables are taken into consideration.
- ❑ Other types of patches, such as kernel patches, will need to stop the R/3 systems. For them, planning certain downtime is required.

We have seen in this discussion that maintaining an optimal level in SAP systems by applying corrections and patches should be well organized, using clearly established procedures. This process will ease the management and control of further installations or upgrade projects.

The next chart summarizes the issue of correcting bugs and applying patches to R/3 systems.

Why deal with this issue	Other issues affected	Solutions
❏ To solve standard application program errors (within R/3 applications and runtime)	❏ Development of programs and reports	❏ OCS/OSS
	❏ Performance	❏ SPAM
❏ To advance functionality	❏ Availability	❏ Testing
	❏ Upgrade	❏ Clear procedures
		❏ Patch levels

Personalizing the System: Towards the Business Client

SAP has always realized that perception and system acceptance by users has much to do with the appearance and functionality of the graphical interface for working with the system.

It is precisely because of the increasing functionality of R/3 that SAP has started to readdress the typical user interface, SAPGUI, and think about a fully functional, comprehensive *"Business Client,"* redefining this term under client/server terminology.

An overview of the new SAP user interface strategy reveals these projected features:

❏ **Personalization Project.** Through this project, SAP's objective is to simplify system use and give it a greater capacity to adapt to the real needs of different types of business users. This means that the options available in different application screens or systems transactions can be different or customizable. As part of the personalization project, SAP provides the following components:

   ❏ *Session Manager* (available since release 3.0D) is an alternative user interface based in a configurable company menu; it allows for quicker and simpler navigation, as well as providing a more flexible way of managing user sessions in several different systems.

   ❏ *Globals* (global field values) can be used to define default values for fields throughout the system. The system will automatically fill out the values corresponding to the globals defined. These values can be applied to every organizational level that can be defined: users, groups of users, client, or the full company.

❑ *Profile Generator* is the authorization system tool that can be used to assign authorization profiles to a group of users to facilitate administration and customization of the security aspects (profiles and authorizations) of the R/3 system.

❑ *Transaction Variants* make it possible to have different screens according to the different uses of the same transaction or business processes. The system will generate a new transaction code for each variant. The user can have the new transactions available in his own menus.

❑ *Shortcuts* are a new user aid for running the most frequent functions or activities. These shortcuts can be defined the same way as in other Windows programs, as icons in the user desktop, included within documents, sent by mail, and so on.

❑ *Java SAPGUI* is the R/3 interface for connecting to the system through an intranet or the Internet, with the fundamental advantage of providing a great degree of independence on the platform when executing transactions. This development has evolved into the Platform-Independent GUI.

❑ *Platform-Independent (Platinum) GUI* is the new generation of SAPGUI, being designed to have the same appearance and work the same way, no matter what the underlying platform and operating system. The design goal is to integrate all new available technologies within the user interface.

❑ **Business Explorer** is the new interface for accessing the collection of reports available in the R/3 system. It is the main user interface or client for the SAP warehouse component known as Business Information Warehouse.

With R/3 release 4.x users can see other interface enhancements, since the application includes *Tabstrips*, which work like folders with tabs. This simplifies navigation within long transactions, specially those used for defining master data.

WEB

Further, updated information about SAP front-end strategy (user interface) can be found at the information center for technology infrastructure, located at **http://www.sap.com/products/techno/index.htm**. Select User Interfaces. There is a lot of documentation about the SAP strategies we have just discussed. Refer also to OSS notes 66971 and 146505 for updated front-end platforms and strategy.

The results of the *personalization* project, as well as the EnjoySAP initiative started in 1998, have created the basis for the new user interface of the EnjoySAP release.

Introduction to the ABAP/4 Development Workbench

This second part of the chapter includes an introduction to ABAP programming language and the ABAP developing environment known as ABAP Workbench. It is a summary of what can be found in *The SAP R/3 Handbook*, updated with new tools and features available since release 4.x

We do not intend to teach how to program in ABAP, just to provide the reader with an introduction to the main features of the programming language and the main concepts and tools used in the ABAP Workbench environment. We try to show how the components of the development environment relate to the R/3 system and what tools are available for developers.

ABAP stands for "Advanced Business Application Programming" and is a fourth generation language; its full name is properly ABAP/4. The release 4.0B has caused the name to change to just ABAP. Although all previous syntax and keywords are maintained, it has incorporated many object-oriented features in a move to make it a fully capable object-oriented language. ABAP is the programming language in which all R/3 business modules have been written and developed. Customers can use it to extend SAP R/3 functionality.

Development Environment of the SAP R/3 Systems

The development environment of the SAP R/3 system is a fully integrated set of development tools, functions, programming language, and data dictionary, grouped together under the name ABAP Workbench. The ABAP Workbench is the core for all the SAP R/3 system business applications and the foundation for developing additional functions and applications for the client/server R/3 system.

ABAP Workbench is intended as a development environment that can cover all the phases of a development project, allowing teamwork, organization, and version management even across SAP systems. It includes the tools required for easily transferring developments among systems, making it completely portable among R/3 systems and thus ensuring information integrity.

For example, most of an R/3 system upgrade consists of a large collection of programs, function modules, tables, and so on, developed at SAP and transferred to customer systems using the transport tools. This process is automatic and almost transparent to administrators.

The main features of the ABAP workbench architecture are:

❑ Distribution of applications among servers; the same application can run on different underlying hardware platforms and operating systems without modification.
❑ Support for common and standard GUIs.
❑ Transparent communication with other systems, with the interfaces provided by the SAP's middleware.
❑ Transparent handling of the underlying database system with ABAP Open SQL, or with Native SQL.
❑ Communication with external applications with RFC, ALE and other standard protocols, with desktop applications using RFC, OLE2, and ODBC. A full list of communication and interfacing protocols can be found in the section on interfacing.

The development work is based on an object repository, which facilitates the creation and maintenance of database definitions, applications defaults, and business rules that can be viewed graphically. The ABAP Dictionary performs central, active management of all application-related descriptive data including table definitions, foreign-key relations, and views.

The full integration of the development environment components means that changes in any part have a direct and immediate effect on all applications using those components.

SAP is based on standards: user interface, database development, communications, and programming. It provides the data model for R/3, containing the relationships between the business applications.

Development Workbench contains a major library of business functions. Customers can precisely fine-tune R/3 to their specific needs.

Introduction to the ABAP Programming Language

ABAP stands for Advanced Business Application Programming. ABAP/4 (ABAP) is a fourth-generation programming language developed by SAP. This is the programming language which SAP has used to develop all the R/3 business modules and applications, including the system management functions. It is available to customers and developers to extend SAP functionality for their particular needs.

ABAP programs are created and maintained using the Workbench tools. The main features of the ABAP programming language are:

❑ It is a fourth-generation language based on structured programming methodologies and similar to "natural English language," which makes ABAP programs quite readable.
❑ It is an interpretative not compiled language. This facilitates testing and running earlier versions of programs without the need for constant compilation.
❑ It can be used for single report list programming (report programs) and for complex transaction processing (dialog programs).
❑ It is a event-driven language.
❑ It is completely integrated with the rest of the Development Workbench tools, such as Screen Painter, Menu Painter, ABAP Dictionary, etc.
❑ It supports multi-language text elements. This means that text elements can be created in several languages without modifying the program source code.

❑ It is similar to many programming languages and includes elements for:

❑ Variable and data type declarations

❑ Flow control elements

❑ Operational elements

❑ Event elements

❑ Functions and subroutines, which can be managed by a central library.

❑ It contains a subset of standard SQL statements enabling transparent database table access independent of the underlying database system being used.

❑ It provides extensive functions for handling and operating data types such as dates, strings, floating point numbers, etc.

ABAP Object-Oriented Features

Since release 3.0 of R/3 there has been a strategic move by SAP to provide the system with a object-oriented technology. This strategy started with some of the system components and architectures such as ALE (Application Link Enabled), with the tool to browse in the Reference Model (Business Navigator), and with the SAP Business Workflow. This strategy is based on Business Objects. A global approach to objects started with R/3 release 3.1, with the introduction of BAPIs; later with release 4.0 the object-oriented technology was enhanced by the Business Framework architecture and ABAP object-oriented features.

These ABAP object-oriented features are based, as is the rest of the R/3 system, on the business objects included within the ABAP Workbench in the Business Object Repository (BOR).

As an object-oriented language, ABAP from release 4.x onward, incorporates technology principles such as *inheritance*, *encapsulation*, and *polymorphism*, to provide the language with advantages such as lower maintenance costs and ease of code reuse.

The basic concepts and features of the ABAP object-oriented programming language are the same as those of other object-oriented languages. The most important are:

❑ A business object, or simply *object*, represents a type of entity, like a customer, a business unit, an account, and so on, containing all its properties. Every object has an *identity* which allows it to be distinguished from other objects.

❑ Object classes, or simply *classes*, specify the structure of the objects belonging to that class and the definition of the interfaces. Classes are useful for grouping objects with the same structure (attributes, methods, events). Generally, objects are defined using classes. The term *instance* is used for objects belonging to a class.

❑ *Attributes* provide the object with its characteristics and describe the current object state.

❑ *Methods* are actions that can be performed with the object and indicate the behavior of the object.

❑ *Events* are used so the object can inform or be informed of any event or state change on the system and can react to those events.

❑ *Interfaces* are another important feature of objects, defining the method in which objects can be used, independent of their internal implementation.

WEB

More detailed information about the ABAP development environment and the object-oriented features of ABAP can be found on the following site http://www.sap.com/products/techno/abapover.htm.

Overview of ABAP Workbench Tools

For developing and maintaining the client/server applications of the SAP R/3 system, the ABAP/4 Workbench includes a group of tools and utilities to facilitate and perform all development-related tasks. Table 5.4 contains a list of these tools classified by the use and purpose of each.

TABLE 5.4   *Overview of Workbench Tools*

For	Tool/component	Is used for
Programming	Dictionary	Defining, maintaining, and storing the data dictionary of the SAP R/3 system. It stores all dictionary objects like tables, relationships, documentation, help information, etc.
	ABAP Editor	Creating and maintaining the ABAP programs; editing function modules, logical databases, and the screen's logic programming.
	Function Builder	Defining and maintaining, administering, and testing the ABAP function modules (general-purpose routines which can be called from other ABAP or external programs using RFC calls). Can be used for designing server or client programs to communicate using RFCs, by creating RFC templates in C or Visual Basic.
	Business Objects Repository	Two main purposes: ❑ It provides all the needed information about Business Objects: types, key fields, access methods, BAPIs, and so on. ❑ It can create business object instances at runtime when receiving object-oriented requests.
	Screen Painter	Designing and maintaining the graphical user interfaces screen in a transactional and client/server environment like R/3.
	Menu Painter	Designing and maintaining the menus for the graphical user interface.

continued on next page

For	Tool/component	Is used for
	Data Modeler	Managing and maintaining the SAP and its own data models using the SAP model known as SERM (Structure Entity Relationship Model). Due to its level of integration with the ABAP Workbench, the Data Modeler can make models using a top-down or bottom-up approach by assigning dictionary tables or views with Entity Types of the Data Modeler.
	ABAP Query	Generating report programs without any programming experience, by navigating the menus that the ABAP Query Administrator creates for different user groups.
Navigating and Information	Repository Browser	Managing and organizing the development objects in a hierarchical form, to allow easy navigation among objects and the development environment. Objects can also be directly managed from the Repository Browser and assigned to other development classes.
	Repository Information System	Navigating and searching for dictionary objects, development objects, and the relationships among objects; can also be used for where-used-list analysis.
	Application Hierarchy	Displaying the development objects from an organizational and application point of view.
	Data Browser	Navigating in the table data of the database; locating and displaying the content of several dictionary objects like tables and views, and their internal relationships. In some cases, new entries can be made (for tables with Maintenance Allowed set).

continued on next page

For	Tool/component	Is used for
	BAPI Browser	Presenting Business Objects in their hierarchy within R/3 and permitting navigation among them.
Debugging and Testing	SQL Trace	Tracking database calls from the system transactions and programs.
	Runtime Analysis	Analyzing the performance of the system calls.
	On-line Debugger	Stopping a program and analyzing the result of the execution of every program statement.
	System Log	Keeping track of errors that occurred during program execution.
	CATT (Computer Aided Test Tool)	Facilitating the testing process; can be used for creating, maintaining, and executing automatic processes of testing and software verification. Tests can be conducted for ABAB Workbench developments as well as for customizing.
Organizing development	Workbench Organizer	Controlling and keeping track of development work and team-related development projects and for managing versions of development objects.
	Customizing Organizer	Managing and controlling modifications to customizing settings (like Workbench Organizer).
	Transport Organizer	Performing and managing the transport of development objects across different SAP systems.

ABAP Workbench Changes Introduced In Release 4.0

Table 5.5 includes a summary of the changes introduced in the ABAP Workbench environment with R/3 release 4.0.

TABLE 5.5   *Changes and Enhancements Starting with Release 4.0*

Modification	Description of Change
New Terminology	❏ ABAP/4 is now known as ABAP
	❏ ABAP/4 Development Workbench is now known as ABAP Workbench
	❏ ABAP/4 runtime environment is now known as ABAP Objects
	❏ Object Browser is now known as Repository Browser
	❏ Function Library is now known as Function Builder
	❏ ABAP/4 Editor is now known as ABAP Editor
	❏ ABAP/4 Dictionary is now known as ABAP Dictionary
Extended Field Names and Name-spaces	❏ Field names can be longer
	❏ Customer developments do not have to conform to SAP naming standards
ABAP Editor Enhancements	❏ Breakpoint icon
	❏ Lower/upper/key word option
	❏ Integration with Notepad for editing
	❏ Compression of structure language elements
Menu Painter	❏ Pushbuttons in the application toolbar
	❏ Name extension for function codes, status names, titles, texts, and documentation
Screen Painter	❏ TabStrip control
	❏ Editorial functions "Undo," "Repeat," "Cut," "Copy," and "Paste" in the graphical Screen Painter
Debugger Enhancements	❏ Improved toolbar
	❏ Scrollable display of breakpoint watch point

continued on next page

Modification	Description of Change
	❑ Improved processing (conditional)
ABAP Language Enhancements	❑ Two new table types (sorted and hashed) that simplify coding
Batch Input Enhancements	❑ Import/export of sessions
	❑ Improved error analysis
	❑ Batch input recorder generates a program that can be altered to customer requirements
Repository Information System	❑ Displaying the external references of an object
	❑ Displaying unused objects
	❑ Processing background list
	❑ Extension of the "Where-used list" function
ABAP Dictionary Enhancements	❑ Views can be buffered
	❑ Database-dependent with disabled indexes
	❑ Common name space for structures and data elements
	❑ Search Helps replace help views and Matchcodes
	❑ Dialog enhancements
	❑ New tab strip control
	❑ ABAP Objects
	❑ Object orientation implemented

Basic Concepts of the Development Environment

The development environment includes hundreds of functions, many of which are quite common in other types of applications, especially the features concerning programming languages, such as a sensitive editor, a data dictionary, function library, debugging facilities, and so on. The SAP R/3 development environment has many of its own functions and features. Within the entire environment there are two basic concepts of particular importance: development objects and development classes.

Development *objects* are all the components of an ABAP application: programs elements (events, global fields, variants, subroutines, includes), program code (functions modules, reports, module pools), transactions, message classes, dictionary objects (tables, data elements, domains, etc.), and development classes.

Development *classes* are logical groups of development objects that are related; they are normally deployed for the same application module, related reports, etc. We investigated this concept in the section on teamwork and the Workbench Organizer. Development classes are particularly important for team development, for the transport system, and for use within the Object Browser, Application Hierarchy, etc.

ABAP Data Dictionary

The ABAP/4 Dictionary is the central Workbench Repository utility, providing data definitions and the information relationship later used in all the business applications within R/3. The ABAP Dictionary can be seen as a logical representation, or a superior layer over the underlying database. As we have said before, the supported database engines must comply with the relational data model. This model is strictly followed by the ABAP Dictionary. It is therefore important to know the basic concepts of relational databases: what functionality it provides, how it establishes the relations between the different objects and elements, and what operations can be performed over the objects.

A data dictionary, in computing terms, is the source of information in which the system data are defined in a logical way. The data dictionary is the centralized and structured source of information for business applications.

The data dictionary is the core of a well-structured development environment. Around a data dictionary can be assembled other components of a development environment, such as a programming language, context-sensitive editors (CASE type), screen painters and handlers, etc.

The elements that make up a dictionary are known as *metadata*, the computing term for the data whose function is to describe other data. The data of the dictionary are not the operational data which tell a customer's address or article price, but a type of data whose function is to define the semantic or syntactic properties of the operational data, such as type, length, relationships, etc. Currently, relational databases and transactional systems in general all have and use a data dictionary as the system core.

An advantage of having a data dictionary is avoiding inconsistencies when defining data types that will later be used in different parts of an application. This will avoid redundancies and considerably decrease the cost of maintenance.

When a type of data is defined in the dictionary, it is available to any program or function module in the application. A change in the definition of a type of data in the dictionary will automatically affect any other data, module, function, or program which has data or variables defined using that modified data type. This can be quite useful in modifying all related data types. At the same time and for the same reason, it requires extreme care not to affect negatively other system parts (other types, or programs) using those data types.

The Role of the ABAP Dictionary in the R/3 Systems

The data dictionary makes it possible to create, modify, or delete data definitions (data types). It is at the same time a great source of information, not only for the development environment but also for the user, since it is a fast and efficient way to answer questions about the entries that exist in a database table, the structure of a table or view, or the relationship between two different dictionary objects.

ABAP Dictionary data are the core of the R/3 development system and the source of every definition within R/3, from the very basic domains to the company model. They are totally integrated with the other tools of the development environment.

The integration of the ABAP Dictionary with the Development Workbench is an *active* integration. Activating any modification in the data definitions will have an immediate effect in all related ABAP programs, function modules, menus, and screens.

Some of the main available functions in the ABAP Dictionary are:

❑ It can add, delete, modify, and, in general terms, manage the definitions of the dictionary data (activation, version handling, etc.).

❑ It preserves data integrity.

❑ It is a central source of information. Information about defined relations between the system tables is available from the dictionary. It allows access to the data directly in the underlying database system. The dictionary tells whether a table is active, empty, or contains data, etc.

❑ It is the central layer for software development. The ABAP Dictionary is an active component of the SAP R/3 environment. Every created or modified element of the data dictionary (every definition) can simultaneously and automatically be used in every software component which includes that definition.

❑ The ABAP Dictionary is integrated in the development environment and in the R/3 application environment using *call interfaces*. With those call interfaces, the programs can directly access the information stored in the dictionary. At the same time, all the Development Workbench tools can directly access the data dictionary for creating menu definitions, generating screens, reporting functions, etc. There is always up-to-date data definition information. For example, once a table is declared inside an ABAP report, there is no need to declare the structure of the table or to declare the name of the table itself. At program generation time, the system directly accesses the data dictionary to look for structure and properties.

❑ The ABAP dictionary can be used for documenting system data.

❑ It ensures that data definitions are flexible and can be updated.

Because the R/3 system works basically as an interpretative method, instead of working with original objects, it actually uses internal representations of objects. With this type of operation system performance is enhanced, and the development tools, screen interpreters, database interface, etc., always access the most-current data.

When any data dictionary object is used in other parts of the development workbench, for example within a source code program, in a screen, etc., the developers only have to enter a table name, or position the corresponding field in the screen. The system automatically knows all the object properties and information and automatically creates and initializes all the work areas, symbol tables, and related areas.

Entering one or more tables names with the ABAP TABLES keyword will make the system automatically know, even in the program edition phase, the properties of the tables and fields making up those tables.

For example, if an ABAP report contains the declaration TABLES: TABNA, all information about this table, such as primary key, indexes, field names, and data types which is defined in the data dictionary will be retrieved when the program is generated. Any change to the table does not require modifying the source code for the program, except when explicitly using field names that have been removed from the table structure. When the programs are called after a table structure change, they are automatically regenerated without user intervention. This means the most updated information is always available and can be retrieved from the ABAP Dictionary.

Introduction to the Business Framework

Business Framework is the architecture established by SAP for componentization. It is an architecture based on integrated and open products, grouped around the R/3 applications. This architecture is perfectly aligned with the SAP strategy to make R/3 the core of a family of integrated products that can be installed, managed, and upgraded independently, without affecting other system components.

Technologically, Business Framework is supported by and founded on the arrival of new integration technologies, based on standard object-oriented interfaces.

The componentization of business applications software has the objective of solving some of a companies' biggest problems in the lifecycle of applications, such as software maintenance. It also makes use of new functionality, versions and technology, whose pace of release and development is not the same as the changing rhythm of business. The Business Framework architecture has opened wide the business door to the Internet world and electronic commerce by using interface mechanisms.

Here is a list of the main features and advantages provided by this type of architecture:

❑ Fast implementation of new functionality by easily incorporating new application components, from SAP or from other partners
❑ Allowing enhancement of functionality using standard interface technology
❑ Application of new technologies without interfering with or affecting other parts of the system
❑ Independence of versions between components
❑ Ability to change or upgrade components independently
❑ Integration of SAP and non-SAP applications
❑ High availability and scalability
❑ Basis in object-oriented technologies.

Business Framework architecture is based on the following technologies:

❑ **Components (or Business Components)**, for providing specific business functionality that can be perfectly integrated with the rest of the R/3 system using standard interfaces. Components have their own development and maintenance cycle.
❑ **Interfaces**, provided by means of BAPIs, the SAP communication technology using interfaces based on business objects. These are used to connect and communicate with different components.
❑ **Integration**, provided by SAP using the ALE technology and SAP Business Workflow. With this technology the system guarantees a total integration of components at the business-process level, so it is independent of the system in charge of the particular business process.

The parts of the SAP system that make up the logical core of the Business Framework are the Reference Model and the Business Object Repository Both components guarantee the semantic integration of business processes.

From release 4.0 the various components of Business Framework can be accessed from the R/3 main menu by selecting the options **Tools → Business Framework**.

BAPIs

BAPIs (Business Application Program Interfaces) are the access methods for Business Objects (BOs) available in the SAP systems, and are managed from the Business Object Repository (BOR) within the ABAP Workbench. The external access to the data and processes of business objects is performed using BAPIs.

For example, the Business Object "Material" includes a process for checking the availability of a material. This process is the "Check-Availability" that can be called using the "Material.CheckAvailibility" BAPI.

Currently, BAPIs are implemented using function modules based on RFC. Some of the advantages of this type of implementation are:

❑ Better integration between standard business applications
❑ Access to business objects using object-oriented technology like COM/DCOM
❑ CORBA compliance
❑ Stability and compatibility with future SAP R/3 releases
❑ Ability to be called from any development platform supporting RFC.

Programming with Business Objects

Access from R/3 applications to business objects within the BOR can be performed in two ways:

❑ Object Oriented (OO) through the BOR:
    ❑ The ActiveX BAPI Control can be used so that client applications on Windows 95 or NT platforms can access the Business Objects making BAPI calls using OLE Automation.
    ❑ The BAPI C++ Class library can be used for accessing each Business Object with related BAPIs.
    ❑ Using SAP's BAPI Java Class, BAPIs can be accessed from any platform supporting Java Development Kit 1.0.2
❑ RFC with the function modules in which the corresponding BAPIs are based:
    ❑ Using the RFC or C/C++ Class libraries, BAPIs can be accessed from any platforms supporting those libraries.

With any of these methods, the programmer must know the BAPI related to the business object to be accessed, and the input and output parameters that must be provided. This information can be obtained using ABAP Workbench tools (BAPI browser, Repository information System, or Function Builder).

CHAPTER 6

Technical Implementation

This chapter deals with the technical activities and issues important—even critical—to successful implementation of SAP R/3 projects and to planning support. These activities and issues are commonly grouped as "Basis" activities.

Technical issues, also referred to as technical implementation, comprise the activities needed within all phases of R/3 projects, from initial project startup to productive operation and beyond.

As we noted in Chapter 2, every implementation project needs a solid technical base and a knowledgeable workforce to support the installation. Underestimating technical issues can ruin not only project realization, but also user acceptance of the new system.

The following list outlines the main infrastructure and technical issues in SAP implementations:

- ❑ Systems landscape
- ❑ Sizing and scalability
- ❑ Choosing platforms
- ❑ Network infrastructure
- ❑ Software installation and systems copy
- ❑ Contingency and availability
- ❑ Backup and recovery strategy
- ❑ Printing strategy
- ❑ Batch strategy
- ❑ Front-end distribution.

In this chapter, the technical issues discussed are mostly those during the preparation and realization phases of the project, before going live.

Other important technical issues like System Administration, Performance & Tuning and System Troubleshooting are explained in Chapter 7. Although it is also useful to manage and tune systems before going live, these issues have a greater impact during the productive operation and support of the systems.

A vital element in technical implementation, though rarely considered, is *people*. Although the system is complex, planning, designing, and managing the SAP R/3 system in not difficult if the right expertise, support lines, and procedures are in place.

This chapter explains a set of elements that should be taken into consideration when starting a SAP technical implementation project.

Every element is important, and the right configuration of every one of them—people configuration used to be known as *training*—is what makes the technical implementation a successful base for the project.

The Scope of Technical Implementation

Looking at the SAP R/3 implementation process from a computing and application point of view, there are two major types of tasks/activities: functional and technical. Previous chapters considered other types of activities like organizational, including for instance, change management.

Despite differing activity types, there is only one major expected result or objective: the implementation of SAP R/3 will solve business issues and will return the expected benefits. Functional activities comprise all those tasks needed to adapt the SAP R/3 software to company business requirements. Technical implementation activities for a SAP R/3 system comprise all those tasks needed to:

❑ Provide technical support for the configuration of standard software to meet business requirements
❑ Maintain and manage the hardware and software used as the SAP R/3 project platform.

The scope of technical implementation issues can be categorized according to:

❑ **What needs to be done:** Activities needed for planning, designing, and carrying out the technical implementation tasks
❑ **In which implementation phases:** Pre-production (preparation, customizing, and development), preparations to start production (going live), and post-production (operation and support)
❑ **In what geographical locations:** Most tasks are location independent, and therefore valid for any region or geography. There are some which are not: technically, these are the network configuration, infrastructure, design, and monitoring, as well as the installation of front-end software and the printing strategy. Technical support for users at remote locations must be taken into consideration as well.

Overview of Technical Activities in SAP Projects

The diagram shown in Figure 6.1 was introduced in the first edition of *The SAP R/3 Handbook*. It has now been slightly modified and updated to reflect valuable suggestions from readers and technical leaders on SAP projects.

The diagram in the figure includes 16 numbered circles reflecting the main activity areas related to technical implementation of a SAP R/3 system. This diagram is a generic approach, or blueprint, to a more detailed definition of a technical project plan that can be adjusted according to project needs and scope.

In this diagram, only three milestones have been established:

❑ **Start.** This is the starting point for the R/3 technical implementation. Usually, this technical starting point occurs soon after implementation starts, during initial project preparation. Previous activities in the overall R/3 project include preparing documentation, like the project plan; defining organization, roles, and responsibilities; and possibly some basic training. The project plan often does not take into consideration all aspects of technical activities and usually underestimates the resources needed to perform them.

❑ **Systems Landscape (Productive Environment) Defined.** At this point, the systems infrastructure might have been correctly sized according to business needs. A suitable systems landscape (development, integration, production) should be defined. The systems architecture design should contemplate additional technological requirements such as network security, contingency, planning, and information integrity strategy. This milestone signifies the beginning of the most critical project, the solving of technical issues before starting productive operation.

❑ **R/3 Going Live.** At this point, end-users start real work, which means entering real data, searching for real and meaningful information, and so on. Going live (productive start) marks the "distance" in terms of transactional data between the development or test systems and the productive one. Availability becomes a critical factor that can severely affect the business.

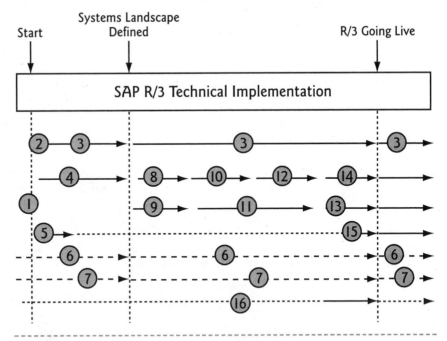

FIGURE 6.1 *Overview of tasks in SAP R/3 technical implementation*

Below is a list of activity areas shown in the previous figure, as well as a brief explanation of the purpose or intended result of each. Timing each phase is a matter of specific project needs, although there are some phases, such as system administration, which are usually ongoing tasks lasting as long as the application itself.

1: Infrastructure and Requirements Planning

This is the first project task involving technical issues: the planning phase where initial infrastructure requirements are specified for servers, workstations, network, and so on. An initial system and network size survey is performed. At this stage it is advisable to procure the development system as soon as possible.

This should be considered an initial sizing that will probably change as the first phases of the implementation start and more information is gathered about infrastructure requirements. Although it is advisable to perform this production systems size survey, it is actually quite difficult to estimate size at this stage. The sizing issue is covered later in this chapter.

2: Development System Installation and Configuration

This includes all the activities needed to install and configure the development environment, where customizing and development are carried out. Activities range from the physical installation of hardware to initial R/3 configuration, including the creation of user master records for those responsible for implementation.

Some of the tasks in the development system installation and configuration are:

- ❏ Installing the hardware, software and the network components
- ❏ SAP R/3 software installation
- ❏ SAP front-end installation (SAPGUI) for the functional and technical group
- ❏ Setup of the SAP Online documentation
- ❏ Protecting SAP super-users
- ❏ Definition of development users and initial authorizations
- ❏ Definition and setup of some printers
- ❏ Definition and implementation of the backup strategy for the development system
- ❏ Delivery system setup and client copy procedures
- ❏ Scheduling cleaning background jobs.

The outcome of these tasks must be a development system ready to start R/3 customizing.

3: SAP R/3 System Administration and Operation

From the moment the development system is installed and configured, the system must be maintained and administered. These tasks will be required as long as the R/3 software keeps running the business applications. The tasks of the R/3 system administration must include technical support to functional consultants.

The issue of Systems Management on SAP implementation projects is covered in Chapter 7.

The mission, roles, and responsibilities of system managers and operators, as well as a description of their tasks can be documented in the Procedures Guide. More explicit information such as the physical and logical description of the systems, as well as detailed instructions for operating the system, can be written down in a SAP R/3

Administration and Operation Manual. Examples of these guides can be found on the Documentation section in Chapter 4.

4: Productive Systems Landscape Definition

Another activity area that is very important because it will set a milestone is to define the productive system landscape and architecture. Support from project management and the functional team will be required. Tasks in this area involve:

❑ Defining the number and type of R/3 systems: production, development, integration, training, and so on. It is important to remember that a systems landscape also includes the definition of a structured client concept and client copy strategy.
❑ Calculating the initial database size and storage growth expectations
❑ Defining systems backup strategy
❑ Defining switchover systems and contingency plans
❑ Sizing the networking needs: calculating expected throughput and bandwidth for LAN, WAN, remote connections, etc.
❑ Defining initial Help Desk strategy for technical issues.

The result of these activities might take the form of an RFP (request for proposals) to be sent to hardware vendors, as well as to form the base technical project plan to be implemented before going into productive operation.

5: Configuring and Managing the Remote Connection with SAP

Just after the development system has been installed, it is very convenient to establish the remote connection to SAP support servers, especially for getting access to the OSS (Online Service System) and to have the infrastructure ready to receive remote services. The OSS is a valuable tool for both functional and technical areas of the whole project. Activities are:

❑ Getting and configuring a remote connection
❑ Registering the connection with SAP
❑ Establishing security policies
❑ Configuring SAProuter
❑ Registering the OSS users.

6: Technical Documentation

This is also an ongoing activity for the life of the project. As we see in the diagram above, there is probably documentation before starting point of the actual technical implementation. Throughout the project, at least the following technical documents must be worked out:

❏ The "Procedures Guide," describing the overall project organization, mission, roles, and responsibilities. This might also include specifications shared by both functional and technical people, such as development methodology for the project or rules for the transport system. It is particularly important to cover aspects such as contingency planning for what to do when systems are unavailable, although this might be a separate manual or document. With this as with other manuals it is also important to define the *change management*: how to handle changes in the systems, in documents, in the organization, etc.

❏ The "Administration and Operation Manual," containing detailed descriptions about the systems architecture, and detailed instructions about full system operations including operating system management, database administration, R/3 management and monitoring, failover operation, backup procedures, etc. The cornerstone to this manual is to include step-by-step instructions on how to perform all tasks needed in the operation of SAP R/3 systems.

❏ The "Technical Validation Test Specifications," a document which can be prepared for testing technical requirements and specifications before the system becomes productive. Tests can include simulating disk or power failures and network line breakdown, deletion of important files, database recovery, archiving, security issues, etc.

❏ The "User Guide." The development of this guide is not actually the role of the technical team, since it should be more functionally oriented to depict users' work in the system business applications. The technical support group might collaborate on initial sections in the guide describing how to move around the system, how to manage passwords, etc.

There are any other documents that do not specifically target technical issues, though these are referred to. Among them are the Project
Plan, the Preparations for Going Live Plan, the Migration Plan, and
so on.

7: Technical Training

Training is a big issue in R/3 implementation projects, as explained
in Chapter 4. There are many options and tools for training. There
are SAP standard courses, knowledge products for self-training, and
so on. Some SAP partners also provide learning services for R/3
applications.

During the project life, companies might contract for technical
consultants to do jobs or tasks for which their own personnel are
not prepared. Knowledge transfer is another way for effective training by actively participating or understanding what other consultants do. This is the "on-the-job training."

SAP R/3 training areas for technical support personnel should
include:

❑ R/3 Architecture and Administration
❑ CCMS
❑ Authorization System
❑ Development Workbench tools, and if needed, ABAP and inter-
faces for configuration and programming
❑ Software Logistics (Transport System)
❑ When the projects require it, add-on cross-application modules
such as Workflow, EDI, ArchiveLink, etc.

Technical staff may have to take not only courses but also prepare
specific training materials for others: think of an introduction to the
R/3 environment for help desk personnel, an overview and the company's specific rules for the Workbench Organizer, transport system
for the development team, use of the business workflow, etc.

The timing for taking or teaching those courses should be included in the project plans and extensive training must be taken by the
R/3 technical group before the system can become operative.

8: Productive Systems Installation and Configuration

This stage marks the beginning of a new phase after the productive systems architecture has been defined and the hardware infrastructure is available. Tasks related to this activity area include:

❑ Installation and configuration of hardware, base software, and network components, including RAID systems, backup devices, etc.
❑ For high availability systems, installation of cluster or switch-over hardware and software
❑ Installation of database and R/3 central instance
❑ When needed, defining and mounting NFS file systems or file shares
❑ Installation of additional R/3 instances in application servers
❑ Initial distribution and configuration of SAP services, including the definition of operation modes (CCMS). (Further tuning and optimizing of the system load is an ongoing task, which should be assumed by activity 2, system administration and operation, after the system starts productive operation.)
❑ Configuration of the SAProuter for accessing SAP remote support servers
❑ Scheduling of periodic background jobs for management tasks, statistics collection, and systems cleaning.

Together with the functional group and based on the procedures guide, define the rules for user master records creation, along with the authorization and profiles concept. Other technical configuration activities for the productive systems continue in activity area 10.

9: Test System Installation and Configuration

This is an optional activity area, needed only for customers who have defined a system landscape including a test system, also known as quality assurance system (QAS).

Tasks are almost the same as for the development system, and basically consist of:

❑ Installation and configuration of hardware, base software, and network components

❑ Installation of SAP R/3
❑ Defining and implementing a backup strategy for this system.

Further tasks will depend on the actual use assigned to this system. A QAS can be used for:

❑ Testing new developments before going productive
❑ Testing data load and interfaces procedures
❑ Testing operating system, software, and R/3 migrations.

With the right procedures defined, it could even become a standby server in emergency situations.

10: Transport System Configuration and Management

Once all the systems are installed and initially configured, it is time to configure the Transport System. The configuration of the Transport System should be the same as that for a group of related SAP systems belonging to a common system landscape, for example, development, test, and production. Since the introduction of the TMS (Transport Management System) the configuration is synchronized automatically. Some of the tasks needed are:

❑ Sharing the common transport directory /usr/sap/trans, either with NFS in UNIX systems or by setting a Global Transport Host using shares on Windows NT
❑ Running transaction SE06 in every system (it is part of the post-installation steps)
❑ Setting the system change option according to system roles
❑ Configuring transport routes and transport layers
❑ If necessary, configuring the TPPARAM file.

Management of the transport system will include such things as defining when and how imports are performed, as well as log checking.

11: Installation, Development, Configuration, and Testing of the Technical Infrastructure

Technical requirements might demand a lot of work in this activity area to get the system infrastructure working properly. Although some tasks might be optional, those implemented at this stage should cover the setup, configuration, and testing of the following technical elements:

❑ Backup and recovery strategy, including hardware and software, integration with the R/3 CCMS, parameter settings, tape labeling and storage, etc.
❑ Widely available software and hardware. If possible test contingency situations: what to do if..., how to redistribute SAP services, etc.
❑ An operator menu: a central place where operators can easily perform the tasks assigned to them. An operator menu can include things such as starting and stopping the SAP systems, scheduling backups, displaying and cleaning log files, disk and file system monitoring, spooling control, etc.
❑ Communication with external systems, including remote communication with SAP support servers
❑ Together with the developers and functional group, prepare the systems for testing massive data loads and periodic interface with the batch input procedures or use of other tools
❑ Test system monitoring with the CCMS, as well as general R/3 administration and operation, including user administration and authorizations, background job management, and extensive database administration procedures
❑ Set in place the technical support strategy.

Some of these tests might be performed using the test system, while others will possibly require the full infrastructure of the productive environment, for instance, the switchover software. In any case, at this stage many backups and recoveries will be needed, so be sure that procedures work properly in every condition.

12: Printing Strategy and Front-end Services

Even in a paper-free computing environment, printing for SAP R/3 installations should not be thought of as an obvious task. Careful planning and consideration are needed to avoid long print wait times and collapsing network lines. A wrongly defined printing strategy might lead to degradation of overall system performance.

This also happens with the installation and distribution of the SAP front-end software and services. So before R/3 productive operation these tasks should also be undertaken:

❑ Carefully plan the printing strategy, considering number, expected volume, locations, critical printing, remote printing, and so on.
❑ Physically install the printers; define and test them at the operating system level
❑ Configure and test the printers within the Spool Administration facilities within the SAP system
❑ Test and avoid situations where printers attached to application servers can lead to inability to do user printing.
❑ If needed, configure and test SAP logon groups
❑ Decide the front-end installation and distribution strategy; install the SAPGUI software and the SAPlogon in all user workstations. Think of migration strategies when there is a need to update the front-end software.
❑ Install the online documentation CD for user access and define the strategy for possible updates.

Both the printing issue and front-end software distribution are discussed in subsequent sections of this chapter.

13: Data Load

This activity area is part of the "preparing for going live" plan. It should be performed with great coordination between the functional and technical teams. Some of the needed tasks are:

❑ Transfer objects and data from the development system
❑ Load master data from legacy or external applications
❑ Implement and test the periodic interfaces with external applications
❑ Manually enter needed data and information
❑ Check consistency of entered data.

14: Final Tests before Going Live

Just as in the previous activity area, this requires a full team effort to check and test overall system functionality. These tests should be supported by "Validation Test Specifications" documents, both technical and functional.

Many tests have been performed in other activity areas. Now it is time to put them all together. At this stage a "stress test" should be defined and performed, simulating user loads, peak times, printing, interfaces, and general user handling of the application. This is also the time to check the quality of the project, including processes and functions, user and administration documentation, etc. As part of the pre-production test, make sure users understand and follow contingency procedures: what to do in case of system unavailability, whom to call, etc.

15: Pre-production Maintenance Service

SAP offers several packages for performing certain maintenance services before going live. The best known is EarlyWatch, but there is also a special Going-Live Service.

As we mentioned in Chapter 1, EarlyWatch is the SAP preventive maintenance service. Before going into productive operation and as a way to validate the productive system parameters and configuration, make sure to contact SAP to perform this first EarlyWatch service. This service requires that the remote connection be set up and established as discussed in activity area 5.

After the SAP specialists perform the system analysis and send the EarlyWatch report, make sure to implement and test the suggested changes and solve the problems found before starting productive operations. Once the system becomes productive, you may or may not decide to keep on with this service.

16: Optional Technical Projects

There are several technical areas that might be implemented in initial R/3 projects. Some of these projects might run along with the initial production preparations or might be part of additional projects. Most of those additional projects fall normally into the "Cross-Application" module areas, where both the design and implementation should be shared by the functional and technical teams.

The following list reflects some of these optional projects:

❑ Implementation of an archiving strategy with or without optical archiving solutions (ArchiveLink). Besides SAP standard software, this type of project requires third-party software and hardware.
❑ Implementation of the SAP Business Workflow
❑ CAD, EDI, mail, or fax integration
❑ Application Link Enable (ALE) scenarios and configurations
❑ Electronic commerce and Internet front-end server setup and installation
❑ Configuration of supported external devices, such as timing equipment, plant control devices, etc.

System Landscape and Client Concept

The R/3 system landscape defines of the strategy for the deployment of the group of systems and clients. A SAP R/3 system is made up of a central database and one or several application servers, based on a client/server architecture. It is identified by a three-character code, known as SID or SAPSID (SAP System Identification).

A client is an organizational concept, defined as a "legally and organizationally independent entity" within a SAP system. It is technically characterized by having its own set of user data and tables. At the database level, a client is a logical subset of table records, achieved by having the client number defined as a primary key.

The recommended group of systems for SAP implementation comprises three types:

❑ A Development system, where customizing and development takes place
❑ A Quality Assurance or Test system, where the previous work can be tested
❑ A Productive system, where actual end-users work with real transactions and operations.

NOTE

System is not necessarily a single hardware server. A SAP system is characterized by having a single database.

There are situations where additional systems might be needed for special, isolated development, hardware testing, training, additional components, disaster recovery, and so on. The minimum environment, however, is made up of two systems: one for development and one for production. In this case, customizing, development, and testing are performed in the development system.

It is essential that any errors, problems, missing entries, etc. found on the productive or test environments be corrected in the development environment for transport to subsequent systems. Otherwise there might be inconsistencies in development on the same object, and a transport could even reverse previous changes. This can be solved by telling clients not to allow changes to customizing and repository objects.

A single system landscape's only advantage is hardware costs; there are many problems and disadvantages: upgrading, client-independent table settings, testing, modification of standard programs, applying patches, and so on.

There are several important points to consider with respect to client configuration:

- ❑ A SAP system is installed with three standard clients
  - ❑ Client 000: SAP Reference client
  - ❑ Client 001: SAP Sample client
  - ❑ Client 066: EarlyWatch service client
- ❑ Other clients (customer defined) start as copies of standard clients (normally of 001), and then can be further copied
- ❑ Client settings (customizing, application, and master data) cannot be merged (this is not supported)
- ❑ There are some tables which are client independent; creating or updating table entries is therefore automatically available in every defined client
- ❑ In the initial stages and maybe during the whole project there will be a need to have several clients: vanilla client for initial project team training and tests, master customizing client, training client, and so on; this may mean that many client copies will be performed
- ❑ Different R/3 application data (for example, FI and SD) cannot be isolated in a client, so it cannot individually be copied or transported

❏ Clients can be open to modifications or protected against transports.

A system landscape comprises both number and type of systems, as well as clients and client configurations. Concerning *productive* clients, Figure 6.2 shows possible configurations.

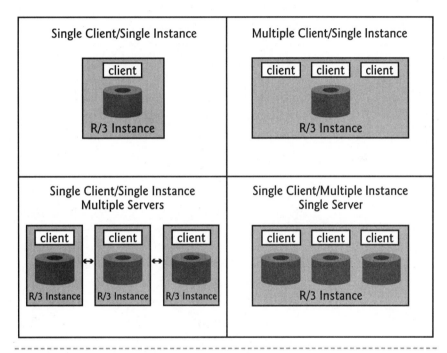

FIGURE 6.2   *Possible client and instances configurations*

Four possibilities are:

❏ **Single client/single instance.** This is the most common configuration for productive operation: a single SAP/DB system uses only one productive client, where all the company business transactions are integrated.

❏ **Multiple client/single instance (known as multiclient installations).** This type of configuration is sometimes chosen for handling several completely independent companies or business areas, etc. There is no integration among clients. Although supported, this configuration has several disadvantages, because of client-independent settings and because all clients are dependent on SAP release. This can require greater coordination efforts between those companies or departments.

❑ **Single client/single instance/multiple servers.** Each SAP system has its own database and instance with a single productive client each. This is a typical ALE configuration well supported by the Business Framework architecture. There is integration between business processes among systems, and systems are independent of SAP releases.

❑ **Single client/multiple instance/single servers.** This configuration comprises situations where more than one SAP system is installed on a single server. This is not a recommended configuration for productive operation since all instances are dependent on operating systems and/or SAP releases. Not only is it more technically difficult to configure and install these systems, but a system breakdown would shut down all instances.

The issue of planning, defining, and configuring a systems landscape is important, because it will have a direct impact on other technical issues, mainly on systems sizing, how the customizing settings and developments are transported to other systems, and how the testing will be performed.

As a result of the systems landscape there will also be impact on the tasks involved in installing and configuring the R/3 systems, copying and transporting clients, and systems management and monitoring.

A well-defined systems landscape will offer several benefits for implementation projects, a few of which are:

❑ Helping to foster an organized customizing process and therefore a better realization phase, thus avoiding common customizing/ development chaos

❑ Saving time in deleting, copying, and transporting systems and clients

❑ Acting as the cornerstone for setting up a stable and scalable systems environment

❑ Helping to avoid unwanted changes or modifications in productive environments, through planning and testing activites.

The concepts discussed give implementers a general idea of the issue of designing a system landscape. The main advice on this topic is:

❑ A system landscape configuration requires careful planning and systems sizing. This should be performed by experienced technical consultants with the involvement of the project manager.
❑ Whatever system and client landscape is defined, it must be clearly communicated to the project team and reflected in the operating procedures, especially for those in charge of developing and customizing.
❑ There is a two-system landscape in the Ready-to-Run R/3. This type of system is mostly preconfigured for a defined number of users.
❑ There is an excellent white paper created by the SAP simplification group (**http://www.saplabs.com/simple**) that is also part of ASAP.

The following chart summarizes the issue of system landscape on SAP Implementation projects.

Why deal with this issue	Other issues affected	Solutions
❑ To set up a stable and scalable systems environment	❑ Sizing	❑ Careful planning and sizing
	❑ Customizing	
	❑ Data Transfer	❑ Communicating concepts and procedures
❑ To organize the realization phase	❑ Systems Management	
❑ To avoid performing unnecessary systems and client copies	❑ Systems and Client Copies	❑ ASAP R/3 System Landscape White Paper
	❑ Testing	
❑ To avoid unwanted changes	❑ Configuring and Managing Transport System	❑ Ready-to-Run R/3
❑ It has a big impact on other technical requirements		

Sizing

In the context of implementation, sizing is a process of analyzing the computing needs of a particular installation and calculating what the systems infrastructure will be in terms of computing power, server distribution, disk space, and network infrastructure.

Sizing is a complex and never-accurate process involving various people and organizations. A SAP customer will usually require the help of the selected hardware vendor and SAP itself. At the same time, these providers will pass on lengthy questionnaires to the customer, whose data will be fed into a sizing application to calculate the estimated size for the system.

The sizing of an overall SAP installation will have a direct impact on the following elements of the technical implementation process:

❑ Installation type—how many servers are needed, what are their intended tasks
❑ Hardware and network configuration
❑ Layout and size of the file systems
❑ Installation of the database
❑ Systems availability
❑ Distribution of servers and services
❑ Load of a customer database
❑ Post-installation steps
❑ Installation of add-on components such as Industry Solutions.

The goal of the sizing process is to define three important figures: how much CPU power will be needed (type of processors, memory, number of servers) for each system within the landscape, how big the databases will be (disk space necessary), and the minimum recommended network infrastructure size to support the SAP R/3 traffic. The quality of the sizing will be as good as the quality of the data supplied by the customer.

Systems Sizing

Sizing SAP systems is based on a unit known as SAPS: SAP Application Benchmark Performance Standard. 100 SAPS are equivalent to:

2000 order line items processed in an hour, or 6000 dialog steps with 2000 postings in an hour. In terms of computer power, sizing can be defined by any of three different methods:

❑ Number of users per application module
❑ Number of dialogs, transactions, and line items per transaction
❑ Additional processing: batch, printing, interfaces.

The first method is the easiest because it is usually simpler to estimate the number of users per application. The second and third are a little tougher because it is difficult to make a realistic estimate of transaction load before being productive. However, an effort to use all three methods should be considered, since the best sizing result will be the one that can estimate the highest systems or transaction load at peak times. For example, if there is a two-hour nightly batch window for running a particular background job requiring 600,000 dialog steps (approx. 5000 SAPS), compared to a daytime need of 200,000 dialog steps/hour (approx. 3400 SAPS), the peak load is in the batch window.

Sizing also depends on the R/3 release. For instance, it was estimated that release 4.0 needed approximately 30% more processing power than the previous 3.1 release.

Concerning user-based sizing, it must be noted that every SAP application module can have different processor power consumption depending on the depth of the transactions, and therefore each is assigned a load factor. An SD transaction requires 3.5 times the load of an FI transaction.

An additional factor in the sizing process is established consumption thresholds. Usually sizing is done for a specific CPU average consumption (normally below 70%), memory consumption (below 80%), and average response time (under 1.5 seconds). The average CPU consumption is usually sized at 33% for dialog processing, allowing an additional 33% for other processing services like batch, printing, etc. The remainder is reserved for peak workloads. This is a generic approach for dialog instances.

Database (disk volume) sizing requires more in-depth business knowledge to be able to fill out the lengthy questionnaires supplied by SAP. Often customers are unable to fill in data accurately.

In these cases, the approach is usually to supply a moderate amount of disk space based on similar configurations and later to monitor system growth and add more disk space as needed. This might have some drawbacks, like file systems redesigns or time-costly database reorganizations.

The main factors that influence the sizing of disk volume require:

❑ The selected database management system
❑ High availability and disk array technology
❑ The number of system clients
❑ Master and transactional data expected
❑ Historical data and time of residence (retention periods).

An easy and early approach to a sizing can be the **QuickSizer** tool provided by SAP through SAPnet (**http://sapnet.sap-ag.de/quicksizer**). With the QuickSizing service, customer can make an initial calculation of CPU, memory and disk resources, based on users by application module, or on a transaction load profile. The results in terms of SAPS and average disk volume requirements are immediately available, and customers can decide to pass on this information to the hardware partner directly from the QuickSizer form.

This self-service tool can be used in the initial project phase to generate an approximate idea for planning systems infrastructure. With the progress of the project, and more usage data available, a double check should be done, either again using the QuicksSizer tool or by directing the information to the selected hardware partner.

Network Infrastructure Requirements

An additional and sometimes underestimated factor for correct overall sizing is the expected network infrastructure sizing and topology. In this case, besides users per module, or transactions rates, there is a location or geographical factor. It is important not only to size the network infrastructure, but also to take into consideration the impact of network availability for an overall SAP systems installations. This issue is covered in the section High Availability later in this chapter.

There are usually two types of network connections which will require an appropriate bandwidth: from the application servers to the database server, and from the presentation servers (usually PCs) to the application servers. A rule of thumb establishes an approximate figure of 1.5Kbits/sec. to 2.5Kbits/sec. between presentation servers and application servers. This figure does not take into consideration other network traffic related to R/3 (printing, download, graphics) or not R/3 related (mail, Internet).

The load between the application server and the database server (when different servers are involved) depends on the overall system load, but a minimum of 10Mbits/sec. should be guaranteed.

To calculate network bandwidth, customers have to know the number of sites and the number of users per site and per module. SAP hardware and technology partners can help in this process. A benchmark-based formula is available for an approximate sizing:

$$C = 16.000 * N / [L * (Tthinktime + Tresponse)] \text{ bit/sec.}$$

Where

C = Required line capacity measured in bit/sec.

N = Number of users

L = Line utilization (0 < L < 1) Values of line utilization higher than 50% are not
     recommended

$Tthinktime$ = Think time between two dialog steps (average = 30 sec.)

$Tresponse$ = Response time (average = 1 sec.)

Usually there are two networks:

❑ A server network, sometimes called a private network, connects application servers with the database server. This should be a high-speed network, using FDDI, Fast Ethernet, or FC technology.
❑ An access network, also known as public network, enables the connection of end-user desktops with the application servers.

A quick recommendation for this typical configuration is to have at least two network cards for each SAP server: one for connecting the server network, and another for the access network. Additional cards can be used to avoid single-point-of-failure or high availability.

Another network consideration in SAP installations is the need to establish a remote connection to SAP support servers, to have access to the OSS or remote services. The connection from a single server using the saprouter utility to enable the connection from other servers suffices.

Finally, remember remote users who connect using modems and phone lines. The common solution for them is the configuration of some type of remote access software (Microsoft RAS or similar programs) for logging into the local network.

Scalability

Scalability is enabled by the nature of the R/3 design as a client/ server architecture. However there are several types of different solutions for increasing the power of a current system:

- ❑ **Vertical scalability** is when new CPU, memory, or disk storage is added to an existing system. The vertical scalability limit resides in the specific limitations of the server model.
- ❑ **Horizontal scalability** occurs when a new server is added to the system landscape, for example, a new application server. It is limited by the processing power of the database server. The rule of thumb states that the workload average of the database server in an overall R/3 installation ranges from 15 to 25%. The good thing about this type of scalable solution is that the R/3 system need not be stopped to install additional instances; also, better distribution and load balancing can be achieved.
- ❑ **Internet scalability** is a way of enabling virtually thousands of users to perform business transactions through the Internet. Scalability can be achieved by adding several ITS servers.
- ❑ **ALE (Application Link Enabled)** is a way of designing a distributed architecture of logically connected SAP systems by using integration scenarios and messaging technology.

Finally, if there is no way to scale current configuration, then a hardware change must be considered. This will imply at least a system copy, plus downtime. Therefore careful planning of infrastructure requirements is a must.

Summary of the Sizing Issue

Remember that sizing is not perfect, and since hardware partners have a competence center in charge of doing sizing and benchmarks, it may be a good idea to a request proposals and do some comparison.

The following chart summarizes the main points of the sizing issue in SAP implementation projects.

Why deal with this issue	Other issues affected	Solutions
❏ It is essential that systems support the expected work load	❏ System Landscape	❏ Quick Sizer
	❏ Performance	❏ Hardware Partner
	❏ High Availability	❏ Double check
❏ To avoid bad response times and gain user acceptance	❏ Going Live	❏ Distributed architectures via ALE might be an option
	❏ Choosing a Platform	
❏ To ensure user access to SAP systems	❏ Costs	
❏ To avoid frequent hardware upgrades		❏ Request for Proposals
❏ To prepare the infrastructure for growth and scalability		

Choosing the Right Platform

Although choosing a platform for running R/3 systems is not a critical implementation issue, a wrong decision might affect several phases of the project and cause serious delays.

All the biggest hardware vendors have superb server platforms for running SAP systems. For many companies with large enough budgets, this will not be an implementation issue, but a statement on their investment sheets. For others, mainly those where IT is leading the project, the question becomes one of great importance.

Input for choosing platforms comes mainly from sizing results. As we noted, sizing is hardly perfect; it is not possible to have every needed piece of data in place from the project start.

Hardware vendor support will be important for several phases of the project, especially when additional hardware is required, or there are malfunctions or configuration problems. For high availability systems, a good maintenance contract and good response times are also recommended.

In critical installations (24 hours/7 days), spare pieces of the critical hardware parts, not sufficiently covered by redundancy in single-point-of-failure, should be on site.

Hardware should be chosen from the SAP certified list. The platforms supported are constantly being updated. For a current list visit the SAP Web page at **http://www.sap.com/products/techno/index.htm** then select **Platforms**.

The decision then should be based on:

❑ Certified platforms
❑ Ability to procure maintenance and support; experience in R/3 should be considered
❑ Alignment of current systems strategy
❑ Confidence and communication with vendor
❑ Accurate sizing.

Finally, although it is often a first consideration, there is cost. These points are summarized in the following chart.

Why deal with this issue	Other issues affected	Solutions
❑ To ensure a stable and scalable platform	❑ Sizing/Scalability	❑ Certified platforms
❑ To avoid unnecessary migrations	❑ Systems Landscape	❑ Benchmarking
❑ To minimize downtime	❑ Costs	❑ Hardware vendors/partners
❑ To minimize hardware/base software upgrades	❑ Systems Management	❑ Customer references
	❑ Testing (stress)	
	❑ Support	

Client Copies and Installing SAP Systems

The R/3 installation process has increasingly eased as upgrades have appeared, because hardware is faster, installation tools have improved, and there is more knowledge in the field. Installing the R/3 system is now an implementation issue only because it is an activity to be carried out and might need to be done several times.

There are some types of installations, systems landscapes, and distribution options which may be quite complex, including high-availability software and hardware. A careful planning of the installation and configuration of the different components is required. For example, to attain better performance, there must first be work done to design the file system layout and disk volumes, mainly to enhance input/output throughput. Bear in mind that overall system installation includes the configuration of back-up and recovery hardware and software, and other possible connected devices.

A topic closely related to system installation, and one is becoming increasingly used, is systems copy, which exists in two types:

❑ **Homogeneous** systems copy, is when the source and target operating systems and database are the same, as in copying an HP-UX/Informix system to another HP-UX/Informix, or NT/Oracle to NT/Oracle. Homogeneous systems copy is often done in installations that want to have a copy of one of their systems for testing or training purposes, perhaps to keep a copy of the production environment to test an upgrade project.

❑ **Heterogeneous** systems copy, is when either the operating system or the database, or both, are different from the source and target systems. This happens when a customer decides to change either hardware vendor or database management system. This type of copy is offered as an SAP OS/DB Migration Service. SAP provides white papers and tools for performing this type of systems copy, but the copy should only be performed by an experienced technical consultant.

Copying Clients

Copying clients is a common task for R/3 system managers, part of the post-installation process and one of the essential elements of the system landscape design, as we noted earlier. This section is intended to remind readers why copying a client is important and how it affects installation, customization, and the software logistics.

Since there is no R/3 tool that separates transaction data from master data, in current versions (4.x) there is no transport tool that can transport just the master data from a test environment to a production environment. This can be done by configuring and using ALE or other third-party data extraction tools.

Copying application data or integrating data from different clients is not supported. This means that copying clients must be closely in line with a convenient procedure for organizing both customizing and development within the system landscape.

A Word about SAP Systems Installation

Installing the SAP R/3 software successfully, providing all requirements are met, is a process that may last from one to two days, depending on options and the processing power of the hardware chosen. This estimated time does not include post-installation steps or basis customization.

A good level of expertise with operating systems (UNIX, Windows NT, AS400, and so on) and management of database systems will ease the way to fast and successful installations. It is also a good idea to know the hotline numbers of the nearest SAP subsidiary and the hardware vendor.

The following summary does not include installation topics such as clusters or switchover systems, or RAID options, since they depend on hardware vendor products and configuration utilities. Standard R/3 installation includes the following hardware elements:

- ❑ One to several server computers, with enough main memory and hard disk space
- ❑ An appropriate network infrastructure
- ❑ Many presentation servers, commonly personal computers, with network interface cards

❑ 99 % of the time there is also a need for LAN servers
❑ One to several printers.

We also have the following software elements:

❑ Server computer operating system and base software kits
❑ Graphical operating environment for personal computers and a supported network operating system
❑ SAP R/3 software kits
❑ A relational database management system such as the SAP information container; it usually comes bundled with the SAP kit.

All these plus additional requirements that might be needed are described on the SAP brochure *Check list—Installation requirements* which comes bundled in the installation kit.

The main steps in an R/3 installation process are:

❑ Planning the installation and getting the latest OSS notes
❑ Installing the hardware, operating system, and base software
❑ Installing the database system
❑ Installing the central instance
❑ Loading the database
❑ Performing post-installation steps (license, front-end, printing, hot packages, and so on).

RRR: R/3 Ready-to-Run

The R/3 Ready-to-Run is a solution from SAP and its hardware partners to offer small- and medium-sized business preconfigured solutions with an R/3 system preinstalled, including the operating system, the database, the network, and even a printer. Customers need only to choose the approximate size in terms of users and modules, and also choose the hardware partner. RRR is available for up to 200 concurrent users.

The RRR solution is meant to save time in technical infrastructure activities, thus reducing the costs. It also includes a special tool and documentation (the RRR Administration Assistant) for administering and troubleshooting the system, so it also can save time in system management and support.

WEB

More information on Ready-to-Run can be found on the SAPnet at **http://sapnet.sap-ag.de/rrr**.

Summary of Systems Installation

The following chart summarizes the importance of the tasks of R/3 systems installations.

Why deal with this issue	Other issues affected	Solutions
❑ It is an important repetitive task in initial project phases ❑ To avoid the bottleneck of not having systems installed	❑ Sizing/Scalability ❑ Systems Landscape ❑ Customizing ❑ Systems Management ❑ Performance ❑ Support	❑ Certified installers and technical consultants ❑ Hardware partners ❑ R/3 Ready-to-Run ❑ Appropriate training

High Availability

SAP defines availability as the fraction of time the system can be used to perform the functions for which it was designed. It is not an isolated hardware or software element, but a property of the whole information system. For a business-critical system, availability becomes a vital factor for nonstop operation. There are complex technical elements involved in planning, designing, and configuring systems to overcome the "availability" issue.

Information Integrity

Information integrity refers to issues concerning the quality and consistency of the data managed by the system (*logical integrity*), and issues having to do with hardware elements and system availability (*physical integrity*).

When there are errors in the system that affect logical integrity, such as wrong user inputs, unintentional deletes, etc., these issues are either solved using application facilities or by having a comprehensive backup and restore strategy. Logical integrity can be a more difficult issue than physical integrity.

Physical integrity and therefore the system availability (for unplanned downtime) can only be achieved by means of redundant hardware components, that avoid *single points of failure*.

In SAP R/3 installations and, any other business-critical applications, advisable hardware and software elements which can be used to avoid system downtime by reducing single points of failure are:

❑ Use of RAID technology for mirroring disks, which can avoid system downtime caused by a single disk failure
❑ Setting up high-availability systems, which can take over other functions in case of system crash
❑ To protect against power failures, systems should be attached to a *UPS* (uninterrupted power supply). Also consider having double power supplies for all hardware elements: disks, servers, network hubs, etc.
❑ Setting up double network links to protect against network failures
❑ Storing backup tapes in fire-resistant cabinets.

Further security can be achieved by defining a disaster recovery scenario. This is a service that can be provided by many hardware vendors as well as by service and consulting firms.

Both logical and physical information integrity issues were considered by SAP and its partners in something started as a "zero downtime" project. Later we discus some of the concepts covered by this project.

High Availability and Switchover Systems

Availability, in a general computing sense, is the period of time in which systems can be used to perform the functions for which they were designed and implemented. The opposite to availability is downtime.

Downtime can be of two natures:

❑ **Planned downtime**, for example to perform offline backups, database reorganizations, hardware upgrades
❑ **Unplanned downtime**, like system crash, disk failure, electrical power failure, software system error, network failure, etc.

Availability is not defined as an isolated hardware or software element, but as a property of the group of systems elements. For instance, when neither the software nor the server hardware presents errors, but network lines are broken and keeping users from performing their work, this is defined as a downtime situation.

SAP project managers should clearly understand that the key measure of systems availability is not the time the servers are up and running (system manager point of view) but rather the perception of end-users.

SAP high availability consists in reducing to a minimum both planned and unplanned downtime. To reach that goal, SAP and its major partners have invested in developing software and hardware solutions. When thinking about availability in the R/3 environment, the following factors should be considered:

❑ What is the availability need of the business? Is it 24 hours, 7 days a week (24/7)?
❑ What are reasons for a planned downtime: software upgrades (R/3, operating system, database)?
❑ What are reasons for unplanned downtime: hardware and software unexpected failures?

Among the first components developed by SAP hardware partners to maximize availability and minimize unplanned downtime were switchover systems (failover systems) and the allied technology. These types of systems consist of a group of hardware and software elements that provide:

❑ At least two servers (normally database server and application server) sharing a common group of disks
❑ Reaction to server, disk, or network failures; when a system crashes, the SAP services are automatically passed on to the standby server, and vice versa

❑ Database software with reconnect capabilities.

A switchover system usually works by dynamic assignment of SAP services to TCP/IP addresses using TCP/IP alias addressing facilities. An advantage of a switchover system is that when hardware upgrades or service maintenance is required, services can be manually switched over to the other system without interrupting normal system work.

Remember that having switchover systems will require an additional SAP license, since they are attached to the network controller card of the server. SAP has usually provided this additional license free when the switchover software and systems are registered.

Extensive information about the specific high-availability issues such as R/3 services, different databases, network, and software issues can be found in the R/3 Online documentation under the CCMS section.

A brief summary of this technical issue is presented on the following chart.

Why deal with this issue	Other issues affected	Solutions
❑ To guarantee systems availability and user operation	❑ Systems Landscape	❑ SAP high availability concept
❑ To protect critical business information	❑ Systems Management	❑ Avoiding single points of failure
❑ To ensure maximum uptime	❑ Systems Installation	❑ Conducting a study of critical elements
	❑ Testing	❑ Switchover and cluster software and hardware
	❑ Backup/Recovery strategy	❑ Maintenance contract with a hardware provider

Backup and Recovery Strategies on R/3 Systems

The backup and recovery strategy is a critical issue in technical implementation and operation of SAP R/3 systems. It is also the only way to protect business-critical information and guarantee a system's operation in any failure event.

Backup and recovery strategies are meant for:

❑ Avoiding loss of critical system data in case of failure (either hardware or software)
❑ Recovering from a logical integrity error
❑ Protecting the business
❑ Allowing full system copies
❑ Safeguarding critical management operations.

When studying what backup strategy will best fit your needs and requirements, first consider the backup factors that can affect the choice of the backup solution or strategy.

The following is a list of factors that directly influence backup strategy decisions:

❑ **System availability.** The first issue to consider is how much downtime for backup your systems can accept. This can range from "no downtime," in other words, a 24/7 systems operation, to other possibilities such as: 24/6, 15/5, etc. For instance, if you decide on 24-hour operation, then your only choice at the moment is to perform the available types of "online backups." If systems only need to be available from 7:00 AM to 10:00 PM and then for four hours for batch processing, then there is a window of five hours (from 2:00 AM to 7:00 AM) when offline backup is possible.

❑ **What to back up.** You must consider if you are going to back up the full system including the operating system files, SAP runtime files, database, etc. It is critical to SAP backup strategy to back up the full database, since this piece of the application changes most frequently. Other system files can be backed up only periodically (say once a week) or on those occasions when changes take place. You can define a consistent backup strategy by having different backup periods for different types of file systems. In SAP installations with an ORACLE database you must also consider the backup of the archive log files.

❑ **Size of files to back up.** Together with the previous factor, the size of the files to back up will affect the time it takes the backup to complete. Also consider the need to estimate growth of the system and database files.

❑ **Backup performance.** Consider the maximum allowed time for a backup to complete. There is an extensive range of possibilities, from 5 GB/hour to 100 GB/hour and more. It all depends on the hardware and software used.

❑ **Type of back up.** You can decide to perform either full or incremental back ups, although for the database an incremental back up is not recommended, since the data file organization means that most of the database files will change whenever the database starts up. The system availability factor is a basis for deciding whether to perform online or offline backups. You can decide to make backup verification or not. A mix and match of available types is also possible.

❑ **From where to back up.** You must also consider if back ups will be performed using the same system where the data is located, or whether a different server will do back ups and restores. Currently, there are many client/server backup solutions. In any case, you also need to consider the CPU, input/output, and network capacity both for the server-to-back up and the server-from-which-to-back up.

❑ **When to back up.** You must decide dates and times for and the frequency of performing backups. This decision will be affected by other factors such as system availability, the expected backup performance, and the size of the files to be backed up. Consider what is the right period between two full back ups, especially for large back up volumes.

❑ **Back up devices.** The hardware market offers everything from simple tape drives to the most sophisticated automated tape robots, which can perform backups using several tapes in parallel. You could also consider backing up to other devices such as disk volumes, optical devices, CD-ROMS, etc. Use volume, performance, and growth factors to determine the most convenient backup device.

❑ **Back up management tools.** Also consider what software or tools to use for managing backup. Try to find the software which offers the most extensive features. It should at the same time be easy to use and above all else, reliable. Another consideration is whether to use the SAP tool for ORACLE and INFORMIX databases, BRBACKUP, or other external tools which can be integrated with it using the backint interface.

❑ **Back up tape management.** In the back up strategy, you must also decide how the tapes, or other back up media, are going to be managed: how to label them, what the retention and recycling periods will be, where to store them, etc.

❑ **Recovery procedures.** Once you decide on a clear back up strategy, the need to restore and recover what was previously backed up can create problems. Defining a recovery procedure is not easy because there are so many possible situations: from simple copy procedure (backup and restore) to a single file missing. The point is to define the possible situations where a restore might be needed and test the procedure.

When checking your requirements against the factors we have discussed you should come up with a solution that best fits company needs. The main concern is to test and monitor the back up and recovery strategy before going into productive operation.

The next section introduces some of the possibilities available for back up strategies. These mainly concern how the back up is performed.

Performing Backups with BRBACKUP

BRBACKUP is the utility provided by SAP to perform backups in R/3 systems when the database system is ORACLE. The Informix database is also supported by the *sapdba* database administration menu for doing backups. In every new release the BRBACKUP tool has been improved, and with releases 4.x there is support for online and offline backups, for resuming a previous backup, for a two-step backup (first to disk and then to tape), and also for backing up other system files besides the database. Using the *backint* interface you can use BRBACKUP together with other third-party software and hardware for greater performance and different management interfaces.

BRBACKUP advantages are:

- ❑ Full support by SAP
- ❑ Integrated with CCMS
- ❑ Comprehensive tape management
- ❑ Integration with *sapdba* and restore and recovery procedures
- ❑ Ability to schedule backups from within SAP R/3.

The main disadvantage of BRBACKUP is that it can be slow and must be run from the same database server, which can affect system performance.

Operating System and Database Backup Utilities

Hardware vendor operating systems usually include some type of backup utility. The database management system also includes backup tools, and other third-party software companies offer backup hardware and software solutions.

Using this type of utility usually confers the advantages of speed and greater flexibility than BRBACKUP. Many back up utilities can run in a client/server mode, avoiding the need for running the backup in the same database server. Some of the operating system backup utilities can back up several servers (several SAP systems, or even application servers) using the same devices. The disadvantage of these solutions is that they are not directly supported by SAP and online backups normally cannot be performed, since the system must be stopped to shut down the database in a consistent state.

The Triple Mirror Approach

This solution is based on both software and hardware elements, and can best be applied in systems with a high availability configuration. Figure 6.3 shows the initial layout.

Every disk has two additional mirrored disks. There is a lot of redundancy since the same information is copied in three different volumes. The backup is performed in the standby switchover system, which has the tape devices connected.

At a certain point the system is stopped to have the database in a consistent state. At that moment the third mirrored disk is detached from its volume, so that two mirrored disks continue normal operation. This third mirrored disk is then passed to the switchover system, which mounts the file systems contained in the disks. It then starts the backup. Figure 6.4 shows the resulting situation.

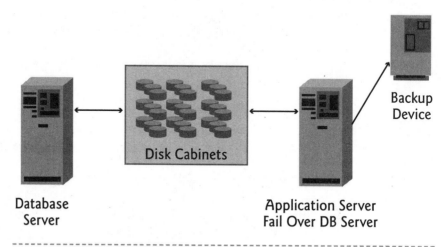

FIGURE 6.3   *Phase I of Triple Mirror*

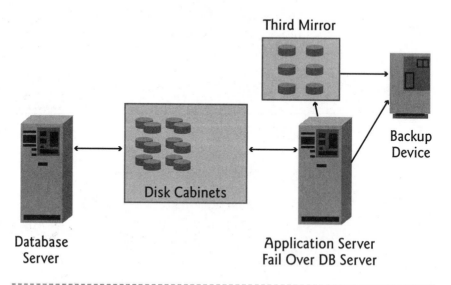

FIGURE 6.4   *Phase 2 of Triple Mirror: Disks are Detached to Standby Server*

At this point, SAP can be started again in the original system. With the convenient hardware and software, the operation of stopping

SAP, detaching the third disk, and starting the application again might take less than ten minutes.

If only one server is used, the third disk must be mounted in different locations, the backup devices must be connected to the database server, and the backup must be performed by the same server, which can degrade system performance. When the backup is finished in the standby server, the third mirror is put back online to synchronize for the next backup, without needing to stop the application again. This synchronization process might slightly affect system performance, especially input/output. The trick is careful measurement of the input/output bandwidth of the disk controllers.

The advantages of this approach are minimal downtime for offline backups and extra safety with the three mirrored copies. In case of failure before the start of synchronizing the disks, a full backup copy resides on the disk of the third mirror.

The disadvantages to this solution are that it is costly and requires many disks and disk controllers. It only allows for offline backup, as the system is briefly stopped. Synchronizing the disks online can be costly in terms of I/O and CPU.

Standby Database Server and the Roll Forward Approach

This solution consists of having an additional server, based on a complete offline copy from the database server. The standby database server can be located in a different building, even many miles away, but connected by reliable network lines.

Once both servers are in the same initial state, the original database server will constantly send the archive redo log files to the standby server, which can then be run (rolled forward) either synchronously or asynchronously so that both servers are almost in the same database situation. The only difference will be the time it takes for the archive redo logs to be sent and then applied.

This solution makes it possible to perform the backups in the standby server. While the backup is going on, archive redo logs cannot be applied, but once it is finished they are all sequentially recovered.

This solution has the drawback that recovery procedures can be more difficult. Another disadvantage is that it can be costly to maintain an additional dedicated server.

However, this approach makes it unnecessary to stop the original database system for backups. This backup solution can also serve the purpose of being part of a disaster recovery situation.

Summary of the Issue of Backup and Recovery

The following is the summary of the importance and approaches of backup and recovery strategy for SAP systems.

Why deal with this issue	Other issues affected	Solutions
❑ To avoiding losing critical business data	❑ Systems Management	❑ SAPDBA/CCMS
❑ It is the only way to recover from a logical error	❑ Performance	❑ Operating system/database backup utilities
❑ To protect business and business operations	❑ Testing	❑ Standby server and roll-forward approach
❑ It can be used for copying systems	❑ Systems Landscape	❑ Third-mirror approach
	❑ Archiving	❑ Backup hardware
	❑ High Availability	
	❑ Sizing	

Batch Processing Requirements

Batch or background processing is the part of the R/3 system that allows users to work independently. This type of noninteractive service can be used to submit programs for execution at the most convenient time, in the background. Background work processors perform this type of work.

Programs for background processing are submitted in the form of *background jobs*. The planning and administration of jobs and control of background processing are part of system management. This section deals with the issue of planning batch requirements for productive operations and the implications this can have for other mainly technical issues.

An effective background processing plan must take into consideration:

❑ The expected batch load, in terms of type and number of jobs, time for completion, and when they are executed
❑ How background work processes can be better distributed among application servers
❑ How operation modes can be defined to make better use of available resources
❑ Whether there is a batch window for processing large volumes of data, and its effect on other operative procedures, such as regular online operations or backup
❑ The influence of batch load on the performance, sizing, and availability of the system
❑ How to perform complex scheduling that is job- and time-dependent
❑ How to synchronize R/3 job execution with external jobs.

All these questions make background processing an important issue for technical implementation tasks.

Why Use Background Processing?

There are several reasons for submitting programs for background execution:

❑ The interactive user sessions are always fighting to get a free dialog work process for their requests.
❑ The maximum allowed time for online execution is defined in an SAP parameter profile (rdisp/max_wprun) which normally is set to 300 seconds. This means that for ABAP programs whose processing time exceeds that value, users would get a TIMEOUT error and an aborted transaction. To avoid this type of error, submit jobs for background processing.
❑ The most important reason to have background processing jobs is to continue working in the system while the program is executing. When working online with a long processing report, you can-

not interact with the system and must wait until it finishes or the dispatcher throws you out if you exceed the time limit. With background jobs, the system does not need user input, nor is this provided within the job definition.

Background jobs are used mainly for the following tasks:

❑ To process large amounts of data; for example, to get a quarterly report of sales, a monthly warehouse movement report, data load from external systems, etc.

❑ To execute periodic jobs without human intervention. Easy examples might be to have jobs for users wanting an everyday report with the total of incoming payments, or an R/3 system manager who must submit periodic cleaning jobs for background processing to take care of deleting obsolete data like old log files, ABAP dumps, etc.

❑ To run programs at a more convenient time than normal working hours, for example at night and on weekends, when there are usually fewer interactive users.

For example, if a report that takes two or three minutes to finish is run interactively, the R/3 session in which the report is executing will be busy until the report execution ends. During that time the user cannot interact with the session. The report could have been scheduled for background processing, by creating a background job and specifying the name of the report. When releasing the job, the system executes it in the background but gives the user the control of the R/3 session so he or she can keep on working and interacting with the system.

Background job execution is handled with the background work processes. The way to implement these will depend on the particular needs of the SAP installation.

In any case, when an R/3 system is installed for the first time, the system configures the background processing system by default in the central SAP instance, with the number of background work processes depending on the hardware configuration.

The number and location of background work processes is configurable both with SAP system profile parameters and with the use of the CCMS operation modes. With operation modes, system managers can define some work processes to work as dialog during certain hours and then switch automatically to background processes without the need of restarting the application server.

Defining Background Jobs

Starting background jobs is a two-step process: first the job is defined and then it is released. When users define a job and save it, they are actually "scheduling" it, that is, specifying the job components, the steps, the start time, and the print parameters. To schedule a job is the same thing as defining it. More precisely a "scheduled" job is a job definition that has been saved.

When users schedule programs for background processing, they are instructing the system to execute an ABAP report or an external program in the background. Scheduled background jobs will not be executed until they are released. When jobs are released they will be sent for execution to the background processing system at the specified "start time."

Jobs will be released automatically if the user is authorized to release jobs, and will automatically start execution in the background system if the "start immediately" option has been set.

Both the scheduling and releasing of jobs require authorizations. Standard SAP users have authorization that allows for scheduling jobs. However, releasing jobs is a task normally assigned to system administrators, which requires another authorization. Protecting the release of jobs with authorization enables system administrators to better monitor and maintain the background system and allows better distribution of the available resources. The drawback is that scheduling jobs is such a common task that it can put too many demands on the administrator's ability to maintain the whole system. Reserve some time for studying which users should be allowed to release their own jobs.

When users do not have release authorization, the start time or frequency they specify does not have any effect at all, except for informing the administrator in charge of releasing jobs of their preference for executing the job. Administrators or users with authorization for releasing jobs can change the start time specifications and the interval.

When scheduling jobs, users can specify several steps, each with a different report or program. Each step has its own attributes, like authorized users or print parameters. The same job can contain steps with ABAP reports and steps with external programs.

When defining jobs, users also have the option of scheduling a program as a separate job, or modifying an existing job not yet processed and adding it to the list of job steps.

Users, and especially administrators, should avoid having too many released jobs in normal operating and working hours, since the system processes the background jobs during online operation when there are available background work processes. Remember that a background job will perform the same tasks as if the functions were performed online. If a background job does lock a table or updates the database it will have an immediate result and can affect the work of online users.

An Approach to Background Processing Planning and Design

An approach for dealing with the issue of background processing consists of the following steps:

❏ Identify and classify jobs according to their function. Usually four job types are defined:
  ❏ *Central jobs* are those for administrative tasks such as periodic cleaning, reorganization, and daily monitoring tasks (examples: performance collector, spool reorganization, and so on. OSS note 16083 includes a full list).
  ❏ *Application jobs* are those needed for specific R/3 application processes. These might be periodic (the dunning program, massive billing calculation, and so on).
  ❏ *User jobs* are jobs defined by users for their regular work, like long-running reports.
  ❏ *External jobs* are used mostly for interfacing with external systems (for example, for sending faxes, loading or sending data to other applications, and so on).
❏ Make a full job list and job documentation, defining the expected run time, whether jobs are critical, who is responsible for job administration, restartability, priority, and dependencies.

❏ Distribute the jobs among available background services. This process might require the definition of additional background work processes, the configuration of operation modes (that can switch the types of work processes), or, if there are not enough resources, the need for the configuration of an additional application server to handle background.

❏ Within system management, define authorizations and clear procedures for the scheduling, releasing, and management of jobs. Also include procedures for error handling.

❏ Monitor background jobs and performance to optimize the scheduling and processing of jobs.

❏ The background processing system has an interface for external management tools, so if job scheduling conditions are too complex, complementary third-party tools might be an option.

The following chart summarizes the technical issues concerned with the planning and management of the background processing system.

Why deal with this issue	Other issues affected	Solutions
❏ To enable the continuity of business processes needing batch data processing	❏ Performance and Tuning	❏ Plan expected jobs
❏ To avoid system resource bottlenecks	❏ Availability	❏ Restrict releasing with authorization
❏ To gain user acceptance through performance	❏ Sizing	
	❏ Authorizations	❏ CCMS operation modes
❏ To maintain a "clean" and stable technical environment	❏ Systems Management	❏ CCMS job monitor
	❏ Backup Strategy	❏ Third-party scheduling tools

Printing Issues in SAP Installations

Printing is an issue that rarely shows up in the radar of the SAP project teams until the start of productive operation approaches.

Then suddenly people realize users don't get their expected printout, they don't yet have solution for barcoding, for printing critical forms which can't wait, for handling large printing volumes, or even for defining the printers in the different geographical locations without affecting system performance or saturating the network bandwidth. Not dealing with printing soon enough can have a direct effect on delaying going live and training programs.

Technically, the R/3 spool work process is the service in charge of formatting spool requests and sending them to the host spool system. Before release 4.0, there was a limit of only one spool work process per SAP dialog instance, and this could cause severe printing bottlenecks. This problem has been solved, although many other technical details must still be addressed.

When planning a printing infrastructure the following printing types must be taken into consideration:

❏ **Volume or mass printing:** Long-running printing jobs sometimes containing hundreds of pages, like the payroll
❏ **Critical printing:** The type of urgent print jobs requiring immediate output, such as invoices, production orders, etc.
❏ **Confidential printing:** The type of output that should be protected against unauthorized access, such as personnel information or budgeting decisions.

Steps in a printing strategy include:

❏ Planning the printing infrastructure, in project preparation or soon after. This will require using the ASAP printing questionnaire. Identify printing needs by departments or applications, type of printing, connection.
❏ Performing a gap analysis between the current printing infrastructure and R/3 printing requirements.
❏ Defining printer groups by printing types.
❏ Defining printers at the operating system level; documenting the print naming conventions.
❏ Defining printers at the SAP level and testing them carefully; documenting the print naming conventions.

- ❏ Appropriately sizing network bandwidth for remote or network printers that must share throughput with other types of non-R/3 printing like desktop applications.
- ❏ Planning printing contingencies; what to do in case of a printer malfunction, or in case the spool server is down.
- ❏ Monitoring printing performance and network traffic.
- ❏ Protecting confidential output printing and devices with authorizations.

For businesses with special large printing requirements there are several complementary output management solutions available on the market.

The SAP printing system provides several access methods or different ways of linking the R/3 print device with the host spooling. Since release 4.0 came out, there are additional and more convenient methods, such as defining device pools and logical devices, which can be used for contingency and even print load balancing. OSS note 19706 ("Tuning the Spooler") contains useful recommendations for matching printing types and requirements with the available access methods.

The following chart summarizes the main topics related to the issue of printing in SAP implementation projects.

Why deal with this issue	Other issues affected	Solutions
❏ To avoid business problems with critical or confidential printing ❏ To avoid delaying going live ❏ To provide full process training	❏ Systems Management ❏ Network Infrastructure ❏ Authorizations ❏ Testing ❏ Training ❏ Reporting/Development	❏ ASAP Printing Questionnaire ❏ Printing Gap Analysis ❏ Output Management tools ❏ Provide contingency solutions for critical printing ❏ OSS note 19706

Front-end Software Distribution

Here we deal with technical activities involved in installing and distributing the client software (presentation) to end-users of the R/3 applications.

As we noted in "Personalizing the System" in Chapter 5, there are many types of available front ends for end-user access. The front-end software allows users to access R/3 applications. The most frequently used and typical user interface is the classical SAPGUI.

For installing and distributing the SAPGUI software, consider the following:

❑ **Desktop requirements for software installations.** These requirements are included in the R/3 standard documentation sent along with the software kits. SAPGUI is not a very demanding software in terms of processing power; for local hard-disk installation of minimum required components only 20M of disk space is needed. The most important thing is that the desktop computer must be connected to the network and be able to access the R/3 application servers using the TCP/IP-supported protocol.

❑ **Location of users and network infrastructure.** The front-end installation strategy must consider the location of users and provide infrastructure for network access, as we have discussed. Strategy for installation on those remote users that connect through modems must be also considered.

❑ **How to install the software.** The goal, especially for large networks and a number of users is to avoid manual intervention. Options for installation are: installing locally on each PC, installing from file servers, or installing automatically with tools for software distribution (for example Microsoft SMS). SAPGUI allows for installation from the command line to ease automatic installation, so there is also the possibility of programming simple scripts that can automatically install the SAPGUI when users access their network accounts.

❑ **Where to install: hard disk or file server?** This question is closely linked to the previous one. The recommendation is to install locally on each PC hard disk and have a backup installation on the network file server. A disadvantage of local installation is the possibly large number of such installations. On the other hand, if software is installed on a file server, the network can be more demanding and if the server becomes unavailable, users will not be able to connect to the systems.

❏ **Handling upgrades.** In close relation to the previous two factors, a front-end installation and distribution strategy must take into consideration a plan for software upgrades and the effect it will have on the network, or on the job load of the people installing the software.

❏ **What to install.** Presentation software includes many optional components besides the mandatory SAPGUI. There are components such as SAPLOGON, Graphical Screen Painter, SAPforms, Excel links, and many more. The options for end-users should not be very complicated. Include SAPGUI and SAPLOGON as a minimum; then, depending on job requirements, the XXL interface, the Session Manager, the CAD Interface, the ArchiveLink Viewer, and so on. Other presentation components are used mainly by the implementation project team for development or interfacing with other components. The procedure for installation must consider how to handle the need for installing new components. An additional consideration is that installation of presentation software must be at least the same release or higher than that of the R/3 systems. For example, users with a SAPGUI 4.5B can connect to a 3.1H system, but the other way around does not work.

❏ **Online Documentation.** Access to SAP online documentation must also be planned. Documentation is usually copied from the CD to a network file server. There is a file, SAPDOCCD.INI, that includes pointers for specifying the language and location of the documentation.

❏ **Other options.** There are other presentation options besides traditional SAPGUI, like SAPGUI on JAVA using a Web Browser, the Session Manager, or even the option of personalizing access with external applications and using BAPIs.

The following chart summarizes the technical issue of installing and distributing presentation software.

Why deal with this issue	Other issues affected	Solutions
❑ Ensure user access to R/3 applications	❑ Network Infrastructure	❑ Software distribution tools
❑ Avoid problems with software upgrades	❑ Systems Management	❑ Alternative front-ends: SAPGUI on JAVA
	❑ Going Live	❑ Login scripts
	❑ Upgrade	❑ Alternative software locations

CHAPTER 7

Going Live, Continuous Change, and Productive Operation Issues

There is a feeling among companies implementing SAP that success is indicated by going live. Often this feeling is also part of the marketing effort of the supporting consulting company. Soon after that, the company realizes that going live has not finished the implementation effort, but is just the beginning of a new phase, a new way of approaching the implementation.

This new phase may have several objectives, such as: implementing new modules or application components that were not part of the initial project, adjusting and optimizing business processes, topping automation with Business Workflow, designing new reporting capabilities, tuning the systems, or adding Internet capabilities or Business Intelligence through Data Warehouse. Whatever it is called, new phase or subsequent project, after going live there are still implementation issues which must be addressed.

The fact that these implementation issues are approached after going live, does not mean that there was no previous work on them. In fact the best and most efficient way to manage production problems is to plan for them from the first project phases.

Topics covered in this chapter are:

❑ Going Llive
❑ System Management
❑ Performance and Tuning
❑ Supporting SAP: Troubleshooting
❑ Supporting SAP: Help Desk Strategy
❑ Upgrade Projects
❑ Continuous Change.

Does an SAP Project Ever Finish?

A project whose phases, tasks, and activities were clearly defined in a project plan can be finished. Ending a SAP implementation project frequently has a reality beyond what was initially planned when the project started.

SAP R/3 as integrated business software, with a philosophy and features, provides solutions for all the business areas of a company.

The application design is meant to gather the best existing business process practices and technology; its capacity for integrating complex and heterogeneous environments is outstanding, and there is constant enhancement and evolution. Finally, R/3 is a product that offers the best support warranty and continuity found on the ERP software market.

SAP's position as ERP market leader forces constant improvement in services and products. As a consequence, R/3 installations, and to some extent R/3 projects, must continue the pace by a process of continuous change.

As we have stated in several sections of this book, companies are in a process of continuous change; they find themselves needing to incorporate business and technical improvements, customize additional functionality, better respond to users and business requests, and so on. These needs, together with the nature of R/3 as a business project, lead to a very long application life; R/3 projects do have continuity.

There are, of course, many differences between the implementation project that "ends" with the "going-live" phase and projects that are in the "support and continuous change roadmap." These differences can be found in the range of applications being deployed, in the chosen implementation strategy, and in the expected life-cycle for the systems.

There are many specific examples of continuity in a SAP implementation project. Answers to the following situations lead to that continuity:

❑ What to do with historical data? When do system data become historical so that they can be taken offline from the database?
❑ What to do to manage the database efficiently when the size is too big?
❑ How to address the customizing of a new module?
❑ How to handle new enhancements or modifications coming from standard SAP release upgrades?
❑ How to manage organizational growth and adapt both the physical (infrastructure) and logical (organization and business processes) design of the system?
❑ How to proceed with the need for new user interfaces, new enabling technologies, and so on?

This is a short list of possible situations for continuous projects. In a live and changing business environment it is not so difficult to establish a stable line that takes into consideration how to handle continuous change, but it is difficult to establish a fixed line for a project end.

The Issue of Going Live

In the SAP implementation project, Going Live and Productive Support is the phase consisting of moving a preproduction environment to a live productive one. Going live marks a major milestone in an implementation project. It is the time when end users start entering data into the system and receiving valuable output and information.

The going live period can take several weeks. Right after starting production, it is characterized by:

❑ Users having problems and not knowing who can solve them
❑ Processes with real data do not work as expected
❑ Many questions on the use and meaning of screen fields
❑ Slow response time by systems and frequent reboots of the application
❑ Printing that does not work
❑ Support personnel who are overwhelmed
❑ Strange errors are displayed on the screen (i.e. an ABAP dump).

In order to make as smooth a transition to R/3 as possible and to get a stable operation as soon as possible, intensive support and support lines must be ensured during the first weeks of operation.

To reach this milestone, the project team must be well prepared for the periods before, during, and after going live. Most important, end-users must be well trained and know how the support strategy works. Going live is a milestone and a critical phase of the implementation requiring the following sets of activities:

❑ **Final preparations for going live**, including the last part of system tests and core transactions. This involves carrying out the transport of customizing settings and other repository objects from development of a quality system to production. There is a massive load of master data. The last part of end-user training and the Help Desk and support plan must be implemented. All system tests and functional tests should have been performed and verified, and critical issues addressed and corrected.

❑ **Cutover process.** Cutover is the final set of activities to get a production system ready for going live. It includes additional transport of customizing settings or repository objects, final conversions and data loads, including manual inputs and the transfer of items or business documents still open on old systems. It also includes the verification and scheduling for execution of interfaces with other systems, when required.

❑ **Going live.** Project management and the steering committee make the decision to go live when all preparations are accomplished and verified: training is complete, technical infrastructure is ready, data have been correctly loaded, system management is prepared, business processes have been verified, and the support strategy and resources are in place.

❑ **First weeks of production support.** This period is characterized by the typical problems described above. In order to make a smoother transition to R/3, a support plan designed in previous phases of the project should now be in place to resolve user and technical issues as soon as possible. These first weeks are also characterized by the work of systems managers to closely monitor daily transactions and performance bottlenecks, in order to take corrective action to tuning and optimize the systems.

Critical to the first stages of switching to R/3 is to have a clear support strategy communicated and understood by the organization. The goal must be a swift problem resolution process, the introduction of a new LOP (List of Open Points), and the procedure to address those points.

On the technical side of the implementation, during the going live phase system managers must closely monitor the workload and performance of the systems, the errors, the longest-running transactions, whether printing is working as expected, security issues, the operation of the background processing systems, and batch workload. These issues are address by an established system management strategy and operation.

Completing the going live phase officially ends the implementation project and is the start of the continuous change implementation phase (forever?).

The following sections in this chapter deal more closely with the issues of productive operation after going live.

Pre-production to Production

Technically, going live requires a production system ready for end-user work. To reach that goal, customizing has been completed, and programs for data loading and interfacing are ready and have been tested, usually in development and quality assurance systems. How is the transfer made? How is the system cleaned? What about test data?

When a proper system landscape has been designed and configured, the best method is always the SAP recommended one: organizing the customizing and development projects, creating change requests, testing, and transporting. This should be done from the beginning of the realization phase. If there are mistakes or changes, corrections can also be transported without side effects. Often lack of knowledge of system landscape issues and unclear procedures plague installations that do not follow this standard.

A full client can be exported from the development or quality assurance system to production. Since a client copy does not include repository objects, which are client independent, this often causes many programs, tables, or repository objects to be missing in the target system.

A third transfer method is to do a homogeneous system copy from the development system to the production system. Then, for cleaning purposes, a client copy with only customizing can be performed in the target system, with later deletion of the original client. This has the advantage of ensuring that everything (customizing, repository and data) is copied, but it also copies unwanted programs or other objects.

Soon After: Some Stories

Soon after the initial excitement and problems of going live there are many dangers waiting behind the organization's door:

❑ Consultants are gone
❑ Key users have a better or different job position, and many migrate to better-paying companies
❑ Documentation is not updated, not handy, difficult to find
❑ Roles and responsibilities disappear behind Alice's mirror
❑ Everybody is too busy to teach new employees.

On many projects during the implementation phases, SAP customers had an excellent team of external consultants and internal analysts, key users, and IT. Implementation was smooth and issues were resolved quickly. A few months after going live, there were no resources to handle all the support issues and problems to keep the system smooth and answer questions that arose.

This is a common situation that emphasizes the need to have post-implementation expertise, up to the point that internal organization is able to handle the questions, problems, and situations that must be investigated. But what does having post-implementation expertise mean? It means managing the knowledge acquired during the project. Either the knowledge is transferred and kept within the organization, or it must be searched for outside. This is a common issue on any kind of project, and in any kind of business: knowledge can be a critical asset. Chapter 4 included an overview of Knowledge Management issues on implementation projects.

Solutions for Going Live

SAP and its consulting partners offer several services to help companies in their going-live process. Well-known services are the *Going-Live Check* and *EarlyWatch*.

Going-Live Check is a SAP consulting service which verifies that the main requirements and preparations have been carried out; it checks on systems resources and the main productive and support strategy, and gives advice on open or weak points found during the check. EarlyWatch is a preventive maintenance service, mainly targeted at the technical infrastructure and systems performance. It is also a common service for continuous support and optimization of R/3 systems.

Very important to the technical strategy for going live are correct use and clear procedures for transporting the customizing and repository objects to a productive environment. This is the only way to guarantee a correct verification of changes and change requests within an R/3 system landscape. Related to organizational preparations, the smooth transition to a new system is also a goal of the change management program, as described in Chapter 4.

For the "soon after" problem and consulting and implementation support, there are knowledge management techniques, tools, and disciplines that will help lower post-implementation costs as well as keep and increase the knowledge assets within organizations.

The following chart summarizes the most important points to take into consideration when dealing with the issue of going live.

Why deal with this issue	Other issues affected	Solutions
❑ To make a smooth transition to new system	❑ End-User Training	❑ Going-Live Check
	❑ Performance	❑ EarlyWatch
❑ To ensure business operations	❑ System Management	❑ Transport Management System
	❑ Support	
❑ To achieve the goals and objectives of the project	❑ Sizing	❑ Change Management Program
	❑ Testing	
❑ To reach the expected benefits of implementing an integrated system	❑ Change Management	❑ Knowledge Management tools

Systems Management

As we have stated elsewhere, the issue of managing the system while providing technical support is important before and after going live because there is need for systems management from the moment the development or integration system is installed and customizing is being performed.

Systems management is the continuous process of monitoring and administering, supporting, optimizing, and securing the systems, with the objective of a stable platform for smooth execution of business processes.

The best systems management is proactive, anticipating tasks and problems, rather than reactive, just waiting for tasks and problems to resolve themselves. A proactive approach to systems management can be achieved by having operating procedures and a daily and periodic checklist, in which the main systems indicators are checked and issues resolved.

Topics concerned with systems management include:

What are the roles in R/3 systems management?

Ideally, systems managers of SAP systems should play several roles, as defined in the operations manual. This will depend on the size, complexity, and scope of SAP systems. Very complex installations require a clear definition of systems administration roles such as: R/3 systems manager, database administrator, network administrator, R/3 operators, transport system administrator, security manager, authorizations administrator, desktop infrastructure administrator, R/3 technical consultant or supervisor, and so on.

ASAP includes an Operations Manual template that can be used as a starting point for defining administration procedures, roles, and responsibilities.

How and when do we train; what skill sets are necessary?

Technical training is a very time consuming activity in SAP implementations because there are many different and complex tasks to be performed, most of them continuously. The complexity of the training is closely related to the many components and layers of the technical infrastructure: operating system, database, R/3 basis components, data dictionary, network, client/server computing, security, authorizations, and, perhaps, development.

SAP has an extensive education offering on technical training, including several Knowledge products and self-training material. The availability of resources, such as a test system, help in the technical learning process. Often hardware partners have R/3 technical consulting services that can aid in the initial phases of systems management while transferring knowledge and experience to customers. Skill sets are introduced in a following section.

How many people are needed to administer SAP systems?

In implementation projects there is always the question of required resources. For instance, if an implementation project lasts for a year, how many basis consultants are needed, and are they needed all the time, or just in some phases? The answer is never accurate. What follows is an estimate based on experience and customer survey answers.

Small and not too complex R/3 installations for up to 50 users and two systems landscapes might have enough resources with two system managers doing most of the tasks, and with the help of external resources for occasional help.

More complex installations and those customers in a continuous process of adding new technical components will require a much larger staff. Experience has shown me that installations implementing at least four application modules, with more than 200 users, more than 100 printers, connecting R/3 with EDI, fax, and external devices, and distributed over several geographical locations, require a minimum of four people for systems management and support, and that is when the appropriate skill sets exist.

Who will support system managers?

System managers can get support and refer their problems or questions to SAP using the OSS or SAP Customer Support. The support of a hardware or software partner will often be required to solve problems with the servers or operating system components. The best support for system managers is to have an updated and accurate documentation of their tasks, roles and responsibilities. The Knowledge Warehouse (infoDB), discussed in a previous chapter, not only advances training but also manages and searches documentation.

Skills Sets for Systems Managers

Project managers and other responsible people in the organization, such as the IT manager, often have questions about the skill sets necessary for the job positions of systems management within the project team.

Here is an overview of the technical areas that need to be supported by system managers or technical consultants:

- ❑ R/3 Administration
  - ❑ Installations
  - ❑ User administration
  - ❑ Security and profile administration
  - ❑ Configuration and management with CCMS: monitoring, operation modes
  - ❑ Client copies
  - ❑ Transport system administration
  - ❑ Management of batch
  - ❑ Frontend installation and distribution strategy
  - ❑ Administration of spool system and printing
  - ❑ Configuring R/3 for remote connection with SAP
  - ❑ Defining R/3-related alerts within the CCMS monitors
  - ❑ Correcting bugs by applying OSS notes
  - ❑ Applying patches (Hot Packages, Legal Change Packages, kernel patches)
  - ❑ Workload analysis and performance tuning
  - ❑ Supporting the functional team with data loads and interfaces
  - ❑ Assisting in the technical areas of cross applications such as ALE, archiving or workflow
  - ❑ Assisting in the connection of external software or devices, such as fax, EDI, mail, GIS, CAD, and so on
  - ❑ Assisting in upgrade projects
- ❑ Database Administration
  - ❑ Design and maintenance of the database backup and recovery strategy
  - ❑ Assisting in tuning the database
  - ❑ Database reorganizations
  - ❑ Managing database space allocation
  - ❑ Rebuilding missing indices or creating new ones
  - ❑ Defining database alerts
  - ❑ Defining the database administration and operation procedures
  - ❑ Planning and design for database preventive maintenance

- ❏ Securing access to the database
- ❏ Assisting developers in tuning customer programs or reports
- ❏ Performing recovery tests
- ❏ Design and documentation of database administration procedures
- ❏ Systems Administration
    - ❏ Installation and maintenance of the operating system
    - ❏ Setup and configuration of the disk volumes and file systems
    - ❏ Assisting in operating system-related tuning
    - ❏ Installation of operating system patches or corrections
    - ❏ Monitoring usage and tuning performance
    - ❏ Backup and recovery
    - ❏ Installing and configuration of additional software
    - ❏ Automating periodic system tasks
    - ❏ Providing support for hardware maintenance or upgrades
    - ❏ Configuring network protocols
    - ❏ Maintaining shared file systems
    - ❏ Controlling system security.
- ❏ Network Administration
    - ❏ Design and configuration of the R/3 server network and the R/3 access network
    - ❏ Configuration and maintenance of the remote connection to SAP
    - ❏ Managing network security
    - ❏ Maintaining the saprouter
    - ❏ Assisting in the configuration of remote connections with R/3
    - ❏ Providing access for remote users
    - ❏ Supporting the setup and connection of external services like Web browsers or the Internet Transaction Server (ITS)
    - ❏ Configuring and maintaining routers and other network devices.

R/3 includes many tools and utilities for managing and monitoring the R/3 systems. An introduction to system administration and the CCMS is included in Chapter 10.

Having an Administration and Operations manual and a process of incidence logging can decrease the time needed to solve problems when similar situations have occurred previously and the resolution procedure is known. The easiest reference procedure for system managers is to search the OSS or request SAP's support.

Planning Systems Management

The process of managing the R/3 system can be eased by careful planning during the implementation phase. Activities to be performed during previous phases include:

- ❑ Training the technical team
- ❑ Planning technical infrastructure and scalability
- ❑ Designing, writing, and maintaining technical documentation
- ❑ Testing systems infrastructure and systems management procedures
- ❑ Carrying out advanced training of the technical team
- ❑ Getting acquainted with the SAP support lines and services
- ❑ Designing a clear Help Desk and support strategy and communicating efficiently
- ❑ Focusing on proactive systems management.

Operation Checklist

One of the best ways to perform proactive systems management is to do a daily and periodic monitoring of the status of the main systems components. This is the operation daily checklist, usually carried out by R/3 operations. The following tables include most of the R/3 indicators that must be periodically checked.

While most checks are performed using R/3 standard transactions, some must be performed at the operating system level using operating system applications and tools.

Checks at the host operating system level and network level include:

R/3 Transaction	Description	Purpose of the Check
—	Status of servers	Check that all R/3 servers are up and running
RZ02	System Monitor	From within R/3, check that all systems are running in their scheduled operating mode Also display the alert view and analyze problems
—	Disk space	Check that no file system is full
—	Backup status	Check the result of backup when it is launched with OS applications or other external software
SM51	SAP Servers	Display all available application servers
SM50	Process Overview	Display the status of processes (continuous daily monitoring task)
OS06	OS Monitor	Display the status of the main OS indicators and analyze if figures indicate problems
AL16	OS Alert Monitor	Display OS alerts for correcting and documenting problems
OS03	Parameter Changes in OS	Check if some changes have been done at the system kernel
—	LAN/WAN	Check the LAN/WAN connections
SMGW	Gateway Monitor	Check gateway connection status
ST08/ST09	Network Alert Monitor	Display, analyze, and document any detected network problems

Checking the R/3 environment includes:

R/3 Transaction	Description	Purpose of the Check
SM21	System log	Display and analyze warning and error messages generated in the previous hours. Errors that generate short dumps should be quickly corrected and documented

continued on next page

R/3 Transaction	Description	Purpose of the Check
ST22	ABAP Dump Analysis	All ABAP dumps should be displayed and analyzed
SM04/AL08	User overview	Display users and their activity. Check unauthorized access and logon balancing. Are there any phantom users (users who have lost their connections)?
SM37	Background jobs	Check that all expected background jobs run successfully and periodic jobs are scheduled and released for the next run. Check the jobs log. Communicate canceled jobs to their owner users.
AL01	SAP Alert Monitor	Check SAP systems alert. Communicate red alerts to system managers.
RZ01	Graphical Job Monitor	Check the runtime statistics for background jobs. This is procedure for optimizing performance of a batch, and for fine tuning the scheduling of jobs and distribution of background work processes.
SM13	Update Records	Check whether the update process is running and active. Aborted update transactions should be analyzed and corrected.
SM12	Lock Entries	Check lock entries. Those entries that remain for a long time in the lock table should be analyzed and corrected.
SP01	Spool Request Overview	Check problems with spool and output requests. Check logs and possible causes of printing problems. Check printer connections and host spoolers. Check possible problems on PC or front-end printing.
SP12	TemSe Administration	Check the consistency of the temporary sequential database and launch a reorganization if this was not scheduled in a background job.

continued on next page

R/3 Transaction	Description	Purpose of the Check
SE01/SE09/ SE10	Transport System Logs	Check all transport logs from the previous period, analyze warnings and error messages and communicate them to the responsible person who requested the transport.
STMS	TP Transport Log/ Transport System at the OS level	Check warning and error messages from the SLOG file corresponding to the TP transport control program.
ST03	Workload Analysis	Display and check the main performance and statistical values of the system. Average response time by process type gives a good idea of possible performance or system problems.
ST02	Buffer Tune Analysis	Display and check the quality of R/3 buffers and analyze red spots (free space problems, swaps, and so on).
SM35	Batch Input Logs	Display and check the periodic batch input logs and communicate errors to the application responsible for correction.
AL11	Display SAP directories	Display the work directory and search for log and error files from the SAP instance. Report any warning or error.

Checking the database is one of the activities most critical to ensuring the consistency and stable operation of R/3 systems. This can be done using SAP tools (*sapdba*) for ORACLE and INFORMIX database, or by using standard R/3 transactions or specific database management system utilities.

R/3 Transaction	Description	Purpose of the Check
—	Check free space	Check and verify the free space on database data devices (tablespaces, dbspaces, etc.) and check space left on the log directory

continued on next page

R/3 Transaction	Description	Purpose of the Check
—	Check DB logs	Check the database alert log
DB12	SAPDBA Logs	Verify the log of last backup and free space in the log directory. Verify the log of the last backup of archive files when necessary.
DB02	Storage Management	Display the status and growth of the database. Monitor the percentage of free space. Monitor database fragmentation and optimizer statistics when necessary.
	Missing Indices	Monitor whether there are missing indices in the data dictionary of the database.
	Critical Space Objects	Check for the existence of any critical object that could cause database problems when it grows
ST04	Database Logs	Display the database error log.
—	DB Consistency Check	Perform a database consistency check
AL02	Database Alert Monitor	Display, acknowledge, and analyze all the database alerts.

SAP Operation and Maintenance: Basic Laws

The following list was first introduced in the *SAP R/3 Handbook* and has now been updated. My experience in several SAP implementations has indicated some operational laws when an SAP system is in a productive state. I am sure this list is not complete, and that you can probably enlarge it. It could be shortened by automating most the entries into fewer, more complete checks.

These are some laws for the technical administration and operation of SAP systems, and in general for planning and design of the technical infrastructure:

❏ Daily tasks are daily!

❑ Do not undersize your SAP systems. Be especially generous with the amount of memory for your application servers.

❑ Backup strategy is the cornerstone to safety. Do not leave room for unconsidered events to happen.

❑ Have enough disks ready and even preconfigured to add extra space to your SAP file systems.

❑ Check database-critical objects. Do not let table spaces grow beyond 85%.

❑ Get (ask for) a test server. It can be useful for operating system, database, or SAP upgrades; also for SAP transports and for a sound and safe backup and recover strategy. Before taking anything to a productive state, test it.

❑ Log your incidences from the very beginning, no matter how silly the solution was. The question is not to find out a wrong permission in a file, but to avoid the situation the next time it happens (and it will).

❑ Monitor your network. SAP client/server R/3 relies on the network. Even if the SAP system is up and running, a network breakdown will have a negative impact on the availability of productive deployment of the system.

❑ Do not forget printers. Have you ever seen the face of a trucker waiting for his transport route for more than half an hour?

❑ Think of what procedures are in place in case SAP becomes unavailable for a long period of time (*long* is of course a subjective qualifier, ranging from 10 minutes to several days). Do not think of how much money the company will lose because of this (this can cause depressions and insomnia).

❑ Contract for the EarlyWatch service. Prevention is better than cure!

❑ Design and communicate a clear procedure for end-user technical support. Don't just put a nice framework on a Web page!

❑ Optimize the infamous Z programs (customer programs). For an unknown reason these are always the programs with longest run-times.

❑ Put a high-availability system in your SAP-life.

Systems Management Summary

Systems management will be the longest activity throughout the SAP life-cycle. As experience is gained through daily administration operations, new projects, and continuous change, there are a few challenges to ensure and guarantee the smooth operation and stability of the R/3 systems. A well-designed system landscape and accurate systems sizing are extremely important for reaching the objective of keeping operations smooth.

Knowledge in the many technical areas and skill sets needed for systems management can be achieved by training, as well as by occasional help from R/3 technical consultants.

R/3 includes many tools to help system administrators in the management and monitoring of systems. There are also many third-party products in the area of systems management, proactive monitoring, database utilities, and backup-and-restore solutions, among others. There are several packages for auditing system usage, additional scheduling utilities, and automatic calls when alerts arise.

The following chart summarizes the issue of systems management in SAP implementation projects and post-implementation support.

Why deal with this issue	Other issues affected	Solutions
❑ To ensure the correct maintenance and the smooth operation of SAP systems	❑ Performance	❑ Administration and Operations Handbook
	❑ Systems Landscape	
	❑ Sizing	❑ CCMS
❑ To support business operations with a stable system	❑ Training	❑ Third-party tools
	❑ Support and Troubleshooting	❑ Advanced training and knowledge management
❑ To help ensure maximum performance and good response times	❑ Going Live	

Performance and Tuning

Performance is the measure of a system's response time to user requests, either interactively or in batch. Performance problems in R/3 systems can hurt the overall acceptance of the systems as well as cause serious financial damage to companies. Therefore this issue must be seriously considered and planned for. Performance and tuning are issues closely linked to systems monitoring and administration.

Performance is affected by following factors:

❑ Systems sizing and hardware resources
❑ Disk input/output throughput
❑ Network infrastructure
❑ Number of concurrent users and workload transaction profile
❑ Background processing
❑ Online reporting
❑ Printing strategy
❑ Locally developed programs and transactions
❑ Size and fragmentation of database
❑ Service distribution
❑ Configuration of technical infrastructure
❑ Buffer resets by transports
❑ Other allied services and applications.

Tuning is the process of optimizing performance, and consists of setting and configuring hardware and software components with the goal of having better system response times. In other words, it is the technique by which the systems do the same processes in less time. To achieve optimal available resources, the system manager and technical consultants must closely monitor systems workload profiles and statistics and take corrective actions. These actions can be performed on:

❑ Scalability, by configuring additional hardware resources if CPU or memory bottlenecks are detected
❑ Operating system parameters and configuration: memory management, disk input/output, and swapping
❑ Database parameters and design

❏ SAP parameters: buffers, processes, instance profile parameters
❏ R/3 service distribution: batch, printing, operation modes
❏ Optimization of programs and reporting
❏ Optimization of database accesses
❏ Archiving.

During the going-live phase and production support activities for a continuous improvement of performance take place. This is usually done by workload analysis and tuning.

Often the most time-consuming transactions are those which have been locally developed. It happens that end users don't like to go through so many R/3 screens to perform a single transaction, so they ask the consulting company to make a new transaction chaining required fields into a single screens. This is a dangerous process, since what used to be several dialog steps, processed at the clerical level (usually measured as a 30-second think time between two dialog steps), is now processed in a row by the system; this can affect performance, especially in those operations where the business process includes dozens of line items.

Frequent transports into a productive system have a negative effect on performance, since, when programs are changed and transported, they must be reloaded into the instance buffers. This causes buffer fragmentation and might provoke buffer swaps and decrease buffer quality.

Workload Analysis

Workload analysis is done by the performance monitors; the goal of the information provided is to optimize the system's performance. This analysis finds out what causes problems and bottlenecks, and those programs or transactions that have a larger than average response time, or consume more system resources. The analysis of the performance data of the R/3 system and the Performance Monitor are the base tools for finding problems and bottlenecks in the system and can be used to take optimization actions.

Workload analysis is based on various monitors:

❑ The performance database of the *Main Workload monitor* (transaction ST03) displays important information about the performance status of the systems.

❑ The *Work Process overview* can be used to display information about current processes status and can find stopped processes or long-running transactions.

❑ The *Operating System monitor* can be used to display important information about operating system activity such as CPU utilization, memory, swap, or disk utilization, and top CPU processes. The monitor collects both snapshot and statistical information.

❑ The *Database Monitor* shows the status of the database and the main indicators of the quality of SQL access, data cache, dictionary cache, and so on. It also displays information about the status and fragmentation of the data files .

❑ The *Buffers Monitor* provides useful information on the quality of the instance parameters for the different SAP buffers and the use of the main memory. Bottlenecks on buffer usage are usually indicated by an excessive number of swaps.

When analyzing performance problems, first analyze whether the full system and every user are affected by the problems, if it always occurs and it is reproducible, or whether it only happens occasionally.

There are many solutions or approaches for improving performance and tuning the system:

❑ Contracting for maintenance services like EarlyWatch

❑ Proactive monitoring and systems management, and performing a documented daily and periodic checklist

❑ Analyzing statistics and load profiles using the Workload Monitor

❑ Checking the quality of development by debugging and optimizing local programs and transactions; SAP tools such as debugger, SQL-Trace, and Runtime Analysis can be a help in this process

❑ Performing extensive system and stress tests

❑ Distributing the load among available instances and servers

❑ Using offline reporting tools

❑ Archiving and deleting obsolete data from the database

❑ Applying patches and corrections to standard programs.

The following chart summarizes the issue of performance and tuning in R/3 systems.

Why deal with this issue	Other issues affected	Solutions
❏ To have the best possible response time for users	❏ Sizing	❏ Workload Analysis
	❏ Systems Management	
❏ To better distribute R/3 services	❏ Systems Landscape	❏ OSS/EarlyWatch
	❏ Reporting	❏ Remote Consulting
❏ Because it is an implicit task of systems management to have a stable platform	❏ Development	❏ Stress tests
	❏ Archiving	❏ Development quality Check
	❏ Applying Patches	❏ Archiving
		❏ Offline reporting

Supporting SAP: The Help Desk

Support for R/3 systems consists of solving all types of problems and questions that arise during the operation of SAP systems. Supporting SAP users and SAP systems is one of the main activities during and after going live. If support is not provided in an efficient and timely manner, users will not be able to perform their jobs as expected, systems will not be stable, many questions will remain unanswered, and many application and technical issues will remain unresolved. This can severely affect business operations.

Reasons why problems exist or can arise include:

❏ System bugs
❏ Human error
❏ Lack of knowledge
❏ Problems with continuous data migration, conversion and interfaces
❏ Technical infrastructure problems with PCs, printing, batch, or network connections.

Problems are better solved when post-implementation support is planned in the first phases of implementation. Typical mistakes and problems in establishing support staff or Help Desk procedures after implementation include:

❑ Lack of proactive support and communication
❑ Lack of training
❑ Poorly documented support requests
❑ An unclear Help Desk process.

A good support strategy is based on proactive systems and application management, as well as on a well-established, trained, and organized Help Desk. Figure 7.1 shows one of many possible models of a Help Desk process within an SAP support strategy.

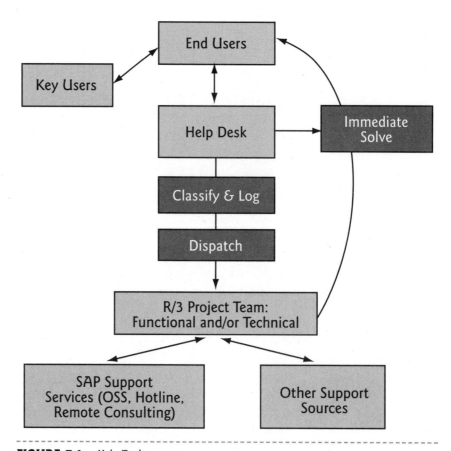

FIGURE 7.1   *Help Desk process*

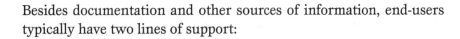

Besides documentation and other sources of information, end-users typically have two lines of support:

❑ Key users or department super-users who are normally close to business operations and who helped during the implementation phase. These people can sometimes help end-users with basic operations questions, doubts, or problems related to the applications they must use.
❑ Help Desk, a the central source of support.

On many occasions, the Help Desk can provide an immediate solution or answer to end-users. For instance, when the Help Desk is aware of a network problem in one of the lines, it can advise how to change a password, SAPGUI connection parameters, and so on. Most typical Help Desks will log and prioritize user calls and dispatch them to appropriate expert support.

Expert support is normally provided by the R/3 project team, both functional and technical, and even by developers. This group of people is more knowledgeable in business processes and systems functioning. They are often responsible for calling back users with an answer and documenting the problem for further reference.

Finally, when the project team is not able to solve a problem, they can use SAP support services such as OSS or the SAP Customer Support and log a call. Other sources of support include hardware partners, the database vendor, or other software or service companies.

Besides having a defined Help Desk process, there are several other requirements for establishing the Help Desk, including:

❑ Defining what will be supported
❑ Establishing levels of priorities
❑ Establishing hours of operation and methods for contacting support and logging calls
❑ Establishing standards and procedures for support
❑ Establishing service levels and response times for call-back
❑ Assigning Help Desk roles and responsibilities
❑ Establishing communication channels
❑ Defining Help Desk logistics: equipment, phones, faxes, facilities
❑ Designing the Help Desk application
❑ Defining the skills and resources needed

❑ Managing the escalation process
❑ Developing ongoing training.

The number of support staff and the skills required will largely depend on the size of the user base, as well as the scope (modules) and status (continuous change and open projects) of the R/3 implementation. For small and closed implementations, a small number of support staff will be necessary, whereas large and open implementations may require a large number of support staff, both technical and functional, including developers.

In cases of medium to large and complex implementations, a larger support and Help Desk staff will be required. This size is closely related to that of the resources needed after implementation (after going live).

Common recommendations for resources after going live are:

❑ Keep at least two consultants or business super-users for each of the R/3 application modules being deployed.
❑ Built a strong technical team, with at least two basis experts plus a system manager and a good database administrator. At least two of these must be familiar with how to monitor performance and tune the systems.
❑ One or two ABAP programmers are required when there are additional reporting needs or developments, and also to upgrade projects.

Large companies and value-contract SAP customers with several R/3 installations and intensive support requirements, are advised to create a Customer Competence Center (CCC).

The task of beginning the planning process for defining post-implementation support is included in the project preparation phase within the ASAP Roadmap.

The next chart summarizes the issue of defining a support and Help Desk strategy.

Why deal with this issue	Other issues affected	Solutions
❑ Help end-users to perform their business operations	❑ Systems Management	❑ Plan the Help Desk
❑ Ensure a stable platform	❑ Troubleshooting	❑ OSS/SAP Customer Support
❑ Obtain user acceptance of the systems	❑ Training	
	❑ Communications	❑ Support Sources
		❑ Customer Competence Center
		❑ Help Desk and call-handling applications

Supporting SAP: Troubleshooting

Previous sections investigated the way problems or errors are discovered or incidences are detected; either from end-users through the Help Desk or by a proactive monitoring and systems management. Intimately linked with the support process, and the cornerstone of efficient support, is a defined and proven method for problem resolution and troubleshooting in the technical, development, and functional areas.

Troubleshooting documentation and methods tell support personnel how to analyze and find the cause of problems; this leads to corrective action in order to solve them. The most difficult task in correcting problems (as in healing sickness) is to make the most accurate diagnostic.

Functional problems must be analyzed and solved by the R/3 project team or by consultants. Basic to diagnosing functional problems is to be able to reproduce them, and when needed, debug them.

Resolution will often mean changing customizing settings, applying patches to standard R/3 programs, or modifying locally developed ones. The process will require making changes in the development system and then testing them before transporting the new settings or objects into the productive system.

A Basic Technical Troubleshooting Handbook

A technical troubleshooting handbook, documenting the basic procedures for problem resolution and problem escalation, is a valuable tool for system managers or technical support personnel. Here is a brief overview or scheme of such a handbook. It can be completed for specific hardware, operating systems, databases, and R/3 system landscapes:

❑ The first step is to identify and analyze the problem
  ❑ Initial Analysis
    – Identify if something has changed: software or hardware installation, scripts, profile parameters, database structure.
    – System (hardware) is down
      • Check console messages
      • Reboot and keep important system log files
      • Check hardware components
        • Analyze with diagnosis tools
        • Escalation procedure: call hardware support
  ❑ Check main log files
    – Analyze with diagnosis tools
    – Startup/shutdown log files
    – Operating system log files
  ❑ Identify other problem in: startup/shutdown, disks and operating systems, database, operational R/3, performance.
❑ Startup and shutdown problems (R/3 and application servers):
  ❑ Check processes or services at operating system level
  ❑ Check that database is up
  ❑ Check the connection with the database (i.e. tnsping, R3trans -d)
  ❑ Are file systems full?
  ❑ Check network problems in the server network
  ❑ For problems after backup, check the backup log
  ❑ Check problems after system crash
  ❑ Check problems with the PDC file server

- ❑ Check file permissions and authorizations
- ❑ Manually start up or shut down the database and then the application server
- ❑ Check hosts and services files
- ❑ Operating system problems:
  - ❑ Check operating system log and event viewers
  - ❑ Check disks and file systems
  - ❑ Check directories and permissions
  - ❑ Check path names
  - ❑ Check security
- ❑ Database problems:
  - ❑ Starting and stopping database
    - – Refer to startup problems
    - – Check database specific error log file
  - ❑ Check database storage status
  - ❑ Check database error numbers
  - ❑ Check database alerts
- ❑ R/3 application operation problems:
  - ❑ Are all users affected?
  - ❑ Is there no work at all, or just limited work?
  - ❑ Check that application servers are available (SM51)
  - ❑ Check standard monitoring transactions: SM50, SM04, SM12, SM13, ST22, SM37, SP01.
  - ❑ Check trace files on the work directory (/usr/sap/ < SID > / < instance > /work)
  - ❑ Check SAP Systems Alerts
  - ❑ Analyze database problems
- ❑ Specific operational problems:
  - ❑ Problems with Printing
    - – Check network
    - – Check SP01 / SPAD spool request logs
    - – Check system log
  - ❑ Problems with Batch Input
    - – Check directories and files
    - – Check SM35 logs
    - – Check system log
  - ❑ Problems with lock entries
    - – Check lock entries

- Check update process
- Call user

❑ Problems with update process
- Check update process
- Check database
- Check network connections

❑ Problems with Enqueue
- Check database
- Check instance parameters
- Check operating system processes

❑ Problems with message server
- Check processes
- Check network
- Check log files at work directory

❑ Problems with background processing
- Check jobs log
- Check background system consistency
- Check file systems
- Check system log

❑ Performance problems:
  ❑ Workload analysis
  ❑ Debugging
  ❑ Runtime Analysis
  ❑ SQL Trace
  ❑ Check for Operating System problems
  ❑ Check disk for input/output bottlenecks

❑ Resolution process:
  ❑ Search OSS or SAPnet for hints, solutions, or workarounds
  ❑ Escalation: enter the message on SAP Hotline or OSS
  ❑ Enter the problem on a hardware partner hotline
  ❑ Follow problems actions and SAP indications
  ❑ Apply patches and corrections, test and verify results

❑ Document problem and resolution.

The following chart summarizes why it is important to have a troubleshooting process in place during and after SAP implementation.

Why deal with this issue	Other issues affected	Solutions
❑ To have a detailed problem analysis method	❑ Systems Management	❑ SAP Support Services (OSS, SAPnet)
❑ To speed up the problem resolution process	❑ Help Desk	❑ Hardware partner
❑ To avoid further problems	❑ Performance and Tuning	❑ Database vendor
❑ To facilitate the search for a stable platform		❑ Knowledge Management tools
		❑ Troubleshooting handbook
		❑ RRR Troubleshooting Roadmap

Upgrade Projects

Upgrade projects consist of migrating an R/3 release to a newer one. The degree of difficulty of this process can range from very simple to very complex, and the main variable that affects it is the degree and quantity of modification to standard SAP, as well as to local developments based on standard SAP programs.

There are of course other variables. On the technical side these include the number and size of the systems or volume of the database. On the business application side, an upgrade can be used to solve business processes not fully covered or not covered at all in a previous version of SAP.

Because an upgrade means changes, some of the change management activities to be undertaken are risk assessment, training, communications, and knowledge transfer. The organization must be prepared for a new change, possibly less difficult than the initial implementation effort.

An important factor in any upgrade project, which becomes critical to the realization of the upgrade on productive systems, is the *time needed for completion*, since it will affect systems availability and therefore business operations.

A new release might require additional infrastructure, such as disk space or processing power. In this case a *new systems sizing* should be requested during the planning phases of the upgrade project.

With respect to the roles and *resources needed* when upgrading R/3 releases, a team similar to that which performed initial implementation is required. The team will be in charge of analyzing the impact of possible business changes, setting up new configuration parameters, developing or modifying ABAP programs and reports, and preparing the technical infrastructure for the new release.

An upgrade may be different in many aspects if performed on a development system rather than on the production system. Though the process will start by upgrading the development system, it can be helpful to have a similar system, or a test system, where the actual productive upgrade can be carried out and *business functions tested* with real data.

An additional factor to consider is what *training* will be needed for both end-users and the project team. Plan for time and resources to gain skills in the new functions, changes, or enhancements provided by a new version.

Approach to an Upgrade Project

Careful planning must take into consideration the special circumstances of inhouse development and customized business processes. An approach to an upgrade project plan can be found on the ASAP Upgrade Roadmap, though the plan, tasks, and activities are limited to projects whose previous implementation did not include enhancements based on standard programs.

SAP's upgrade tools include the PREPARE program to verify and check systems and warn of requirements to be met before starting an actual upgrade.

During the actual realization of an R/3 release upgrade each system in the landscape is upgraded in the order defined within the transport routes: it is usual to start with development, then progress to the quality assurance system, and then to production. Time and effort needed for upgrading each system will probably not be comparable because of hardware differences and database size. Problems and errors detected on previous upgrades will be better solved in following updates. The order of the upgrade is also important for transporting object adjustments, which will only be possible by following defined transport routes.

R/3 includes two main modification adjustment transactions, known as SPDD and SPAU, that are used for adjusting dictionary and program objects that could have been modified on customer systems before the upgrade. In good upgrade projects the adjustments are performed only on development systems that will later be transported to QAS and production.

The adjustment of modifications is performed first during the actual upgrade, where the tool will stop so that developers and consultants can analyze the differences between modified objects and new objects. When doing this process, customers can decide to keep the old modifications and adjust them to new objects, or to keep new objects by overwriting previous ones. The SPDD and SPAU transactions show a list of the modified SAP objects.

Especially in installations with complex modifications, the adjustment process can be one of the more time consuming activities of the upgrade. It is therefore vital to perform the adjustments on the development system so that on subsequent systems these objects can be automatically transported.

The upgrade usually is limited to maintaining the operation and business processes as they were before the upgrade. The main problems are the locally developed transactions, especially those first copied from standard processes and then modified and enhanced. After the upgrade, a company might decide to perform additional customizing. Two types of customizing can be done after an upgrade:

❏ **Upgrade customizing** consists of restoring the functionality and business processes settings as they were on the previous release.
❏ **Delta customizing** consists of performing additional customizing activities to make use of the functionality delivered with the new release.

One of the usual and initial problems in starting an upgrade is to find unconfirmed and even unreleased *repairs*, that is, corrections to programs or objects that were not originally developed on the system in which they were modified. This type of problem is usually discovered by the PREPARE program, although it will require manual resolution by developers and system managers.

Before going-live with the new release, remember to plan for training, handling new documentation, and communicating efficiently to end-users the changes they will find.

Finally, a crucial success factor in upgrade projects is extensive testing of all the business processes, printing outputs, and technical infrastructure, including a new stress test where the peak workloads can be verified. This procedure can be eased when documentation of previous implementation testing exists.

Repository Switch

For performing an upgrade process using SAP tools there are three upgrade strategies available which will affect the total downtime of the process. These strategies are based on what is called the *Repository switch*. This consists of having shadow tables while the system is running. At a certain point there is a switch between the actual productive repository and the one loaded in the upgrade. The three upgrade strategies or modes are:

❑ **A_switch.** Using this strategy the R3up tool imports a substitution set in parallel to the productive operation. All user transactions up to the first half of the upgrade are saved using database mechanisms. A full recovery of the database is guaranteed, before the switch or after, though a full offline backup is needed after the upgrade. This method requires a shorter downtime than A_off. On the other hand, a considerable amount of additional disk space will be needed during the upgrade.

❑ **A_on.** This is very similar to the A_switch method, but user transactions are saved during the entire upgrade. It is the method with the shortest downtime, but requires the maximum amount of additional disk space. There is no need for a full offline backup after the upgrade.

❑ **A_off.** This method is equivalent to having productive user operation stopped during the full upgrade process. It is the method with the longest downtime in terms of production use, but is the process with the shortest runtime. It requires very little additional disk space compared to the other methods. The only possible recovery is to the state previous to the upgrade.

Not all these upgrade types are supported for all databases engines. For instance, for upgrading to 4.0B on a SQL-Server database, only the A_Off mode is supported.

The decision about which strategy to use is mainly based on the maximum possible downtime; that must take into consideration the time needed for a recovery of the system in case serious problems arise.

The following chart summarizes the topics of release upgrade projects.

Why deal with this issue	Other issues affected	Solutions
❑ To enable new functionality	❑ Sizing and Technical Infrastructure	❑ ASAP Upgrade Roadmap
❑ To solve current release problems	❑ Systems Management	❑ Procedure Model
	❑ Development	❑ Upgrade Customizing/Delta Customizing
❑ For legal or technical reasons	❑ Control of Scope	
	❑ Customizing	
	❑ Change Management	❑ Testing tools
	❑ Testing	

Continuous Change

The change management discussion in Chapter 4 introduced the importance of handling all types of changes to overcome problems that can undermine an implementation. Although there is a different goal for post-implementation support, change management is still required to solve issues related to the ongoing operation and enhancement of the systems.

Good management of continuous change starts by applying all lessons and experiences learned during the implementation so that best practices can be reused and previous mistakes do not take place.

There are many issues in managing continuous change that depend on the implementation strategy initially chosen. In phased or rollout implementations, continuous training and support must be provided throughout all company divisions, business units, plants and geographical locations.

The post-going-live period is often characterized by the implementation of additional modules like cross applications such as Workflow or Internet-enabled transactions and components.

Continuous change is the process of analyzing and planning the requirements for:

❑ Ongoing communication of changes, additions, and enhancements
❑ Training for new users
❑ Advanced training for remaining project team members and technical support
❑ Maintaining and updating documentation, standards, and procedures
❑ Preparing for the new project and its impact on existing systems.

It is common to find many problems after the implementation project team is disbanded, although some customers see the switch from implementation to post implementation as injecting new blood and new enthusiasm. This is sometimes because consultants no longer rule and have passed control to in-house personnel. Continuous change must also take into consideration the organizational impact and risks of new projects and new people.

CHAPTER 8

Implementation Subprojects

Often a project is so concentrated on streamlining the most important business processes that there is little or no focus on dealing with special implementation issues that relate to all the business applications and the full implementation project. These are *cross-application* implementation subprojects. In this sense, the term *subproject* means a smaller project within an overall implementation project.

Implementation subprojects includes those implementation tasks and activities that must be dealt with by both technical and functional teams and often include a great number of organizational problems.

Except for the most critical issues, like basic authorization settings or forms needed for printing, these activities are often just partially covered or are not covered at all. Some of these issues are often postponed for a better time. This is a clear case for archiving or reporting. Certainly some of the implementation issues presented in this chapter will sooner or later be matters for careful planning and additional resources. These issues are not new to project and implementation managers.

SAP solution sets, ASAP, and the Procedure Model include activities or even full work packages for dealing with these issues. For instance, establishing key reporting requirements is part of the conceptual design "Define Function and Processes."

As indicated in a previous paragraph this type of issue involves functional and technical activities together, which makes communication *protocols* and project management two essential points for the success of these project activities.

Dealing with Reporting

Only meaningful data become information, and only information can trigger decisions. Business operates based on information, and even better when information becomes knowledge. It is therefore essential to get "information" out of the immensity of data held in a transactional system, so it can be transformed into knowledge that consequently enables or triggers decisions and actions for improving competitiveness and efficiency.

Reporting capabilities fill the gaps in business information requirements. The benefits of an integrated business system largely depend on the use of information companies can get out of it. As we have stated, reporting is the way to get that information. It is therefore important to address this issue in any implementation project: every company must decide on reporting needs and strategy.

The reporting problem, the reporting issue, the strategy or the approach to reporting can be analyzed from two perspectives during an SAP implementation project:

❑ **From the project team perspective, during implementation phase.** What are the reports needed and what are the best R/3 reporting options? How will the reporting strategy be set up?

❑ **From the user perspective, during the productive operation phase.** Where do I find a report I need? How do I use it or print it? How can I create a new report or enhance an existing one?

These perspectives should coalesce when the project team defines and designs a reporting strategy for users and productive operation. Often end-user training does not adequately address user reporting requirements.

A third, overriding perspective is that of project managers or implementation leaders, who might ask how a reporting project will affect other implementation issues, such as the scope of a project, system performance, programming required, or printing. They may also be concerned with other implementation activities that can help solve the reporting problem, such as the change management program.

A *report* is a program designed to select and extract data from the database and present the output information either on the screen or on a printing device. In SAP terminology the term report is often used analogously to program. We discussed differences in Chapter 5; a reminder, reports can be considered as programs that produce listings that usually do not update the database data, while ABAP *programs* can be considered as transactions for performing functions or business operations; often they can change the database data.

Reports or output to users is usually presented in two ways: in display mode, where information is shown on users' screens, and in print mode, on paper or other media. This fact is important to stress when training end-users who previously always needed a printed report, often custom made.

From the point of view of people needing information, reports are needed both internally and externally. External users of reports include tax authorities, auditors, or financial analysts. Internal users include most operational system users, who must select and extract information from the system to take a business decision, continue the business process chain, or trigger a subsequent operation.

Why Is Reporting an Implementation Issue?

Reporting can become a big problem during and after implementation. If any user needs timely information to continue the business operation, or make a decision, the report should be immediately available, otherwise, work might stop at that point. Warehouse stock must be known to plan for future purchase requisitions, or the dunning report for unpaid bills must be available.

In this section some of the problems in dealing with reporting are highlighted so that preventive or corrective actions can be taken. The importance of the reporting strategy and approach during an implementation project is further highlighted by the fact that most companies spend much money and effort in developing custom reports and printouts. A wrong approach to reporting can be very costly.

In the first place, reporting must be addressed from the point of view of the expected final results or benefits for end-users. Users put information into the system for performing business processes. They often need information for completing or interlocking those business processes. Often, this information (in the form of a report) can be displayed on the screen. However users encounter many problems trying for efficient use of this input and output information. Some of the most common reporting problems that users find when starting to work with the R/3 systems are:

❑ Standard reports are not found (hidden, titles misleading, etc.)
❑ There is no clear documentation on the purpose or outcome of reports
❑ It is not clear if the report is the appropriate one
❑ There is no clear path from which to select and run reports

❏ Users either cannot, or find it very difficult to, modify the reporting options or tree structure
❏ Users do not know how to run a report
❏ Users do not know how to print a report
❏ Users do not know how to mail a report.

Then there is the debate about whether online reporting is appropriate in transactional systems, or whether it is possible to decouple the reporting requirements to an offline environment.

R/3 is a transactional (OLTP) system, where data are put into the system to perform one or many business transactions that make up business processes. One of the advantages of the SAP R/3 system is that it can process the information and provides results in real time. Results are output in the form of reports, either on the screen or through the spool system.

Reporting on the transactional system can have a severe impact on performance, availability, system management, and related productive tasks such as printing, authorizations, and backup. There will always be the question of balancing the benefits of having online information so that the decision process is quicker, against the effects that heavy reporting might have on system performance.

Finally, there is the problem of designing the appropriate reporting strategy during the implementation phase: planners must know the reporting requirements, the tools, and the activities that must be carried out to fulfill the expected objectives. These points are investigated in following sections.

Reporting During Implementation Phases

For the project team and the end customer there are significant challenges in addressing the reporting issue, because reporting is often neglected during implementation.

Is reporting a technical issue that must be addressed by technical consultants and programmers, or it is a functional issue to be addressed by consultants and key users?

Reporting is included in this chapter as an area within SAP cross-application components, where both technical and functional teams are involved. Doubts or responsibility conflicts can be automatically solved when the team as a whole focuses on the common objective of providing the reporting information required for the business.

Reporting requirements are usually not clearly defined, and the only requirements baseline is previous system reports. Users normally need to have at least the same reports they used with previous business applications. During this phase, one of the main activities within the reporting strategy is to compare the reports of legacy systems with those of the R/3 system. The project team needs to listen to end-users' reporting requirements as well to support the migration process from previous system reports to new ones.

During this activity, one of the most common problems is that there is little effort to search for and explore available standard reports. Instead, implementation teams spend much time and money custom developing reports that were available in the legacy systems. Often the problem is not that the information required is not available on R/3, but that it is not the same as in older reports.

In some cases, previous reports are just regular standard transactions, which provide the information required on a real-time basis, without the need for running additional programs. In other cases, the information fields will have changed, sometimes significantly. This problem becomes one of finding the appropriate reports and reporting options within the many possibilities of R/3.

Release 4.0B introduced the *General Reporting Tree*, an evolution from Report Navigator on previous 3.x releases. This tool is a central repository for reports and report documentation. It can be used for searching for reports, executing them, modifying their structure by adding new reports, or configuring the tree to required, so unneeded reports can be deleted. Trees, in the form of tree variants, can be customized by users. They include search facilities that can be performed by module, title, or keyword. Reports include brief descriptions or notes that can be helpful for identifying their purpose or use, as well as a list of related reports. Users can also record their own documentation for reports.

However, the common practice in many implementation projects is to develop custom reports, expending effort and resources. There are several problems in developing custom reports:

❑ ABAP programming is required and must be provided by trained in-house programmers or IT personnel, or by contracting for external programming resources. This is costly.

❑ Reports are not well documented, and are hard to maintain.

❑ Access to reports is not clear, so either specific reporting transactions must be developed, or users must know the exact name of the report to execute it.

❑ There are more chances of programming bugs or performance problems than with standard reports.

❑ There are no OSS notes on custom reports.

❑ Business process integration is usually forgotten.

Areas for potential problems should be handled by leaving the development of custom reports to those cases when other R/3 standard reporting tools cannot be applied. It will be an activity of the implementation team to design the approach to reporting for the different business areas.

A final reporting-related issue in implementation is the relationship between reporting and the Change Management program. Information availability and new reporting options such as online and real-time reports, drilldown or interactive reports, and other reporting capabilities are factors of change. They can influence responsibilities, relationships, coordination, middle management, and other cultural or departmental work patterns. As with any other change, this will involve an additional risk that must be assessed and addressed in order to avoid resistance. In the case of reporting, resistance is usually translated into a request for the legacy system reports—consequently custom-developed reports.

Before describing a possible approach to the reporting within SAP projects, the following section introduces some of the common concepts, tools, and options for dealing with reporting.

R/3 Reporting Options and Tools

As we have noted, one of the most common reporting problems for users is to find the report or the appropriate reporting tool information requirements. There are many reporting options and tools. Some are designed for specific application reporting, while others are general-purpose tools that can be used in all applications. A brief summary of the main reporting options follows. More information can be found in R/3 online documentation. Especially interesting in this area are the excellent books *Reporting Made Easy* by the Simplification group.

❑ **Standard predefined reports** can be found normally in the same application areas where users perform their business operation tasks. They are usually accessed through either List or Information System options in the Application menu. All these reports are also found in global or general repositories.

❑ The **General Reporting Tree** is the central repository of R/3 standard reports. It can be accessed by selecting **Information System → Report tree** from the main menu. This is the SAP tool recommended for finding reports. The reports contained within the report tree are organized in hierarchical structures within application-specific folders. These structures can be customized to include user-defined reports. Figure 8.1 shows the initial general reporting tree.

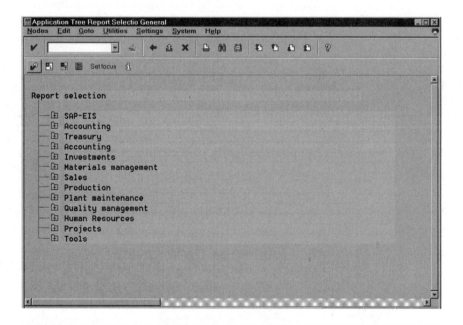

FIGURE 8.1   *General Reporting Tree*

❑ **ABAP Query**. SAP provided a report development tool for use in any application area. ABAP Query can be used (without any programming knowledge) to create reports by selecting fields and output reporting options. ABAP Query can be accessed from any R/3 window by selecting **System → Services → ABAP Query** or from the main menu by selecting **Information systems → Ad hoc reports → ABAP Query**, or by entering transaction code SQ00 on the command field.

❑ **Report Writer and Report Painter** are two R/3 reporting tools that use a graphical report structure to define reports. They are well suited for reporting on numerical figures, especially for mass production ones like month-ends. These tools are not available for all applications. The main application areas that can use Report Painter/Report Writer are FI, CO, and PS. Report Painter is a simpler interface than Report Writer and does not require any programming. Report Writer is the execution engine, and any report created with the Report Painter can be edited and further enhanced with the functions of Report Writer. These tools can be accessed from the R/3 main menu by selecting **Information systems → Ad hoc reports → Report Painter**.

❑ **Drilldown reporting.** The main feature of this reporting option is its interactive functionality that allows users to analyze data by "drilling down" into the reports. Some of the functions are quick summarization, levels of detail, sorting, categorizing, easy navigation, hiding columns, and so on. The option is available in most of the financial and controlling applications, as well as in Project System and Real State among other locations. It is particularly suited to working with EIS and the Profitability Analysis (CO-PA).

❑ **Report Specification Form** was developed by the Simplification Group and can be found as an appendix to the Book 1 of the *Reporting Made Easy* guides. It can be used for specifying report requirements so that standard reports can be identified or used for analyzing

❑ **EIS (Executive Information System)** is an information system available for analyzing data coming from several R/3 application modules. It is aimed at upper management, to provide a view of the main business figures and factors influencing business operations. EIS can be accessed from the R/3 main menu by selecting

Information systems → Executive information system. It is also accessible from within the financial modules.

❏ **ABAP Reports** are the customer-developed programs with reporting purposes.

❏ **OLTP (Online Transactional Processing)** includes transactional systems (such as R/3) based on operational data.

❏ **OLAP (Online Analytical Processing)** is a type of decision support software that can be used to analyze data coming from operational (OLTP) systems. This type of system can usually build multidimensional views of the data, and is the basic analysis tool used in Data Warehouse systems.

❏ **Business Information Warehouse** is SAP's independent data warehouse solution that seamlessly integrates with R/3, providing an OLAP environment as well as powerful reporting options. An introduction to the Business Information Warehouse is included later.

❏ **ABAP List Viewer (ALV)** is a collection of function modules that programmers can use to simplify and enhance the development of report lists.

❏ **OIW (Open Information Warehouse)** is the predecessor SAP's solution to the Business Information Warehouse. It includes an Excel front end that must be installed as an additional component of the SAPGUI. It can be used for extracting and unifying data from several of the R/3 information systems. More information on OIW can be found in R/3 online help under the CA-Cross Application section.

❏ **Web reporting** is the feature of SAP's Internet-enabled applications for helping users run R/3 reports using a Web browser.

❏ **Third-party reporting tools.** There are a number of software vendors who offer interesting general reporting tools and applications which are very user-oriented. Some of these tools have direct links with R/3 metadata and data repository, and also offer the possibility of integrating data from R/3 with legacy systems.

The Business Information Warehouse

Business Information Warehouse (BIW or BW) is the SAP Data Warehousing solution introduced in 1997 as a major component of the Business Framework architecture. BIW is an independent system with its own release and upgrade cycles, and can extract data from R/3 systems that have different release levels. As with other Business Framework components, communication between Business Information Warehouse and R/3 is implemented with BAPIs.

The importance and use of data warehouse and mining techniques have been increasing rapidly during the last few years, in the search for business intelligence. Fast data analysis has become key in making business decisions.

Data Warehouse and analytical tools used to unleash the meaning of huge amounts of data are thought of as integral components of getting business knowledge feedback. Figure 8.2 shows the role of Data Warehouse and the analysis process in getting a broader base of business knowledge that can provide feedback to the process of continuous change and improvement in companies.

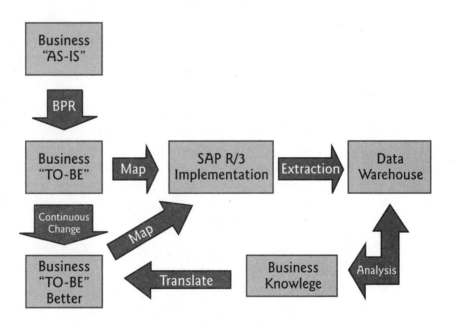

FIGURE 8.2   *Data Warehouse as feedback to business knowledge*

We have included an overview of BIW within the reporting issue. Its analysis capabilities, its own database, and its decoupling from the transactional system make a data warehouse an excellent independent reporting environment. One of the objectives of BIW is to help making reporting and data analysis simpler and more efficient.

Figure 8.3 shows an overview of the SAP Business Information Warehouse architecture.

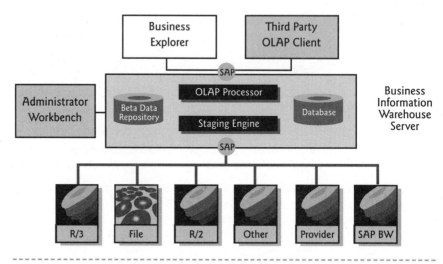

FIGURE 8.3   *SAP Business Information Warehouse   Copyright © SAP AG*

The SAP BIW is an evolution from the Open Information Warehouse, including a standard analysis tool environment that fits perfectly with R/3 systems and provides a powerful reporting solution.

SAP strategy is to position BIW as a ready-to-go warehouse, comprising all the components required by a global data warehouse architecture, including all the tools for designing, extracting, building, and managing the system:

❑ **OLAP processor** (server) with the data and information models from the R/3 system. BIW includes information models and report libraries for all the R/3 business areas.

❑ **Metadata repository** to manage and control the full data warehouse environment

❑ **Administrator Workbench**, the central data warehouse management tool, which can be used for maintaining and extending the BIW

❑ **Business Explorer** is the user interface based on Excel and Internet technology. It contains a large standard report library, as well as the required analysis tools. Business Explorer works as an information catalog allowing users to browse through the available information from R/3 business applications. The analysis tools that can support complex and multidimensional analysis based on different data views are also a central component of Business Information Warehouse.

BIW also includes the processes that can automatically extract data from R/3 systems, as well as from other external data sources. These are represented by a *staging engine* with integrated data staging routines that normally run in the background supplying BIW with current data from data sources, such as R/3 and non-R/3 systems. These routines can run at predefined update intervals and are managed from the Administrator Workbench.

SAP BIW is based on BAPIs, which provide a large degree of openness and extendibility so that BIW can be integrated with other applications, data sources, or tools. This system is tailored for all types of users, and as an alternative or a complement to the R/3 standard reporting options, it can help reduce the load and impact on performance of extensive online R/3 reporting.

BIW is based on the SAP Business Framework Architecture and uses the R/3 Basis system and technology as middleware, making it as safe, open, scalable, and reliable as R/3. There is a smooth integration between the BIW metadata repository and the ABAP repository, so that changes in objects and processes can be immediately transferred to BIW.

Users can employ the provided and predefined BIW reports or can use them as models for custom reports. The Excel spreadsheet makes analysis and reporting quite simple. Just as other SAP components do, the BIW also includes *wizards* for creating new reports, as well as many functions to help users customize their own reporting and analysis environment.

Another key point in the SAP BIW strategy is the very low implementation cost, since the kit includes all the required models, configurations, and staging services to work with R/3 data out of the box. This means data modeling is needed only for special purposes or when loading the warehouse with external legacy systems.

Approach to Reporting

In order to handle reporting during and after implementation, to make this project more cost effective and to satisfy end-user requirements, various points should be taken into consideration. While reporting might not be a critical success factor for the overall SAP implementation, it can be costly, it can severely affect other implementation activities, and at the same time it can delay the benefits of integrated R/3 applications. For these reasons, reporting is important and should be addressed early in implementation phases.

ASAP includes the first reporting activity in the Business Blueprint phase, within the Business Process Definition work package. This activity is to Determine Reporting Requirements, and the objective is to develop a conceptual design for the company's reporting needs. At this stage, the project team must examine whether specific business processes need to be reported, the contents of the reports, and possible reporting options for addressing the requirements. Basic notes for initial approach to reporting are:

❑ Reporting requirements must be addressed from the point of view of the business processes being implemented rather than from the point of view of previously available reports on legacy systems.

❑ Follow the recommended approach when R/3 reporting options and capabilities can be exploited, rather than the costly method of developing custom reports from scratch.

❑ Find out whether information is needed on a real-time basis, or if reports can be scheduled for nightly background processing or taken to an offline reporting system.

Later, in the Realization phase, ASAP includes the Create Reports work package, where information needs and specific reports are identified and detailed definitions are created for starting the report search, selection, and development. It is important in this phase to create test procedures to check the validity and quality of the reports.

Tests on reporting, mainly for those identified reports that can severely affect performance, will help to define any additional technical requirement, such as service distribution or system landscape design.

Reporting is a never-ending story of user requirements during implementation and after R/3 productive operation. For this reason some effort must be dedicated to end-user training in R/3 reporting. It is difficult for new R/3 users to understand that the system can provide online information just by running simple standard queries or transactions. Users need to know what information is available, where these query functions are, how to find them, and how to use them.

For projects where reporting is an essential part of the return of information, the project organization should include a reporting consultant, or even a full reporting team.

Summary of Reporting

The following chart summarizes the topics and solutions for reporting within SAP implementation projects.

Why deal with this issue	Other issues affected	Solutions
❏ Information is the cornerstone of business decisions ❏ Avoid uncontrolled reporting requirements	❏ Development and Enhancements ❏ System Management ❏ Technical implementation (sizing, printing, performance) ❏ Project Scope ❏ Archiving ❏ System Landscape ❏ Time and Ccosts	❏ *Reporting Made Easy Guides* from the Simplification Group ❏ R/3 Information System ❏ Report Painter/Report Writer/ABAP Query ❏ Custom-made reports ❏ Business Warehouse ❏ Third-party reporting tools

Testing Activities on
SAP Implementation Projects

Testing is the process of verifying that the work done achieves the expected goal. Testing is one of the few processes that can guarantee the quality and reliability of applications. The objective or goal of any task should have been previously stated, so the test can verify the results.

During SAP implementation, testing is a daily activity, the only way to verify that everything works as expected. However, many projects deal with testing activities in an uncoordinated way, often forgetting important tests or test conditions, or being tolerant toward "small" failures, without preventing the larger impact of those small failures.

Testing is present in every phase and every activity of the SAP implementation project, and also in the productive phase, in new applications, new components, developments, add-ons, technical infrastructure changes, upgrade projects, and others. Tests will be an issue of any implementation with the following objectives:

- ❑ To ensure processes work as designed
- ❑ To guarantee the quality of the overall project
- ❑ To avoid technical risks
- ❑ To anticipate solutions to potential problems
- ❑ To reach a stable platform for running SAP systems
- ❑ To help in the decision-making process on many project issues.

There are several types of tests done on the SAP projects; the most important are briefly explained.

Business Process Tests

One of the main testing tasks during SAP implementation projects is to check and verify that all the core R/3 transactions behave as designed and provide expected results, which is critical for going live. Business transactions are usually tested during the customization or realization phase, but there are some important points to consider:

❏ Full business processes, from beginning to end must be tested. This includes those horizontal transactions crossing several modules, like a sales order that could go to production, materials management, purchasing, delivering, billing, and accounting.

❏ All business processes should be tested before stress tests take place.

❏ Transactions showing bad performance (slow response time) should be analyzed. Problems with performance might be related to program bugs, a development change, or customizing settings. Changes should always be performed on development systems so that they can be tested and later transported.

❏ Critical transactions to be tested include the most frequently used, and those which are critical for the daily operations. These transactions should also be put into perspective, with conditions as close as possible to real operation. For instance, some critical transactions might work well with some data or data volumes, but not when tables reached a certain volume. The same thing might happen with date-dependent transactions. (Witness the Y2K problem.)

❏ It's quite important to test carefully those transactions that have been custom developed.

❏ Business process tests should also include testing output, such as reports, printing, mailin, or faxing.

A general word of caution: testing both standard and custom transactions requires as real an environment and data as possible. Performance can differ markedly when the database tables are nearly empty, and when they have thousands or even millions of records.

Stress Tests

Stress tests are a simulation of peak or high workload that can be run to analyze system performance under these circumstances. This type of test is essential to ensure that the system will be able to support the expected user and transaction load under peak circumstances. Stress tests consider several important performance factors:

❏ The system sizing is checked, including technical components such as CPU, memory, database volume

❑ The main systems and tuning parameters can be tested and verified
❑ Different workload scenarios can be tested
❑ The areas of potential problems can be discovered
❑ Alternative configurations, such as different server and services distribution, can be tested
❑ System management procedures can be tested
❑ Realistic expectations regarding workload throughput can be tested.

Stress can be handled in two ways: by real user interaction and simulation, where users are logged on and perform predefined testing scenarios, or by automating stress tests using scripting tools that can simulate standard transactions of the R/3 business applications

Stress tests are normally considered to have three phases: review, test, and report. Initially the functional configuration and technical infrastructure is reviewed and prepared for simulating the most real conditions possible, keeping in mind the possibility of going back to the initial test status (backup/restore) so that tests can be repeated. The second phase is the actual testing, where the system is set under test conditions. Finally, test results are reviewed so that problems are evaluated and corrective measures can be taken. Often tests must be run several times to validate the corrective measures.

Technical Infrastructure Tests

These tests include all those issues normally part of the technical implementation, which ensures a stable platform as well as data integrity and security. Among these tests are:

❑ Backup and restore tests
❑ Contingency and disaster recovery tests
❑ Availability tests
❑ Development tests
❑ Data load tests
❑ Cutover tests
❑ Going live tests
❑ System management and monitoring tests
❑ Tests or verifications of the transport system
❑ Authorizations and security tests

Procedural Tests

Finally, as a behavioral test, it must be verified that collaboration and communications channels work by testing how people perform their role resolution:

❑ Test the transport request procedure
❑ Test the batch procedure
❑ Test the daily checklist procedure
❑ Test the users leaving the company procedure
❑ Perform other defined procedures tests.

The following sections include an approach to testing and testing activities from the perspective of the automating tools.

Best Practices in Automated Testing

The following is an extract from the booklet *Best Practices Guide to Automated Testing*, developed and published by Autotester Inc., one of the world's leading providers of automated software solutions. Autotester offers several tools for handling all types of R/3 automated testing and these have been successfully deployed in many SAP installations. The next sections are copyright by Autotester Inc., and are printed with permission.

The Case for Automated Testing

Today, rigorous application testing is a critical part of virtually all software development projects.

As more organizations develop mission-critical systems to support their business activities, the need is greatly increased for testing methods that support business objectives. It is necessary to ensure that these systems are reliable, built according to specification, and have the ability to support business processes. Many internal and external factors are forcing organizations to ensure a high level of software quality and reliability.

Some of the most commonly cited reasons requiring organizations to adopt software quality initiatives include the increasing quality standards of application end-users, regulated quality standards of application end-users, regulated quality requirements, out-of-control maintenance costs, and missed deployment schedules. Application managers and developers increasingly use testing to support the goals of their organization and ensure applications performs as designed.

Why Automate the Testing Process?

In the past, most software tests were performed using manual methods. This required a large staff of test personnel to perform expensive and time-consuming manual test procedures. Owing to the size and complexity of today's advanced software applications, manual testing is no longer a viable option for most testing situations.

Every organization has unique reasons for automating software quality activities, but several reasons are common across industries.

Using Testing Effectively

By definition, testing is a repetitive activity. The very nature of application software development dictates that no matter which methods are employed to carry out testing (manual or automated), they remain repetitious throughout the development lifecycle. Automation of testing processes allows machines to complete the tedious, repetitive work while human personnel perform other tasks.

Automation allows the tester to reduce or eliminate the required "think time" or "read time" necessary for the manual interpretation of when or where to click the mouse or press the enter key. An automated test executes the next operation in the test hierarchy at machine speed, allowing tests to be completed many times faster than the fastest individual. Furthermore, some types of testing, such as load/stress testing, are virtually impossible to perform manually.

Reducing Testing Costs

The cost of performing manual testing is prohibitive when compared to that of automated methods. The reason is that computers can execute instructions many times faster, and with fewer errors than individuals can. Many automated testing tools can replicate the activity of a large number of users (and their associated transactions) using a single computer. Therefore, load/stress testing using automated methods requires only a fraction of the computer hardware that would be necessary to complete a manual test. Imagine performing a load test on a typical distributed client/server application on which 50 concurrent users were planned.

To do the testing manually, 50 application users employing 50 PCs with associated software, an available network, and a cadre of coordinators to relay instructions to the users would be required. With an automated scenario, the entire test operation could be created on a single machine having the ability to run and rerun the test as necessary, at night or on weekends, without having to assemble an army of end-users. As another example, imagine the same application used by hundreds or thousands of users. It is easy to see why manual methods for load/stress testing are an expensive and logistical nightmare.

Replicating Testing Across Different Platforms

Automation allows the testing organization to perform consistent and repeatable tests. When applications need to be deployed across different hardware or software platforms, standard or benchmark tests can be created and repeated on target platforms to ensure that new platforms operate consistently.

Repeatability and Control

By using automated techniques, the tester has a very high degree of control over which types of tests are being performed, and how the tests will be executed. Using automated tests enforces consistent procedures that allow developers to evaluate the effect of various application modifications as well as the effect of various user actions.

For example, automated tests can be built that extract variable data from external files or applications and then run a test using the data as an input value. Most importantly, automated tests can be executed as many times as necessary without requiring a user to recreate a test script each time the test is run.

Greater Application Coverage

The productivity gains delivered by automated testing allow and encourage organizations to test more often and more completely. Greater application test coverage also reduces the risk of exposing users to malfunctioning or non-compliant software. In some industries such as healthcare and pharmaceuticals, organizations are required to comply with strict quality regulations as well as being required to document their quality assurance efforts for all parts of their systems.

Results Reporting

Full-featured automated testing systems also produce convenient test reporting and analysis. These reports provide a standardized measure of test status and results, thus allowing more accurate interpretation of testing outcomes. Manual methods required the user to self-document test procedures and test results.

Understanding the Testing Process

The introduction of automated testing into the business environment involves far more than buying and installing an automated testing tool. In fact, effective automation is predicated on the idea that a manual testing process already exists since there is not a technology in existence today that performs automatic testing. So it is recommended that testing organizations begin their testing projects with a structured approach.

Within the testing environment, a quality assurance process is defined as a set of related steps designed to ensure or verify that a software application meets the requirements of the business user.

Before attempting to automate a test, a solid grasp of basic testing processes is needed, as is an understanding of what automated testing can accomplish, and an idea of which tests are good candidates for automation.

In fact, not all tests should, or can be, automated. When a company is considering which tests to automate, focus should be placed on those manual tests activities which take the longest time to set up, including manual tests that require the highest number of repetitive tasks and run the most frequently.

Automated testing should be used to augment current testing methods, and the process of planning for automated testing should be an extension of the current test planning process.

Typical Testing Steps

Most software testing projects can be divided into general tasks or steps.

- ❑ **Test Planning.** This step determines which applications (or parts of applications) should be tested, what the priority level is for each application to be tested, and when the testing should begin. Applications with high levels of risk or heavy user volumes are identified.
- ❑ **Test Design.** This step is for determining how the tests should be built and what level of quality is necessary for application effectiveness. During this phase, individual business requirements and their associated tests should be addressed within an overall test plan.
- ❑ **Test Environment Preparation.** This step of the testing process is concerned with establishing the technical environment that the test(s) will be executed in. Without this step, the investment in test automation is at risk because of the inability to re-execute the tests.
- ❑ **Test Construction.** At this step, test scripts are generated and test cases are developed based upon the test plans created during the design phase. Most of the time spent in automated testing is typically in the test construction phase.
- ❑ **Test Execution.** This step is where the test scripts are executed according to the test plans. As test execution is the most tedious and repetitious step during a manual testing process, the automation of this step is where the most significant time savings are made.
- ❑ **Test Evaluation.** After the tests are executed, the test results are compared to the expected results and evaluations can be made about the quality of an application. At this stage, application errors or problems are identified and appropriate corrective actions can be considered. Decisions can be made as to the readiness of the application for release.

Identifying Test Requiring Automation

Most, but not all, types of tests can be automated. Certain types of tests, like user comprehension tests, tests that run only once, and tests that require constant human intervention are usually not worth the investment to automate. The following are examples of criteria that can be used to identify tests that are prime candidates for automation.

☐ **High Path Frequency.** Automated testing can be used to verify the performance of application paths that are used with a high degree of frequency when the software is running in full production. Examples include: creating customer records, invoicing, and other high volume activities where software failures would occur frequently.

☐ **Critical Business Processes.** In many situations, software applications can literally define or control the core of a company's business. If the application fails, the company can face extreme disruptions in critical operations. Mission-critical processes are prime candidates for automated testing. Examples include: financial month-end closings, production planning, sales order entry, and other core activities. Any application with a high degree of risk associated with failure is a good candidate for test automation.

☐ **Repetitive Testing.** If a testing procedure can be reused many times, it is also a prime candidate for automation. For example, common outline files can be created to establish a testing session, close a testing session, and apply testing values. These automated modules can be used again and again without having to rebuild the test scripts. This modular approach saves time and money when compared to creating a new end-to-end script for every test.

☐ **Applications with a Long Life Span.** If an application is planned to be in production for a long period of time, the benefits from automation are greater.

Task Automation and Test Setup

In software testing, there are many tasks that need to be performed before or after the actual test. For example, if a test needs to be executed to create sales orders against current inventory, goods need to be in inventory. The tasks associated with placing items in inventory can be automated so that the test can run repeatedly.

Additionally, highly repetitive tasks not associated with testing can be automated utilizing the same approach. For example, when establishing base training data for an application training class, the procedure could be automated to avoid performing repetitive tasks for each iteration of the class.

Who Should be Testing?

There is no clear consensus in the testing community about which group within an organization should be responsible for performing the testing function. Many organizations make quality testing a responsibility of the development staff. The rationale for this type of arrangement is that the persons who developed the application are the ones best suited for finding and alleviating errors.

Others feel that the testing function should reside within the scope of a separate testing group that is independent of the development staff. Their argument hinges on the fear that application developers are too closely involved with the application to be useful for finding its problems.

Still others feel that testing should be the right and responsibility of the end-user groups who will actually use the application. This line of reasoning implies that the end-user is the final judge of whether or not an application meets the necessary requirements and is ready to be deployed.

Indeed, it is not as important who does the testing, but that the testing be done to support organizational goals and objectives. Clearly, where the responsibility resides for testing should be based upon the organization's unique circumstances and resources.

General Concepts in Automated Testing

Testing is now an accepted and vital part of any software development project. Automated testing is recognized as a cost-efficient way to increase application reliability, while reducing the time and cost of software quality programs. AutoTester offers the following information on the methods and applications of automated software testing.

Common Types of Testing

❑ **Functional.** Functional testing evaluates whether an application communicates and works with other elements in the computing environment. Integration of testing ensures that complex system components can share information and coordinate to deliver the desired results.

❑ **Regression.** Regression testing is used to ensure that new or updated versions of an application work as planned. Regression tests examine new versions of the application to ensure that they do not produce negative effects on other parts of a system. Most Year 2000 system testing is regression testing.

❑ **Load/Performance.** Load/performance tests examine whether the application functions under real-world activity levels. This is often the final stage of quality testing, and is used to verify that a system can handle projected user volumes and processing requirements.

Testing and the Development Life Cycle

In years past, application testing was the last phase of most software development projects. However, as organizations increasingly recognized the risks and costs associated with deploying faulty applications, testing has become a key part of virtually every stage of the development process.

By testing from the requirements phase to the end user acceptance phase, developers can dramatically increase the quality and reliability of virtually any application.

During This Testing Cycle Phase	**These Tests Are Recommended**
Requirements definition stage	Test planning and definition
Functional specifications	Test design
Design specifications	Test suite creation
Coding/assembly	Test suite creation
Testing (functional, integration, stress)	Test suite execution

continued on next page

During This Testing Cycle Phase	These Tests Are Recommended
Deployment	Test analysis
Maintenance	Test modification
Redevelopment	Test maintenance
Testing (regression)	Test suite execution

ASAP Approach to Testing Activities

ASAP methodology proposes to define a testing strategy during the initial project preparation phase, within the Project Procedures work package. The purpose of the Define Testing Strategies activity is to establish an overall procedure, approach, or strategy for all testing tasks during the project. Strategy must include all types of tests as well as the procedures. In most work packages during ASAP, specific test plans will be prepared and performed.

Two main ASAP work packages that include the main test activities are:

❑ **The Final Integration Test in the last part of the Business Blueprint phase.** The integration test is a process-oriented test. The purpose is to ensure that R/3 has been correctly implemented according to company or business requirements. This activity includes design of the final plan for the integration test, where the scope, scenarios, and test processes are specified. The purpose is to verify the functional (business processes) environment that has been customized, and all the dependencies, such as interfaces, reports, or enhancements. These tests are normally performed on the Quality Assurance System.

   ASAP procedures include the definition of test cases and scenarios, as well as priorities, impacts, and coverage. To aid users, it includes a sample integration test procedure and instructions which can save time for the project team.

❑ **Conduct System Tests during the Final Preparation phase.** System tests should verify the technical infrastructure as well as the procedures defined for managing and supporting the system. These extensive tests include volume tests, stress tests, system administration tests, disaster recovery, backup and recovery, and so on.

❑ The CCMS alert monitors and operations mode should be tested (Systems Management)

❑ The procedure describing what to do when alert thresholds are reached should be reformed

❑ The escalation procedure should be reformed

❑ Volume tests on critical business transactions and as a result, tuning should be done

❑ Stress tests, measuring system performance and data volume growth against different peak workload profiles, should be reformed

❑ The technical team must perform all the system and infrastructure tests: backup and recovery, switchover system, service distribution, operation mode change, start and stop, CCMS monitors. The technical tests must be also include a contingency plan and test, where critical situations are tested, for instance by simulating single points of failure or point-in-time recovery.

❑ The functional team must complete and perform all the critical business process tests, including output information like forms and reports.

❑ A Going-Live check service and/or an EarlyWatch session must be conducted.

SAP Test Workbench and CATT

SAP is well aware of the importance of testing and testing tools in implementation projects. Since the early releases of R/3, SAP has provided the CATT (Computer Aid Test Tool), as an integrated component within the ABAP Workbench; it includes all required functions for creating, executing, and maintaining tests modules and procedures.

CATT can be used for recording transactions that can later be executed using different variables and parameters, making it a valuable testing tool for customizing adjustments, changes on programs, or adding new functionality.

On a higher level, SAP has included a Test Workbench as the central place for organizing and managing the R/3 system tests. The

Test Workbench organizes tests on different hierarchical levels: test catalogs, test plans, and test packages. Each of these levels allows for flexible organization and planning of testing activities, organization, reutilization of components, setting test status, as well as logging and documenting results. The Test Workbench component can use all the utilities of the CATT tools.

Summary of Testing

The following chart summarizes some of the major topics of testing during SAP implementation projects.

Why deal with this issue	Other issues affected	Solutions
❑ To ensure processes work as designed	❑ All technical and infrastructure issues	❑ Plan and document test procedures
❑ To guarantee the quality of the overall project	❑ All development-related issues	❑ Assign testing responsibility
❑ To avoid technical risks	❑ Modeling Processes	
❑ To anticipate solutions to potential problems	❑ Going Live	❑ Benchmarking
❑ To reach a stable platform for running SAP systems	❑ Training	❑ CATT and the SAP Test Workbench
	❑ Documentation	
❑ To help in the decision-making process on many project issues	❑ Costs	❑ Third-party test scripting and automation tools

Archiving Projects

In a general sense, archiving is the process of storing documents in an archive storage location. In SAP R/3 as in many other systems there are two types of archiving: *Application Data Archiving*, or just data archiving, and *Document Archiving*, commonly known as optical archiving.

R/3 data archiving selects and moves the application data that are no longer needed online from the R/3 database to an external archiving storage. A key point in this process is that the application data are deleted from the database but are still accessible from the application: the data stays in a *near-line* status. Application data archiving within the R/3 system becomes a very important issue especially after the systems have been in production, since the data volume usually increases. This has direct effects on many technical issues such as performance and system management activities.

On the other hand, *document archiving* is the process of linking original documents with R/3 documents, as in linking an R/3 invoice with the image of the invoice. The original documents are usually entered into the system by scanning.

SAP ArchiveLink is an interface between the R/3 systems and archiving solution that can store electronically both archive files (from data archiving) and optical documents (from document archiving). Both types of archiving usually allow for managing optically stored documents two ways: not only by storing, but also by fetching and reading.

When dealing with implementation issues or subprojects, the focus is on data archiving over document archiving, since the first is a mandatory project, while the second is an optional one. However, for reference, a brief introduction of ArchiveLink and optical archiving appears below.

SAP ArchiveLink

The SAP ArchiveLink, as its name indicates, is meant for establishing *links* between R/3 business applications and the archiving system. SAP ArchiveLink is an interface between the R/3 systems and external optical archiving systems. The archiving systems usually run in a separate and isolated server. Figure 8.4 shows an example of a typical archiving architecture.

To make ArchiveLink work as intended, there must be a third-party archiving solution, certified to work with SAP ArchiveLink specifications. A list of supported certified archiving solution can be found at **http://www.sap.com/products/compsoft/certify/imaging.htm**.

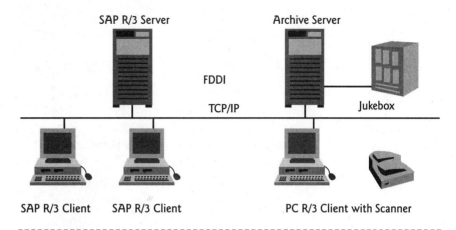

FIGURE 8.4 *Classic archiving architecture*

The ArchiveLink system is made up of several interfaces:

❑ **Interface to R/3 applications.** ArchiveLink administration tools are used to establish the settings needed for linking business documents with the archive systems.

❑ **Interface to archiving servers.** This provides communication between R/3 servers and the archive servers to perform such archiving operations as storing, retrieving, deleting, and other functions. This interface is basically accomplished using message exchange with the RFC (Remote Function Call) protocol.

❑ **User interface.** This contains the application tools for users to display archived documents in the front-end (SAPGUI) workstation. It can also include a scanning interface for transferring scanned documents from a user workstation to the archive server.

Optical Document Archiving

Reason companies decide to archive documents electronically include:

❑ Legal dispositions
❑ Disputing of contracts
❑ Inspection (taxes, audit)
❑ Historical analysis and research, etc.

There are several clear advantages to an archiving system that works closely with business application software (R/3):

❑ It greatly decreases paper flow and handles only one reference copy of the archived documents.
❑ There are fewer storage requirements for archived documents than in physical paper storage in binders and cabinets.
❑ An optical archiving system provides quick retrieval and processing of documents, allowing simultaneous access by several people.
❑ Archiving provides secure and long-term storage.
❑ Optical archiving can be useful for optimizing the business process by affording users online access to the original information as quick as possible.

Document Archiving Concepts

The most important terms to understand in working with the ArchiveLink interface include:

❑ **Document.** ArchiveLink considers a document to be a set of logically connected pages; this might range from a single page to a very long print list.
❑ **Archive.** An archive may have two meanings:
  ❑ A *physical archive* is the storage medium (disk, CD-ROM, WORM, etc.) containing documents
  ❑ A *logical archive* is a group of documents which logically belong together (they are from the same department, module, year, etc.).
❑ **Technical document class.** The technical document class establishes a correspondence between archives and the archive formats. ArchiveLink assigns technical document classes to different categories of documents, so that the archive format can later be interpreted by the ArchiveLink Viewer (user interface).
❑ **Object types.** Object types are the familiar application business objects, a concept similar to that introduced in Business Workflow. They include the definition of methods that specify the actions a user can perform with the documents which belong to that object type. In the ArchiveLink interface, this is an impor-

tant concept since the archiving of document types is always related to object types.

❏ **Document types are a way to classify objects.** An object type might have more than one document type. Several document types can be assigned to the same document categories.

❏ **Incoming documents (NCI).** These documents, also known as *Non-Coded Information documents* or *originals*, can be considered as *images*, i.e. documents which have been introduced into the system with an scanner. Their information is actually a raster image (binary data). Another example of NCI documents is incoming faxes. There are three different possibilities in R/3 for entering NCI documents into the system and linking them with the applications: advanced entry, simultaneous entry, and late entry. When CI documents are stored in the archives, they need to include a description file to allow them to be indexed.

❏ **Outgoing documents (CI).** These documents are also known as *Coded Information documents*. They are generated with the usual data processing functions (often with the SAP print spooler), such as print lists and archive files. CI documents can be sent directly to the archive.

Archiving Administration Concepts

The SAP ArchiveLink system requires that some administration tasks be performed in order to create the necessary links between the business objects of the SAP applications and the documents stored in the archive system. These tasks consist basically of defining the archives and assigning the object types and document types to the archives and the link tables.

The logical configuration and settings for the different components of the archiving systems are managed from the monitor administration tool. To access this tool, from the initial R/3 screen, select **Tools → Administration → Administration → Process technology → Optical Archive → Monitoring**. The archives are identified by an *archive ID* which can be accessed by an RPC address or RFC destination.

Links define the place where the object is to be archived, as well as the link table which manages the relation between SAP objects and archive objects. The link tables contain references including the corresponding SAP object identifications and the archive document identification.

ArchiveLink manages references to archive objects so that SAP applications store the archive documents with their own object keys; there is no need for the applications to maintain a direct reference to the archived object.

ArchiveLink Customizing

Configuring and customizing the whole archiving process, although not difficult, is not an obvious task. Understand that archiving always requires a third-party archiving solution, and therefore there is additional hardware and software to set up and configure. Some of the steps needed to customize ArchiveLink are:

❏ Install and set up the archive server, both hardware and software
❏ Configure the communication path between the R/3 servers and the archive server
❏ Install and possibly configure the presentation servers (SAPGUI); for the scanning workstation install ArchiveLink and scan software
❏ Configure and customize the archiving from the Archive Monitor: archive IDs, communication queues
❏ Configure output devices as archiving devices for print list support
❏ Customize the document types and link tables which will be handled by ArchiveLink
❏ Configure the settings to allow the input of NCI documents, for all types of entries
❏ Configure application settings for output document (CI) archiving.

There may be other steps required for customizing, depending on the particular customer configuration and certified software chosen.

It is beyond of the scope of this book to describe each of the required steps. Look up the extensive information available in SAP online documentation, particularly in the guides *WF ArchiveLink: User Guide* and *WF ArchiveLink: Interfaces*.

Application Data Archiving

There are many reasons to address an application data archiving project. Since the daily business operational work increases R/3 data volume, it will directly affect the time needed for backup and restore operations. Archiving can be used to reduce the amount of data in the database, since the data archived is no longer part of the database. For example: if a customer database is 100 GB and grows an average of 5 GB per month, in 5 years it will grow to at least 400 GB; if the time needed for backup of the 100 GB was 4 hours, after 5 years it could be 16 hours. If the regular retention period for documents is 6 months, the database size could be stabilized to about 140 GB.

Database growth directly affects the system's performance: there are many system reports that must search for and select records from the database tables. Even in the case of using indices, there will not be the same response time when scanning big tables as there is when scanning smaller ones.

System management is also affected by archiving. The growing volume of data will make system managers periodically add disks, disk volumes, and disk controllers and configure RAID systems—the frequent file system reconfigurations that will affect uptime. At the same time, database administration will be affected when reorganizations are required.

Application data archiving is particularly important for those installations expecting a considerable growth in their database. For the typical SAP project a life-cycle of at least the coming 10 years is common.

Besides technical considerations about the importance of archiving, there are other requirements for considering an archiving project: legal and fiscal requirements, audits, warranties, or historical data analysis.

Features and Requirements for Archiving Solutions

The R/3 system includes several functions for managing application data archiving and archive files. The core archiving management transaction is **SARA → Tools → Administration → Archiving →**, but there are many links to this transaction within the R/3 application modules. When navigating from specific business functions, the system automatically selects the archive object.

An *archive object* describes the database objects that must be grouped together to have a full business object, independent of other data or operations performed at the moment when the object is archived. An archive object represents a full business operation or commercial transaction that has been completed, with no related open items, and whose retention period has been reached.

SAP's data archiving concept is based on the Archive Development ment Kit (ADK). This component is a group of specific archiving function modules positioned between the application and the archive itself, ensuring that, although the data no longer exist in the database, they remains accessible to the application. The ADK includes all the functionality required for the archiving process.

Archiving processes are based on archive programs. The basic archive program selects the data to be archived from the database, based on selection criteria and other conditions set in customizing. It then builds a logical data container (*archive file*) and flags the records selected for deletion. The deletion from the database is performed by a *delete program*. The R/3 system verifies that this will only delete data that have been previously archived successfully. Other archiving programs are in charge of analyzing data, fetching and reading data from archive files, or reloading. Not all archive programs are available for all object types.

As we noted earlier, there are several requirements that any archiving system and archiving process must address:

❑ **Legal requirements.** Most countries impose rules on companies for making data available for tax or legal purposes, so that archives should be stored in a way that can be easily restored and analyzed by authorities, if they are ever requested in the future.

❑ **Hardware independence.** Archive files should be stored so they are independent of the hardware and code page used; this makes them retrievable by other hardware systems.

❑ **Software independence.** The archive objects must include additional information such as table and field definitions, since the data structures should be accessible even in the case of software upgrades.

❑ **Data interdependence.** In an integrated system such as R/3, many data objects have many dependencies on other objects, and are only meaningful when combined. It is important that the archive system check any dependencies, so that, for instance, some objects must be archived in parallel, or require that preceding objects be previously archived. Consider the Network Graphic shown in Figure 8.5 where purchase documents, purchase requisitions, deliveries, and billing documents must be archived before the sales documents can be archived.

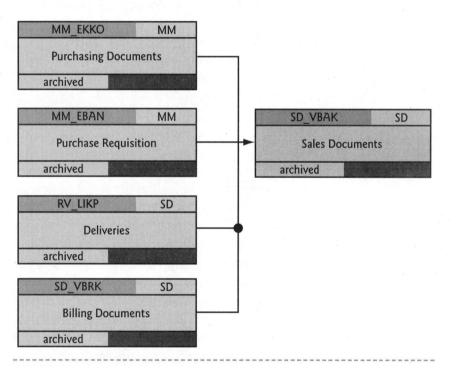

FIGURE 8.5   *Archive Object network graphic*

❑ **Organizational dependencies.** Many data types and data structures are closely linked with the defined organizational structure of companies, such as business areas, cost centers, sales areas, and so on. In case companies change their organization, and consequently the system setting, the archive system must ensure that data are still meaningful, so the organizational information must be included and stored.

An additional consideration is what to do with local developed objects (the infamous *Z objects*) and their dependencies.

The R/3 archiving system complies with all previous requirements, and facilitates not only the selection and management of archive objects, but also the development of additional archive programs with ADK.

Approach to Archiving Projects

Traditionally, both the Procedure Model and ASAP have included little information and few strategies for archiving projects. The reason is that these projects become more important after the system is in productive operation. However, during the initial project phases, the draft of the archiving strategy should be defined and the project initially planned. There are several considerations for archiving that can affect customizing settings.

Archiving is clearly an implementation subproject or a project of its own, where:

❑ A project plan for archiving should be designed. Project managers or experienced consultants should design the archiving plan.
❑ An archiving project team should be established and roles and responsibilities defined. The team should include technical and functional members, key users, and a database administrator.
❑ A third-party archiving solution that is ArchiveLink compliant should be chosen and procured.
❑ Productive operation of archiving requires that different users periodically perform archiving runs or, if these are scheduled, be in charge of checking the results of archiving processes.

Usually the functional departments, with the help of consultants and database administrators, are in charge of selecting data that can be archived and the type of access that will be required. This is a difficult task because users always want all data to be accessible online. An effort should be made to define retention periods, application dependencies, and requirements for access types.

The selection of the data to be archived is usually performed in two steps:

❏ Finding and determining which database tables and which application data are constantly increasing

❏ Determining the technical and functional conditions for archiving, such as the volume of the data, and the applications or legal requirements.

Activities after selection of the data to be archived include:

❏ Technical archiving customizing, including selection of storage media, installation and configuration of the archiving solution and customizing of the ArchiveLink settings

❏ Functional customizing, where the process owners decide on the settings of their archiving objects

❏ Testing archiving runs on the Quality Assurance System, and archiving going live by transporting settings and scheduling archive runs.

Figure 8.6 shows a generic approach to an R/3 application data archiving project.

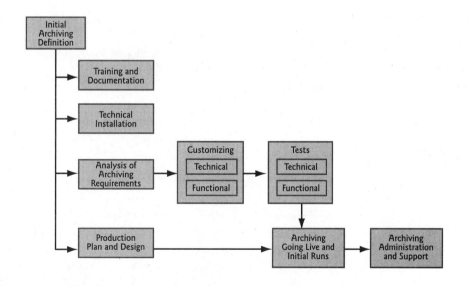

FIGURE 8.6   *Example of archiving project*

An interesting paper, *Managing SAP R/3 Archiving Projects* can be found on the SAPnet. This is an excellent guide for archiving projects. SAP has also included an innovative service offering known as Remote Archiving Service to support their customer's archive projects.

Summary of Application Data Archiving

The following chart briefly summarizes the topics and issues that must be taken into consideration when dealing with application data archiving. An important point is that archiving should be dealt with as soon as possible. Otherwise, when the pressure of database growth is too great, there will be additional problems such as those that derive from the long time that initial archiving runs will require.

Why deal with this issue	Other issues affected	Solutions
❑ To overcome all problems caused by database growth	❑ System Management	❑ Plan an archiving project
	❑ Performance	
	❑ Sizing	❑ ADK and ArchiveLink
❑ To maintain a stable platform	❑ Reporting	
	❑ Backup/Restore	❑ Remote archiving service
❑ Legal and tax requirements	❑ Development	
❑ Audit	❑ Time and Costs	❑ Third-party archiving products
❑ Historical data analysis		

Security on SAP Systems

Addressing security within implementation projects has the objectives of protecting valuable business data and ensuring continuous and stable systems operations. Often security is just considered as the design and realization of the authorization concept. Profiles and authorizations are key to providing access to needed transactions and to ensuring secure access to sensitive data. The security strategy must also consider all the layers and components of the SAP system. Figure 8.7 shows the SAP security concept.

Layer	Components	Security Aspects
Presentation	GUI, frontend	Access control/password, SNC, integrity check
Application	Application modules, work processes, enqueue server	Authorizations, locking of used objects
Database	Relational database	Access protection of R/3 data, logging, administration
Operating system	UNIX, Windows NT, OS/400, S/390	Access protection of R/3 data, operating system commands, administration
Communication	SAP router, network, SNC	Access control lists, SNC, OSS-API V2, SAP router

FIGURE 8.7   *SAP security concept*

Security must address the presentation layer, the application layer, the database layer, and also the network. Security must also address the overall system landscape: development system, quality assurance system, productive system, and any connected complementary system, whether it belongs to the SAP Business Framework architecture or not.

All security aspects on R/3 systems components are based on restricting access to each of the system's layers to authorized users or external systems. The following sections briefly introduce some of the security concepts for each layer.

Security at the Presentation Layer

Security at the presentation layer is based on restricting access to the SAPGUI, or other user interfaces connecting to the R/3 systems. Measures that can be considered include:

- ❑ Security at the desktop operating system, such as local network passwords
- ❑ Using passwords in screen savers
- ❑ Setting expiration dates on passwords
- ❑ Setting automatic logoff after an specific idle time
- ❑ Protecting Internet access with the use of firewalls

❑ Using automatic virus detection programs
❑ Protecting anonymous ITS users by defining an R/3 service user of a background type which cannot interactively access R/3.

Security at the Application Layer

This is probably the layer requiring most effort, since security here is based on restricting access to business transactions to users connected to R/3 systems. At the application layer, security is closely related to the R/3 authorization concept described in detail in our discussion of the implementation issue.

Basic security measures at this layer are:

❑ R/3 access should be provided to system parameters that restrict password lengths and logon attempts and impose password expiration dates.
❑ Restrict and change standard super-user passwords, basically by disabling SAP and DDIC and creating other super-user master records.
❑ The authorization profile SAP_ALL should be avoided by any users, including developers, except for super-users.

Extensive information about authorization and profiles is included later in this chapter.

Security at the Operating System Layer

The SAP R/3 system installation only sets a limited number of user accounts at the operating system layer: basically the SAP administrator and database administrator (on UNIX systems). Other created accounts provide service privileges on Windows NT systems. There are often administrative accounts with full access privileges such as *root* on the UNIX system or *administrator* on the Windows NT system. Other user accounts must be set up for technical teams or programmers for the execution of interfaces with other systems.

Security at the operating system layer must be provided by restricting access to those system accounts, and by strictly controlling passwords and physical access to server consoles.

Other security measures can be enforced by setting access permissions for critical files and directories. This can be achieved by Access Control Lists and operating system security features. Shared file systems must be also protected so that only certain operations and users can access those files and directories.

Database Security

The database layer of R/3 systems include a database user, SAPR3, that owns database objects, and gives permission for accessing, deleting, and updating data. Different database engines include their own administrator ID that can also access and modify database data and structure.

Security at the database layer is enforced by changing user ID passwords, which is standard in all R/3 installations. Both users, SAPR3 and administrator, should be handled with care.

Although it is possible to access the database using interfaces and tools, non-R/3 access should be granted only in read mode, since the R/3 applications and data models are what ensure application and data integrity.

Remember that the most important point in ensuring data integrity is a consistent backup and restore strategy.

Security at the Network Layer

Between all previous layers is the network or communication layers, where security must be enforced by protecting and restricting the communications between the different layers, and also between R/3 systems and external systems.

Network security includes all the communication hardware such as routers, cables, modems, or network interface cards. Remote communications can be secured based on user names and passwords and call-back procedures.

R/3 includes SAProuter software that acts as a firewall and can be used to check connection routes and restricting permissions by the use of a routing table that grants or denies access to servers and services. This service is also used to allow SAP remote connections.

Remote connections with SAP support servers are usually set up to allow outgoing connections, so that SAP customers to allow that permit open the connections that permit access to SAP consultants.

SAP has provided an interface for using external security products with R/3 systems known as SNC (Secure Network Communications). Products that can be used include smartcards, single sign-on, or other types of security coding such as cryptographic tools. SNC can be used with the SAProuter to provide secure communications through Internet and WAN connections.

Another security interface that enables communication between R/3 and external security tools and applications is Secure Store and Forward (SSF). It allows the use of digital signatures and can be used for all types of documents or files being transmitted from or to the R/3 system, including electronic payments, orders, and Internet transactions.

The ASAP Approach and Activities for Security

The ASAP solution set includes several security activities and tasks in different work packages. The core security project is based on the authorization concept, explained below.

During the Business Blueprint phase, ASAP includes tasks for securing the development system, so that only the project team and other authorized members have access to the R/3 system and components. At this phase, technical consultants should make a draft plan for the security strategy, including all layers. In installations where security is considered a critical issue, a security administrator should be appointed.

The Realization phase includes activities that must deal with security aspects of production and the quality assurance system, as well as the authorization concept. This phase will again require a close cooperation by project team members, including key users, and business process owners.

During the Final Preparation phase, team members responsible for security must perform all the tasks that ensure secure access to R/3 systems, including tests that guarantee security in the production environment.

As a general approach, ASAP defines some points considered critical for dealing with R/3 security aspects:

❑ Application security provided by the SAP Authorization concept must be defined and implemented before going live.
❑ Security must be provided on all system layers, including network and communications.
❑ Remote communication must be secured by using SAProuter and other security products based on interfaces such as SSF and SNC.
❑ Access to computer rooms and other technical equipment should be restricted and secure.
❑ If Internet applications are implemented, security measures such as installing and configuring firewalls are critical.

Summary of the Security Concept

The following chart includes a summary of issues and problems affected by the SAP Security Concept.

Why deal with this issue	Other issues affected	Solutions
❑ To protect valuable business information	❑ Authorizations	❑ Security team
	❑ System Management	❑ SAProuter
❑ To secure all R/3 system layers	❑ Backup Strategy	❑ SNC and SSF
		❑ Authorization project
❑ To ensure a stable environment		

R/3 Authorization Projects

The authorization system of the SAP R/3 groups together all the technical and management elements that grant access privileges to users to enforce the R/3 system security.

An *access privilege* is a permission to perform a particular operation in the SAP system. Access privileges in the R/3 system are granted to users by assigning authorizations and profiles. Entering such profiles in user master records enables users to use the system.

The main features and concepts of the SAP R/3 authorization system can be summarized as follows:

❑ The authorization system is based on complex system objects with multicondition testing of system access privileges. It tests multiple conditions before granting users permission to perform tasks in the system. A multicondition access test is defined in an authorization object. An example of multicondition testing is allowing users to create, display, or delete information from a purchasing center, but only to display information in another purchasing center. The table below illustrates this concept:

User	Purchasing center	Permissions
FREDSMITH	001	Create, Delete, Display
FREDSMITH	002	Display
JGALPJR	002	Create, Delete, Display

❑ The authorization system uses authorization profiles to ease the maintenance of user master records. Authorization profiles are groups of authorizations. Instead of entering every authorization in user master records, administrators need only enter profiles.

❑ Authorization profiles can be either simple or composite. Composite profiles contain other profiles.

❑ The authorization system uses an activation method. When authorizations or profiles are created or modified they must be activated to become effective.

❑ The SAP authorization system provides mechanisms for distribution of the maintenance tasks related to users and access privileges, like assigning authorizations, activating profiles, managing new authorizations, etc. A single super-user can do these tasks or they can be divided among several administrators.

The R/3 system includes many predefined authorization and profiles that cover most of the usual needs for assigning access privileges. Before creating a new profile, try to use an existing predefined profile.

The complex objects of the R/3 authorization system are structured in a hierarchical but flexible way, as shown in Figure 8.8. The main elements of the authorization system are introduced below.

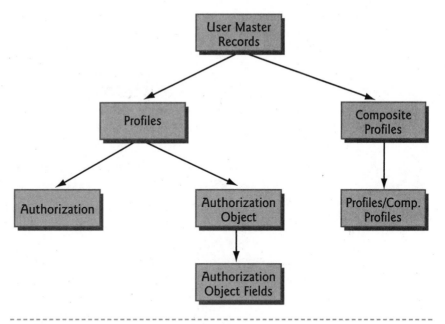

FIGURE 8.8   *Authorization system hierarchy*

R/3 User Administration

Users of the SAP R/3 system are defined internally within the same R/3 system by the means of *user master records*. There is no need for user management at the operating system or database level, except for one special user (in the case of Windows NT) or two (in the case of UNIX) defined in the standard installation: `<sid>adm` as SAP administrator and `ora<sid>` as SAP database administrator with Oracle databases.

Users are defined and maintained, and the security of the system enforced in user master records, with the use of the SAP R/3 authorizations and profiles. As with much of the rest of the R/3 system, where there is a material master, a vendor master, and so on, for the user administrative and management functions there is also a user master.

The user master records define user accounts for enabling access to the system. They contain other screens with additional fields apart from the *User ID*, some of which are just for information purposes (though still important). Some others can really make life easier for both users and administrators.

SAP R/3 users are defined in the system in user master records. These records contain all the access information needed by the system to validate a user logon and assign access rights to the system, like the password and authorization profiles. There is much extra information in a user master record, like the default screen the user will see on initial logon, what printer is assigned by default, address, phone number, etc. Some of the fields are just for information purposes, while others have a direct effect on the users' working environment.

To reach the user maintenance functions via menu options, from the main menu select **Tools → Administration → User maintenance → Users**.

To perform functions over a group of users, the system includes some options under the menu **Utilities → Mass changes**.

The easy part of user administration deals with things such as creating user master records, changing passwords, helping users define their own default values, and organizing the user maintenance tasks.

Overview of the Authorization System

The main concern for system administrators and project managers when implementing the R/3 system is how to enforce the right security methods so that users can access the business transactions and information they need. The SAP system provides a comprehensive and flexible way of protecting data and transactions against unauthorized use.

In the user master records, users are assigned one or more authorization *profiles*. These authorization profiles are made of a set of *authorizations*, which give access privileges for the different elements of the system. Authorization objects contain a range of permitted values for different system or business entities within the R/3 system.

To a SAP administrator or support personnel, user handling should not be of major concern if certain rules and guidelines are followed from the beginning of the project. This does not apply to authorization and profile maintenance, a matter of joint effort between the SAP functional and technical people. This is because usually SAP system managers do not have to deal with such things as giving certain users access to specific general ledger accounts, cost centers, or production plants. It is the role of customizing specialists, developers, or business consultants to define entities that should be protected by means of authorization objects and to assign or create the corresponding profiles. This task is important and might take a lot of time to accomplish depending on the degree of security protection, number of users, and modules being implemented.

Authorization Profiles

An authorization profile contains a group of authorizations or access privileges. Profiles are assigned to users in the user master records. A profile could represent a simple job position since it defines the tasks for which a user has access privileges. Every profile can have as many access privileges (authorizations) as desired. Profiles can contain authorization objects and authorizations.

Changing the list or contents of the authorizations inside a profile will affect all users given that profile. Changes become effective next time the user logs on, not for current logged-on users.

Composite Profiles

Composite profiles are sets of authorization profiles. A composite profile can contain an unlimited number of profiles and can be assigned to users just like profiles in the user master records. Composite profiles are suitable for users who have different responsibilities or job tasks in the system. These profiles are sometimes known as "reference" profiles for assigning a larger group of access privileges. They are able better to match users with several responsibilities.

Making modifications to any of the profiles in the list included in the composite profile will directly affect the access privileges of all users having that composite profile in the user master record. When profiles are displayed on the different SAP screens, there is a flag indicating whether the profile is simple or composite.

Authorizations

The R/3 system uses authorizations to define permitted values for the fields of an authorization object. An authorization might contain one or more values for each field of the object.

An authorization object is like a template for testing access privileges, and consists of authorization fields that define the permitted values for the authorization.

An authorization is identified by the name of an authorization object and the name of the authorization created for the object. An authorization can have many values or ranges of values for a single field. It is also possible to authorize for every value (entering an asterisk "*") or for none (leaving the field blank).

Authorizations are entered in authorization profiles with the corresponding authorization object. When an authorization is changed and then activated, it will immediately affect all users whose user master records contain a profile with that authorization.

The technical names for authorizations and authorization objects have a maximum of 12 positions, but usually they are displayed in the system using short descriptive texts.

For customer-created authorizations the only name restriction is not to place an underscore in the second position of the technical name. Every customer-created system object should also comply with SAP standard style guide and begin with a Z or a Y to distinguish it from the SAP original objects, thus avoiding the possibility of being overwritten by a system upgrade.

Authorization Objects

An authorization object identifies an element or object within the SAP system that needs to be protected. These objects work like templates for granting access rights by means of authorization fields, which permit performing complex tests of access privileges.

An authorization object can contain a maximum of ten authorization fields. Users will be permitted to perform a system function only when passing the test for every field in the authorization object. The verification against the field contents is done with the logical AND operator. A user's action will be allowed only if the user authorization passes the access test for each field contained in an object. With this mechanism, the system can perform multicondition tests. As with authorizations, in maintaining authorization objects, the system displays not the names but a descriptive text for each object.

Authorization objects are grouped in object classes belonging to different application areas. These are used to limit the search for objects, making it faster to navigate among the many R/3 system objects.

SAP predefined authorization objects should not be modified or deleted, except on the instruction of SAP support personnel or an OSS note. Deleting or changing standard authorization objects can cause severe errors in programs that check those objects.

Before an authorization object is to be modified, all authorizations defined for that object must first be deleted.

To use the OR logic for giving users access to certain functions, define several authorizations for the same object, each time with different values. In the user master records, assign each of these profiles, which are linked with the OR login. When the system tests whether the user has access privileges it will check each authorization to see if the assigned values comply with the access condition. The system will allow access to the first authorization that passes the test.

Authorization Fields

Authorization fields identify the elements of the system to be protected by assigning them an access test. An authorization field can be a user group, a company code, a purchasing group, a development class, an application area, etc. There is one authorization field found in most authorization object: the "Activity." This field defines the possible actions that could be performed over a particular application object. For example, activity "03" is always "Display," so if an authorization contains two fields like "company code" and "activity," if the company code field is "*" (meaning all company codes), it means that the user with that authorization can only "display" the company codes.

The list of standard activities in the system is held on the SAP standard table TACT. The relationship between the authorization objects and the activities is held on table TACTZ. Not all authorization objects have the "activity" authorization field.

Authorization fields are the components of authorization objects as we stated above. Fields are also part of the standard ABAP function call AUTHORITY-CHECK.

When maintaining authorization the system does not display the real names (technical names) for the fields, but shows a description for each field. Table TOBJ contains the fields associated with each authorization object. This is how the SAP system knows which fields belong to an authorization object. The fields in an object are associated with data elements in the ABAP Data Dictionary.

Authorization fields are not maintained from the user maintenance menu, but have to be defined within the development environment.

Normally users need not change standard authorization fields, except if adding or modifying system elements and if those elements should be tested with authorizations.

Profile Generator

Creation, modification, and assignment of authorizations and profiles is a complex task within an SAP implementation project, as we have noted. This task is often underestimated in the planning charter, and in order to overcome the problem of missing authorizations and the inability to work normally, there is a natural tendency to assign full privileges to many users, who might have problems and also seriously threaten security and control.

Time and effort needed for authorization tasks, together with customer requests, made SAP design a tool to reduce the time needed for implementing and managing the authorizations, thus decreasing the implementation costs. This tool is known as the *Profile Generator*.

The Profile Generator is a SAP utility available from release 3.0F and productively onward since release 3.1G, whose goal is facilitating user authorizations and the management of user profiles. It can be used to automatically create authorizations and profiles, and easily assign them to users.

The profile generator can be accessed from the main menu by selecting **Tools → Administration → Users → Activity groups**, or alternatively by entering transaction code PFCG in the command field.

The Profile Generator only generates simple profiles. When these profiles have been automatically generated with the PG, they cannot be maintained manually.

This is a big difference from manual profile management, for authorization objects, and for later assignment to users. With the profile generator, the management of authorizations is built based on the functions and tasks users will perform with R/3. The profile generators are in charge of selecting and grouping the authorization objects.

The definition of profiles in the PG is based on the possibility of grouping functions by *activity groups* in a company menu, generated using customizing settings. The menu will only include those functions selected by the customers.

Activity groups form a set of tasks or activities that can be performed in the system, such as running programs, transactions, and other functions that generally represent a job role. The activity groups and the information they include are what trigger profiles to be automatically generated.

ASAP Approach to Authorization Activities

The authorization strategy is an implementation issue that many people have seen as a nightmare. It is complex and time consuming, and often the project team does not address it with enough resources. However the authorization system is the only way to ensure maximum system security and provide users with privileges to perform their job tasks.

The problem of the authorization system is that it must reflect the functions performed by people within different business areas. Those functions are often not well known or defined.

The authorization project must describe in detail what authorizations and profiles are required. In order to do that, the best approach is to build up a job role diagram, by functions and users, showing the transactions that can be executed and the authorizations required. The functional team usually performs this activity, since it is normally most familiar with the transactions and authorization objects associated with user profiles and job tasks.

ASAP includes the *Authorization Made Easy* guide, based on the Profile Generator tool. This guide can be found on ASAP or on the Simplification Group Website. ASAP establishes the role of the security manager, in charge of implementing the R/3 security concept.

The manager's main and most difficult task is to document job roles within the company and the business areas. This is usually with a matrix of activities and R/3 transactions and can be very complex. To simplify this task, user groups with the same or similar jobs should be defined so that authorization profiles can later be assigned to individual users.

The authorization system should be first designed and implemented in the development system, for later transport into Quality Assurance and the Production System.

The realization of the authorization project is mainly performed with the Profile Generator tool, used for creating activity groups that join R/3 transactions and tasks. These groups can later be assigned to individual users. A prerequisite for creating activity groups is to generate a company menu that reflects a subset of the transactions selected with the Enterprise IMG. This menu is used to select transactions to create activity groups. The Profile Generator includes standard predefined activity groups and is also used for easy maintenance of authorizations; it assigns users as many activity groups as required for performance of their tasks.

During the Project Preparation phase there is a first authorization activity *Define system authorization standards for the project team*, within the work package Project Procedures. The purpose of these early tasks is to define and limit the number of super-users within the project team and to start the authorization concept. This effort in security will ensure that users do not make unintentional changes to areas out of their responsibility.

During the Business Blueprint, there are authorization tasks within the Develop System Environment work package. Project team user masters are created with the required authorizations according to roles and responsibilities. At this stage it is recommended that an authorization administrator sets up those user masters and authorizations and start the overall authorization concept.

The Realization phase includes a specific work package, Establish Authorization Concept, where the detailed design of the authorization concept for end-users is performed, activity groups are implemented, and authorization management procedures are defined. This work package considers the authorization concept within an overall security strategy. Final activity within the work package includes the testing and validation of the authorization concept before approval.

Authorization activities are implicitly included in the Final Preparation phase, in the System Management tests, and in the End-User Training.

Finally, the Going Live and Support phases must address the issue of the problems raised by missing authorizations and validate access rights for end-users. At this stage, the authorization administrator is in charge of providing new authorizations or modifying existing ones, according to the degree of new developments, the incorporation of new end-users, or new application modules.

In case of R/3 upgrade projects, the release notes usually include all necessary modifications and adjustments to standard authorizations and profiles.

ASAP includes the following general advice for success during and after the implementation of the authorization concept.

❑ Clear authorization procedures are critical for maintaining and supporting the authorization system. They must be known and understood by the user community.

❑ Complex authorizations require dedication and resources.

❑ It is possible to define authorizations based on organization units (positions) rather than by direct assignment to users. This would require the activation of the Human Resources Organizational Plan.

❑ R/3 has an extensive reporting and auditing system for checking users, authorizations, and profiles, including change documents. Unauthorized modifications can easily be traced. These functions can be accessed from the main menu by selecting **Tools → Administration → User maintenance → Repository Infosys**.

❑ Take the concept very seriously and avoid problems: information is valuable and sometimes sensitive; protecting it is critical.

Summary of the Authorization Concept Issue

The following chart summarizes the issue of handling users and authorizations in a SAP implementation project.

Why deal with this issue	Other issues affected	Solutions
❑ To enforce security to critical data	❑ Security	❑ ASAP approach to security and authorizations
❑ To enable users access to job tasks and information	❑ Training	❑ Profile Generator
	❑ Systems Management	❑ *Authorizations Made Easy*
	❑ Change Management	

Putting the Ribbon on the Package: SAP Business Workflow

In its simplest meaning, a workflow is a set or sequence of logically related activities. In the SAP R/3 workflow system, an activity can be any type of business operation that can trigger a report, a transaction, a message, or other things. The SAP R/3 applications are a set of integrated applications already acting as a type of workflow, where data and information cross functional borders.

The SAP Business Workflow is a tool that can logically integrate and automate transactions belonging to different application modules. This feature ensures the adaptability of R/3 functions to specific customer needs.

Implementing SAP Business Workflow scenarios is not just an issue, but rather a project that can provide further benefits to the overall system. The Workflow allows a clear business path that incorporates both information and action.

The SAP Business Workflow integrates the functionality of the various R/3 modules. It is application independent and does not restrict or change R/3 standard transactions. The SAP Business Workflow uses existing programs and transactions, but can be considered as an upper layer over the transaction layer.

The SAP Business Workflow surpasses other typical "messaging" or "electronic signature" workflow tools, which are very document oriented. Although these features can also be covered with R/3 workflow management tools, SAP enables a "business process"-oriented workflow, fully integrated within the R/3 application modules. The goal of the SAP Business Workflow is to automate business processes. Many advantages result from a information technology tool at the service of business goals. Among the advantages and possibilities of the SAP Business Workflow are:

❑ It automates and organizes the processing of related work steps.
❑ It facilitates communication between the people in charge of performing related tasks and speeds administrative processing, thus avoiding "waiting" times and resuming work after a previous process. This factor allows decisions to be made more promptly and directly influences the expected productivity of employees.
❑ It fosters a better and more flexible organization structure that is more business process oriented and uses fewer individual assignments to jobs.
❑ In workflow processing, the employees have a better vision of their contributions and responsibilities, and of the relationships established in the process chain.
❑ It decreases the time spent searching for information and the risk of duplicate entry of information.
❑ It can be used to reduce the complexity of business processing, seamlessly integrating successive tasks and providing a better response time to management, customers, suppliers, etc.

Where Workflow Can be Useful

There are many areas where Workflow can be useful within R/3, including:

❑ Checking for availability
❑ Tracking projects
❑ Approval operations: planning, budgeting, purchasing requisitions, vacation entitlements, etc.
❑ Expense claims
❑ Managing job applications
❑ Sales order processing
❑ Releasing production orders
❑ Processing and management of documents
❑ Archiving
❑ Monitoring deadlines
❑ Organizing and tracking activities.

Concepts and Components in SAP Business Workflow

SAP subdivides the Business Workflow components into three different categories:

- **Definition tools.** These are meant for defining tasks, object types, roles, events, and full workflows.
- **Runtime system.** This includes all the components needed for the processing of workflows. There is a Workflow Manager in charge of controlling and coordinating workflow. The runtime also includes an event manager and the work item manager for controlling the execution of individual steps, deadline monitoring, etc.
- **Information system.** The workflow also includes several options for displaying and reporting user activity within the workflow system, as well as for tracking and correcting errors.

To reach the Workflow components, from the initial R/3 screen, select **Tools → SAP Business Workflow**.

There are three options in Business Workflow:

- **Organizational Plan (transaction code PP70).** This is a transaction belonging to the Human Resources module, but it is closely integrated with SAP Business Workflow, so that the workflow tasks can be linked with agents from an organizational point of view. This linking is based on jobs and positions, so that any and all employees with the authorizations required for executing the tasks will receive the workflow. The system does load balancing and ensures that only one task is processed at a time. This feature greatly increases efficiency by automatically considering changes in organizations.
- **Process Structure (transaction code SWLW).** This is for defining organizational structures, but includes most functions for the workflow runtime and reporting systems. It is meant for users who, although responsible for organization management, should not define workflow tasks, events, etc.
- **Development (transaction code SWLD).** This contains all the definition, runtime, and reporting options available for the Workflow, including those of the Organization menu. It is meant for the developers of workflow tasks and associated objects.

Among the definition tools is a graphical workflow editor for configuring and setting the execution rules or instances of the workflow. Figure 8.9 shows an example of a standard graphical workflow definition.

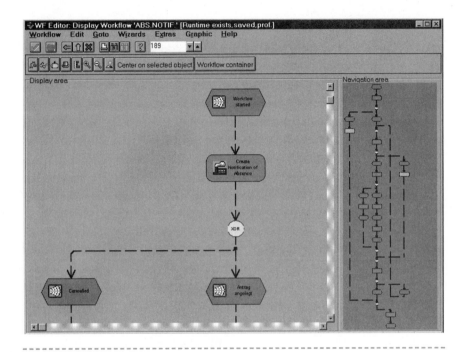

FIGURE 8.9 *Graphical Workflow Editor*

The workflow management system is responsible for controlling and monitoring all the work steps, determining the processing state of a process, and initiating or triggering the successive steps. The most important concepts when working or setting workflow tasks are:

❏ **Workflow definition.** The description of a workflow process. The workflow process is made up of a set of steps or tasks, which can be processed sequentially or in parallel.

❏ **Tasks.** In a general sense, these refer to descriptions of activities. Within the SAP Business Workflow there are:

❏ *Single-step tasks* that describe the most basic or elementary business activity. These tasks always refer to a single method that is performed over a business object. This terminology clearly leads to a certain object-orientation approach within the SAP Business Workflow, which will be discussed later.

❑ *Multi-step tasks* that describe several steps belonging to a logically related sequence of a business process. These tasks refer to a workflow definition.

SAP provides s*tandard tasks* (single-step tasks) and *workflow templates* (multi-step tasks). *Customer tasks* (single-step) and *workflow tasks* are defined by the customers.

❑ **Roles.** These refer to the person or persons that are assigned to process a particular task. The roles are resolved at runtime by the role resolution component of the workflow using the rules that have been previously defined.

❑ **Work items.** The name for the runtime execution or representation of the individual steps (single-step tasks) which are sent to the corresponding Integrate inbox for processing. The work item manager is responsible for assigning these work items to the processing agents and for monitoring deadlines.

❑ **Events.** Events are entities that trigger, start, or end a workflow. The event manager is responsible for managing events. They are part of the object definition and used to flag status changes.

❑ **Containers.** These are data structures that store the definition and execution components of a workflow. They are used for exchanging information between the components of a workflow definition, as well as between the workflow and the applications.

❑ **Binding (or binding definition).** The specification of rules to ensure that the application programs which are to be activated receive the correct information and that the result is reported back to the workflow management system.

Workflow and Flexible Organizational Management

Besides technically customizing and configuring the SAP Business Workflow management system, the first thing to set for working with the workflow is an organizational model or plan for the company.

Integration of organizational management in SAP Business Workflow allows tasks to be linked with agents through an organizational assignment. This assignment is used to determine the "correct" agent and allows the workflow management system to assign tasks actively.

The organizational plan represents the structures and division of a company. It is used for the whole business workflow, which can run across several or all R/3 business applications.

The Workflow is configured and defined so that it automatically performs role resolution: you define the rules, the workflow establishes the person holding the position in charge of the next activity in the process.

Business workflow tasks are linked or assigned to position descriptions according to an organization model, rather than to particular persons. If employees leave the company or change position, a new person can be assigned to the position, and the workflow automatically adjusts the routing. It's possible for more than one authorized employee to perform the same task. The workflow system supports automatic load distribution of tasks within a group of users having the same position or activity profile.

Workflow Customizing

Before the SAP Business Workflow functions can be used, there are technical settings which must be performed.

Since version 3.0F, R/3 has included an "Auto customize" function that makes it possible to configure the workflow at the "push of a button." To perform this customization, access the IMG from the Business Engineering menu. From the IMG hierarchy, find the SAP Business Workflow customizing options under **Basis Components → Business Management**. When you click on the execute button of the option **Maintain standard settings for SAP Business Workflow**, the system displays the necessary steps to customize the workflow runtime system and the development environment, showing the actual status of each step. Figure 8.10 shows an example of this screen.

To start workflow customizing, click on the Automatic Customizing button on the application toolbar. When all the steps are correctly defined, the "lights indicator" becomes green, and the system is ready for working with the Workflow.

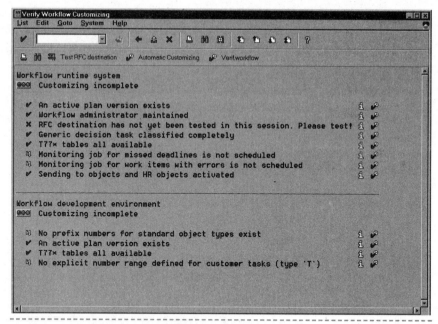

FIGURE 8.10   *Workflow customizing*

Objects, Wizards, and Forms

SAP has been constantly adding capabilities and features to the Business Workflow. Since release 3.0 the interface between the SAP business workflow and the actual business application has been designed using an object-oriented approach.

Available business objects are kept in the Business Object Repository that contains the directory of objects together with related attributes, methods, and events.

From the workflow management transactions, look up the available object types. With the object-oriented approach, the system can:

❑ Perform some processing on business objects by applying *methods*
❑ Read and evaluate the characteristics of an object by reading its *attributes*
❑ Respond to events using the *status changes* of objects.

Release 3.1 introduced Workflow wizards to further ease and automate the creation of workflow tasks by using predefined forms and guided questions.

Workflows can be started from MAPI-compliant clients such as Microsoft Exchange, Outlook, or Lotus Notes, and are also Web-enabled so that they can also be launched from Web browsers.

With SAPforms, Workflow can be connected with Exchange Forms, so that workflow tasks can be triggered using forms from the desktop, even in offline operation.

CHAPTER 9

Overview
of R/3
Applications

This chapter is intended to serve as a quick reference to readers not familiar with the SAP R/3 application modules. It contains brief descriptions of the different components of the system and their main features. The objective of this chapter is to present and synthesize the main features and possibilities of R/3 application modules. The simplest way to get more information about R/3 is to refer to SAP online documentation. There is also extensive information in the SAP Web pages.

R/3 applications or functional modules are divided in three closely related areas: financials, logistics, and human resources. In addition to specific business applications, there are special R/3 components that interact with the standard modules and are aimed at specific industries. These components or specific functional applications are known as Industry Solutions (IS). Some of these solutions (Retail, Public Sector) are being introduced in the standard system from release 4.0. An introduction to available and future IS modules is presented at the end of this chapter.

There is also a set of cross-application modules or components, usually known as CA modules, which can be used as independent add-ons or across several or all R/3 applications. These CA modules are generally positioned between the technical and functional areas of the system. Some of the components usually classified among these modules are: SAP Business Workflow, ArchiveLink, SAP Communication Services (SAPOffice), CAD Integration, and Document Management System.

The R/3 application modules include hundreds of predefined business processes ready to customize to specific business and information needs.

As we have stated elsewhere, R/3 applications work in an integrated way. Just as there is integration in the real business life between logistics and financial processes, there are the same links in the software business intelligence and reference model.

Despite the large number of modules and module components within application areas, these applications work just as well when used independently. For instance, some companies decide just to implement some of the R/3 modules. It is quite common to start with financial components, such as the general ledger or the controlling modules, and then to begin other projects to implement materials management or Sales and Distribution. This latter is often the starting point for companies in the distribution or manufacturing sectors.

R/3 is a live product with a fast and continuous path for development of new releases and functionality. The following sections in this chapter reproduce the most important features of R/3 applications, from a SAP marketing perspective, but also offer a synthesis and selection of features. Since this chapter is to be used as a reference, readers may find some of the processes are not sufficiently covered. For more information they can consult online documentation, SAP Web pages, or SAPnet.

It is not the purpose of the following sections to teach readers how to configure these modules, since a specific and deep knowledge is required, as is a relationship among applications, which is beyond the scope of this book. There are specific training courses as well as several manuals and guides on customizing a module. However, what is really needed is through knowledge about actual business processes and how companies do business.

Financial Application Modules

The SAP R/3 Financial applications provide users a complete view of their finance and accounting functions, and include an information system and report generator to facilitate the decision-making process. Applications from the FI modules are designed to fill the needs of small- and medium-sized companies as well as multinational corporations, allowing users from different countries and with different currencies to use the system at the same time, in an appropriate language. The main applications of the financial modules include:

❑ FI–General Ledger
❑ CO–Controlling
❑ EC–Enterprise Controlling
❑ IM–Investment Management
❑ TR–Treasury.

The following sections introduce each of these components.

FI: Financial Accounting Applications

Financial Applications are usually generically known as module FI, and provide the functions and processes needed for the operating aspect of general ledger and financial information for a company. These applications are tightly connected and integrated with other financial applications like treasury and overhead cost controlling, as well as with several parts of human resources like payroll and travel management. The Accounts Receivable (AR) application and Accounts Payable are directly integrated with the sales and distribution modules (SD) as well as with Purchasing. Table 9.1 shows the applications or components that make up the FI module. Each contains a full range of financial business processes and related functions.

TABLE 9.1   *FI–Accounting or Financial Modules*

FI-AA	Asset Accounting (traditionally knows as AM or Asset Management)
FI-AP	Accounts Payable
FI-AR	Accounts Receivable
FI-GL	General Ledger
FI-LC	Legal Consolidation
FI-SL	Special Purpose Ledger

Figure 9.1 shows the R/3 menu with each of the accounting applications in release 4.0B.

An important feature of financial accounting is its ability to generate in real time the current balance as well as the profit and loss statements. The FI module covers all company accounting needs, at the local and international levels. It is prepared to work with multinational companies. It can work with multiple currencies, which are converted to the local currency associated to the company, and its multilingual capabilities facilitate interchanging texts between different divisions in a company or group.

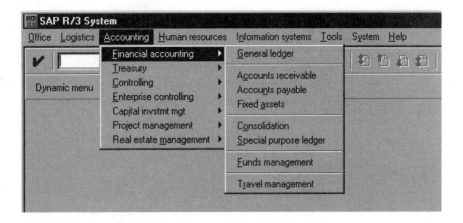

FIGURE 9.1   *Financial accounting application modules*

FI-GL: General Ledger

The main function of the FI-GL module is to keep a record of all accounting postings that take place in the company. It is totally integrated with the rest of the R/3 application modules, which guarantees that every time a business transaction takes place in any module which has any accounting implication, the FI-GL module registers that operation. This module makes it possible to choose the scope of accounting: company codes or business areas.

The main features of the module are:

❑ Automatic registration of accounting statements both in general ledger accounts and in consolidation accounts. This accounting is done simultaneously.
❑ When accounting postings·related to cost accounting objects are made, there will automatically be a document posting in the controlling module.
❑ A complete information system with tools for evaluating all accounting data. It provides real-time analysis with account information, balance status, etc. The system permits the definition of several versions including different information and comparison analysis between versions. Several plans can be done with different versions.
❑ Information can be analyzed on the screen on an individual or global basis: a single accounting document can be displayed, as

can an accounts summary, monthly totals, balance status (with profit and loss statements), and so on.

FI-AP: Accounts Payable

This submodule is in charge of processing all the administration concerned with accounting for payments to vendors. It is intimately related to the Purchasing application. The main features of the Accounts Payable application are:

❏ Functions for payment entry can be done using either standard R/3 transactions, the Internet, or EDI, among others. The application includes two ways of generating payments. The first is using a payment program which automatically creates all outstanding payments which meet preselected requirements. The second is by using a manual payment transaction, where each payment is registered.

❏ Management of payment notifications allows the system to generate, either manually or automatically, all documents containing information on payment details and their corresponding accounting documents (invoice number, vendor reference, and so on.)

❏ An application for calculating interest rates can figure out the total due for each payment according to the applicable interest rate and payment method defined for each vendor.

❏ Management of correspondence includes all documents to be sent to company vendors (payment notifications, extracts, balance confirmations, letters, open line items, and so on.)

FI-AR: Accounts Receivable

The main goal of the Accounts Receivable module is to manage the account information of the company's customers. This module includes tools for controlling and keeping records of the individual and collective status of every customer. Postings on Accounts Receivable are also automatically posted into General Ledger Accounts. The FI-AR application is completely integrated with the Sales and Distribution (SD) module, since it is in the sales area that the functional data is generated.

The functionality is very similar to that of FI-AP, and includes specific functions such as:

❑ **Credit management.** The system facilitates definition of credit control areas that can be used to give credit limits to a group of customers or to specific customers.

❑ **Dunning program.** This facilitates the task of controlling debtors. The application makes it possible to establish different dunning levels and to define different procedures for each level.

FI-AA: Assets Accounting

This is the module responsible for managing all the fixed assets in the enterprise. It includes the tools needed for all operations related to the accounting of fixed assets. The system automatically determines and calculates depreciation values, interest, etc. The AA application includes an information system which makes it possible to perform a wide range of standard analyses (depreciation, total values per fiscal year, per investment type, per cost center, and so on) as well as flexible analyses defined by users. It also includes tools facilitate multiple simulations, a great help in studying the best way to making investments in fixed assets.

The FI-AA component is integrated with the other systems modules:

❑ From the Plant Maintenance (PM) module users can define maintenance activities which make up investments which link with AA.

❑ When there is any change in the value of the company's fixed assets (appreciation or depreciation), these are noted in the FI module. If these changes should also be reflected in the cost accounting, this is linked to the CO applications.

❑ If there is any purchase (from the Materials Management module) of fixed assets, the purchase and invoice can automatically affect the AA module. If the fixed asset is directly produced by the company, the affected module is PP (Production Planning).

FI-LC: Legal Consolidation

This application makes it possible to legally consolidate different companies which make up a corporation, or, on a lower level, to consolidate business areas, business units within a company, or profit centers. The system permits canceling of internal accounting processes between areas to be consolidated.

LC also includes the interfaces needed to transfer all the information to the consolidated entity. It also includes tools for monitoring and analyzing the consolidation status. The information system includes all reports needed to verify and test the result of consolidation operations.

There is a new module in Enterprise Controlling, knows as EC-CS which has a similar functionality, and it will soon replace the LC module within FI.

CO: Cost Accounting Applications

The CO module, also knows as Controlling or Cost Accounting, is used to represent the cost structures of companies and all factors that influence those costs. This is commonly known as *internal* accounting as opposed to *external* and official accounting, required by tax authorities and represented within the FI applications module.

This module includes areas such as overhead cost control, product costing, profitability analysis, and activity based costing.

The Cost Accounting applications are designed to answer key questions about the cost of a product or service. In order to answer this type of question the cost controlling functions of the CO module use various valuation strategies and quantification structures, making it possible to plan the cost of goods produced in the most realistic and accurate form.

The functions in the Controlling Application module are based on "account assignments" objects: cost centers, cost objects, orders, and projects. However, the main operative and transactional object is the cost element, which is defined as a cost-relevant item; it can also be a revenue item. With the help of real and planned data, the system makes possible quick acknowledgment of the weak points in the production process.

The main components of the CO module are listed in Table 9.2.

TABLE 9.2   *Components of the Cost Accounting Module*

CO-OM	Overhead Cost Control
CO-PA	Profitability Accounting
CO-PC	Product Costing
CO-ABC	Activity Based Costing

CO-OM: Overhead Cost Control

Overhead Cost Control functions are used to monitor internal costs and activities. They can also be used to plan and allocate costs. The main account assignment object used is the cost center, where the overhead costs are assigned.

Cost centers are a way to define different areas and subareas within the organization. Using cost-center accounting, the company can have a better knowledge of where costs are being incurred. R/3 also provides functions for cost-center planning and budgeting, with the corresponding approval process, and including extensive reports and tools for analyzing and summarizing the cost-center accounting data.

R/3 includes different ways to allocate overhead costs, in order to achieve a better understanding of the real source of the costs. This CO component is also used for reconciliation with the general ledger accounts of Financial Accounting.

CO-PA: Profitability Accounting

The CO-PA application includes two main components: Profitability Analysis and Profit Center Accounting. The Profitability Analysis component of the CO module is used to analyze the different sources of company revenues. In CO-PA, revenues are assigned to market segments. It is possible to define any type of market segment and make distinctions between products, business areas, customers, sales organizations, and others. Later these market segments can be evaluated according to the revenue margins they have produced.

Profit Center accounting is also used to analyze revenues (profit and loss) from an internal point of view. This is accomplished by defining profit centers that can be divided geographically (regions, areas, plants), by product (range, divisions), or by function (sales, production).

The CO-PA module uses SAP standard master data such as customer, products, and so on. It also allows for including additional characteristics to define *profitability segments* that are used for the profitability analysis. There is a planning function for creating profit plans. Planning can be carry out either as account-based or cost-based.

This application is closely integrated with Sales and Distribution by means of a direct transfer of sales orders and billing documents into CO-PA. This transfer can be evaluated to determine actual costs. These are the actual postings that make the most important data into CO-PA. By means of cost transfers, CO-PA also can be linked with cost center accounting, project system, FI account postings, and orders received in MM.

Just like most of the R/3 application modules, the CO-PA component can become a valuable tool for the decision-making process, since its provides market-oriented information that can be used to select customers, determine which are the best distribution channels, modify prices, and so on.

CO-PC: Product Costing

This is the application component to use to calculate the actual cost of manufacturing a product or providing a service. It can therefore provide crucial information such as the price that makes a product profitable. At the same time it helps optimize the cost of the products manufactured.

This CO component is closely integrated with the rest of the CO module, as well as with other R/3 applications. It provides information that can be used in profitability analysis, cost object controlling, and MM for evaluating material and stock. The information from product costing can be used to update the material master so that cost estimates can be used as standard prices. It includes many functions that can be used for cost planning and for performing simulations.

CO-ABC: Activity-Based Costing

In Activity-Based Costing, the R/3 system performs a cross functional approach to cost optimization. CO-ABC charges organization overhead to products, customers, sales channels, and so on. Figure 9.2 shows the relationship of ABC with other CO applications.

In order to have a more realistic view of costs and to optimize the process chain, the CO-ABC component can be used in parallel with regular cost accounting, or can be actively integrated with product costing.

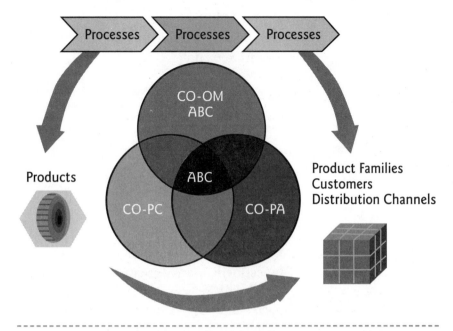

FIGURE 9.2   *Activity-based costing in the R/3 system   Copyright © SAP AG*

EC: Enterprise Controlling

The Enterprise Controlling module is important for the management and decision process. It is in charge of monitoring critical success factors in the evolution of the enterprise as well as figures that the financial controller considers key.

The EIS (Executive Information System), one of the module components, is basically a collection of tools for filtering and quickly analyzing the most important company data; this is a way to obtain the most current and important information about business status. This information can be represented in standard or custom graphical reports.

With the Management Consolidation system (EC-MC module) information and data from the different company subsidiaries, even from different countries and different legal requirements, can be passed to the system, which automatically performs all the necessary jobs to obtain consolidated information.

The EC modules are also designed for analyzing the profit of independent business units. The system automatically extracts and groups information it needs for performing the full process. The next table contains the list of the components included within the EC application module.

TABLE 9.3   *EC: Enterprise Controlling Components*

EC-EIS	Executive Information System
EC-MC	Management Consolidation
EC-PCA	Profit Center Accounting

IM: Investment Management

The Investment Management module is an application that SAP introduced with release 3.0. It is designed for planning and managing budgets and capital investment projects. It can also be used for monitoring bookkeeping functions associated with work-in-progress assets within orders and investment projects.

The main components within this module are Capital Investment Management (Programs) and Tangible Fixed Assets (Measures).

TR: Treasury

The Treasury modules of SAP R/3 integrate forecasts and the management of cash resources with financial and logistical applications. They provide the necessary tools to analyze budgeting, the processing of electronic account settlements, the market in foreign currencies, etc. The Treasury module is divided into four main application components. (see Table 9.4).

TABLE 9.4   *Treasury Application components*

TR-CM	Cash Management
TR-FM	Funds Management
TR-TM	Treasury Management
TR-MRM	Market Risk Management

Figure 9.3 shows the integration between Treasury modules and the FI application.

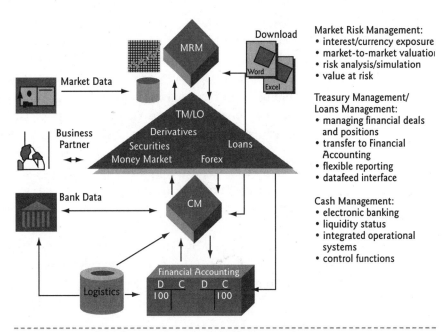

FIGURE 9.3   *Integration of treasury components   Copyright © SAP AG*

TR-CM: Cash Management

The Cash Management application can be used to analyze all the transactions dealing with the company's cash management. The main objective of this application is to keep a register of the input and output of cash and to control and plan liquidity to ensure timely payments by the company.

The Cash Management system includes the following main functions:

❑ **Cash inflows and outflows.** Used to register and monitor the input of all cash transactions, incoming and outgoing payments, bank postings, and so on. This can be done either manually or automatically by electronic banking. This tool makes it possible to have in real time all information related to cash accounting postings, providing for better and efficient planning of liquidity.

❑ **Liquidity planning.** With this functionality treasurers can evaluate company liquidity based on a specified time horizon. It allows for partial evaluations by defining or grouping different risk levels. The analysis of liquidity can be performed using different validity periods (short-, medium- or long-term).

❑ **The Payment Proposal list.** Using this, companies can monitor cash flow and therefore can anticipate and plan for future payments. This information can be compared with planned data.

❑ **A cash concentration functionality.** This is an effective financial planning tool for managing in one target account the balances of a group of accounts. At any moment and depending upon cash needs, companies can make financial planning for all cash transactions (payments, payment advices, account transfers, and so on). The system includes an interactive way of managing and implementing a concentration strategy.

❑ **Management of incoming payments.** This is integrated with financial accounting, so each time a payment is settled, this is automatically posted in the accounts receivable application and data of the cash management are also updated.

TR-FM: Funds Management

The Funds Management application can be used to control and manage the company's budgeted funds. To ease the management, the company can be divided into areas of responsibility for the budgeted funds. (Each of these areas is known as a financial management area). The TR-FM application can be used for monitoring all the payments and expenditures related to those FM areas.

The main processes covered by this application are:

❑ Complete control of budgeted funds in order to manage each of the phases: budget definition and creation, approval and release, extensions, modifications, and so on. It is possible to work with several budget versions; these can be compared or one can operate between them, facilitating budget modification and simulations.

❑ Assignment of funds to specific resources within the company. The application can be used to establish individual funds for specific proposals. Budgeted funds can be managed for each objective across the planned horizon. The budgeted funds can be proportionally distributed to the fiscal periods in which they are used.

❑ Monitoring budget status and selection of the work horizon, by fiscal periods, or by total budget.

❑ Drill-down reporting can be used for defining and customizing report layouts according to information need for funds: work horizon, responsibility area, data classification, ratios to analyze, summarization levels, and so on. The system can activate alarms to prevent fund overflow. The information system can also work with historical fund data and make comparisons between real and planned data.

❑ Total integration with other modules, so that all committed transactions in other business areas can affect the funds budget associated with the area. Modules integrated with Funds Management are:

  ❑ *Financial Accounting*, by means of incoming and outgoing payments, invoices received and issued, bank operations, and so on

  ❑ *Materials Management*, when there are goods receipts, consumptions, goods issued, purchase orders, etc.

  ❑ *Assets Accounting*, used when doing new investments.

TR-TM: Treasury Management

Treasury Management is a component of the Treasury model that includes all the functions related to performing cash transactions, analyzing current liquidity, risk positions, currency exchange, and so on. This application groups the functions needed by the Treasurer. The TR-TM application includes tools to analyze and plan liquidity, to report on market data risks for the short-, medium- and long-term. It has an information system that can be used to perform all types of analysis using the information generated by all Treasury transactions. This application also allows transferal of information to spreadsheets on PC, when users need a more specific analysis.

TR-MRM: Market Risk Management

Market Risk Management is a recent incorporation into the TR module in the latest release version 4.0. MRM functions use simulation and analysis tools to analyze and predict market risks in areas in which the company operates. TR-MRM incorporates access to all financial transactions of the company (cash operations, forecasting, financial postings, and so on), so that with all the information centrally treated, it can use the information analysis for each of the business environments in which the company operates. An important function for companies operating in several countries is the ability to establish currency exchange rates and risk margins for the currencies being used.

With simulation, the system can establish what-if scenarios and perform detailed analysis to better know market risks.

Logistics Application Modules

The Logistics modules represent the largest number of applications and business processes within R/3. They are in charge of managing the full supply chain of companies: from material procurement to product delivery and customer billing.

Logistics application modules include a comprehensive number of standard business processes, all necessary analysis tools, and predefined reports to help in the decision-making process. These applications are perfectly integrated and relate to the financial and human resource modules.

The main Logistics applications include following modules:

❑ LO–General Logistics
❑ MM–Materials Management
❑ PM–Plan Maintenance
❑ PP–Production Planning
❑ QM–Quality Management
❑ SD–Sales and Distribution
❑ PS–Project System

Figure 9.4 shows the main menu for the Logistics applications.

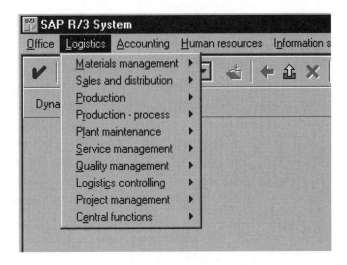

FIGURE 9.4 *Main menu options of logistics applications*

LO: Logistics General

Logistics General applications contain the intelligence engine of the R/3 logistics system. This is a set of tools and a report for analyzing and managing the status of company logistics. It also carries out a forecast of the supply chain. These applications are used by the other logistics applications. Table 9.5 lists the components of the LO module.

TABLE 9.5 *LO: General Logistics modules*

LO-ECH	Engineering Change Management
LO-LIS	Logistics Information System
LO-MD	Master Data
LO-PR	Forecast
LO-VC	Variant Configuration
LO-EHS	Environment Management

MM: Materials Management

The Materials Management module is part of the logistics applications of the SAP R/3 system. The functionality provided by this module is based on logistic operations on materials: acquisition, procurement, requirement planning, inventory management, physical warehouse management, and invoice verification.

The Materials Management module includes all the activities related to acquisition and procurement (purchasing) and control (inventory, warehouse).

Table 9.6 lists the MM application components.

TABLE 9.6   *Materials Management modules*

MM-PUR	Purchasing
MM-IM	Inventory Management
MM-WM	Warehouse Management
MM-IV	Invoice Verification
MM-IS	Information System
MM-CBP	Consumption-Based Planning
MM-EDI	Electronic Data Interchange

MM-PUR: Purchasing

The R/3 Purchasing application includes an extensive group of operations such as quotation requests, purchase order limits, vendor price comparison, agreements, order status, and so on.

The Purchasing module includes a comprehensive range of operations and functionality:

❑ **Management of purchase requisitions** with manual or automatic creation (using materials planning) of a document with the material needs from any of the requesting departments in a company.

❑ **Quotation management** which makes it possible to create and maintain quotations received from every provider, make comparisons between them, and create a purchase order for the best offer.

❑ **Purchase orders** function to make a formal order for materials to a specific provider (vendor), including data about quantity, prices, delivery dates, conditions, and so on. It includes a release strategy for order, in which there is control for managing purchase orders.

❑ **Info records (relationship between vendor and material).** Using these master data records, each vendor can be related to each of the materials sold (price, pricing conditions, quotations, delivery tolerance dates, vendor evaluation data, etc.)

❑ **Determination of sources of supply.** This function automatically proposes the best vendor, using information it already has when making a purchase order.

❑ **Purchase agreements** register outline agreements and contracts with vendors. Contracts have validity dates and quantities or total values for each material. With this procedure, every time an order is issued, the system automatically relates it to the contract and establishes price conditions and details agreed upon with the vendor.

❑ **External services management.** This performs a full cycle of handling the requisition of external services: requests the provider, requests for quotation, formal service orders, and acceptance.

MM-IM: Inventory Management

The MM-IM module contains tools to control and manage company stocks. IM contains direct links with purchasing and quality control applications.

Inventory Management is a great planning tool, with functions for comparing ordered materials against those received. IM always provides an updated stock control, since goods movement is immediately reflected in the system.

Stock management is performed dynamically so that it is possible to know instantly any materials situation in company warehouses. With this module the system always keeps stocks updated, since every materials movement is automatically registered in the system. It contains direct links with the purchasing module, quality management, sales and distribution, and production planning. Stock management also directly links with financial modules since with every stock movement (input, output, transfer) an accounting document is automatically created to reflect the difference in value produced by the movement, and another document to reflect the settlement made over the cost-object related to the operation, for instance a cost center, an order, a project, etc.

Another function of this module is the physical inventory of the warehouse, which makes it possible to take partial or total inventory of materials and then account for inventory differences.

MM-WM: Warehouse Management

The Warehouse Management module allows management of complex warehouse structures and physical control of the storage areas. It allows different storing strategies as well as picking mechanisms custom designed for every need. This application makes it possible to control all materials that by nature are dangerous and require special handling. This module links perfectly with other R/3 logistics modules such as Materials Management, (MM), Production Planning (PP), Quality Management (QM), and Sales and Distribution (SD).

MM-IV: Invoice Verification

With the Invoice Verification module R/3 provides the right tool so the company can avoid paying more than necessary for materials received. It manages information directly from accounting modules, cost control, and asset management.

Invoice verification uses purchase order and goods receipt information to register and account for the invoice. This operation not only checks if the invoiced quantity corresponds to that received, but also verifies the correctness of the accounting value; that it is between the tolerance limits defined for the purchase.

The Invoice Verification module does not include management of payment to the provider. The invoice, once created, and once all possible checks are made (for instance exceeding delivery dates, tolerance, etc.), is released for the payment. The payment itself is located within the Financial modules.

MM-IS: Information System

Within Materials Management, there are the following information systems (or collections of reporting programs and facilities):

❑ Purchasing Information System
❑ Inventory Control
❑ Vendor Evaluation.

Purchasing Information System and Inventory Control are two information systems within the Logistics Information System (LIS) of the Logistics General (LO). These two systems were described earlier in this module.

The application for vendor evaluation defines a collection of variables which can be associated with each provider (delivery dates, prices, degree of meeting agreement terms, etc.) with the aim of retaining and statistically measuring, analyzing, and evaluating the service offered by each provider. This information system is integrated with the Quality Management module (QM).

MM-CBP: Consumption-Based Planning

Materials planning in R/3 is based on warehouse stock and the information of historical consumption data for each materials.

Within consumption-based planning there are three types of strategies:

❑ **Reorder-point planning.** For every material this establishes a stock from which the system will automatically generate purchase requisitions.
❑ **Forecast-based planning.** With this option the system calculates future material needs based on historical consumption data. The planning horizon can be set to short-, medium- or long-term (daily, weekly, monthly, by fiscal period, etc.).
❑ **Time phased planning.** This planning variant is meant for materials that must be delivered precisely by the provider on a fixed and periodic schedule. With this strategy, planning establishes the same fixed date (for instance the same weekday) for replenishment.

MM-EDI: Electronic Data Interface

This component is in charge of the electronic interchange of information corresponding to documents related to purchasing management (request for quotations, purchase orders, invoices, etc.) For interchanging information EDI uses message formats. R/3 can work with its own format, known as IDOC. Incoming or outgoing messages must be formatted following IDOC. R/3 works with external EDI subsystems, which code and convert IDOC formats into the EDI format of every country.

PM: Plant Maintenance

The PM module is in charge of the complex maintenance of plant control systems. It includes support for graphical representations of plants and can be connected with Geographical Information Systems (GIS). It also contains detailed plant diagrams.

PM also includes support for the management of operating and maintenance problems, equipment, costs, and purchase order requisitions. A complete information system allows for rapid identification of weak points and plans preventive maintenance.

Table 9.7 shows the main application areas of the PM module.

TABLE 9.7   *Plant Maintenance module components*

PM-EQM	Equipment and Technical Objects
PM-IS	PM Information System
PM-PRM	Preventive Maintenance
PM-PRO	Maintenance Projects
PM-SM	Service Management
PM-WOC	Maintenance Orders Management

PM-EQM: Equipment and Technical Objects

This component of the PM module is used to register information on all the aspects that must be involved in plant maintenance. Besides registering data for each aspect, it includes the structures and relationship among them. For instance, a complex machine is made up of many pieces that must be included in the maintenance schedule.

There are many different types of technical objects. Among the most important are:

❏ **Equipment.** Each piece that makes up a tool or piece of equipment must be maintained individually. Each piece of equipment can have its own documentation, with a history of its revisions and repairs.

❏ **Functional locations.** Technical objects have different functional locations within a plant that are organized in hierarchical form, depending on function or on location within the plant. This way the system can plan and work on each object on a individual or collective basis.

❏ **Object networks.** This is used to link technical objects, for instance, those which make up a production line.

❏ **Bills of Materials.** BOMs are structures used to establish the complex relationship between the components of a technical object. They can have their own technical documentation, such as text documents, CAD drawings, and so on.

PM-PRM: Preventive Maintenance

The PM component is in charge of planning and performing the operations dealing with preventive maintenance in a full plant. All the work that must be done for preventive maintenance can be established by defining task lists for each of the technical objects to be maintained.

The system includes functions for establishing task periods, which can be based either on specific time periods or on counters defined for each technical object. These counters can be established based on the performance of the defined object. For example, preventive maintenance can be established for a specific machine, to be performed after 2000 hours of operation, or after specific power consumption.

PM-PRO: Maintenance Projects

This is a component closely linked to the Project System (PS) module. Functions from this application can use the structure of a defined project to incorporate maintenance tasks. Within a project structure users can define maintenance orders including the list of tasks to be performed. Maintenance tasks are also incorporated into the budget assigned to the project and their costs can be monitored and controlled at any time.

PM-SM: Service Management

This component is designed for complete administration and control of the services requested by customers, for every phase of a service: planning, request, acceptance, and billing.

The list which follows notes the main functions offered by Service Management:

❑ **Management of Warranties.** This application covers warranties for service management. Users can include types of warranties, attach information to be included within the warranty and establish the period of warranty.

❑ **Call Management.** Within R/3 the call management functions cover the entire service life-cycle. *Service notification* describes the type of service requested, the tasks to be performed, and where and by whom the service call is generated. The *processing of a service notification* is converted into a service order to the customer that includes all the requested services, and a maintenance order with the data of the tasks to be performed, the materials, resources and costs. The *completion of a service notification* indicates the acceptance of the received services, and the technical documentation for those services is generated for later analysis. At any time, users can perform a detailed analysis of the status of each call.

❑ **Service Billing.** The billing of services can be calculated based on service requisitions or services actually performed.

Service Management functionality is closely allied to the other modules of the R/3 system:

❑ Service needs are registered using order requisitions and, later, purchase requisitions; delivery and subsequent billing are done within the Materials Management application.

❑ Cost associated with each service and its settlement is measured against target cost within the Control module.

❑ When the company offers services to its customers, the conditions and descriptions of available services are defined in the Sales and Distribution module (SD).

❑ Serial number management within the Logistics General (LO) module can be used for individual treatment of each material. Service management can thus be performed on materials with a serial number.

PM-WOC: Maintenance Order Management

The management of maintenance orders can be used to better control maintenance tasks. Among the functions of this application are establishing planning for all the tasks that must be performed for each act of maintenance: reserving the materials needed for the maintenance, planning the work associated to each maintenance order, related costs, documents and necessary forms, and so on. With maintenance order management, the time needed for reaction to emergencies can be greatly reduced, since the orders include definitions for the requirements to solve problems.

This application can also keep a record of the realization of each task and know orders in advance, using the associated status to post accounting documents, make settlements of the cost objects, and maintain the history of maintenance orders.

PP: Production Planning

The business processes in charge of controlling, managing, and planning production are a very complex component within the SAP R/3 logistics application.

The PP module contains applications for the different phases, functions, and methodologies used for production planning: product quantities, types, material requirements and the supply chain, as well as the process of production itself. Figure 9.5 shows the PP application components menu.

The Production Planning and Control System module includes the functionality to meet the needs for Manufacturing Resource Planning (MRPII), as well as the functions related to Customer-Oriented Manufacturing Management System (COMMS) and Enterprise Resource Planning System (ERP). The components of the Production Planning module are also closely integrated with other R/3 applications such as Sales and Distribution (SD), Materials Management (MM), and others. PP module establishes strong links with all functionality related to production processes: customer requirements from the sales and distribution modules; goods movements from warehouses or factories, or the management of external sources of supply (MM); automatically generated financial statements (within the Financial Accounting module); the transfer of production costs to the different cost areas of the company (Controlling module); the management and control of the time used or planned for each of the production processes (Human Resource Management); quality control for all the materials involved in the production process (Quality Management); etc. PP also has an information system completely integrated within the Logistics Information System.

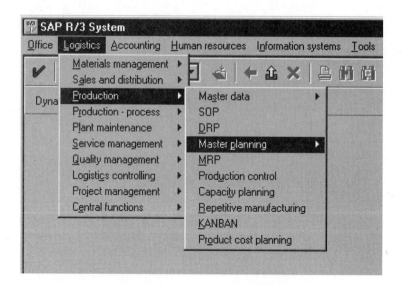

FIGURE 9.5   *Production planning application components*

Table 9.8 lists the main components or applications within the PP module.

TABLE 9.8   *PP: Production Planning applications*

PP-ATO	Assembly orders
PP-BD	Basic data
PP-CRP	Capacity Requirement Planning
PP-IS	Information System
PP-KAB	Kanban/Just-in-Time
PP-MP	Master planning
PP-MRP	Material Requirements Planning
PP-PDC	Plant Data Collection
PP-PI	Production Planning for Process Industries
PP-REM	Repetitive Manufacturing
PP-SFC	Production orders
PP-SOP	Sales and Operations Planning

The functions of the PP module are grouped into two parts: production planning and production management.

Production Planning and Control

There are several different ways to use production planning within R/3 PP module:

❑ **Sales & Operations Planning (SOP).** This has a set of tools for establishing production planning based on sales forecasting. The system is able to design a plan using a multiple-level hierarchy. SOP can foster a plan made with sales information but also using other information, such as purchase requisitions, goods delivery, stock levels, open orders, etc. SOP makes it possible to plan different scenarios with different planning horizons and can establish comparisons among them.

❑ **Forecasting.** This tool, related to production planning, has as its goal to establish forecasts based on historical data to anticipate future needs. Planning can be based on stochastic models (moving average, constant model with exponential smoothing, trend model with exponential smoothing, seasonal model with exponential smoothing, etc.).

❑ **Master Planning.** This application can be used to manage the master data for finished goods for production planning. To establish a plan, sales order information, demand planning, or stock replenishment plans are used. The module includes demand management, production planning, and master production scheduling (MPS).

❑ **Material Requirement Planning (MRP).** The aim of this application is to determine the required quantities for each material in order to create automatic production orders. To do so, this application needs information on the stock in each warehouse, material purchase planning, and planned production orders. The PP module can do global or selective MRP, acting on different levels. It can plan for a single material, a group of materials, or all the materials from a plant. MRP execution proposes and automatically defines the production needs or sources for external supply for each date in the plan horizon.

❑ **Distribution Resource Planning (DRP).** This allows for global planning of the needs of a distributed environment with several R/3 installations. DRP permits analysis of the needs in a global way and plans the production, taking into consideration the needs of every installation within a corporation.

❑ **Long-term planning.** This is a PP tool that uses forecast information about stocks and planned sales to anticipate supply needs and calculate the potential bottlenecks for each work center. This is extremely useful information for the purchasing department, since the automatic generation of forecasts, can be used to establish outline agreements and vendor delivery plans. Long-term planning includes functions for defining several versions within the master plan. This feature can be used for simulations and comparisons between versions. Different scenarios can be defined for long-term planning. For each of the scenarios, the system will handle the information separately. Once the simulations and tests with different versions are completed, the demand program can be replaced.

❑ **Capacity Requirements Planning (CRP).** This set of tools can be used for defining and calculating the capacity for each work center. It can graphically display the results of the planning process. Then capacity can be evaluated and planning for production orders can be carried out using the resulting data on work center capacities.

Production Orders

The functionality associated with production orders is the main link between different production plans and manufacturing. All the production process is centered on the production order, which includes all required information, such as operations, materials, capacities, and generated costs.

The production order cycle reflects each of the phases within the production process:

❑ **Creation of production order.** Normally the order is created when the date for the previously defined opening period is reached. Production orders can be based on planned orders. The process of creating a production order requires detailed information about associated materials and quantities, operations, and work center capacities. Once the order is created, the system adds the Bill of Materials (BOM) and the route to the order. The system can also work with alternative routes and BOMs. Finally, the system reserves the components in the list of materials needed for the order and charges identified work centers.

❑ **Order release.** This happens before a production order can be processed. Before order release the system checks to verify the stock existence of the components in the list of materials and that there is enough capacity in the work centers in which the order will be processed. Order release can be carried out individually or collectively, in order to speed up the process. Once the order is released, all associated documents can be printed: control list of operations, picking list, and so on.

❑ **Order confirmation.** Once the order has been processed the system must be told it has been finished. Order confirmation is used by PP to inform plant planning to update information. The information forwarded includes: produced quantities, consumed quantities, scrap, times, and ending dates. Part of this information goes to the Cost Controlling (CO) application, and other part is integrated with the Human Resource System (corresponding to the time used by employees for carrying out the operations).

When the order is confirmed, the stock for those materials included in the order is automatically updated, and the general ledger account associated with finished goods is increased by the valuation of the product standard price.

The Production Planning module distinguishes several types of production:

❑ **Make-to-Order with Assembly Orders.** In this type, production orders are generated based on sales orders, so that there is a tight integration between production orders and sales. When a sales order is created, the system automatically generates a procurement element for the MRP, checks the availability of all necessary components for production, and makes reservation for production capacity and availability of work centers. The system can then calculate the date for the delivery of the sales order from the manufacturing lead time.

❑ **Repetitive Manufacturing.** This type of production work is normally carried out with similar groups of products. Production is not controlled by individual orders, but using production plans linked to the production master plans for each line. The system can work with different production versions, making it possible to establish different routes for the same product. In order to plan production, a period-based planning table is used. Repetitive manufacturing can also work with production plans, with plans for specific products, or with user selection through the "planning ID." To facilitate the tasks, R/3 includes a graphical interface for managing the planning table in an interactive form: it has tools for line balancing, collective planning, detailed capacity information, and so on. Production costs are automatically routed to the associated cost centers.

❑ **Engineering-to-Order with Project System.** This type of production is integrated with the R/3 Project System (PS) module. It is oriented to production within long-term projects. All the production control is inside the PS module.

❑ **Just-in-Time and Kanban.** R/3 PP supports both the Just-in-Time and the Kanban methods for production. These are completely integrated with the Cost Controlling (CO) module and the MRP functionality. The control cycle defined in Kanban is based on a replenishment strategy derived from the balance between input and output requests within the production circuit. R/3 includes a tool for managing the procurement and supplies flow within the production circuit, known as KANBAN Board. This tool obviates the need for working with cards to control the flow between different containers.

PS: Project System Management

Project System is a global and sector-independent solution for the monitoring and control of every task involved in a project. It can be applied to any type of project: investment, marketing, research, installation, and so on.

From the point of view of business processes, any type of project must go through the following phases:

❑ Concept/Design
❑ Structuring
❑ Cost and Date Planning
❑ Budgeting
❑ Realization
❑ Closing.

Project System supports the management of a project throughout all life-cycle phases. Before defining and realizing specific projects, the system allows for definition of standard structures, which can be used as models or starting points for creating new operative structures.

The R/3 Project System includes graphical tools that allow creation of project structures using standard techniques such as Gantt charts and network diagrams. PS also incorporates standard system interfaces with support for PDC (Plant data collection) and for popular PC applications such as GRANEDA, MS Project, MS Access, and spreadsheets.

There are two basic structures specific to Project System. The WBS element (work breakdown structure) is used to make a hierarchical structure of projects, and the network can be used to define (with a maximum level of details) all the tasks, relationships, and resources needed.

The Project System includes all the components that support the project management for each of the phases previously defined:

- ❑ PS–BD: Basic Data
- ❑ PS–OS: Operative Structures
- ❑ PS–PLN: Planning
- ❑ PS–APP: Budgeting
- ❑ PS–EXE: Realization
- ❑ PS–IS: Information System.

PS-BD: Basic Data

The Basic Data component of the PS module is meant to define and use *project templates*. It can be used to define standard structures used in the Project System, like WBS, networks, and milestones. It can also include data from other modules or cross applications that can be used in operative and standard structures, like human resources data, capacities, product resources and tools, materials, equipment, project texts and documentation, and so on.

PS-OS: Operative Structures

The Operative Structures component of the PS module is used to specify the necessary data for completely describing a project and the needs it generates.

The *Work Breakdown Structure (WBS)* is a way of defining projects in a hierarchical form. The projects are made up of a project definition containing common data for all objects in the project, and on which all WBS elements are dependent. Every WBS element can be made up of other WBS elements, until the desired level of detail is reached. Those making these hierarchical structures must remember that this definition will be the base for planning, time and cost control, and the project budget.

The WBS elements include operative flags for specifying whether they can be used for planning costs, and if they can receive income or costs. WBS can be linked with texts and documents.

The next important operative structure is the *network*, consisting of a header, containing all the common data for objects depending on the network, and activities that can be made up of other operating elements. There are functions in the system to define time and logical relationships between the network operations.

There are three types of activities:

❑ **Internal processing** activities are those operations or activities performed by the internal resources of the organization. To define these activities, the system uses the concept of *work center* to represent the internal resources of the organization and its capacity. Work centers can be equipment, persons, groups of persons, and so on, according to the capacities assigned to them.

❑ **External processing** activities are those operations that will be executed or performed by external resources. When defining a need for an external processing activity, the system automatically creates a purchase requisition.

❑ **Cost activities** can be used for planning and notifying costs, without making a detailed definition and description of the content of the activity.

Activities can be further composed of other activities, known as *activities elements*, that can be of the same type as described above. Users can also link materials, documents, texts and production resources, and tools to the network activities.

When material needs for a network activity are defined, the type of procurement can also be specified. When there is an external procurement, the system can generate purchase requisitions, and for internal procurement, it can generate stock reservations. Projects can manage their own stocks; these are treated as special stock and include all the materials needed for the project.

The system can use *milestones* in WBS elements as well as in networks. These milestones are used for analyzing the progress of the project and can also be linked to predefined functions.

For each WBS element and network, the Project System also defines the settlement rules by assigning cost objects and the percentages in which costs will be settled. The objects receiving the settlements are: general ledger account, cost center, order, WBS element, asset, material, network, profitability segment, sales order, cost object, and order position.

A strategy for automatically creating the settlement rule can be established in the network based on the rules defined for the WBS element. Commonly, in a generic case and considering the relationship to the phases of the project, the process for defining operative structures will be:

❑ Creation of a project definition corresponding to the conceptual design phase

❑ In detailed design or structuring, creation of a hierarchy of WBS elements, with as many levels as needed; networks are defined with their operations as well as the interaction between activity or network and WBS element

❑ Control of project status and activities by using system status and defined status values, which can be configured by the users. Through user status management, the project can include additional controls.

PS-PLN: Project Planning

The planning component of PS includes the project planning tool, based on Gantt charts, that can be used to define the operative structures of a project, as well as to set date planning on a global basis for all the project elements. There are also functions allowing for independent definition of the planning of costs, dates, and finances.

PLANNING OF DATES   The desired method for planning (top-down or bottom-up) can be predefined. There are also several types of dates. In WBS elements, dates can be planned as basic dates and forecast dates. The dates on the network are calculated by the system based on the duration of the activities and the defined programming method, except for restrictions on completion dates, which can be manually updated. They can later be transmitted to the assigned WBS elements as programmed dates. With a mix of all possibilities, the system can be used for choosing and defining the planning method that best suits each case.

COST PLANNING   The R/3 system can contain several versions of cost plans and make comparative analysis using the PS information system. The planning of costs for WBS elements can be performed using three different methods:

1. **Structure costs planning**, where the global costs for WBS elements are planned. This is a method that allows for yearly plans.
2. **Detailed planning**, used for making plans for each cost class within a WBS element and year. This type of planning can make distribution by period, of the planned costs for each cost class.
3. **Individual cost calculation**, used for planning costs based on involved resources, both internal and external.

All planning methods can be used simultaneously. It is quite common to have information with different levels of details, according to the specific WBS element, when realizing the planning process. The planning of costs in the networks is done using the relevant costs of the resources included in the network.

FINANCIAL PLANNING   Financial planning is used for forecasting income and expense flow, yearly and by defined periods, for each WBS element.

PS-APP: Project System Budgeting

The budget is the authorized framework for the costs associated with projects. It can be done using planned costs. Budgeting is based on total values for the WBS elements of a project, and it is possible to distribute the budget over several years.

The project system uses different types of budgets. The *original* budget is the initially assigned or allocated budget; it can be later modified. Budget *updates* occur when it is necessary to make corrections or amendments to the original budget. These updates can be either supplements, which increase the budget, returns that make it lower, or transfers between WBS elements. The *current* budget is calculated based on the original budget and the modifications introduced by the budget updates.

Releasing the budget is a process that allows the use of allocated funds. Some organizations clearly distinguish between budget allocation and the authorization for using it. Based on the allocated or released budget, the system performs availability control to define the tolerance limits above or beyond the budget. Reaching the tolerance limits can activate several system actions such as warnings or error messages.

Taking into consideration the hierarchical structure of the WBS elements, all different budget views or displays are intertwined:

❏ The *distributed* budget for a WBS element is the sum of the budgets assigned to the hierarchically dependent WBS elements.
❏ The *distributable* budget corresponds to the difference between the current budget and the already distributed budget.
❏ The *assigned* budget corresponds to the total committed and real budget.
❏ The *accumulated* budget is the sum of the annual budgets.
❏ The *remainder* is the difference between the global current budget and the sum of the annual budgets.

PS-EXE: Realization

The Realization component supports most of the functions corresponding to realization phases and project closing. The notification of dates and real cost is carried out inside this module component. The real dates in the operations of a network are registered in the notifications. The updating of dates for WBS elements can be defined for manual entry or by notification of the assigned operations.

The real costs of a WBS element are entered through:

❏ Notification of operations
❏ Billing of internal activities
❏ Costs transfer
❏ Determination of charges of general costs
❏ Goods receipts for purchase requisitions charged to the project
❏ Goods issued for reservations.

It is important to remember that the integration of real costs for WBS elements can be done in two ways: by settlement or by assignment.

REAL COSTS INTEGRATION BY SETTLEMENT   Where there is a goods receipt for a purchase requisition settled to a network or to a WBS element, the costs are directly posted to the corresponding element. The real cost collector will be the network or the WBS element.

REAL COSTS INTEGRATION BY ASSIGNMENT   When any of the following cost collectors—network (which can be known as *PS order*), CO order, maintenance order, or production order)—are assigned to a WBS element, the costs remain in that order until they are settled to the WBS element. However, with the reports of the Information System, users can perform a cost analysis using the assigned WBS element.

Within this module the main processes of the closing phase are:

❑ Determination of overhead surcharges to general costs
❑ Cost settlement to the WBS elements and networks to the cost objects established on the settlement rules.

It is from the operative structure component that the last two tasks of the projects are performed: closing the operative structures by changing the status of networks and WBS elements to CLOSED, and project archiving.

PS-IS: PS Information System

The PS Information System can be accessed from inside the module or outside it from the general information system facilities. Internal PS module information can be obtained by using:

❑ **The structures/dates component of the Information System.** This provides mainly technical information about the progress of the project. It includes information about all objects that make up a project and its hierarchical structure, including date and status information. Together with current project data, it allows for recovery and analysis of data from previous versions, as well as different versions of planned costs, and archived data.
❑ **The costs/revenues/payments menu.** Different levels of details, the summarization of current budget, costs, and payments data are used.

Using the integration reports, the system can provide aggregated data based on the characteristics defined in the classification system. The reports from the resources component include data external to the project system and provide information about capacities and materials management based on the purchasing documents created from projects.

The Integration of PS with Other Modules

One of the main advantages of the R/3 Project System management module is the inherent integration of PS with the rest of the R/3 applications. The following paragraphs briefly describe the way in which this integration is achieved.

INTEGRATION WITH MM   When creating a purchase document and making a reservation, these operations can be posted against WBS elements. With these operations, when making a goods receipt in the first case or a goods issue in the second, the associated costs are directly posted to the WBS element. A tighter integration can be maintained when project needs for materials or services are defined in the activities of related networks. R/3 automatically generates purchase requisitions and corresponding reservations, which will be posted to the network.

INTEGRATION WITH IM   An investment program is a hierarchical structure. The last level of this structure is an investment measure. These investment measures are a first-level WBS element and CO orders. To manage investment projects, integration with IM is carried out in a natural way, since these projects are really the investment measures that make up the investment program.

INTEGRATION WITH SD   In this case there are two possible ways for integration. A sales order, or a position within an order, can be posted to a WBS element so that costs received by the project can be analyzed for revenues corresponding to the sales of the project. There is the possibility for tighter integration when automatic definition of projects from sales orders are used. The material to be sold is assigned to a standard network. If configurable materials are used, the project can also be defined based on the characteristics of the material by using a variant configuration.

INTEGRATION WITH PM   Maintenance orders can be assigned to a WBS element. For instance, in the case of a project with a warranty during a specified period after the delivery, if maintenance orders are assigned to a corresponding WBS element, the system can analyze the maintenance costs together with the other project costs.

INTEGRATION WITH PP   A production order can also be assigned to a WBS element for projects that include internal production.

INTEGRATION WITH FI   The Project System can be used to carry out the financial planning for the cash flow of a WBS element. There is also an indirect integration of real costs derived from the integration with MM.

INTEGRATION WITH CO   PS receives internal costs through the billing of activities, overhead surcharges, distribution, and so on. A CO order can also be assigned to a WBS element.

INTEGRATION WITH AA   Projects can be defined so that the created WBS elements have an associated "work-in-progress" asset. It is also possible to make a direct cost settlement from a project to an asset.

QM: Quality Management

The Quality Management module (QM) is that group of applications within R/3 in charge of managing the functions related to quality management and control. As an integral part of the R/3 logistics applications, the QM components include the functions and tasks related to quality planning, control, and inspections, as well as compliance with international normalized quality standards. The R/3 system as a whole and the independent R/3 applications always include efficient quality control of all the business processes they manage.

The main tasks of the QM applications have to do with the quality control of the sales and distribution processes (for example, deliveries to customers), material management (for instance, quality data linked to materials, quality control of goods receipts, provider qualifications and assessments, and so on), the plant maintenance (quality inspection of the components of each plant, materials for repairs, and so on), and with production planning (quality control of finished goods, in-production operations, and so on.)

Table 9.9 shows a list of the components within the QM module:

TABLE 9.9   *Quality Management application components*

QM-PT	Quality Planning
QM-IM	Quality Inspection
QM-CA	Quality Certificates
QM-QC	Quality Control
QM-QN	Quality Notifications

QM-PT: Quality Planning

The Quality Planning component of QM includes a set of tools and functions for easing the process of planning quality and organizing inspection plans.

The most important functions within Quality Planning are:

❑ Management of master data (basic data) related to the inspection plan (materials, providers, info records, catalog, inspection characteristics and methods)

❑ Inspection planning, used to define all information associated with inspection plans: characteristics of inspections, operations, and the equipment involved.

❑ Control of quality inspections of the procurement process (purchase requisitions, goods receipt, provider selection, and so on)

❑ Quality control on the production processes: capacity planning, production control, quality inspections associated with production lots, and so on

❑ Quality control for sales and distribution, such as the operations of delivery to customers, picking orders, and so on.

QM-IM: Quality Inspection

Quality inspection is carried out on different inspection lots created in the system. An inspection lot is a set of a group of materials created with the purpose of performing a quality inspection. The creation of lots can be defined either manually or automatically, from different points of the supply chain:

❏ In goods movement (goods receipts from purchase orders to providers, goods issues, goods transfers between plants, and so on).
❏ In the production processes, associated with production orders
❏ In the process of delivery to customers.

Finally, once the quality inspection is performed on an inspection lot, the system can save two types of results: planned and unplanned. The system can keep information on possible errors or malfunctions detected during the inspection and, depending on the defined degree of control, can store the information using different levels of detail, on either a summarized form or a detailed one.

QM-QC: Quality Control

The Quality Control component is one of the most important applications within the QM module. Quality management is based on analysis of the information generated in the other QM components: Planning, Inspection, and Notification. The system makes possible automatic determination of samples according to the desired level of quality to be defined.

The application includes graphical tools for facilitating analysis of the registered data. The information system is prepared to use standard and flexible tools that can define information structures to perform analysis resulting in inspections and quality notifications. The quality management information system is included within the Logistics Information System (LIS), located within the Logistics General (LO).

QM-CA: Quality Certificates

This QM component is used for including documents on specific logistic operations that can be used to certify the components or associated processes. For example, in some industries, such as chemical or pharmaceutical, it is mandatory for goods deliveries to attach a quality certificate including information about the production lot of each product (expiration dates, dangerous components, and so on.) All the information attached to the certificate is collected from several associated master data (materials, inspection plans, production lots, and so on).

The certificate generation can either be manually or automatically created, according to previously defined profiles (certificate profile and automatic certificate determination profile).

QM-QN: Quality Notifications

The objective of quality notification is to enhance the system with a powerful tool for storing and communicating incidences and problems related to the management of quality. The notification can register information about malfunctions in materials or services, customer complaints, delivery damage, and any other quality-related issues. This component is closely allied to the notifications of the Plant Maintenance (PM) and Service Management (SM) modules.

There are three different types of standard notification: customer complaints, complaints about sales representatives, and internal problems. It is also possible to define additional types of notifications according to the type of management and of the notification needs identified in the company business.

The notification functions give the quality management system the efficiency to dynamically manage the incidents detected. The process could be as follows:

❑ Detect the problem or incidence and describe it in the system
❑ Analyze the problem and define the cause
❑ Correct/solve the problem.

The problems or defects detected and registered make up a database that can later be used to speed up and automate the management of notifications. The system can automatically notify based on previously registered malfunctions or problems.

SD: Sales and Distribution Module

The Sales and Distribution (SD) module consists of a collection of applications for supporting the needs of the business areas related to selling activities and management, such as sales orders, promotions, competition, quotations, call management, planning, marketing campaigns, and so on. These applications are closely allied within R/3 and interact with the other modules, mainly with Materials Management and Financial Accounting. The module's most important components are: Sales Support, Sales Order Management, Delivery, Transport, Foreign Trade, Billing, and Sales Information System.

A noticeable feature of the SD module is the system's ability to obtain in real time information on product availability in order to make quick quotations. Customers benefit from better and faster service and can receive direct confirmation of their orders by mail, fax, or other media.

The functions of the Sales and Distribution module can be used also to define and manage pricing structures and conditions; the link with financial accounting and controlling allows immediate updates of accounts receivable and billing.

Table 9.10 lists the main SD module components.

TABLE 9.10   *Components of the Sales and Distribution module*

SD-BIL	Billing
SD-CAS	Sales Support
SD-EDI	Electronic Data Interchange (EDI)
SD-GF	General Sales Functions
SD-SIS	Sales Information System
SD-MD	Master Data
SD-SHP	Shipping
SD-TR	Transportation
SD-SLS	Sales

Figure 9.6 displays the SD menu options, corresponding to each of the application components.

SD-CAS: Sales Support

The SD module contains a group of tools to facilitate the management of sales and make sales administration more efficient. The objective of this application is to simplify and automate all the processes related to the pre-sales activities, such as customer inquiries and quotations, so that users can be free of routine tasks.

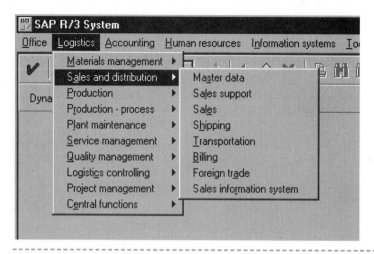

FIGURE 9.6   *SD applications menu*

Sales support functions are closely linked to the sales information system; the most representative are the following:

- **Contact people.** SD helps gather detailed information on contacts who are potential customers or are relevant to the business (contact type, way to locate, personal data, responsibility within the company, and so on). Besides the contact personal data, the system can store the contact history used for each potential customer.
- **Information about the competition and its products.** In order to better know the status of the competition and its products, SD can store detailed and individual information for each competitor. Data about a competitive company can be kept on the competitor master, and its products can be saved on the material master. This information can be used to perform product comparison between a company's own products and those of the competition. Besides product data, the system can contain descriptive notes to facilitate comparative analysis.
- **Sales activities.** This functionality makes it possible to perform a control of the various contacts with each customer. Users can store the different types of sales activities carried out with each customer (call management, letters, personal visits, presentations, and so on) and use this information to assess the effectiveness of sales management.

❑ **Direct marketing.** SD includes a direct mail function to facilitate the creation and later follow-up of a massive mailing campaign.

SD-SLS: Sales Order Management

The objective of the SD Sales Order Management component is to speed up and automate routine processes, thus increasing the efficiency and reliability of the sales chain. Full sales management, from any of the phases in the circuit, is based on linked documents to guarantee correct workflow without the need for printing documents.

The main types of documents within the SD module are:

❑ **Sales Inquiry.** This is the first document in the sales order cycle. It stores information requested by the potential customer that may be used in future sales documents or in global evaluation with the rest of the pre-sales documents.

❑ **Sales Quotation.** When a customer requests information on price, availability, delivery dates, and so on, the system creates a sales quotation. This document can also be generated with information available in an Inquiry Document.

❑ **Sales Order.** The sales order is the main document of sales processing. It makes a formal commitment with the customer using relevant sales data: products with quantities, prices, delivery dates, contact people, descriptive texts, taxes, measurements, and so on. All this information can be automatically proposed by the system using master data on material, customer, price conditions, customer-material info records, etc. Linked with the order, the system automatically performs several functions to facilitate sales processing, like price determination, availability control, delivery planning, route determination, shipping point, and so on.

❑ **Contracts.** Contracts are documents that reflect business agreements with customers including the global delivery quantity of a list of materials, or the global price of the sale. Contracts are signed with a period of validity and can include a delivery plan. Once the contract is created, sales orders are issued against it.

❑ **Cash Sales.** These documents speed up the sales process. Once the sales order is created, the system automatically generates the delivery order and the billing information.

❑ **Consignment orders.** Goods are delivered to the customers and not paid for until the customer uses them. Reposition orders are used to establish the quantities needed in the consignment stock.

❑ **Returns.** These documents reflect the returns of part or all of a sales order. They include reasons for return, like malfunction, damages, goods on customer test, and so on.

SD-SHP: Shipping and Delivery Processing

The main function of the delivery-processing component is to guarantee the distribution process to customers and to make it more efficient. The whole delivery process is based on shipping points defined for every organization. The shipping point is an organization element that defines the type of equipment and the choice of transportation used (truck, train, ship, air). The main activities in this functionality are:

❑ **Delivery creation.** Within R/3 the creation of the delivery document does not require entering information, since all the data are obtained using the system's master data. When creating the documents the system determines products and quantities, route information, expedition location, export information, weights and measures, lots, packing proposals, and so on.

❑ **Picking.** This function is linked to delivery. Within the system, picking indicates the physical location of the goods that must be picked, the best moment for picking, the serial numbers associated with the selected products, and additional information. Picking management can be performed collectively in order to improve efficiency, as when optimizing routes within the warehouse to minimize the time required for the physical picking.

❑ **Packing.** The packing functionality of the SD module can associate with material information about packing attributes, like type, measurements, weight and volume tolerance limits, and others. It then can create transport units to ease the process of delivery (product grouping, label printing for facilitating handling), automate and speed up the management of packaging, and so on.

❑ **Information Management.** Documentation linked to full delivery processing (delivery notes, transport notifications, picking lists, etc.) can be displayed on screen or printed on paper. R/3 also includes alternative methods for output like fax, Internet, telex, and EDI.

SD-TR: Transportation

This SD functionality is able to monitor and plan transportation management. Its main objective is to guarantee delivery by speeding the process and making it more efficient. An important point in this module is that the cost of transportation directly affects the product cost.

The SD module includes the necessary tools for optimizing transport and consequently the incurred cost. The transportation planning functions can organize transport (best dates, means of transport, carrier, and linked documentation), specify routes, and monitor the shipments. This component also has an associated information system with many reports offering detailed information about transports routes, shipments, and so on.

SD-FT: Foreign Trade

The goal of this SD component is to manage exports and international trade in the most efficient way. The foreign trade application can automate all the necessary information needed for this type of commerce. Once this information is stored in the system, it is automatically attached to the documents needed for foreign trade. The system collects the information in order to make export declarations and meet the regulations of the countries with which the company is doing business (declarations of INTRASTAT, EXTRASTAT, NAFTA, MITI, etc.). The system includes standard interfaces (via EDI or ALE) than can be used for communication with other systems and for the exchange of needed information to speed up the process.

SD-BIL: Billing

Billing is the last process in the sales chain. The main functions within the Billing application are issuing invoices based on sold goods or services, issuing pro forma invoices from sales orders or shipments, cancellation of billing, etc.

The billing process within R/3 is closely integrated with the Financial Accounting and the Control modules. All the invoices, cancellations, and credit operations have corresponding statements within the accounting application (both when issuing the invoice and when issuing the payment). Integration with CO can be used for assigning charges as well as revenue to different cost centers, projects, profitability segments, and so on.

Another important functionality within Billing is *Pricing*. Price determination in the invoices has some flexibility, and includes such items as copying prices, discounts, or recharges from the sales orders; entering them manually; using dates for price determination; and so on.

The SD module includes three different billing methods:

❑ **Separate invoice** for each delivery on customer site
❑ **Collective invoice**, including several orders and several deliveries per order; a single invoice can be created including all sales transactions
❑ **Separate invoices**, where a single order with its respective delivery order is converted into several invoices.

SD can carry out a date strategy for invoicing each sales order:

❑ **Periodic Billing** can be used for establishing a periodic and constant invoicing calendar (monthly, quarterly, etc.); the system will automatically issue the invoice when the due date is reached
❑ **Milestone Billing** is performed according to a group of milestones used to divide the total bill; when each milestone is reached the system issues the corresponding partial invoice.

Human Resources Application Modules

The HR modules include all necessary business processes for efficient management of human resource needs: applicant screening, payroll accounting, personnel development, or time management. As with the rest of the SAP applications, the aim of the HR module is to enter data once, so that it will be available to other related applications, like accounting, plant maintenance, or business workflow.

The HR applications include full support for salary administration and payroll, work schedule models, planning, travel expenses, and so on.

The HR modules and their associated business processes are country-specific areas, since the software must adhere to specific country laws concerning employment, taxes, benefits, etc. For this reason SAP includes different procedures and transactions for different countries.

Two main application areas can be distinguished within the Human Resources module: PA–Personnel Administration and PD–Personnel Development.

Tables 9.11 and 9.12 list the HR application components within PA and PD.

TABLE 9.11   *PA: Personnel Administration modules*

PA-APP	Applicant Management
PA-BEN	Benefits
PA-EMP	Employee Management
PA-INW	Incentive wages
PA-PAY	Payroll
PA-TIM	Time Management
PA-TRV	Travel Expenses

TABLE 9.12   *PD: Personnel Planning and Development modules*

PD-OM	Organizational Management
PD-PD	Personnel development
PD-RPL	Room Reservations Planning
PD-SCM	Seminar and Convention Management
PD-WFP	Workforce Planning

IS Modules: SAP Strategy for Vertical Industries

To become more competitive in the ever-changing and global economy, companies need to reduce their costs and provide added value to their products and services. These objectives and needs require that a company make important investments in systems and information technology. These require not only a tight integration of business processes, but also must satisfy the exclusive requirements of the relevant business market segments.

To complement the comprehensive set of functions and process models included within R/3, SAP is constantly developing and enhancing IS (Industry Solutions) packages aimed at specific vertical industries. These are optional packages that integrate perfectly with the rest of R/3 applications.

Using the solid business process platform provided by the R/3 core applications, SAP strategy has been directed toward complementing and enhancing solutions from different perspectives: vertical solutions for specific industries, extended supply chain management, and business intelligence.

These specific packages are also a way for SAP to extend its strategic position and broaden the software market to other industries as it searches for a bigger market.

Available or announced IS solutions SAP has developed or is in process of developing are:

- ❏ IS-B: Solution for banks, financial industries, and market risk management
- ❏ IS-H: Solution for hospitals and healthcare institutions
- ❏ IS-IS: Solution for insurance companies and currency markets
- ❏ IS-OIL: Solution for oil industries
- ❏ IS-Media: Solution for the communication and publishing industries
- ❏ IS-PS: Solution for administration and the public sector
- ❏ IS-Retail: Solution for retailing companies
- ❏ IS-Utilities: Solution for utilities industries
- ❏ IS-Telecom: Solution for telecommunication operators
- ❏ IS-Automotive: Solution oriented toward automobile manufacturing industries

- ❏ IS-Consumer Products: Solution for consumer products industries
- ❏ IS-Aerospace & Defense: Solution oriented toward air and military industries
- ❏ IS-Chemicals: Solution for chemical industries
- ❏ IS-Engineering & Construction: Solution for construction and engineering companies
- ❏ IS-Pharmaceuticals: Solution for pharmaceutical industries.

The list is constantly growing and even includes different components for the same vertical industry.

WEB

An updated list and more detailed information about existing and announced industry solutions can be found at the following Internet pointer **http://www.sap.com/products/industry/index.htm**.

To develop a specific solution for vertical industries, SAP created ICOEs, Industry Centers of Expertise, now known as IBUs, Industry Business Units, and established close partnerships with customers, consulting companies, and software companies. With this approach, implementation and development can be achieved in less time, providing faster benefits to customers.

The IS packages are generally a collection of specific business processes, translated into a set of integrated transactions, programs, screens, and documentation, and installed as an add-on component, closely integrated with core R/3 business processes.

CHAPTER 10

Basis R/3: Architecture and System Management

This is another reference chapter presenting an overview of the SAP R/3 Basis System including common practices of SAP system administrators. This chapter is summarized and updated from several chapters and sections of *The SAP R/3 Handbook*, the book dedicated to the Basis System. The following sections explain basic concepts using clear terms for understanding by non-technical Sappers.

To understand all implications of SAP implementations, it is also important to comprehend the system's technical architecture: how it works, the main processes, how communications are handled, the available options for SAP communication with other systems, the actual role of the database, and how the technical infrastructure is administered and monitored.

SAP R/3 has a solid design based on the principal of a modular multitier client/server whose components are the process and the software models ready to offer the client/server and applications services.

The following sections in this chapter include definitions of the components that make up the system and how are they related. Using this approach we will be able to grasp clearly how the client/server architecture of SAP is defined and implemented.

The R/3 Basis System and middleware work exactly the same whatever the underlying operating system or relational database management systems. The only differences are in administration utilities specific to operating systems and databases incorporated into the R/3 system.

Basis Components (BC) Module

The R/3 *basis software* is the set of programs and tools that interfaces with the computer operating system, the underlying database, the communication protocols, and the presentation interfaces. This software enables the R/3 applications (FI, CO, SD, PP, and so on) to have the same functionality and to work exactly the same way no matter what operating system or database the system is installed on. The R/3 basis software is an independent layer that guarantees the technical integration of all application modules. When the basis software is referred to in this sense, is generally known as the *R/3 com-*

mon kernel or *R/3 middleware*. Kernel and middleware have become generic computing terms widely used: *kernel* usually is referred to as the core or nucleus of a system; *middleware* means a set of programs that allows an independent interface between an upper layer and a lower layer (it stands in the *middle*).

These terms are also referred to as the *R/3 Basis System* or simply *R/3 Basis*. Besides the interfaces with other systems, elements such as the operating system, database, network and user interface, the tools and components of the R/3 Basis provide:

❏ The environment for R/3 applications. This is built on the ABAP development workbench and the ABAP Repository, which includes the ABAP Data Dictionary (centralized logical repository with all the business and system data). It also has Workbench and Customizing Organizer and the Transport system to facilitate the modification and enhancement of the system and the integration of new developments across systems. The second part of Chapter 5 includes an overview of the main components of the ABAP Workbench.

❏ System administration and monitoring tools, including a common printing system and a complex and comprehensive set of management transactions within the CCMS (Computer Center Management System) used for monitoring, tuning, and controlling the R/3 system.

❏ Architectural software of client/server design, specifically suited to scalability. It allows the distribution of available resources.

❏ Authorization and profile management tools that take care of user management and internal access control of system and business objects.

❏ Database monitoring and administration utilities.

As shown in Figure 10.1, the R/3 middleware uses common APIs (Application Program Interfaces) and has the function of interfacing with the underlying operating system, the database, the communication protocols, and the GUIs. The features of the R/3 basis system that enable this type of interface are:

❏ The client/server architecture and configuration
❏ The use of relational database management systems
❏ Graphical user interface design for presentation.

It is based on standards: C and C++ for the programming of the runtime environment, open and standard SQL for embedded SQL calls inside ABAP to interface with the database, communication standards like TCP/IP or RFC, and standard graphical interfaces like Microsoft Windows (3.11, 95, 98 or NT), Motif or Macintosh.

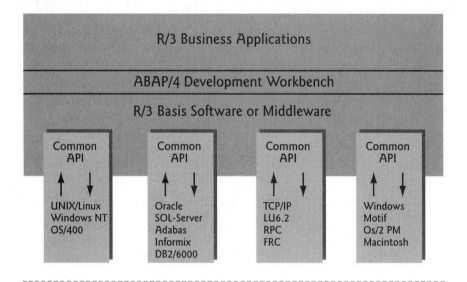

FIGURE 10.1   *SAP R/3 middleware*

Concepts of R/3 Architecture

The R/3 system has some widely used terms to which SAP gives a specific meaning. This section includes terms needed for a clear understanding of the architecture of SAP R/3. You can also find brief definitions of these and other important terms in the Glossary provided on the attached CD-ROM.

SAP System Identification (SID)

The SAP System Identification, commonly known as *SID* or *SAP-SID*, is a three-letter or digit-code (for example, C11, PRD, E56, etc.) that uniquely identifies a single SAP system (a single database). For example, an R/3 installation of one server running and containing the database (database server) and several servers running the application logic (application servers) is identified by a single SID.

However it is possible under certain circumstances and with some database systems, to have two or more full R/3 systems (database + applications) on a single server. That means the server might be running two or more SIDs.

Client Concept

A client is defined as a legally, financially, and organizationally independent unit within the R/3 system; for example, a company group, a business unit, or a corporation. R/3 systems can be configured as single-client or multiclient implementations. However, as indicated in Chapter 6, multiclient implementations must be handled with special care since the repository as well as the independent tables will affect all clients.

At the beginning of the technical phase of the R/3 implementation, just after installation of software, one of the first things that must usually be done is to copy one of the standard clients included in the package. With this copied client, customers can make tests, do training, or start real customization. SAP comes with three standard clients: 000, 001, and 066:

Client 000 contains a simple organizational structure of a test company, and includes parameters for all applications, standard settings, configurations for the control of standard transactions and examples to be used in many different profiles of business applications. For these reasons, 000 is a special client for the R/3 system since it contains the client-independent settings.

Client 001 is a copy of the 000 client, including the test company. If this client is configured or customized, its settings are client dependent. It does not behave like 000. It is reserved for the activities of preparing a system for the production environment. Customers usually reserve this client as a source for copying it to other new clients.

Client 066 is reserved for SAP access to its customers' systems to perform the EarlyWatch service.

The R/3 System includes tools for creating, copying, transferring, resetting, deleting, and comparing clients. When the loads of individual clients differ, the buffer manager of the application service is able to respond and allocate resources appropriately. The *client* is the first field when logging on to the system. More information about the SAP client concept is described in a SAP white paper, "The multiclient concept of R/3" to be found on SAPnet.

Transactions

Generically, a transaction is an operation that lets a user make changes to a database. The overall R/3 System must be seen as a business *transaction* processing system. The whole data flow that runs across application modules is executed using transactions.

In the SAP system, a transaction is a sequence of logically related steps, known as dialog steps, using screens in which data are introduced. This causes the generation of other events. There is a special transaction monitor, the *SAP Dispatcher*, which handles the sequence of those steps.

The final task of a transaction is to modify the information that ultimately goes into the database. The database is not updated until a transaction has finished. For consistency, if the transaction has not finished, all changes are still reversible.

The transactions usually contain two phases: an interactive phase and an update phase. The interactive phase might be made of at least one step, but can have many. This phase is responsible for preparing the database records that can update the database. The update phase might have many or no steps. This phase processes the previously prepared records and updates the database.

Since many users can access the same information, in order for the transactions to be consistent there is a lock mechanism during the time the processing of the transaction in taking place.

All the transactions in the R/3 system have an associated *transaction code*. A fast and useful way to move around the R/3 system is to type the transaction code directly on the *command field* of an R/3 window.

The available transaction codes are held on table TSTC. To see this table, from the main screen menu, select the following options from the menu bar: **Tools → ABAP Workbench → Development → Other Tools → Transactions**. Or, type **/NSE93** in the command field and then click on the possible list arrow (down arrow to the right of the field).

Dialog Steps

A dialog step is a SAP R/3 screen which is internally represented by means of a dynpro. A *dynpro* (dynamic program) consists of a screen and all the associated processing logic. It contains field definitions, screen layout, validation and processing logic, etc. A dialog step is controlled by a dynpro.

Processing logic means that the dynpro controls what has to be done before the screen is displayed (process before output or PBO) and what has to be done after the user finishes entering information (process after input or PAI).

A user navigating in the SAP R/3 system from screen to screen is actually making dialog steps. A set of dialog steps makes up a *transaction*.

The System Interfaces

In this section the main system interfaces are described in more detail. The R/3 middleware or common kernel is made up of central interfaces. These are:

- ❑ The interface with the operating system
- ❑ The interface with the database
- ❑ The interface for presentation
- ❑ The communication interface, a special type of interface which is directly or indirectly present in the other three types.

For compatibility and portability reasons, all these interfaces are grouped together in the central interface functions of the SAP system kernel. The interfaces in the SAP system are a group of software programs running as *daemon processes* in the UNIX operating system, or as *services* on Windows NT.

Operating System Interface

One of the main tasks of the basis system is to guarantee the portability of the whole system. That is done using an internal SAP portability layer. This layer offers to the applications the services nearest to the system, like message handling or memory management, independently of the platform and optimized for performance. The inherent openness of R/3 allows it to run over different operating systems, which have to be POSIX standard compliant. Figure 10.2 shows a list of technical and platform environments supported by SAP R/3. Please refer to the SAP web page for an updated list.

Presentation	Java AWT	Web Browser	MS Windows	OSF/Motif*	OS/2 Presentation Manager	Macintosh*
Communication Middleware	COM/DCOM ActiveX	CORBA		http XML		MQ–Series MSMQ
Language	ABAP Objects		C/C++		Java	
Database	Adabas**	IBM DB2 /UDB /400 /390	Informix	Microsoft SQL-Server		Oracle

Operating System	UNIX							Windows NT		Midrange	Mainframe
	Compaq Digital UNIX	HP UX	IBM AIX	Linux***	Siemens Reliant UNIX	SUN Solaris		Microsoft Windows NT	Microsoft Windows NT	IBM OS/400	IBM OS/390
Architecture/ System	Alpha	PA	Power PC		MIPS	SPARC		Alpha	Intel	AS/400	S/390****
	Compaq	HP	IBM Bull		Siemens	SUN		ACER Amdahl Bull Compaq Data General DELL Fujitsu Hitachi HP	Intergraph IBM ITAUTEC Mitsubishi NEC NCR Sequent Siemens Unisys	IBM	IBM Amdahl Fujitsu Comparex Hitachi

FIGURE 10.2   *SAP supported platforms   Copyright © SAP AG*

Process control is over the system interfaces. Its mission is to offer services like scheduling, memory management, and similar tasks that could be partially done by the operating system software; SAP executes it internally for performance and portability reasons.

The R/3 system runtime environment (known as R/3 kernel) is written in standard C or C++, but all application programs inside R/3 are written in the interpreted programming language ABAP.

The components in charge of controlling the user dialogs are the dynpros. The technology base for the R/3 applications is made up of the interrelation of the dynpro interpreters and the ABAP language. Both use for their tasks the global image of the data environment of R/3, which is held in the ABAP Dictionary. The runtime environment of the R/3 applications consists of two processors: one for the dynpros and the other for the ABAP language.

From the point of view of the operating system, the runtime system of R/3 can be seen as a group of parallel processes (*work processes*). Among these processes there is a special one, the *dispatcher*, which controls and assigns tasks to the other processes.

The Dispatcher Process

The SAP dispatcher is the control program that manages the resources of the R/3 applications. It works like a typical transaction monitor which receives screens and data from the presentation services and passes them to the corresponding work processes. Figure 10.3 below illustrates this concept.

The work processes are special programs in charge of various specific tasks. Using client/server terminology, a work process is a *service* offered by a *server* and requested by a *client*. The dispatcher manages the information exchange between the SAPGUIs and the work processes, enabling users to share the different work processes available.

The main tasks of the dispatcher are:

❑ Balanced assignment of the transaction load to the work processes
❑ Buffer management in main memory
❑ Connection with the presentation level
❑ Organization of the communication processes.

The logical flow of execution for a user request is:

1. The user enters data in the presentation server; the data are received by the SAPGUI, converted to an SAP format, and sent to the dispatcher.

2. Initially, the dispatcher keeps data in the request queues, where the dispatcher later takes them and process them one by one.

3. The dispatcher allocates the user requests using the free work processes. The real execution takes place inside the work processes themselves.

4. At the end of execution, the results of the work process task goes back to the SAPGUI through the dispatcher. SAPGUI interprets the received data and fills up the user screen.

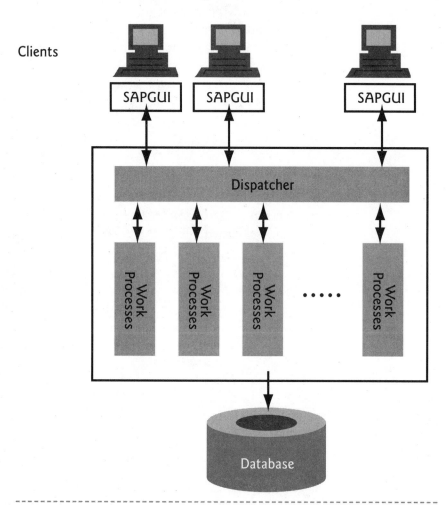

FIGURE 10.3   *Scheme of the Dispatcher Process*

SAP has optimized the data flow between the presentation and the application servers. Typically the quantity of data which goes in the network from the dispatcher to the SAPGUI does not exceed 2K (for dialog processes), except for local printing or download/upload operations. Communication is established via standard TCP/IP sockets.

On each application server there is one dispatcher, but multiple work processes.

NOTE

If an application server (hardware point of view) is running more than one SAP "instance" (application server from a software point of view) there is one dispatcher for every instance.

Work Process Architecture

A work process is a program in charge of executing the R/3 application tasks. Each work process acts as a specialized system service. From the point of view of the operating system, a group of parallel work processes makes up the R/3 runtime system.

As shown in Figure 10.4, a work process consists of a task handler, a dialog or dynpro interpreter, an ABAP processor, and a database interface. The work processes execute dialog steps for the end users. These steps generally relate to the processing or display of a single screen, which means that right after one work process finishes the execution of a dialog step for a user session, it is immediately available for use by another user session.

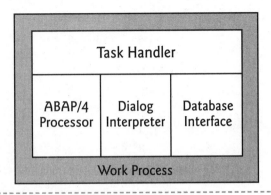

FIGURE 10.4   *Work process architecture*

With the later SAP releases after 4.x, the group formed by the ABAP processor and the dialog interpreter is known as ABAP virtual machine (ABAP VM)

For its processing, each dialog step needs code, dictionary objects, and data. These elements may come from the database server or from the memory buffers that reside on the application server. The dialog processes usually request read-only information from the database and rely on other types of work processes for read-write information.

The activities within a work process are coordinated by the task handler. It manages the loading and unloading of the user session context at the beginning and at the end of each dialog step. It also communicates with the dispatcher and activates the dynpro interpreter or the ABAP processor, as required, to perform its tasks. The database interface allows the work processes to establish direct links with the database.

The work processes might need the same data for more than one dialog step; in these cases, these data are held in shared memory areas (buffers), available for other work processes. It must be noted that users of the same or similar R/3 business applications, like FI (financial accounting) and CO (controlling), logging into the same application servers will benefit from this feature, since they will very often access the same tables. If these tables already reside on the buffer areas, the system does not have to go to the database to get it, and thus performance is improved.

Work processes make use of two special areas: *paging* and *roll*. The paging area holds application program data like internal tables or report listings. The roll area holds the user context data entered in previous dialog steps and other control and user information like authorizations. When there is main memory available, these areas are held in the main memory of application servers, otherwise they are "paged out" or "rolled out" to physical disk files. The sizes of these areas are configurable using SAP system profile parameters. With release 3.0, SAP established new memory management for R/3; so, for instance, the paging file is no longer used except for special conditions.

The system shared-memory areas contain also read-only images of other parts of the R/3 system, like the program or table buffers. The sizing and configuration of these buffers is very important for the overall performance of the system. The configuration and refresh rate of these caches is critical to the overall performance of the system.

To make more efficient use of available resources, work processes are run in parallel, which makes this architecture especially suitable for multiprocessor equipment, able to run the group of work processes distributed among different CPUs.

The number of available work processes per application server is configurable using the appropriate SAP system profile parameters, but is dependent on the hardware system's capacity.

There are several types of work processes: dialog, background, update, enqueue, and spool. The R/3 runtime system also includes three other special types of work processes or services: message service, gateway, and the system log collector.

Since the work processes are in charge of executing the ABAP programs and applications, a group made of a dispatcher and a set of work processes is known as an application server.

The R/3 Work Processes

Every work process specializes in a particular task type: dialog, batch, update, enqueue, spool, message, and gateway. The last two types are somewhat different from the rest. In client/server terms, a work process is a *service*, and the computing system that is running the particular services is known as a *server*. For example, if the system is just providing dialog services, this will be a *dialog server*, although it will commonly be called an *application server*.

The dispatcher assigns tasks to the free work processes, making optimal use of system resources and balancing the system load. The dispatcher knows the pending tasks and distributes them according to the processing type of the defined processes. The differences among the various work processes only effect their mission or special services, assigned to the work processes through the dispatching strategy.

Dialog Work Process

The dialog work processes are in charge of the interactive tasks of the R/3 system, that is, mainly to service the online work of users. A dialog work process performs the dialog steps corresponding to the interactive user sessions.

A job is held by the dispatcher in the request queues after user input is assigned to the next free work process. The dialog work processes execute just one single dialog step at a time and become immediately free for the next user request (dialog step), which will be assigned by the dispatcher. This means that the dialog work processes can be constantly switching between different user sessions. This type of processing allows a great deal of resource distribution, because otherwise the system would need as many dialog work processes as the number of expected interactive users. This works exactly the same way as multiuser operating systems.

The number of dialog work processes and other types of processes per application server is controlled by means of SAP profile parameters. Refer to the CCMS section of SAP online documentation for information on profile parameters.

Depending on the type of business transactions users are working on, a dialog work process can support from five to more than ten simultaneous users each. It means that ten dialog work processes could theoretically support around 100 users. However, this is just a rule of thumb. Tuning this parameter means that if users have to wait long to get a free work process, the parameter should be increased. This has some limitations, like the total number of processes running on the server and the availability of main memory.

When there is a large number of concurrent interactive users expected in an SAP R/3 system, there will certainly be a number of application servers. Some of these application servers can become special dialog servers, containing a dispatcher process and a number of dialog work processes.

Dialog Step Data Flow

Figure 10.5 shows the flow of a user request through the different components and processes.

Initially, the user enters data into the screen fields and presses the < **Enter** > key. These data are received by the SAPGUI process, converted to an internal format, and immediately sent to the application server dispatcher (1).

The dispatcher checks to see if there are work processes available for processing the dialog step. If there are not, the request will go to the request queues (2) until one becomes available.

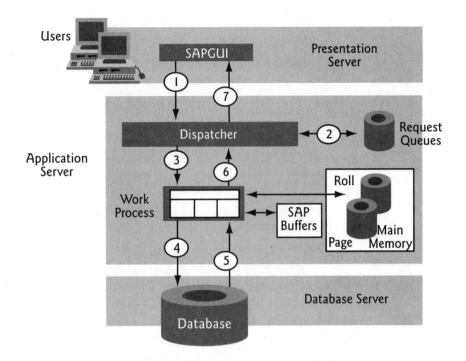

FIGURE 10.5   *Data flow of dialog steps*

Once a dialog work process is available, the dispatcher will send the user data to the work process (3). Within the dialog work the task handler is in charge of assigning the corresponding tasks to the internal components (dynpro or ABAP), using the SAP memory buffers, the roll and page area for user context storage and switching, and finally sending an SQL request to the database (4).

The database system will send the requested data back to the work process (5), which in turn will pass it to the presentation server (6). The SAPGUI formats the data and fills up the screen for the user (7).

The time it takes from step 1 (user request) to step 7 is known as *response time*.

The response time will be one of the main indicators of how healthy (well-tuned) the system is.

The SAP instance profile parameter **rdisp/max_wprun_time** controls the maximum allowed time for interactive execution of a dialog step, and usually has a default value of 300 (seconds). The parameters show the length of time in seconds that the dispatcher will allow the work process to run. When this value is reached, the dispatcher will stop the work process and the user will get a TIME_OUT error.

Background Work Process

The background work process is in charge of executing ABAP programs, or external commands or programs which have submitted for background execution.

From an administrative point of view, the background work processes correspond to the batch jobs queues. The programs or commands submitted for background processing will be executed in the planned time by the background work processes. The sequence of program execution is scheduled with *batch jobs*.

Every job can be made of one or several steps that are consecutively processed. A step is an ABAP or an external program

There are many types of jobs and different ways to submit them for execution. Normally, these background jobs are not processed until the system reaches the planned time for execution.

Background processing is very useful for submitting programs requiring long processing times, since interactive execution would exceed the allowed processing time (**rdisp/max_wprun**) and thus abort with a TIME_OUT error, as indicated in the previous section.

There is a batch scheduler which takes care of initiating the jobs at the specified time. The system allows for periodic job execution. This means that programs are submitted with a repetition interval, and when the jobs execute themselves, the first thing they do is to plan a new execution at the required interval. This feature is very useful with control or cleaning jobs within R/3.

The background process can be further organized into different types of job queues based on the priorities needed in the particular installation.

Background jobs are vital to the daily management and operation of the system.

With the utilities within the CCMS (Computer center management system), administrators know how the dialog and background work processes can be automatically switched with the use of *operation modes*.

Spool Work Process

The spool work process is in charge of formatting the data for printing and passing it to the host spool system. Spool requests are generated during dialog or background processing and are held on the spool database, indicating the printer and the printing format of the spool request. The data are kept in a special area, known as *TemSe* (temporal sequential objects).

When the data are going to be printed for the spool job, an output request is generated and is executed by the spool work process. Once the spool work process has edited the data for printing, it sends a print request to the operating system.

The number of spool work processes per instance is limited to one spool work process per host. Notice that if a host is running two SAP instances, just one spool work process is allowed. SAP might solve this restriction in upcoming releases.

Enqueue Work Process

The enqueue work process is in charge of the lock management system. It allows multiple application servers to synchronize their access to the database and maintain data consistency.

In order for the system to run in a consistent manner it needs to ensure that a transaction whose dialog steps are handled by different work processes retains its assigned locks until the end of the transaction or the intentional release of the lock, even when work processes are switched.

Before release 4.x one, and only one, enqueue process could exist for a single SAP system. However this has changed and now more that one enqueue process can run if specific conditions are followed.

The function of this work process is to protect applications from locking themselves during data access. For that reason, a locking/unlocking mechanism must be present. This is the function of the enqueue work process.

The locks (enqueues) are managed by the enqueue work process using a lock table, which resides in main memory. When the processes receives a locking request, the enqueue work process verifies that the requested lock object does not interfere with other existing entries in the lock table.

The ABAP applications logic considers that data modifications are usually done when a previous read has taken place. For that reason, the locking requests are made before the data reading requests.

SAP has designed the locking mechanism so that each lock needs to be respected not only by the application server executing the transaction, but also by all other servers within the SAP system. That is the reason why each R/3 system contains only one enqueue process (also known as *lock manager*), which monitors the assigned locks throughout the system. The fact that there is only one enqueue server is of particular importance for getting a real fault-tolerant SAP R/3 system.

Lock Objects

The lock objects are special types of objects defined in the ABAP dictionary. The locking type can be shared (type S) or exclusive (type E). Exclusive locks are used to avoid parallel modification of the data, which means that exclusively locked data can only be displayed or modified by one user.

With the shared mode, several users can access the same data in the same type of display mode. As soon as any user processes the data, the remaining users do not have further access to them.

When the lock objects are defined in the dictionary, there are two ABAP function modules automatically generated, one for the locking of the object (enqueue) and another function to unlock it (dequeue). These functions are respectively called at the beginning and end of a transaction. If for some reason there are problems between the locking and unlocking of an object, it will remain locked until the administrator manually deletes the lock.

Update Work Process

The update work process is in charge of executing database changes when requested by the dialog or background work processes.

The dialog work processes can generate database modifications with corresponding instructions to the database server, independently of whether these work processes run on the same or different machines than the database.

However, when the ABAP language element, CALL FUNCTION...IN UPDATE TASK is executed, it raises the order for the modification to occur in the update server, which, generally, runs on the database server, a shorter communication path. Specific update work processes will then modify the database accordingly.

It is recommended that the update service be in the same server as the database for better performance. However with fast network controllers, it does not make much difference if the update server is on a different host than the database.

The update is an asynchronous process, which means that update requests are processed in the moment and order they arrive at the work process. This makes a more homogeneous response time. The drawback is that a transaction might not have finished when another update transaction is waiting.

If, for any reason, the update transaction cannot be completely accomplished, the user will get a system message and an express mail. Sometimes the failure is due to database problems, like table-spaces or dbspaces becoming full.

If the transaction could not finish correctly, the systems rolls it back. The *rollback* of a transaction is possible because there is a dialog part separate from the update part. The dialog program first generates log records in the VBLOG table. These are then processed by the update program (run within the update process), once the dialog is finished.

The log records, read by the update work process, contain all the information necessary to make the modifications. During the update phase the database is modified.

The update of a log record can have several parts, known as update components. This division makes it possible to structure the objects that make up the update transaction components according to their importance.

An update request can contain a primary update component (V1) and several secondary (V2) components. The time-critical processes are held inside the V1, the less critical in the V2.

To be able to initiate the V2 components of the log record, the V1 components must have finished. However the V2 components can be executed in any order, even in parallel if there are enough update processes defined. The execution of primary components (V1) corresponding to different log records can be also done in parallel using several update work processes.

Before release 3.0 of R/3, there was only one type of update work process taking care of both V1 and V2 components. As of release 3.0 onwards, a new profile parameter has been established to indicate also the number of update work processes for secondary components.

The important profile parameter is: `rdisp/vbname = <instance name>`. This is a common parameter for the full SAP system and is therefore normally in the DEFAULT.PFL file.

The other parameters `rdisp/wp_no_vb` and `rdisp/wp_no_vb2` indicate the number of update work processes of type V1 and V2, respectively. These are defined inside the instance-specific profile parameter file.

If there are error situations during the update, these cannot be solved with user on-line actions. The active update process component is stopped. If the errors occurred in the primary component (V1) of a log record, the modifications are rolled back. The log record receives a corresponding status flag and is not taken out of the VBLOG table. The subsequent V2 update actions are not executed.

However, if the interrupted or error component is a of type V2, only the modifications done by this particular component are rolled back. The corresponding log record is marked with a status flag and is not deleted from the table. The other components can follow normal update processing.

After an error situation or update interruption the system automatically notifies the user by express mail about the aborted update. It is then possible to evaluate and treat the update according to the error message received.

Message Server

The message service is used by the different application servers to exchange data and internal messages. It does not have the structure of the typical work process described earlier, although it also acts like a service.

The message server routes the messages between application servers. Since release version 3.0 it has also been used for license checking and work load balancing, together with the SAPlogon utility.

There is only one message server per SAP R/3 system. The message server process makes the application server exchange brief internal messages: update start, enqueue, dequeue, batch job start. Communication is established among the dispatchers using the TCP/IP network protocol and the sockets defined in the *services* file.

Every application server has a unique name for the message server. All application servers can differentiate among update, enqueue, and batch and spool servers and set those services active by indicating an "address" to the message server.

The location of the host running the message server is configured in the DEFAULT.PFL common profile. The parameter is rdisp/mshost = <hostname>. Notice the difference from previous parameters (update or enqueue services), where the value of the parameter pointed to the instance name. In this case the value is a hostname, included in the standard hosts database of the TCP/IP protocol. The particular host is not restricted to the database server. It can run on any of the hosts that make up the SAP client/server system.

The way this service is started is also different from other work processes. It has its own start execution line in the start profile. The next chapter includes more information on start profiles.

Gateway Server

The gateway service allows communication between the R/3, R/2, and external applications. It is a CPIC handler that implements the CPIC protocol for communication and is commonly known as the SAP gateway.

The function of the SAP gateway is to exchange larger amounts of data between application servers; the message server only exchanges brief internal and control messages. The communication agents can be located on the same system, in another R/3 system, in an R/2 system, and also in an external program.

The Interface with the Database Management System

The database is the technical heart of the SAP R/3 system. It is not only the central source of information for the company's business data, but also the container of user information, software components, documentation, and administrative statistical data to be used when managing or monitoring the system.

The SAP R/3 underlying database acts as the main container for all the information managed by the system. The database includes almost everything users can see on their screens: program source code, screens, texts, menu options, customer information, printer definitions, statistical information, transactional data, etc.

The database interface supports relational databases from various vendors.

Its main task is to convert the SQL requests (ABAP Open SQL) from the SAP development environment to the database's own SQL requests. During the interpretation of the ABAP open SQL statements, the database interface makes a syntax check to verify that the statement is correct, and it also automatically tries to make an optimal use (reuse) of the SAP buffers in case a similar SQL statement was requested previously. These buffers are held locally in each application server main memory.

Another way for direct access to the database is to use ABAP native SQL statements. With ABAP native SQL calls, a developer can make specific database SQL calls which are not supported using the standard ABAP open SQL statements, although there is the risk of creating non-portable code.

The database interface also has a cursor caching method. *Database cursors* are like portions of memory which are allocated by the system to process SQL statements. A cursor caching method means that the system tries to reuse the access paths previously used to process SQL statements.

One of the most important logical parts of the database is the ABAP object repository, which contains:

❑ **ABAP dictionary.** The central source for the definition of objects like type and length of fields, indexes, table relationships, and so on. In database terms, this type of definitions is known as *metadata*. The dictionary is intimately connected to all parts of the business applications and is a core part of the ABAP development workbench.

❑ **The ABAP source and executable programs.** Since ABAP is an interpreted language, it can be dynamically regenerated by the application servers (remember the ABAP processor inside the work processes).

The Data in the SAP System

The database of course includes the data themselves. SAP distinguishes three different types of data: master, control, and transaction data.

Master data contain information that does not change very often like vendors, customers, materials, user names, printer definition, addresses of suppliers, etc. This is a type of data is usually used the same way for similar objects.

Control data are held in control tables and include system and technical functions of the SAP System.

Transaction data contain the most volatile information and are frequently used in day-to-day business operations, like customer orders or accounting transactions, such as payments, debits, credits, etc.

Types of Tables

The SAP-declared dictionary tables have corresponding structure in the physical underlying database. The R/3 system handles different types of tables.

SAP *transparent tables* are structures that exactly match underlying database tables. This means that with certain database knowledge you can view or manage these tables directly from the database's own utilities. However, users are advised not handle data outside R/3, since it might provoke serious inconsistencies and data loss.

Other table types managed by SAP, which will eventually disappear, are *cluster tables*, which are structures made of several SAP tables related using foreign keys, and *pooled tables*, corresponding to a set of tables stored in a single table.

The ABAP Dictionary in the Development Environment

The database interface sends the data read from the ABAP dictionary tables to the ABAP programs by placing them in special work areas (memory buffers known to the work processes). The database interface gets the modified data from those areas and sends them to the database.

Software developers can easily declare and work with such areas, since the dictionary is integrated with ABAP. Within an ABAP program, the developer can create additional tables that exist only as long as a program is running. These internal tables can be dynamically enlarged so that it is not neccessary for developers to know in advance the amount of memory the internal tables will occupy.

The Presentation Interface

The presentation interface is the component in charge of making the presentation and the handling of R/3 functionally equivalent, no matter what type of front end is used.

For each user session there is a SAP process (SAPGUI) which enables the use of all available presentation possibilities in the corresponding Windows software. These processes (historically known as terminal processes) are in charge of, among other things, managing the graphical elements of the R/3 System.

The connection between the SAPGUIs and the SAP dispatcher is made with an optimized protocol, in which small data packages are sent through the network.

In the SAP R/3 system, all the menu options, buttons, and even most of the graphical elements are inside the database. This means that the real screens are not held in the PC software, but are sent on demand. The time it takes to go from one screen to another is longer for the first people to log onto the system. As the buffers become full with cached data, this time noticeably decreases.

The presentation interface allows for upload and download functions from the application server. It also includes possibilities for file transfers and communication with popular Windows applications like MS-Excel, MS-Word, MS-Access, etc. when using a Windows-based front end.

Another feature available in the presentation interface is the SAP graphic utility which permits the establishment of a dialog between the ABAP application and the graphic utility in the presentation server, for extracting data to make graphical representations of the information.

Communication Protocols and Interfaces

Inside R/3, communication is an overall process which involves most of the components of internal and external systems. Communication among systems, modules, and components is based on protocols. The R/3 basis system supports all standard and de facto standard communication and networking protocols.

At the operating system level, the protocol used is TCP/IP. Communication with the database is accomplished using Remote SQL calls. Between applications there are many different programming interfaces that use an underlying communication layer, including CPIC, RFC, ALE, EDI, etc.

The communication interfaces are deployed to integrate all layers of the client/server architecture, from database server to application server to presentation servers. They also define channels for the exchange of electronic information, like input of data from external systems and exchange of standardized business information using ALE, EDI, and the Internet. The communication interfaces are also deployed to send and receive mail from the exterior world (Internet for example) using a standard X.400 mail protocol.

At the programming level, the R/3 systems use the CPIC protocol for program-to-program communication and also include support for Remote Function Calls (RFC) and the Microsoft OLE interface.

SAP also provides support for connecting and exchanging data and information with traditional mainframes using SNA or other standard protocols. The system has utilities which enable communication and exchange of data with special peripheral devices like presence card readers, production plant devices, etc.

RFC: Remote Function Calls

RFC is a standard programming interface for remote calls between programs located on different systems. This means that functions developed or existing in a system can be remotely called by another local program. This is particularly useful for data manipulation and processing load balancing between systems. Even when the same functions exist on both systems—called and caller—this is a way of making another system send or receive data; the remote CPU will assign the needed resources.

RFC is a higher level logical interface than CPIC, and makes life easier for programmers since they do not have to worry about implementing communication routines. With the RFC interface, function calls can be accomplished between two SAP systems or between SAP systems and external systems (for instance with Microsoft Windows applications).

The library functions included with RFC support the Visual Basic and C programming languages.

The RFC interfaces basically come with two services:

❑ **A calling interface for ABAP programs.** Any ABAP program can call a remote function using standard programming sentences, providing the remote system has allowed the module to be called remotely.
❑ **An RFC API (application program interface) for programs other than ABAP (non-SAP).** SAP even provides an RFC program generator to help implement RFC partner programs in external systems. With these API calls, external programs can call ABAP function modules in SAP R/3 systems (also in R/2). At the same time, with the RFC API, ABAP programs can use functions provided by external programs.

SAP online help and the documentation print files include extensive information about remote programs with RFC and the RFC API.

SAP Instances

A SAP *instance* is an administrative entity which groups together R/3 components that offer one of several services. These offered services are started or stopped together. All instance components are configured using a common instance profile. A centralized SAP R/3 system is made of an unique instance. Another feature which distinguishes the instances is that every SAP instance has its own buffer area, so it is allocated to its own main memory space.

SAP distinguishes the concepts of *central instance* and *dialog instance*. Every SAP system has just one central instance, which from installation forward contains all basic services, like the message server, gateway, update, enqueue, dialog, spool, and background. Dialog instances only contain a set of basic services like dialog and background work processes.

Administrators can later customize all the services and server locations by means of SAP instance profiles. A central system can be further configured to a distributed system, creating additional instances offering additional services. The usual way of configuring the system right from the box is to have just one instance per computer. However, providing systems have enough main memory and processing power, additional instances an be installed, and this has some advantages.

SAP Services Distribution and the Client/Server Architecture

Distribution in a general sense means sharing something among several individuals. In SAP R/3 systems there are many processes, services, printers, users, etc. Since SAP R/3 is based on a client/server software concept, distributing the SAP R/3 system means sharing the provided services among the clients and servers to optimize performance and availability and to balance the load of the system.

In this section the practical aspects of the client/server components of the SAP R/3 system are introduced, and the benefits of using this architecture are discussed. We deal with such things as identifying what parts of the system can be distributed and planning such distribution. We also describe the main factors to consider when setting up the different parts of R/3: sizing, network, load balancing, and availability.

The following sections describe other important and practical details of R/3 system distribution: SAP instance profiles, the operating system directory structure, the process of starting and stopping the system, and what programs are available in the runtime directory.

When the system is set up there are details which change depending on whether a central system or a distributed system is built. Here we find things like setting up the central system log (the main repository for R/3 problem and error messages) and buffer synchronization (so that users don't say: from this system I can see this data; I cannot see it from the other one).

For installations considered small in terms of number of users (this is relative, but we will say less than 100), there might not be more than one computer server for running SAP applications. In that case every service is running in the central system: database, central instance application server, background services, etc. The only distributed component is the presentation server (SAPGUI) running on a Windows PC or similar machine. With such installations, a factor to consider in distribution is the printing strategy, which could be handed over to the presentation servers (normally Windows PCs) through the SAPLPD protocol.

Centralized SAP Installations

In the case of centralized installations, system layout looks like Figure 10.6. If the server is powerful enough, this can be a suitable installation for a larger SAP user population. Moreover, this can be a good fit for starting the R/3 implementation, since the fact that it is a centralized configuration does not mean it cannot scale up to meet the growing demands of the system, nor that it is *not* client/server from a software point of view.

In centralized SAP systems configuration, the central sever is in charge of every R/3 service, so we can think of it as distributing "time" among services. Time can be distributed among some work processes like dialog and background by means of *operation modes*. Operation modes are a way to define how many processes will run during a certain period of time and to make the system automatically switch the types of work processes at another period of time.

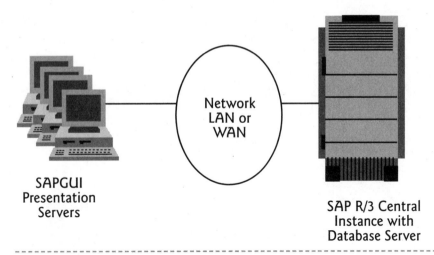

FIGURE 10.6 *Centralized SAP installations*

A single centralized instance contains a set of services that are started and stopped together. Commonly, right from a new installation, the instance name is DVEBMGS00 (notice the letter corresponds to the different work processes and the last two numbers, 00, are the SAP System Number).

When the computer shares these services and the database, this is usually called the central instance or database server instance. However the database could also be installed independently on another computer. Thus, a central instance configuration is made of: application server (dialog, update, background, spool, and enqueue services), a message server, a gateway, and the database system. This is a common configuration.

The advantages of this type of centralized installations as opposed to distributed installations are:

❑ Less management load for installing and administering the system
❑ Less hardware maintenance
❑ Less network load.

The disadvantages are:

❑ No possibility to distribute SAP services; they all reside on the same central server.

❑ Performance degradation; CPU has to share its resources among database services, SAP work processes
❑ Less availability; if the server goes down, everything goes down.

From a hardware point of view, we will add additional servers (application servers) to perform the R/3 application logic on behalf of or cooperating with the central system. This kind of configuration is known as a three-tier server system, as depicted in Figure 10.7.

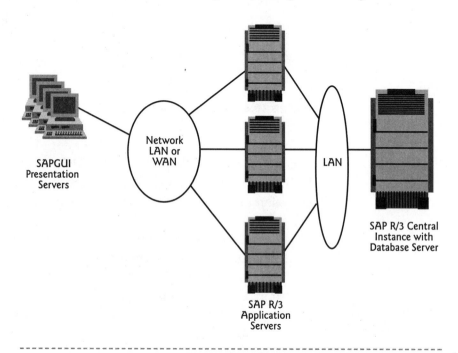

FIGURE 10.7   *Three-tier client/server installations*

Factors for Distributing SAP

The factors to consider when planning the distribution of the R/3 system among several servers are:

❑ **Sizing** (application modules deployed, number of users, geographical location of users) and the system's expected performance
❑ **SAP Services.** Where to place background, dialog, spooling, message server, update, etc.; also about how many to have

❑ **SAP Profiles.** In distributed configurations, profiles must be shared among the application servers

❑ **Load balancing.** SAP can be configured automatically to balance the load on the system

❑ **File and program locations.** In distributed configurations there are two options for where to place the runtime programs: either on the local disks or shared through the network (NFS in UNIX systems, shared on Windows NT); there is also the option of setting a mixed environment: some servers with local programs and some others mounting those directories over the network

❑ **Backup and recovery strategy.** Can differ slightly from central configurations in the sense that all servers must have a recovery procedure in case of disasters or data loss

❑ **Printing strategy.** As introduced in Chapter 6, printing should not be underrated in SAP implementations; with several servers there are more available options to define a better printing strategy

❑ **System monitoring and maintenance.** Additional work procedures must exist to manage and monitor the additional servers

❑ **Network configuration and monitoring.** Minimizing the communication delays can be a crucial issue for distributed SAP servers. SAP R/3 is a client/server application that requires the TCP/IP transport protocol for communication between SAP servers. Remember that the network is one of the critical elements in client/server computing

❑ **Maintenance and operation.** Even if the group of the SAP database server and associated application servers can be monitored from a single system, there is, of course, more maintenance and system management when the R/3 system is distributed.

SAP Client/Server Architecture

As stated in the overview to Chapter 1, the SAP client/server architecture can consist of several application servers from a software point of view. These servers can run distributed on separate computers (hardware point of view).

Between the SAP application servers of a SAP system, there are client/server relationships in which a server performs tasks for other servers, or functions as a client of the same servers. For example, a server can be running the message server for the rest of the system, but at the same time be a client of the update service provided by a different server or servers. Presentation servers (normally PCs) are clients of the application servers, and these in turn are clients of the database server. This is what forms the client/server architecture.

The advantages of a distributed client/server architecture are:

❑ Services with intensive input/output demands can run separately on different computers, without affecting the performance of the central functions.
❑ Interactive user load balancing can be achieved.
❑ Higher system availability and performance exist.
❑ High scalability is achieved by adding additional servers.
❑ Flexibility; there are many options available depending on the particular needs of an installation.

Disadvantages of these architectures are:

❑ Higher network loads due to increased data communication exchange among servers.
❑ Management and maintenance of a distributed system is more complex.
❑ Service configuration and distribution is not a trivial task.

SAP Servers

The SAP R/3 system is made up of a group of servers and a group of services. Depending on the function they perform, there are three types of servers:

❑ The database server basically contains the database engine and associated processes.

The database layer contains the database system used by all servers. Since all database system used by SAP supports remote SQL, it can run separate from the rest of the SAP system.

Notice that what distinguishes one SAP system ID (SID or SAPSID) from another is the unique database for each system.
❑ Application servers, running the SAP services.

The application-server layer contains a SAP kernel that can run ABAP programs. This consists of a dispatcher task and a group of work processes. The dispatcher allocates the resources needed to perform the request to its work processes, which then carry out the request.

We should point out the difference between an application server and a SAP instance. The distinction is made on the basis of the hardware or software concept of client/server computing. A hardware viewpoint of an application server denotes a computer running application services, while the software viewpoint denotes a group of processes running under the same parameters, with just one dispatcher and sharing a common memory pool. This means that a SAP instance is conceptually the same as an application server from the software point of view. Remember that if the server computer has enough memory and CPU power it could have room for several SAP instances. Nevertheless, if the server computer running the application services has just one SAP instance (which is very common), then the server computer, the application server, and the SAP instance are the same.

❑ Presentation servers, running the SAP front-end interface.

The presentation-server layer is responsible for displaying the SAP user interface, sending output to the user, and receiving user input to be sent to the application layer of the system. This layer, commonly known as SAPGUI, is available on different platforms like UNIX, Macintosh, OS/2, and Windows, and is the latest and most popular SAP interface.

SAP Services

Service types are the server work processes in charge of providing and executing the system tasks. The types of services correspond to the work process types as introduced in previous sections. Having specialized services makes it possible to support the distribution of the workload by the R/3 system components.

The service types are:

❑ **Dialog.** Performs the dialog steps or interactive processing. With the use of the CCMS operation modes these services can automatically switch to background processing services. This is very useful when dividing daily and nightly workload.

❑ **Background.** Executes programs submitted for background processing. These services can switch mode with the dialog services.

❑ **Update.** Executes database changes when requested by dialog or background. For better performance it is recommended that the update service be in the same server as the database. There are update types 1 (U1 or time critical) and 2 (U2 or noncritical).

❑ **Spool.** Responsible for formatting data for printing and passing the print job to the host spooler system.

❑ **Enqueue.** The lock management system service. Allows multiple application servers to synchronize their access to the database to maintain consistency. In current R/3 versions, if the database is installed on only one server computer, only one enqueue server per SAP system is needed.

❑ **Message Services.** Routes messages between application servers. Version 3.0 also uses them for licensing. Only one message server exists per SAP system.

❑ **Gateway.** Implements the CPIC protocol.

Depending on the distribution of the SAP servers, the services will be located on the same or different computers.

Guidelines for Distributed Configurations in R/3

As with most large computing applications, there is no formula that will result in a perfect setup of the system distribution from the start. Systems work load is not constant; software upgrades, user population growth, and some type of technical changes always take place. SAP R/3 is no exception; therefore the correct distribution is a matter of knowing the factors that influence the system, and daily monitoring to watch the most relevant figures and take corresponding action.

A distributed SAP R/3 system will be a group of a database server and several application servers. A distributed SAP R/3 system is also a group of server processes (services).

Guidelines to plan the best approach for an R/3 system distribution include:

1. The database server is a critical point in the whole configuration: without database there is no SAP. The underlying database engine processes are those that ultimately access the data for reading, updating, inserting, or deletion. This means that this server will support the biggest input/output load and can become a real bottleneck for the whole system. Depending on the particular sizing and needs of each installation, there are a few things to take into consideration:

   ❑ Keeps users from logging on to this system by means of network configuration, load balancing setup, or by removing the dialog processes. Leave one or two dialog processes for administrative purposes.

   ❑ When installing, plan the file system layout carefully, for security and performance reasons. If the system requires a very high throughput, think of placing the database files over several different volumes, and share the load of the disk controllers carefully. Your hardware partner can help with this.

   ❑ A database server can be installed in a completely separate system, so it would not contain any of the SAP-provided services. The CPU then would not have to share its resources between the database and the SAP work processes. The convenience of this type of configuration will be the result of analyzing the load and correctly sizing the system.

2. Network load between the database server and the application services can become quite high. Size the network accordingly using high-speed connections such as, FDDI, ATM, or FC as supported by the relevant hardware.

3. There should be common file locations. When R/3 services are distributed among several application servers there are at least a couple of shared directories: one for the instances profiles (/**sapmnt**/ < **SID** > /**profile**) and another for the central system log on UNIX systems (/**sapmnt**/ < **SID** > /**global**). Decide whether to share the executables runtime directory /**sapmnt**/ < **SID** > /**exe**. Often this directory is shared by means of NFS (network file system).

❏ Service distribution.

❏ Presentation services should be run only on PCs or dedicated workstations.

❏ Dialog services should be moved out of the database server and placed on the specialized dialog servers. Monitor the number of available waiting dialog processes. If there are too few, users won't be able to log on.

❏ Background processes; at the very beginning of an R/3 project you do not actually know how much background job load the system will have. When starting to monitor in the productive phases, it will be possible to adjust the number and placement of the needed background work processes. It might even be necessary to leave a whole application server as a specialized background server. In any case, be aware and use the CCMS operation modes. With the configuration of the operation modes the system can automatically switch the work process type to background during a defined period of time. For example, it is very common to make some of the dialog work process switch to background during the night. In periods of light interactive dialog load, think of placing background processes in the database server, since they will be processed faster there.

❏ The update server should be as close to the database server as possible. If the database server also includes the central instance, which is very common, leave the update server there.

❏ The message server plays an important role for application server communication and load balancing. Think of placing this service in an application server, since it also will be called by the presentation service interface of the end-users.

5. For load balancing, end-users should connect to the SAP R/3 system as transparently as possible in terms of which physical application server they log onto. With the help of the message server, the SAPLOGON utility, and the SMLG transaction, you can define the instances to which users can connect. This facility is very useful in contingency events and for a better use of common memory buffers. For example, if one server goes down, users can still connect to the R/3 system.

6. In a distributed system, a wrong printing strategy can lead R/3 average response times to miserable figures. SAP systems should

distinguish between the spool work process, in charge of formatting and sending printing jobs to the host spooler, and the host spooler itself. The section on printing strategy in Chapter 6 includes recommendations for planning printing strategy; consider having a dedicated server for critical print jobs. The same physical printer can be defined with different logical names—with each logical name a different host spooler, for example. It is also possible to define a PC as a locally attached printer in the SAP spool system.

7. Backup is an essential part of any system implementation strategy. With distributed R/3 there are only slight differences in backup strategies that have a single server or several. The most important data to be backed up is the database, which is unique. There is of course the SAP and database runtime environment to back up. The strategy must define the procedure to recover an application server if there is any kind of physical error. Considering that most instance data files are temporary, worry only about recovering the operating system and the directory structure for the instance. To be even safer, consider putting some type of disk mirroring on the application servers, which usually do not need much disk space.

8. Number of SAP instances per host. Finally, it might be advisable further to distribute the services, having additional instances in a single computer server, provided there is enough CPU power and main memory. The benefit of this is that logon balancing is easier, memory can be better used, and there is more choice for service distribution. The drawback is that there is no unique SAP system number; some instance parameters, like central logging must be changed; and additional instance profiles must be maintained.

The Administration of SAP Systems

Administration tasks deal with the basic monitoring and management of the components in the SAP R/3 system.

The R/3 system offers an extensive collection of programs, menus and utilities for performing administrative tasks. Most of them are located under the functions provided in the **Tools → Administration** menu.

The basic utilities include the following:

- ❑ Checking the consistency of the system installation
- ❑ Displaying and monitoring all the application servers
- ❑ Displaying and monitoring the system work processes
- ❑ Displaying and monitoring the user sessions
- ❑ Posting system messages to all logged users of a SAP/System to inform them of any particular event such as closing the system for upgrades, backups, etc.
- ❑ Preventing all users from accessing specific transaction by means of locking and unlocking transactions
- ❑ Managing the SAP update records in charge of performing the changes in the database
- ❑ Displaying and managing the SAP lock entries on the database objects
- ❑ Managing and understanding the temporary sequential objects (TemSe) database
- ❑ Using the client copy functions
- ❑ Managing and executing external operating system commands
- ❑ Analyzing the dump files generated by abnormal termination of ABAP programs
- ❑ Using the tracing and logging facilities to analyze system problems
- ❑ Executing Data Archive sessions.

Basic SAP R/3 System Management

The functions available for the basic administration of the SAP system form a group of transactions that should be performed on a regular basis in the daily operation and management of the system. These functions are the responsibility of the R/3 system administrator and/or the system operator. Whenever a problem is detected during basic administration it must be reported and solved as soon as possible.

Administrators can help prevent problems by following certain monitoring practices. In the event of problem detection, the monitoring and administration facilities can help isolate the problem and solve it more quickly. Having an operator's or administrator's manual and maintaining an internal incidence log will greatly reduce the time it takes to solve a particular problem in cases where it has happened previously.

If a problem cannot be solved quickly enough, SAP system administrators should call the SAP hotline or use the online service system (OSS).

The Computer Center Management System (CCMS)

CCMS is a collection of tools and utilities for monitoring, managing, and configuring the R/3 system. The CCMS tool set supports most of the system management functions needed for an R/3 system from within. It provides a series of graphical monitors and management utilities, including functions for:

❑ Starting and stopping SAP instances
❑ Monitoring and analyzing the workload on the underlying operating systems, network, database engine, and the SAP system itself
❑ Automatic problem detection with use and configuration of alert thresholds
❑ Definition of operation modes with 24-hour unattended work process automatic reconfiguration
❑ Instance profile checking and maintenance
❑ Logon load balancing
❑ Backup planning.

The CCMS manages a huge amount of highly technical information, which can only be understood by those with a deep knowledge of the operating system, underlying database architecture, network, and R/3 internals.

CCMS is a great management tool for R/3 administration that includes virtually hundreds of functions. This implies an overwhelming amount of information that is not always easy to understand. It is usually more practical to get acquainted with the most common concepts and the most useful operations of the CCMS. Then, to get deeper details and further help in any part of the

CCMS, make use of all the help options in the R/3 system, especially by pressing the F1 key for any available field, and then Extended Help function on the specific topic. If deeper technical information is required, refer to the SAP online documentation on CCMS.

Below are the main concepts to become familiar with when operating the CCMS:

❑ **R/3 Instances.** An instance defines the resources needed by an SAP application server, such as memory configuration, number and type of services provided (work processes), etc. Every R/3 instance has its own memory buffers and is controlled by a single dispatcher process. R/3 instances are identified with an instance name, normally with the syntax <hostname>_<SID>_<system number>, for example: k2p01_TT1_00. For every R/3 instance the system creates separate directories under the **/usr/sap/ < SID > /SYS** directory, automatically generates the instance profiles, and inserts entries in several operating system files like the **/etc/services** and the **/usr/sap/trans/.sapconf.** R/3 instances are created when the R/3 system or additional dialog servers are installed.

❑ **Instance profiles.** The SAP system profile files include the group of parameters which sets the values for the resources needed by the R/3 instances, as well as for the number and location of the R/3 services in a SAP installation. These files are initially generated when the SAP system and additional dialog instances are installed. From version 3.0 onward, these files can be maintained only with utilities available within the CCMS.

❑ **Operation modes.** With operation modes, system managers define how they want the SAP services to be allocated and started in the configured R/3 instances. The modes main use is for automatically switching work process types to make better distribution of available resources. For example, operation modes can be defined to have many dialog work processes during normal working hours and automatically switch to background work processes during night operation for processing background jobs scheduled at night.

❑ **Control panel.** The control panel is a central monitor which presents an overview of the whole SAP system status. From it most management functions can be performed, such as changing operation modes, and starting and stopping instances. The control panel includes many different views for displaying status, alerts, and performance or error information.

❑ **Monitors.** R/3 includes several monitors, both list-oriented and graphical, for online monitoring of the system. Monitors display the alerts defined in the system. They can be configured to work dynamically to refresh the information at periodic intervals. This feature and color coding combine to make a valuable tool for fast problem detection and correction.

❑ **Alerts.** Alerts are important predefined system events which are constantly monitored. SAP includes alerts for the database, the operating system, the network, and R/3 components. System managers can define alert thresholds, i.e. the values which will make the system show an alert message when a specific event or system condition occurs. Alerts can be simple warnings or critical errors. For example, system managers can configure the alert thresholds to trigger an alert when a file system exceeds 80% of the available space.

❑ **Performance and workload statistics collectors.** The R/3 system incorporates several collector programs and background jobs which keep a record of both current workload statistics and a history of workload for the operating system, the database, the network, and the R/3 system. The different workload monitors permit a detailed analysis of performance problems and are extremely helpful for preventive maintenance of the whole system.

Administrator Duties with the CCMS

The available facilities provided within CCMS should be regularly used and maintained by system administrators to keep operations smooth and make the most of available resources. The information recorded with the CCMS monitors and collectors is also needed by SAP personnel when troubleshooting customer systems and performing EarlyWatch sessions.

In general, system administrators should:

❑ Configure the CCMS for:

❑ Instances and operation modes
❑ Alert thresholds
❑ Submitting the performance collectors
❑ Logon groups
❑ System for scheduling backups and other database activities (i.e. CBO in Oracle databases).
❑ Use the CCMS for:
❑ Online alert monitoring
❑ Performance problems analysis
❑ Importing and maintaining the SAP system profiles.

Although the CCMS is shipped right after a SAP installation with some default values to provide the basic functionality of the system, before using the full capacity of CCMS, there is some configuration work to do. Refer to SAP online documentation for details.

CCMS since Release 4.x

With the introduction of releases 4.0, 4.5, and EnjoySAP, R/3 includes new functions and tools for global systems management. In this area, SAP strategy is to convert CCMS into a centralized management and monitoring system component that is active and dynamic and can be used for decreasing the support and maintenance costs of SAP systems.

The two main new features are a monitoring architecture based on objects and the possibility of integrating CCMS with external tools and applications using BAPIs.

Among the external tools that can be linked through BAPIs are those that can perform functions such as:

❑ General Administration
❑ Management and Scheduling of Background Jobs
❑ System Usage Audit
❑ Printing.

Among features introduced or enhanced since release 4.0 are the following:

❑ A new object-based monitoring architecture

❑ An easier way to analyze and interpret workload statistics
❑ New ways to improve the system load distribution among work processes (dialog, jobs, update, spool, and so on)
❑ Enhancement to the Background Job system, including new possibilities for scheduling jobs
❑ Additional printing options, including new access methods, device types, forms, and support for Output Management tools
❑ New tools for most of the database management functions within and outside the R/3 system.

SAP Database Administration

While the ABAP Dictionary includes a logical view of data for business applications and for the development environment, the underlying relational database management system is used by R/3 as the physical container for system and business information. This section introduces some of the important aspects of the administration of the underlying database system. Remember that management functions and available tools differ depending on the chosen database engine.

One of the databases most often chosen by SAP customers is Oracle, for its availability on all supported platforms and operating systems. Others that are supported and are growing in popularity include Microsoft SQL Server, Informix, ADABAS D, and the different variants of IBM DB2.

R/3 database administration is an important task within overall R/3 technical implementation and support. It is a common one in many database-oriented applications (most current business applications). This role is commonly referred to as DBA (database administrator).

SAP has included many monitoring functions for managing the database from within R/3, and for those tasks which cannot be directly performed within R/3, it has provided a comprehensive tool for making the administration of the database easier. This tool is a character cell menu-driven program called *sapdba*, available for Oracle and Informix. It greatly facilitates database administration for R/3. However, in order to use the facilities provided by *sapdba*, a good knowledge of the database architecture is required.

The database systems used on SAP installations also include their own management applications; for instance, in the case of Oracle, DBA can use the Enterprise Manager, or the programs *sqldba*, *svrmgr23,* or *svrmgr30* according to their releases. These are database administration tools that can manually issue SQL statements for managing, monitoring, and performing database operations. SAP recommends not using these tools for changing system data, since this action might cause severe inconsistencies in the system. Use the tools only at the request of SAP personnel or as instructed by official notes or documentation.

A well-defined database administration is also a critical factor for successful support and maintenance of the whole SAP R/3 system. The following list reflects only some of the tasks usually assigned to DBAs:

❑ Design and maintain the physical database layout, covering such things as ensuring that data segments and index segments are located on different volumes, managing the location of main files, sizing and forecasting database growth, etc.

❑ Help and actively collaborate with the rest of the R/3 technical staff in system sizing and design

❑ Perform database backups, including the backup strategy definition: what to back up, when, where and in what time frame. Also be responsible for defining tape and volume management, tape drive maintenance, checking backup logs, etc. Within the backup strategy, do not neglect recovery procedures, which are at least as important as the backup itself; in the SAP R/3 environment it should be good practice to test thoroughly the backup/recovery strategy before going into productive operation.

❑ Perform database security maintenance, such as user and password administration, checking and monitoring database network connections, and possibly database accesses, using external tools (such as ODBC, RFC, external remote SQL tools, and so on).

❑ Check and monitor database performance. Tasks should include a daily or periodic checklist of database status, including fragmentation level, number of extents, overflow problems, file system problems, etc. Within the R/3 environment, this task also includes the maintenance of the main profile parameter files, such as init<SID>.ora, init<SID>.sap, and others.

❏ Do database storage management, including tasks such as adding data files to table spaces, modifying internal storage parameters, taking care of the log archive area, and backup of these archived logs, planning database reorganizations, designing and performing exports/imports, etc. It is also recommended to draw a map of the *sapdata* file systems, including the table spaces and data files.

❏ Perform database problem analysis and escalation procedures. Actively report, solve, and document common database problems. Consider using a tool for reporting incidence.

❏ Become familiar with the ABAP Dictionary and collaborate also in development of new objects; especially when new SAP applications are getting ready to go productive.

Bibliography

Nancy H. Bancroft. *Implementing SAP R/3*. Greenwich, Manning Publications Co. 1996.

Rafael Barreda *Aprendizaje. La Función de Educación en la Empresa Moderna*. Madrid, Editorial Conorg.1994.

Carla, O'Dell, and C. Jackson Grayson Jr. *If we only knew what we know*. New York, The Free Press, 1998.

Change Management White Paper, Walldorf: SAP AG, 1998.

Doane, Michael. *Capturing the Whirlwind*. Sioux Falls, The Consulting Alliance, 1997.

Michael Doane. *In the Path of the Whirlwind*. Sioux Falls, The Consulting Alliance, 1997.

José Antonio Hernández. *Asi es SAP R/3*. Madrid, McGraw-Hill, 1998. (available only in Spanish)

José Antonio Hernández. *The SAP R/3 Handbook*. New York, McGraw-Hill, 1997.

John P. Kotter, Ed. *Leading Change*. McGraw-Hill Interamericana of México.

Douglas K. Smith. *Taking Charge of Change*. Reading, MA, Addison-Wesley Inc.,1996.

INDEX

Note: Boldface numbers indicate illustrations.

A

ABAP programming language, 3, 20, 25–27, 30, 34–36, 98, 100, 226–239, 251, 447, 448, 453
  Application Hierarchy, 232, 236
  application link enabling (ALE), 227, 229
  attributes, 230
  BAPI Browser, 233, 242
  BAPIs, 229
  batch input enhancements, 235
  Business Framework, 229
  Business Navigator, 229
  Business Object Repository (BOR), 35, 229, 231
  Business Workflow, 229
  call interfaces, 238
  Call statements, 207
  changes with release 4.0, 233–235
  classes, 230
  communications, 227
  compilation, 228
  Computer Aided Test Tool (CATT), 233
  Customizing Organizer, 233
  Data Browser, 232
  data dictionary, 35, 227, 231, 234, 235–239, 447, 466–468, 489
  Data Modeler, 232
  database management, 227, 467
  Debugger, 233, 234
  development environment, 227–228, 235–236
  distributed applications, 227
  dynpros, 35
  Editor, ABAP, 231, 234
  encapsulation, 229
  enhancing SAP systems, 201–202
  events, 230
  features of ABAP language, 228–229
  field names, 234
  Function Builder, 231, 234, 242
  Function Library, 234
  global objects, 229
  graphical user interfaces (GUI)

  support, 227
  identities, 230
  inheritance, 229
  instances, 230
  interfaces, 230
  language enhancements, 235
  List Viewer (ALV), 338
  locking problems, 215–216
  maintenance issues, 216
  Menu Painter, 231, 234
  metadata, 35, 236–237
  methods, 230
  multi-language support, 228
  naming standards, 234
  Native SQL, 227
  Object Browser, 234, 236
  object linking and embedding (OLE), 227
  object-oriented features, 216, 229–230
  objects, 230, 234, 236
  On-line Debugger, 233
  open database connectivity (ODBC), 227
  Open SQL, 227, 466
  patches, upgrades, 36, 221
  polymorphism, 229
  Query, ABAP, 232,337
  Reference Model, 229
  remote function calls (RFC), 227, 470
  remote processes, 227
  report system customization, 200–201, 228
  Reports, 338
  Repository Browser, 232, 234
  Repository Information System, 31, 232, 235, 242
  reusability of code, 216
  Runtime Analysis, 233
  Screen Painter, 231, 234
  SQL Trace, 233
  support, 227
  System Log, 233
  transparency, 227
  Transport Management System (TMS), 36

  Transport Organizer, 233
  upgrades, 36
  virtual machine (ABAP VM), 456
  Workbench, 34–36, 59, 198, 215, 226, 227, 230–233
  Workbench Organizer, 35–36, 233, 236
Accelerated SAP (ASAP), 19, 22–23, 48, 49, 51, 54, 60, 78, 80, 83, 88, 92, 93, 97–98, 122–131, **124**
  Accelerators or tools, 23, 59, 80
  archiving, 366
  authorization, 381–383
  Business Blueprint, 126
  Business Engineer, 126
  Business Process Master List, 126
  change management, 126, 154–158, **155**
  communications, 178–179
  cutover, 129
  data loads, 129
  end-user acceptance, 129
  Going Live, 130–131
  Help Desk, 129–130
  organization of implementation project, 138–139
  preparation for implementation, 125–126, 128–130
  Process component, 22
  quality checks, 95
  Question & Answers database, 126
  realization phase, 127–128
  Reference Model, 126
  Roadmap, 22, 123, 125, 183, 318
  security, 372–373
  Services, 23
  Solution Sets, 23
  support, 129–131
  TeamSAP, 22, 123–126
  testing procedures, 355–356
  training end-users, 129
  Upgrade Roadmap, 324
  verification of implementation scope, 129
Accelerators or tools, ASAP, 23, 59, 80
access control (*See also* authorization), 371

493

About the Authors

J. A. Hernandez is an SAP R/3 senior consultant and team manager at Digital Equipment Corp., and the author of *The SAP R/3 Handbook*. He has been leading an SAP implementation group at a large telecommunications company. For several years he worked on SAP projects as technical leader in one of the biggest R/3 implementations in Europe. He has also been teaching some of the training courses of the SAP Basis System. Besides that, his main area of knowledge in SAP R/3 is the technical implementation of R/3 systems.

J. R. S. Elechiguerra works as an SAP R/3 consultant for Digital Equipment Corp. He has specialized in the ABAP/4 Development workbench and several functional modules like SD. He has been teaching the entire SAP Basis training courses and for more than four years has actively participated in many successful SAP projects in Spain and Portugal, both in the technical and functional areas.

E. R. Bueno is a senior software engineer at Digital Equipment Corp., with more than twelve years in the computer industry. Mr. Roca has become one of the most experienced engineers and technical leaders in successful implementations of SAP R/3 systems in Spain. His main areas of expertise are in the ABAP Data Dictionary, Printing Issues, Implementation Plans, Quality Plans, and Cross-Application modules. He has also been a trainer of many of the Basis modules of SAP R/3 as well as the technical leader of a large implementation in Barcelona.

S. A. Servera is an experienced consultant and project manager at CSC/Ploenzke, one of the most successful SAP partners in Europe. For the last three years he has participated in several SAP implementations and has become one of the most knowledgeable experts in all aspects of R/3 Reporting.